THE PHILOSOPHY OF AMERICAN EDUCATION

The Philosophy
of American Education

G. MAX WINGO
The University of Michigan

D. C. HEATH AND COMPANY

*To Mary, who spends her days
in the schools doing the things
her husband mostly talks about.*

Preface

I have written this book for those who are approaching their first comprehensive study of American conceptions of educational policy and educational philosophy. In this sense my book is a textbook. I have well-defined ideas about what a textbook can do and what it should not be expected to do, and I have tried to construct this text in accord with these ideas.

In the first place, when a student approaches a field as diverse and extended as philosophy of education, he needs something to help him fit together the things he reads, the ideas he hears in lectures, and the practices he observes in schools. A textbook can help him identify the important problems in the field of educational theory together with the solutions that have been proposed to solve these problems. Thus, it can serve as a means for orientation in a marvelously complex field of study.

Secondly, a textbook is not an encyclopedia or a simple repository of factual material. A book that is to serve the purpose of a text must explain technical terms, must give examples wherever these are possible, must relate novel ideas to understandings already possessed by the student, and must help the student fashion and organize his own structure of knowledge about the problems and issues with which philosophy of education is concerned.

In the third place, since virtually all instruction at the college and university level is necessarily group instruction, both teacher and students need something that provides a common base of experience from which other inquiries and studies can develop. The textbook, properly used, provides an organization that prevents aimless wanderings through the vast literature of a field, yet encourages individual and group initiative in discussing and analyzing ideas and branching out to consider in detail issues that the text does not develop fully.

The low status that textbooks endure in some quarters is often owed as much to the way in which they are used as it is to their technical and literary qualities. It is important for students (and their instructors as well) to realize the inherent limitations of a text, however well it may have been prepared. There is no substitute for first-hand contact with the classic works of a field of knowledge. A textbook can help by identifying important original sources for the student and assisting him in interpreting and analyzing these works. If a book does these things well, and if the student in reading the text is encouraged to push his own way into the fundamental literature of the field, then the most important purpose of the textbook has been achieved.

The function of a textbook is not to tell people what they should think and believe; at least this is most certainly the case in the philosophy of education. A textbook will serve its real purpose when it helps a student understand what the major questions are and the variant answers that have been given to these questions. There is plenty of room in the literature of a field for books that advocate acceptance of particular bodies of ideas. When a book is designed in this way, however, it is no longer a textbook and it cannot serve the peculiar function of a text.

There are at least three different levels at which the study of philosophy of education may be carried on. The first of these is primarily descriptive and the effort involved is directed at comprehending the existing status of educational thought and practice and the grounds on which various ideas and practices are alleged to rest. At a second level, philosophy of education has a normative function. In this respect, it is concerned with proposing ends or objectives that are proper for the educational enterprise, together with means that may be employed to attain these ends. At yet a third level, philosophy of education is concerned with identifying and analyzing premises on which conclusions are based and with the function of language in educational discourse.

All of these approaches are important and any student who gets very far into a real study of the field will soon find himself involved in all of them. However, one has to start somewhere, and it is my own view that the most fruitful place to start is with the living reality. Therefore, since this book is designed as introductory to the field, it is primarily descriptive of contemporary thought in educational philosophy.

In presenting a panorama of the philosophy of education in the United States, I have attempted to relate various traditions to the social context in which they exist and function. Accordingly, I have proposed that the prevailing tradition in American education is fundamentally conservative and is linked in certain ways with a wider and more inclusive social conservatism. The other traditions in education and philosophy are presented as protest movements against various aspects of the dominant tradition. In doing this, I have had to develop various classifications—particularly in the case of educational conservatism—that to some people may seem excessively arbitrary. I am sure that anyone who tries to analyze and classify ideas in a field as eclectic as American educational policy immediately lays himself open to the charge of cutting the pattern to fit the cloth.

For myself, I regard classifications as useful intellectual instruments that, used judiciously, help us grasp the broader significance of ideas and events and not as unchanging categories into which ideas and events must be stuffed at any cost. Therefore, I have no quarrel with those who may find my own classifications unsuitable in certain respects and who would substitute some scheme of their own. The point on which I will not yield is that philosophies of education can be studied profitably only within their cultural context and in terms of the functions they perform in that context.

When a writer finishes a book, he begins to think about the debts he owes to others: the teachers he has had, the books he has read, the conversations with colleagues and students that stretch back over the years. My debts in this respect are so great that there is no hope that I can ever acknowledge them specifically. I am grateful to The Macmillan Company, the Yale University Press, and the National Society for the Study of Education for their generous permission to quote extensively from their publications. I am also indebted to Marilyn McGuire, who with intelligence and patience prepared the final manuscript, exercising a measure of forbearance that can be appreciated only by those who have seen the quality of my own orthography, and who in the end was kind enough to say she found it interesting.

Ann Arbor, Michigan
July 6, 1964   G. Max Wingo

Contents

Preface

Epilogue

PART ONE

Philosophy and Education

*The investigation of the truth is in one way hard,
in another easy. An indication of this is found in the
fact that no one is able to attain the truth adequately,
while, on the other hand, we do not collectively fail,
but everyone says something true about the nature of
things, and while individually we contribute little or
nothing to the truth, by the union of all a considerable amount is amassed. Therefore, since the truth
seems to be like the proverbial door, which no one
can fail to hit, in this respect it must be easy, but the
fact that we can have a whole truth and not the particular part we aim at shows the difficulty of it.*

—ARISTOTLE

Metaphysics, Book II (Translated by W. D. Ross), *The Basic Works of Aristotle*
(Ed. Richard McKeon), New York: Random House, 1941, p. 712.

CHAPTER ONE

Philosophy and Education

Our concern in this book is with American education and our primary interest, therefore, is with the institutions and traditions that make up our system of schooling from the lowest to the topmost levels of the organization. We are concerned with the programs these schools conduct, the purposes their programs are designed to serve, the methods and materials of instruction teachers employ in their work. However, it is not our intention to study these matters in isolation as if they were independent phenomena. Our understanding and assessment of them will have meaning only as we see them in the larger context from which they have emerged and in which they operate. An educational system is more than the concrete embodiment of philosophical ideas, or scientific ideas, or economic ideas, though in some measure it is inclusive of these and many more as well. It has often been argued that the school represents ultimately a crystallization of ideas (and ideals) about the nature of man and his place in the scheme of things.

The school is an institution responsible for certain specialized services involved in inducting the young into social life. It is never possible for the school to transmit the entire intellectual and social heritage. Choices must always be made about the areas of knowledge to be transmitted, the intellectual and practical skills to be developed and the value concepts to be stressed. These choices tend to be made in terms of the values that prevail in society and those values that are dominant will be expressed in choices concerned with the purposes and programs of the school.

In societies that are relatively stable there can usually be widespread agreement about the portions of the cultural heritage to be transmitted by formal educational means. The theory of education in such societies operates as a kind of rationale and synthesis of prevailing and accepted modes of education. There is a minimum of friction and debate on educational questions. But in societies that are in a state of transition and disruption, the case is very different. It is a widely accepted thesis of cultural anthropology that societies in process of transition suffer loss of traditional values and this loss is connected with the growth of cultural confusion and the development of social crisis. Mr. Ralph Linton, for example, had said that the stability of a society depends in large measure on wide acceptance of a common core of values and beliefs. Outside this common core there are various peripheral ideas and ideals among which men are free to choose. When social change is accelerated, the common core becomes indistinct and men no longer perceive with clarity a central core of universals. The allegiances of citizens are pulled in many directions. The alternatives become confused with the constants, and the result leads to increasing social disorganization.[1]

Under social conditions of this kind the stresses and dissentions in society find ready expression in the debate over educational policy. Those who resent fundamental changes in the social structure, and who feel threatened by them, make heavy demands on the school to preserve the *status quo*. People who feel themselves in opposition to the old order and who welcome change demand in turn that the school throw its influence in the direction of new curriculums, new services, changed values. Friction grows, name-calling becomes common, and the theory of education loses its character of detachment and becomes evangelical. The view represented here is that the stability or instability of society is not a function of the prevailing modes of education. In fact, those modes of education are themselves manifestations of the stabilities and instabilities of the social order.

The idea around which this book is organized is that American society is involved in a great process of transition in which our whole way of life is being transformed. The common core of ideas and beliefs that once constituted the basis of cultural solidarity is dissolving. It is no longer possible to perceive with clarity what is constant and what is open to choice. The turmoil, therefore, that is everywhere so evident in American education is a reflection of the larger confusion in American society. This educational confusion and conflict cannot be understood, nor can a way out of it be found, until we become intelligent

[1] See: Ralph Linton, *The Study of Man*, New York: Appleton-Century Crofts, Inc., 1936, p. 282 ff.

PHILOSOPHY OF AMERICAN EDUCATION

about the underlying conditions that generate it. Education is always a function of the total social pattern and there is no point in examining philosophies of education as if they were *sui generis* and thus independent of any social context. Many traditions have gone into the making of American society and much of the instability of contemporary life is owing to the fundamental incompatibility of the most important of these traditions. The conflicts and uncertainties generated by these incompatibilities are the genesis of our educational controversies.

There are various possible approaches to a study of the theory and practice of education in a society. The approach taken in this book is what we may call philosophical because it represents an effort to take the most comprehensive view of educational activity in its social context. Philosophical thinking at its best is in part concerned with the specialization, intellectual rigor, and concern for detail that are also characteristic of scientific analysis. But at the same time philosophy is also concerned with wholeness and with the effort to synthesize experience; characteristics that in some measure are typical of common sense. Perhaps we can say, then, that whereas the common man is not particularly concerned with specialization and the scientist typically is not concerned with wholeness, the philosopher ultimately must be concerned with both.

We are now ready to embark on a long and complicated inquiry into the character of the educational enterprise in America. We can anticipate that our task is not simply one of identifying a common body of belief and practice that can be labeled "the philosophy of American education." Rather we are committed to a study of various traditions about education that in these days are contesting for the acceptance of our citizens. Some of the differences among these traditions are deep and bitter. Whether they are capable of being reconciled remains for the time being, at least, an open question.

Our immediate purpose in this chapter is to consider how philosophy can be of assistance to us in comprehending the character of education in America. Perhaps the best place to begin is with a consideration of the relative roles of theory and practice, particularly as these relate to the conduct of such an activity as education, which everybody recognizes as an eminently practical undertaking.

THEORY AND PRACTICE

A common distinction of everyday discourse is that between theory and practice. Individuals vary in their attitudes toward the importance of the two components. Some people profess a strong preference for practice, emphasizing that the work of the world is done by practical people, the "doers" who get things accomplished. On the other hand, there are people whose greatest admiration and approval are reserved for the theorist—the man of ideas, whose work must go on often without much immediate reference to the practical consequences of theory. The doer is interested in bringing about change, influencing the course of events in the world, and bringing new events into being. The theorist, however, is more interested in ideas in themselves and his search is for discovery, understanding and synthesis in the realms of fact and of value.

A common instance of the clash of ideas about the respective values of theory and practice often occurs in contemporary science. While the achievements of science rest ultimately on basic or "pure" research—that is, research not connected immediately with any practical or applied situation, this is not always understood by the layman and perhaps even on occasion by some scientists. Traditionally, it has been easier for scientific workers to get support for practical and technological research than for pure research, although there are signs that this condition is changing somewhat in the direction of greater appreciation of basic theoretical work.

If a situation of this kind occurs in the field of natural science, consider what it must be in a field of endeavor such as teaching, which manifestly is a practical occupation. Those who are responsible for the work of the educational world are doers. They are teachers and administrators and members of boards of education. It is their business to make decisions and to act and they usually have little time for speculation and disinterested analysis. After all, schools must be maintained, school programs must be planned and established, there must be teachers in classrooms with some kind of plans and methods for carrying out the work. Typically, the really important matters so far as teachers are concerned are teaching method (including social discipline), curriculum, and instructional materials. To administrative personnel the important matters are curriculum, personnel, finance and public relations. All of these areas are practical. They are the primary concerns of the doer. In fact, it is not unusual for the practical educator to harbor deep-seated feelings of suspicion of those who are the theorists of educational activity. The attitude of the practicing teacher or administrator may sometimes be similar to that of the practical business man when he asks about some economic or social theorist, "Has he ever met a payroll?"

This same attitude more often than not is encountered by instructors in professional courses for the training of teachers. Typically, the courses students like best are those in which they can see most clearly the relation between what is done in college classes and the specific work they will have to do as teachers. It is not surprising, therefore, that student teaching and similar work that brings the student into contact with the reality of the school are generally the most popular courses in teacher-preparation programs.

In fact, teachers in preparation, as well as those already practicing, find little difficulty in enumerating the things they really want to know about. They want a good mastery of the subject matter they will be called on to teach. They want to know about good methods for teaching the material they are charged with teaching. They are interested in materials to use in the classroom. There is universal concern among teachers about the problems of social control of students—usually called "discipline." All teachers want to know in general what is expected of them, what objectives they are supposed to achieve, and how their work will be evaluated by the administration and ultimately by the community.

Although we will not take the time to do so, it would be possible to make a similar list of the practical concerns of educational administrators. The administrator's mind-set of practicality is not fundamentally different from that of the teacher, nor is there any reason to believe that his attitude towards educational theory is really any different.

These attitudes are important and should be respected within the teaching profession, as well as in institutions that prepare people for educational work. After all, if an individual cannot master the elements of the craft to a reasonable degree, he cannot be a teacher. If he cannot in some way fashion a tenable approach to teaching method, if he cannot devise a workable program for his classes, if he cannot manage the relations in his classrooms so that a reasonable degree of social discipline is maintained, he cannot be a teacher. He cannot even hold a position and collect a salary. It is no wonder, then, that these considerations usually occupy the attention of teachers often to the exclusion of more abstract matters.

Does this mean that theory really has nothing to do with the practical work of the practicing educator? Does it mean that teacher-education institutions should concern themselves exclusively with teaching the practical aspects of the teacher's art? Is it reasonable to expect that those who serve society in the role of teachers should be thoughtful about that role and that their concern should go beyond the immediate problems of the day-by-day routine of the school? In a time of cultural transition and with the resulting upheavals in society, can teachers and school officials content themselves with established ideas and established routines, as important as these may be? It is peculiar to a time of social disorganization that all men are called to make decisions they would not be faced with making in more settled times. Educators, since they occupy positions of strategic importance in society, are called upon to make decisions that will inevitably affect the lives of many people.

Behind every approach to teaching method, behind every plan for administrative organization of the schools, behind the structure of every school curriculum stands a body of accepted doctrine in the form of assumptions, concepts, generalizations and values. In short, every practical approach to the art of teaching is shored up by some constellation of accepted *ideas*—some ideology. Very often, however, the very presence of this ideology goes unnoticed. Its acceptance is largely unconscious and based on tradition. Only rarely is ideology subjected to careful critical analysis and on the occasions when such analysis is made there are certain to be outcries from various segments of society, for men always find it difficult to see their cherished ideas submitted to objective scrutiny.

Perhaps in a time of relative cultural stability accepted modes of education and their attending ideology can operate with apparent satisfaction. If this is true, it is largely because in such settled periods the cultural focus seems clear and distinct. Men find but little difficulty in perceiving what is focal and essential and what is peripheral and secondary. In such times theory and practice are united, though the unity may be unconscious in the minds of a majority of practitioners. Thus, under these conditions, teachers teach as they do because their ways are the "right ways," the established ways. The subject matters they teach are those "everybody knows" we ought to teach in school. The value concepts teachers seek to transmit to their students, whether by precept or example, are those "eternal verities" to which all "good citizens" give allegiance.

Under such conditions as these very little strain is put on the teacher's reflective and analytic powers. There is no reason for him to feel impelled to reflect on the body of accepted ideas that determine what he does as a teacher, in truth he might very well find such speculative activity frowned upon in his community. Generally in his training as a teacher he is told what the correct subject matters are, how they should be presented, and to what end. The emphasis is placed on his development of facility in the practical affairs of teaching, not on the analysis of ideas. Similarly, the administrator and the members of the school board see their task as implementing the "wishes of society." These "wishes," it is maintained, are not only worthy but also clearly known.

In these circumstances the life of the teacher can be comfortable and secure —though perhaps sometimes on the dull side. But this security of life and professional conviction depends on a corresponding stability in the pattern of culture and no culture is ever completely stable. Conditions of the kind described above have been rare or non-existent certainly for more than a century and perhaps really in the whole post-medieval world. The dichotomy of theory and practice in education exists because the ideology of education has been brought into question by certain momentous developments in the pattern of modern culture. The influence of natural science and scientific method has been at work undermining, at least in the minds of increasing numbers of people, the old certainties about the ends, the contents, and the means of education. Altered conceptions of human nature, new theories of social and political life, profound developments in pure science and consequently in technology have robbed the old traditions of a measure of their vitality and influence.

And so, theory, by necessity, becomes a matter of real concern not only to the educational reformer, who seeks to transform, but also the conservative whose deepest desire is to retain and consolidate the existing pattern. Whether we think of ourselves as liberal or conservative, radical or regressive, we cannot escape in these times the necessity of attending to our basic ideas. The luxury of operating our schools on the basis of ideas "everybody knows are right" is gone, providing it ever really existed at all. The educational conservative now finds that he must advocate his cause not merely through the reiteration of the accepted "truths" of educational practice, but also through a demonstration that the ideological implications of these "truths" are coherent and consistent.

And in the same way, the would-be reformer finds it necessary not merely to advocate certain new ideas about practical concerns, but he also is forced to explicate the body of doctrine related to these ideas and which in turn lends support to the practicalities themselves. A certain lag between theory and practice is probably always present in any period, but the question of today is not so much the relation of certain practices to an accepted body of theory, it is rather the question of what practices and consequently what theories are to be accepted. Thus, in unsettled times, at least, the theory of education becomes controversial and dialectical. In a word, it becomes philosophical.

THE USES OF PHILOSOPHY

Philosophy is one of the oldest and most respected provinces of knowledge. Traditionally, it has been regarded as the great synthesizing and speculative discipline and the history of philosophy is a record of achievement of some of the greatest intellects of the west. It is common for professional philosophers to insist that philosophy is first of all an autonomous discipline, that it concerns itself with certain subject matters and certain kinds of questions and that it has its own methods of inquiry and analysis. It is possible, in fact, to study philosophy with virtually no attention or concern for any practical implications, just as one can study mathematics or physics as "pure" sciences independent of any of their practical ramifications. A philosopher, Plato said, is a spectator of all time and all existence. To Aristotle the philosopher was one who is concerned with the "first causes" of things. The history of philosophy is replete with definitions of this kind that portray philosophy as love of wisdom in the grand manner.

Traditionally, western philosophy has concerned itself with certain categories of questions. These conventional categories of philosophy are usually described as being three in number:

1. METAPHYSICS. This category deals with questions relating to the nature of reality. Metaphysical questions are those concerned with the nature of Being in itself, as contrasted with being in the form of the entities with which, for example, physics or some other science deals. Metaphysics is often thought of as the search for that which is ultimately real. To many traditional philosophers metaphysics raises the ultimate philosophical question. Very often in philosophical writing the term is made synonymous with ontology and readers will find the two terms used interchangeably. There are distinctions between the two

terms but these are not of great importance in the matters dealt with in this book.

Cosmology, which is often thought of as a sub-category in metaphysics, deals with questions about the ultimate nature of the universe as a whole.

2. EPISTEMOLOGY. This category is often referred to as "the theory of knowledge." It is concerned with questions about the nature and limits of human knowledge. Some important questions in epistemology are about: (a) The nature of cognitive processes; (b) The sources of human knowledge; and (c) Methods of validating ideas.

3. AXIOLOGY. The questions in this category are about value. General axiological questions are those related to the source and nature of standards (norms) for value and the processes by which these standards are applied in making judgments (the process of valuation). Axiology is considered to have two sub-categories, *ethics* and *esthetics*. Ethics deals with the problem of value as applied to human conduct. Esthetics deals with the problem of value as applied to works of art, criteria for beauty as opposed to ugliness, and the nature of experience when it is concerned with beauty.

To these categories we should perhaps add *logic*, a field of study in philosophy that deals with the rules of inference. Conventionally, logic is thought of as *formal* and *deductive* and as *scientific* and *inductive*.

It should be understood that questions originating in any of the philosophical categories are interrelated. Thus, problems that are considered primarily to be axiological generally have important implications in epistemology and metaphysics. Metaphysical questions most always involve important questions in epistemology and axiology, and so on.

Customarily, the common man—the doer—thinks he has little in common with the philosopher whose concerns so obviously are with matters that go beyond the scope of ordinary vision and understanding. Though the ordinary man may often harbor deep-seated doubts about the "practicality" of the philosopher's speculations, nonetheless he has usually stood in awe of them. And this awe is only slightly diminished when he hears of such recondite subjects as philosophy of law, philosophy of science, or philosophy of education. To the unphilosophic, law, science, and education are understandable terms; above all, they imply practical matters, pursuits that make a difference in human lives and affairs. To be sure, science is known to have its theories, law its general principles of jurisprudence and education its theories of objectives, curriculum and method. But what has philosophy to do with these? Of what use is philosophy in conducting our schools? What kind of bread can philosophy bake for education?

Those who ask this question are entitled to a reasoned answer and the fact is that there is more than one answer to the question. One of the uses to which philosophy is sometimes put is to make it the original source of certain ideas from which it is held the practical matters of education *can be derived by a series of logical inferences.* For example, suppose we learn from philosophy (that is, from some philosophical "system") that ultimate reality is of such and such a nature. To take an example, say we learn from Plato that ultimate reality is of the nature of universal ideas or *Forms* and that these Forms are knowable only through the rational operations of the mind, not through the senses. We learn further that although the things and events we encounter in our sensory experience depend on the Forms for their very existence and character, those things we know through the senses are not real in the sense that the Forms are real.

From these ideas (which we are taking as demonstrated philosophic "truths") it is held that we can deduce certain principles for education. We can say for one thing that the existence known by the mind is of a higher order than that known through the senses. And we can infer, further, that the activity of the intellect, which opens the way to an understanding of that which is ultimately real, is higher than physical activity that deals merely with the world of sense. It must follow then that education should be concerned with the training of the mind, that is, with man's rational powers and this should take precedence over any training in manual and manipulative pursuits.

Now if these things be true, it is said to follow that the curriculum of the school should be one designed for intellectual training, that it should be based on abstractions and symbolic materials—that is, on ideas—rather than on things. And it follows from this that teaching method should emphasize the training of the powers of reason and it should serve to communicate to students those Truths that hold on all occasions, regardless of time, place, or circumstance.[2]

If Platonism can be described accurately as philosophy in the "grand manner," perhaps we can describe the logical derivation of practical ideas for education from metaphysical premises as philosophy of

[2] The derivation of a scheme for practical educational ideas from a set of metaphysical assumptions is, of course, far more complicated than this account would indicate. However, my purpose at this point is not to give a complete exposition but to indicate the general direction of thought such philosophizing takes. For examples

education in the "grand manner." In fact, to many practitioners in the field of educational philosophy this is what the term really means. In their judgment this logical mating of theory and practice is the only sound conception of the uses of philosophy in the educational enterprise. It must be admitted that intellectually this is a tidy approach to educational philosophy. In fact, by this approach it is possible to build a whole system of ideas about what educational practices ought to be without once taking the trouble to observe the character of any existing school or the social context in which the schools must necessarily exist. To some people, it is this attitude of detachment that can make educational philosophy academically respectable.

An instructor, therefore, looking at the matter in this way and wishing to make his course in philosophy of education respectable academically, will often begin with the study of certain epistemological and metaphysical theories and after an analysis of these philosophical matters will proceed to demonstrate that certain propositions in metaphysics or epistemology or ethics imply logically certain conclusions about the objectives of education, the character and content of the curriculum, and the principles of educational methodology.

One thing it is important to note about this is that such an inferential process furnishes a ready-made device for judging the validity of practical educational ideas. Plainly, under this view, false ideas about education are either those that are derived from false premises, or those that are false because formal errors have been made in their logical derivation. Therefore, it is possible to say, as indeed one writer has said, that certain educational practices (in this case those of progressivism) are *necessarily* bad because they are related in the logical sense to an untenable and false philosophy, namely pragmatism. Since there can scarcely be anything more convincing than logical necessity, it does not appear worthwhile, according to this view, to spend time considering educational practices that are already known to be false. The wise thing to do would be summarily to dismiss these ideas and search for others whose validity can be inferred from a firm philosophical base.[3]

As neat and attractive as this approach to philosophy of education

of this conception of the uses of philosophy see: Harry S. Broudy, "How Philosophical Can Philosophy of Education Be?" *The Journal of Philosophy,* 52:612–622 (October 27, 1955); Kingsley Price, "Is a Philosophy of Education Necessary?" *The Journal of Philosophy, Ibid.,* pp. 622–633; Richard K. Morris, "The Philosophy of Education: A Quality of Its Own," *Harvard Educational Review,* 26:142–144 (Spring, 1956).
[3] See Albert Lynd, "Who Wants Progressive Education?" *The Atlantic Monthly,* 191:35 ff. (April, 1953).

may seem, there are certain questions that need to be raised about it. For one thing, the whole enterprise depends on the correctness of the assumption that the relation between, say, propositions in metaphysics and ideas about school practice is a logical one, logical that is, in the sense of a necessary relation between premise and conclusion.

If we say that A implies B, this means that the existence of B necessarily depends on the existence of A and also that the fact of B presupposes A in the sense of logical necessity. But can we say in the same fashion that since ultimate reality is of the nature of ideas it necessarily follows that the school should be concerned exclusively with intellectual training? If the two inferences are really the same kind of logical relation, then it must be possible to say that intellectual training as the exclusive role of the school can be true only if reality is of the nature of ideas—which patently is false since there are many conceivable reasons for postulating intellectual training as the sole role of education. The difficulty with this whole deductive approach lies in the impossibility of demonstrating a true logical dependency between propositions in any brand of pure philosophy and propositions about practical educational operations.[4]

There is a further source of evidence of the untenability of this perception of the role of philosophy in educational theory. The whole idea involves the presumption that there is some set of metaphysical (or epistemological, or ethical) premises that are known to be true and which imply logically certain educational practices and not others. If this is true, where are we to look for these universal, fool-proof philosophical premises? Certainly there seems to be little point in looking for them in the history of western philosophy for if there is a field of knowledge that involves more disagreement on basic issues than philosophy it is hard to know what it is. Whose premises are we to take? Plato's, Aristotle's, Locke's, Kant's, Hegel's, Descartes', James', Dewey's —whose? How are we to know which of these to select? While all of them may be mistaken, there is no possibility they can all be right, for they are obviously contradictory of each other in many important respects. If we accept the idea that philosophical premises can be made to yield conclusions about the practices of education, it seems clear that unless we all begin with the same premises we cannot hope to emerge with the same conclusions. Since there is no promising sign that we are

4 For a study of this question see: Hobart W. Burns, "The Logic of the 'Educational Implication'," *Educational Theory*, 12:53–63 (January, 1962). See also Sidney Hook, "The Scope of Philosophy of Education," *Harvard Educational Review*, 26:145–8 (Spring, 1956).

very near to being in agreement on philosophical premises, how can we hope ever to come to any agreement on practical educational issues?

A book of essays[5] on educational theory written by eminent contemporary philosophers provides an instructive example of what happens when educational ideas are conceived as logical implications of certain philosophical premises. At least three of the authors of essays in this volume come to near perfect agreement on what the curriculum of the schools should be. But these conclusions are arrived at supposedly by way of three different philosophical systems: idealism, realism, and existentialism![6]

How are we to account for this curious situation? Historically, protagonists of the two traditions have thought that idealism and realism are poles apart as philosophical systems. Certainly it is a common notion that existentialism developed, partly at least, as a serious protest against the influence of older philosophical systems. If educational theories are related to philosophical premises in the logical sense, we should ordinarily expect that different philosophical premises would yield different educational conclusions. In this case they do not. Why?

One possibility is that the philosophical premises with which the three authors begin are really identical, although expressed in different words. This would account for the identity of their conclusions but it is doubtful that this idea will hold up under analysis because it is possible to demonstrate that there are genuine philosophical differences among idealism, realism and existentialism as systems of thought. The reasonable conclusion seems to be that the three essayists really arrived at their conclusions about the curriculum on some basis other than inferences from propositions in metaphysics and epistemology. In other words, this case furnishes no clear evidence that the relation between philosophical premise and practical conclusion is a necessary logical one.[7] This may be part of the reason that practicing teachers and ad-

[5] *Modern Philosophies and Education*, 54th Yearbook of the National Society for the Study of Education, ed., John S. Brubacher, Chicago: University of Chicago Press, 1955.

[6] Readers may find it an interesting intellectual exercise to trace, if they can, the paths of reasoning that lead the idealist, Theodore Greene; the realist, John Wild; and the existentialist, Ralph Harper to their substantial agreement on the character of the school curriculum. See *Ibid.*, Chapters II, IV, and VII.

[7] In an interesting paper Joe R. Burnett argues that propositions in philosophy and theology can have a logical relation to propositions about practical school operations without this relation being a strict one of premise to conclusion. See his: "An Analysis of Some Philosophical and Theological Approaches to Formation of Educational Policy and Practice," *Proceedings of the Seventeenth Annual Meeting of the Philosophy of Education Society*, published by the Society, 1961.

ministrators so often harbor a deep suspicion that philosophy really bakes no bread at all in the practical field of education.

Perhaps the trouble lies ultimately in an original and unwarranted assumption that the only respectable approach to philosophy of education is the effort to imitate philosophy in the grand manner, that is, through trying to derive ideas about education from great systems of speculative thought. Suppose as an alternative we should take as a maxim the words of William James when he said that philosophy is simply an unusually obstinate attempt to think clearly. Under this view the role of philosophic thought is to push more deeply than we ordinarily do into the problems that affect the lives of men, to examine the hidden assumptions and implications involved in them, to lay bare the contradictions and inconsistencies that corrupt them, and ultimately to come to some reasoned conclusions and courses of action.

Certainly no one doubts that one whole class of questions of major concern to us today is composed of questions about educational policy. As a people we are sorely perplexed as to what actions we should take in the process of educating our young. Teachers and administrators do not need to be apprised of the fact that there are numerous persons and groups of persons who are more than eager to tell them how to run the schools. Advice on any aspect of education is not difficult to come by in these days, and the recommendations with which school people are assailed cover a broad spectrum. One of the hard lessons a teacher must learn is that not everybody can be pleased. Not every item of advice can be taken. Not every cherished tradition can be honored. There comes a time—and, understandably, many educators strive to put it off as long as they can—when a choice must be made. Many have tried to cope with this condition by bending in whatever direction the wind is strongest, and most of these have paid the price of their vacillation and inconsistency.

If we can agree with James that philosophy is an unusually obstinate attempt to think clearly, then perhaps we can conceive philosophy of education as a stubborn attempt to think clearly about the problems of education. If we accept this notion, we are committing ourselves to the idea that the primary subject matter of educational philosophy is not metaphysics or epistemology or axiology but problems of educational policy. These are problems in their own right, and they do not owe their existence or importance to any prior philosophical premises.[8] They are,

[8] An interesting essay on this point is: Foster McMurray, "Preface to an Autonomous Discipline of Education," *Educational Theory*, 1:129–140 (July, 1955).

in fact, generated by certain specific historical and cultural developments. The reason for trying stubbornly to think clearly about the problems of education is to try to find our way out of an ideological wilderness. In the next chapter of this book, the effort is made to show something of the vast dimensions of this wilderness.[9]

The important problems of education are those of objectives, curriculum, method, and administration. These are the fundamental concerns of all practicing educators; they are also the concerns of all citizens who are genuinely interested in the welfare of the schools and the educational enterprise. If we err in thinking about the practical aspects of education, our error stems not from the fact that we are thinking about the wrong questions, but that we are not thinking clearly and deeply enough about them. We are not being sufficiently obstinate in pushing the questions as far as they ought to be pushed.

We have remarked before that all schools have some objectives. Sometimes these objectives are clearly known and consciously accepted; sometimes they are unconsciously held and therefore uncritically accepted. All teachers adopt some approach to teaching method. They choose, on some kind of basis, to employ certain techniques rather than others. All schools have a program of some kind, that is, a curriculum. In some fashion somebody has made decisions that certain subject matters and activities will be included and that some will be excluded. After all, the school program cannot embrace all possibilities that present themselves. Likewise, all administrative organizations have some kind of design and structure which create in turn certain kinds of relations between teachers and pupils, parents and teachers, teachers and administrators, and school and community.

The real question is which of the alternative possibilities with respect to objects, method, curriculum and administration are most promising with respect to the cultural condition in which contemporary society finds itself. There is the further problem of harmonizing our conceptual and practical approaches to these matters so that a socially-relevant, coherent, and consistent body of educational policy emerges. This means that superficial considerations will not suffice. Social relevance and internal consistency will need to be sought after stubbornly. We have

[9] In this connection Sidney Hook has said: "A philosophy of education, worthy of consideration, will not develop as a result of philosophers *applying* their philosophy to questions of education. It will develop when philosophers and educators, as well as other intelligent citizens, concern themselves with questions of education, explore their bearing on conflicting value commitments and seek some comprehensive theory of human values to guide us in the resolution of conflicts." Sidney Hook, *op. cit.*, p. 148.

15

already had enough of educational philosophers' creating private utopias by "applying" their philosophical premises to educational questions. And we have had more than enough of the superficial practicalism of the professional educator.

We should understand that the search for educational theory does not take place in a vacuum. There is no possibility that we can wipe the slate clean and create a new and ideal philosophy of education that will (or should) supersede all other philosophies. If the purpose of this book were simply to present in ordered detail a "system" of educational philosophy that could be recommended as the official and accepted philosophy of American education, its task would be far simpler than it actually is. The real philosophic task that confronts us is not to begin all over again with forming a "new" educational theory but to take stock of where we are and go on from there. The role of philosophy is to assist in finding ways of educating our young that are more effective, more in harmony with the aspirations we profess, and more in accord with the demands industrial society and cultural transition lay on us.

There are many voices to be heard these days about how our schools should be run. The search for educational policy must begin with an understanding of where we stand presently. A first task, therefore, is that of analyzing and understanding the status of educational theory which is current. It means a careful scrutiny of those traditions that today are competing for acceptance by American citizens. In this analysis we must be as obstinate as we know how to be in pushing the questions as far as they will go.

A PLAN FOR ANALYSIS

The major portion of this book is devoted to an analysis of five general traditions, all of which have some degree of influence in American life today, and all of which have some important things to say about American education, its potentialities and its prospects. These traditions embrace much more than educational ideas. They must be thought of, in fact, as proposals for ways of life in which all important elements of human culture are represented. A signal fact for our own purposes is that all these traditions take education seriously. In all of them, perhaps save one, there is found a distinct body of doctrine about the aims, the contents, and the modes of education. The proponents of these traditions earnestly attempt to persuade others that their particular doctrines are right and should be accepted. Most of the knowledgable proponents of these traditions are aware that their educational ideas do not stand alone, that they have an organic connection with other elements in the tradition. They are aware that a consistent body of educational doctrine is not achieved by picking and choosing from various philosophical systems, in about the same way a man assembles his lunch in a cafeteria line.

The primary concern of this book is with philosophy of education and, for that reason, with fundamental questions related to the operation of the schools. Therefore, in the analysis of each tradition we will begin with the specific proposals of that tradition for educational objectives, curriculum, and method. In every case the first attempt will be to understand as clearly as possible the specific proposals in the tradition with respect to educational practices; what is proposed as the aims of the school, what kind of program should be carried on, and what kind of teaching methods should be used.

This is the beginning of the analysis, not the end of it. Beliefs about educational practice are related to other kinds of beliefs. An important dimension of an idea is the way in which it is related to other ideas, and therefore, an important purpose of our analysis is to trace out as far as we can the interrelated concepts that form a total body of ideas about education.

To illustrate the kind of analysis proposed here, let us take one of the major categories of questions with which philosophy of education is concerned, namely teaching method. This, as we have said, is a matter in which every teacher must come to some decision. Every teacher, on some basis, concludes that he will teach reading or mathematics or history by means of certain techniques rather than others. Now it is reasonable to assume that involved in this choice is the teacher's belief that his chosen method of procedure will result in more effective learning by his students than would result if he employed some other approach. The claim is not made that this is necessarily true, but it must be admitted that very few teachers would be likely to adopt a methodology on the grounds that students would learn less through it than by any other known approach.

Suppose we should ask the teacher—or he asks himself—on what grounds do you conclude that your chosen approach will result in more efficient learning? Various answers, of course, can be given to this query. The teacher may say that other teachers he has known have found this to be a "good" method or that certain experimental studies have shown this to be true. This kind of reply, while important, can be no more than a partial answer, and if we push more vigorously we will gain an answer—at least from most moderately sophisticated teachers—that his chosen methodology is to be preferred because it is consistent with certain principles of learning. In other words, the teacher indicates that his teaching method is coherent with certain principles of the psychology of learning.

When this kind of answer is given, we are no longer talking exclusively about educational practice. We are talking about educational practice in the light of psychological theory, and psychological theories are in part being used to sanction certain educational practices. There are, of course, various facets of psychological theory that apply to educational method. There are psychological theories with respect to perception, to cognition, to motivation, to emotion, to personal adjustment, and so on. The whole argument in essence is that approaches to teaching method should be examined in the light of their consistency with certain theoretical formulations in such social sciences as psychology and sociology. These are fields in which a determined effort has been made to apply scientific method to the study of human behavior and to arrive at general theoretical formulations that will account for various aspects of human behavior.

In this connection it is possible to take the position that sound factual knowledge about human conduct in all its manifestations can come only through the kind of investigations conducted by social scientists. This does not mean that everything about human conduct is known at present or that everything ever will be known. All it involves is the assertion that when we gain grounded and trustworthy knowledge about human behavior it will be through the operations of social and biological scientists. Those who take this position, and the number is probably increasing in this country, are making scientific method and its products the criterion for tenable ideas about human behavior and ultimately about educational practice. They are advocating that the source of some ideas about educational method can properly originate in social science, that one criterion for the validity of an idea about educational method is its coherence with established scientific fact, and another criterion is the experimental testing of educational methods.

There is considerable agreement today about this kind of connection between educational method and social science, but this agreement is very far from being complete. There are various kinds of objections.

18   PHILOSOPHY OF AMERICAN EDUCATION

One is that social scientists themselves are far from being in harmony with each other on many matters of alleged fact. If we examine psychological literature, for example, we find not a theory of learning but theories of learning. We find not a theory of motivation but theories of motivation. Which of these are we supposed to take for the appraisal of our ideas about method? Social science, it is argued, cannot, at least as yet, offer the firm theoretical base that is needed for the appraisal of educational practices.

But this is not the only argument, for in the opinion of many people the greatest defect in the scientific approach is that science simply does not deal with certain matters of very great importance to education and to educational method. The area of human behavior, they say, in which such social sciences as psychology, sociology, political science and anthropology are relevant is limited. There are, in fact, vast dimensions of human life that these sciences never touch and never will be able to touch. Yet these dimensions are of as much importance in the consideration of educational method as theories about learning behavior.

Those who argue from the insufficiency of science point out that what is needed in the appraisal of method is a complete conception of human nature and such a conception goes beyond anything that is the real business of social scientists. It is important, for example, to know what the destiny of man is, and surely this is not a question in social science. It is important to know what the good life for man is, for it is axiomatic that educational method is designed to help men realize the good life. While it may be important to know by what processes men learn, providing one can ever find out, this knowledge tells us nothing about what men ought to learn.

It is argued further that by method we mean a means to an end, and unless we are aware of what ends are to be achieved, we are in no position to make any judgments about how they are to be achieved. What are the ends of man: pleasure, success, happiness, spiritual salvation, or what? Consult the sociologists and you get no answer. Consult the anthropologist and perhaps you can get information about how this matter is conceived in various societies, but you do not get an answer to the question asked.

Those who hold that science is insufficient to deal with the whole of human nature insist that if we are to think clearly about the problems of education we will need to push the questions further. Psychological theories, they say, imply something broader than is found in psychological science. Theories of learning imply a general theory of knowledge. And a theory of knowledge deals with the nature and the limits of all human knowing and the criteria that are needed to distinguish between truth and falsity.

Similarly, it is said, what men ought to do is often a very different thing from what they actually do. To speak in terms of good and bad, desirable and undesirable, is to speak of value and hence of norms or standards. Social scientists can describe how men in various periods of history and in different cultures have conceived value norms, but the social scientist is not equipped to give us the kind of answer we are seeking.

And finally, it is argued, we must push the question to its ultimate point. Can we, for instance, assume that standards for value are to be found in the fleeting everyday experience of the world of sense? Can our sensory awareness really furnish a basis for knowledge of value? The answer that is often given is in the negative. We must look for answers to the value question, it is said, in realms that transcend the flux of sensory experience, realms of being that exhibit such properties as stability and universality and these are attributes that are not typical of the sensory world. So we come to the ultimate question, "What is real?" Are there other realms of existence that lie over and beyond our mere sensory experience? If there are, then how can we have knowledge of these dimensions of reality?

And so, what begins as a consideration of one aspect of the practical enterprise of educational method becomes a philosophical inquiry, though the original object was not to fabricate a philosophy of education but to try to think clearly about methods of teaching. Not everyone who is an educator pushes the question as far as it will go. Many remain always at the first level. They adopt their teaching methods by deliberate imitation or inherit them from their ancestors in about the same way they inherit their religion and their politics. They do not take the trouble to inquire about the interrelationships of their methodological ideas with other ideas they hold. Fortunately, there are always some who approach their teaching responsibilities thoughtfully. They are willing to think as clearly as they know how about the problems of education and when they make the effort they find, as Max Black has said:

> All serious discussion of educational problems, no matter how specific, soon leads to consideration of educational *aims* and becomes a conversation about the good life, the nature of man, the varieties of experience. But these are the perennial themes of philosophical investigation. It

might seem a hard thing to expect educators to be philosophers. But can they be anything else?[10]

It must have been similar considerations that led John Dewey at an earlier time to say: "The philosophy of education is not a poor relation of general philosophy even though it is often so treated even by philosophers. It is ultimately the most significant phase of philosophy."[11]

SUMMARY

The general plan for our inquiry can now be summarized. Attention will be given first to certain major traditions that have influenced the character of western culture. The major thesis is that there are fundamental inconsistencies and conflicts among these traditions and that it is these conflicts that are in large measure responsible for the conflicts that plague educational theory today. These matters are considered in the chapter immediately following.

The remainder of the book after Chapter II is concerned with a detailed analysis of five traditions, all of which, it is thought, have important things to say about education. These traditions are more than educational theories; most of them, in fact, represent comprehensive views of the nature of man and of human society and in every case the specific educational proposals contained in these traditions are related to such other social institutions as politics, economics, religion, and philosophy. In our analysis we will begin with the specific educational proposals involved in the tradition being studied. When we have grasped the general structure of its educational thought we will inquire into the relation of these practical ideas to other kinds of ideas that are important in the tradition.

[10] Max Black, "A Note on Philosophy of Education," *Harvard Educational Review*, 26:154–5 (Spring, 1956), p. 155.
[11] *Problems of Men*, New York: Philosophical Library, 1946, p. 165.

CHAPTER TWO

Conflicting Traditions

in American Society

In the preceding chapter it was suggested that the confusion and acrimony that beset educational theory and practice in America today are themselves products of certain fundamental conflicts in this society. These underlying conflicts are occasioned in important respects by the competition of traditions—the breakdown of the old and the struggle of the new for dominance. In terms of Linton's[1] analysis, referred to in the preceding chapter, what was once the central core of tradition has become indistinct. We can no longer discern with much clarity that which is focal and essential and that which is peripheral and of only passing importance. Consequently, in our efforts to come to some agreement on the theory of education we find ourselves a house divided and the division is not into two parts but many. As Aristotle observed in surveying the state of education of his own time:

> For mankind are by no means agreed about the things to be taught . . .
> The existing practice is perplexing; no one knows on what principle we
> should proceed.[2]

It is almost certain that there were numerous citizens in the Athens of Aristotle's time who were sure they knew on what principle education should proceed. The point of Aristotle's observation is, of course, that it was not possible to get agreement in the community on any common principle. Over two thousand years later we find ourselves in the same

[1] See ante, p. 2.
[2] Aristotle, *Politics*, Book VIII, Chapter 3, Jowett translation.

predicament. There is no scarcity today of people who think they know with the greatest certainty what principles should govern education, but we, too, are unable to find agreement.

We do not have agreement and it seems unlikely that we will get it until such time as the general condition of society becomes much more stable than it presently is. No one living now knows how soon we may succeed in crystallizing a central core of tradition and value which will give direction and steady purpose to our educational thought and practice. Nor does any man know now, except in the broadest outlines, what the character of this core of tradition is likely to be. We can say with confidence that we will not have widespread agreement on modes of educating the young until we have in some way achieved reasonable agreement on the central values to be achieved.

The position taken here is that although the process of cultural change is so monumental that no one man, nor even a generation, can make much impact on its direction and character, still ideas and convictions do have a part to play. This is to say that in a time of upheaval as far reaching as that of the present age, there are choices to be made and no man can escape them. Even those who refuse to take a stand on any important issue, preferring, as they say, to maintain an "open-minded" attitude, are choosing to throw what influence they have in the direction of the *status quo*.

Men can choose blindly and with little thought about the significance of their choice. This is not necessary, though it may happen often, for man can also choose with awareness of the import of his decisions. To choose wisely about education or politics, or religion or any other matter of high moment, men must apprehend as clearly as they can the direction in which their choices point. This effort to foresee what will happen if such and such a course of action is taken can be guided only by previous experience—individual and collective. The future is always unclear and unpredictable in many of its important aspects, but our ability to control it will depend on our success in using the experience we have gained to interpret the possibilities that lie ahead. The development of culture is not capricious. What happens in one age emerges from the conditions that went before it. Cause and effect relations obtain as much in the process of cultural change as in any phenomenon of nature.

Today western culture and western education are a welter of conflicting traditions. Some of these traditions are products of ages far removed from ours in historical time. Others stem from the modern world. These traditions are about man and his relation to the world. They deal with human nature and destiny, human knowledge, the good life, the problem of good and of evil. They incorporate all of these and at bottom they are in conflict. It is these conflicts that plague our efforts to design an education suitable for man in the contemporary world.

The purpose of this chapter is to create a kind of backdrop against which variant philosophical traditions current in American society may be analyzed. It is assumed that readers of this book are already conversant from their studies in history and related fields with the major traditions that have gone into the shaping of the American mind. Our purpose here, therefore, is not a comprehensive exposition of these cultural traditions, a procedure that is obviously impossible within the limits of space available; rather, our purpose is to recall the salient aspects of these traditions to mind so that they may be available to us in conducting our educational inquiry. If we are to be able to choose wisely among the alternatives our times present, we must be aware of the issues with which our decisions inevitably are involved.

THE LEGACY OF ANTIQUITY

There are two great bodies of tradition in the west whose origins lie far in the past. Both of these traditions have exerted great influence on the development of western culture and they still are potent factors in shaping the mind of contemporary man. One of these traditions stems from the flowering of Hellenic culture whose essence is to be found in the great philosophical works of Plato and Aristotle. The other is the Hebraic-Christian tradition whose influence on the western world has been so great as to beggar description. No assessment of the state of contemporary society can be made apart from the effects of these historic influences.

The Classic Tradition

The Greeks set the problems with which western philosophy has dealt for more than twenty centuries. One of the doctrines of Greek thought which has had great effect on subsequent cultural history was the crystallization of a dualistic concept of human nature. The idea that man is composed of two factors, one physical, the other non-material, was not original with the Greeks. Such ideas are found among primitive people and are important in primitive interpretations of nature. But the Greeks brought this idea to a level of sophistication which went far beyond the simple animism of the primitive.

Body and soul, the two components of Greek dualism, were made the basis for theory of knowledge, ethics, politics, and education. Man is conceived as a physical body and an immaterial principle, soul. The two are separate entities but they operate together, each affecting the other. The ideal of the Greeks was a man in whom these factors were in perfect accord, when reason controlled the baser appetites of the body and all was one harmonious relationship.

To the Greek the term soul did not have the same meaning it came to have in the Christian tradition. Soul was primarily the vitalizing or energizing principle which gives life and motion to body, and the presence of soul distinguishes the animate from the inanimate. Soul gives to living things certain natural powers or potencies. There are various levels of these powers, but the very highest power is unique to man. This is the power of reason. It is man's rationality that distinguishes him from all other animals and is, therefore, that which defines his essential nature.

From this basic dualism various theories of ethics, politics, and education emerged. First of all, since soul is the higher principle of personality, the activity of soul is a higher form of behavior than the activity of the physical body. Since the Greeks did not believe that an excellent soul could exist in a weak and underdeveloped physique, they made physical exercise an important part of the education of children and youth. But of physical work the Greek had the lowest possible opinion.[3]

This contempt for productive work had two dimensions—one theoretical, based on the soul-body dualism, the other practical and based on the reality of Greek social and economic life. Though we usually think of Greece as the cradle of democratic government, the fact is that Greek democracy rested on an economic basis of chattel slavery and an artisan class which was not enslaved, but which did not enjoy the rights of full citizenship. These artisans and slaves were the hewers of wood and the drawers of water for the city. The citizen, that is, the free man, had leisure to cultivate the powers of reason, to reflect on philosophy and other high matters. Physical labor was considered

[3] For a summary of the Greek attitude towards manual labor and trade see: G. Lowes Dickinson, *The Greek View of Life*, Ann Arbor: The University of Michigan Press, 1948, Chapter III.

unworthy of the citizen, for labor warps and disfigures the body, making a man old and weak before his time and enervating the soul. Both Plato and Aristotle agreed that mechanical and mercantile occupations are so unfavorable in their effect on soul and body that free citizens should have none of them. The proper activity of the free man is the activity of his rational powers which constitute the higher portion of his nature. True, he must have enough of worldly goods to sustain him in comfort, but if he must toil for these in field or shop he can never be a happy man.

The theoretical dualism now emerges as a theory of education. Just as there are activities which are appropriate to slaves—servile activities —so are there also activities which are appropriate to free men—liberal activities. The servile arts are the arts of the physical body; the liberal arts are the arts of reason. Thus we come to the oldest, the most difficult, and the most persistent idea in all of western educational theory, an idea which today is at the center of our own controversy over education.

What is a liberal education? In Greek culture the answer was simple. A liberal education is one which is appropriate to a free man, free in the political sense, but also free from the degrading necessity for practical work. The servile arts are illiberal by their very nature, but at least some activities can be liberal or illiberal depending on the motive for their pursuit. Aristotle was precise on this point:

> There are also some liberal arts quite proper for a free man to acquire, but only in a certain degree, and if he attend to them too closely, in order to attain perfection in them, the same evil effects will follow. The object also which a man sets before him makes a great difference; if he does or learns anything for its own sake or for the sake of his friends, or with a view to excellence, the action will not appear illiberal; but if done for the sake of others, the very same action will be thought menial and servile.[4]

The idea of liberal education was a product of Greek culture. Its social, as well as theoretical origins, have been studied exhaustively. When this idea passed over into medieval education and most particularly when it entered into the cultures of the Renaissance world, it lost its clarity, if not its appeal for many people. In subsequent chapters the part this ancient educational idea plays in modern theories of education will be discussed. Before we leave this subject, however, there are two other ideas derived from the Greek dualism which are closely related to the liberal idea of education. These are the Greek conception of

[4] Aristotle, *Politics*, Book VIII, Chapter 3, Jowett translation.

PHILOSOPHY OF AMERICAN EDUCATION

education as a process or discipline and the essential duality of knowledge that is central to the Greek tradition.

In Greek thought the mind was conceived as an aggregate of specific natural powers or faculties. In the beginning of life these exist in potential only, in the same sense that the oak tree is potential in the acorn. In order for their potential to be realized they must be developed through the proper discipline. Thus, such a faculty as memory or judgment can be developed by exercises in memorizing or in making judgments in logical discourse. The primary aim of education is to develop the arts of knowledge, it is not to acquire vast amounts of information. The Socratic method as it is revealed in the Platonic Dialogues is not a method of transmitting information, but rather a method of cultivating methods of inquiry and dialectic. Part of the Greek contempt for the Sophists stemmed from the Sophists' advertising themselves as dispensers of knowledge on any subject. Aristotle's comments on their teaching were withering. On one occasion he compared the Sophist to a shoemaker who took an apprentice, presumably to teach him the art of shoemaking. But this shoemaker instead only gave the apprentice several pairs of shoes of different sizes. Like the Sophist, he could not distinguish between an art and its products.[5] To the Greek mind, then, the purpose of education was the perfection of the intellectual powers which men have by their nature, and education was conceived as a disciplinary process—the development of the arts of knowledge. The Greek educational ideal was wisdom not erudition.

The other element in the Greek tradition that bears on this analysis is the dual conception of knowledge in which knowledge based on reason is regarded as superior to that based on sense experience. This is a central theory in Platonic philosophy, a system of thought which consistently gives sense knowledge an inferior status in the order of knowledge. In the Republic (Book VI) Plato emphasizes the superiority of the rational over the sensory forms of knowledge, calling the latter images or shadows about which only opinion can be had, while reason can know Truth as it is embodied in the Forms or Ideas. Thus, there is an order of knowledge beginning with sense impression (opinion) which apprehends only the changing flux of things, and ascending to reason which, through dialectic and logical insight, apprehends Truth. Not all men can attain to rational insight, in fact most of them are

---

[5] Aristotle, De Sophisticis Elenchis, Chapter 34, 184a, translated by W. A. Pickard, Cambridge. A denunciation of the Sophists by Plato is found in The Republic, Book VI.

bound to the animal level of sense impression. Only those who are capable of reaching the ultimate height of rational insight are worthy to rule the state. The rest are to perform the menial work of the city or protect it against its enemies. The just state, Plato thought, was that in which each man performed the work he was fitted for and did not interfere with the work of others.

The keystone of the classic tradition is Reason. The Greeks were not ashamed to be animals, but they saw man as a rational animal who could control his appetites and regulate his life in accord with rational principles of ethics. Education was the process of perfecting those natural powers of intellect which all men have—though some have them in greater measure than others. The good life is that in which all elements of man's nature are in harmony; when his lower nature has been perfected through training in right habits and his ultimate or rational nature has been perfected through liberal education.

The Hebraic-Christian Tradition

There are striking differences between the Hebraic-Christian and the Greek conceptions of man and the world in which he lives. Whereas Aristotle had taught that the earth and all species had always existed in their present form, the Hebrew accounted for the existence of the universe in terms of a specific act of creation. The creation of the world was a single planned act in which man was the last and supreme object. Man was created by God in His own image, and he was endowed with attributes similar to those of the Creator: mind, moral consciousness, and free will. Unlike his Creator, man is also a carnal creature, subject to the appetites and lusts of the flesh; prone to temptation and sin. In the beginning man had enjoyed a state of grace, but this he had lost by his failure to obey the word of God. All mankind is marked with the brand of this original sin and human nature therefore is depraved.

But God made possible a means of salvation and provided a way which man could attain the state of grace he had lost. A promise was repeated through the years by the Prophets who foretold the coming of a Messiah, the redemption of the people, and the establishment of the Kingdom of God on earth. According to Christian doctrine, the first of these events occurred when God sent his only Son into the world to teach the people and, through His own suffering and death, to expiate the sin of man and offer salvation to all who would believe. Among the Jews salvation was regarded as collective. It would come to the people as a whole. In Christian doctrine salvation is of the individual through his profession of belief and membership in the Christian community.

As in the Greek tradition, a fundamental dualism is involved in the Hebraic-Christian interpretation of the nature of man. But this dualism differs in certain important respects from that of the Greek. Man is conceived as being composed of a physical body and an immaterial soul. The body is mortal and its existence ends with death, but the soul is immortal and will pass from this earth to another world where it will continue its existence through all eternity. To the Christian communicant life on this earth is a prelude to that which is to come. Where each man will spend eternity depends on how he endures the test which earthly life places on him. The immortal part of him can spend eternity in paradise where the soul can regain its complete nature, or it can suffer the unspeakable torments of hell. This life, therefore, has no intrinsic importance except as it is a means of transition to the hearafter. If the just suffer in this world, at least they will know peace in the next, and what is a few score years here as compared with the prospect of eternity?

Salvation comes as a result of believing in God, of accepting the grace which His Son made possible, and in obeying the commandments of God. Here we discover another difference between Greek and Jewish thought which is of the greatest significance. Where the Greek had depended on the natural powers of reason to reveal the truth, the Hebraic tradition was built on the belief that knowledge of God's ways are revealed to man, not through any rational process, but directly from God. The ultimate source of truth is God's word and this is revealed to man through the prophets. To the Greek mind this can be interpreted as anti-intellectualism at its most flagrant, for truth becomes a matter of faith rather than rational demonstration. Thus, the great dichotomy between faith and reason developed, a problem which has haunted western culture for centuries and has not yet been laid to rest either by ecclesiastical scholarship or the sophisticated naturalism of modern science.

Primitive Christianity was not an intellectual movement, nor was the Founder of Christianity a scholar grounded in the subtleties of metaphysics. He preached a simple ethic based on love and held out the promise of redemption through emotional acceptance of salvation. His initial appeal was largely to common people who found no intellectual barriers to the acceptance of the doctrine. Furthermore, the leaders of the early Christian communities had a profound suspicion of pagan learning and philosophy was forbidden to communicants as a symbol of the corruption of a decadent society which was shortly to be destroyed.

The synthesis of Greek and Christian traditions was one of the momentous events in the evolution of western culture. This great process of acculturation took many years. The infusion of Greek philosophy into Christian theology began initially with the growing influence of Stoicism and Neo-Platonism. St. Augustine, greatest of the early church fathers and Bishop of Hippo, had been trained in philosophy in his youth. It was through the influence of men of this stature that the process of rationalizing Christian doctrine on the basis of Greek and Roman philosophy was begun. This ultimate achievement in this process was realized in the 13th and 14th centuries after western scholars had recovered the works of Aristotle, particularly the *Organon* and the *Metaphysics*. The final synthesis of these two traditions was achieved by such scholars as Albertus Magnus and most notably, of course, Thomas Aquinas, whose writings still define to considerable extent the philosophical position of the Roman Catholic Church. It was thus that the *Philosophia Perennis* was born; the great tradition of the union of faith and reason which has waxed and waned over the centuries that make up the modern era but which has never died. Today it offers again a spirited challenge to the dominant tradition in American culture and education, a challenge which will be examined in detail in a later chapter.

The Greek and the Hebraic-Christian traditions are the legacy of the ancient and medieval worlds to modern culture. Though they are old in time, they are still important strands in the fabric of contemporary society. Though Christianity dominated western society for a thousand years, uniting men in a great community which knew little of national or geographic boundaries, providing a measure of cultural stability which the civilized world has seldom seen, ultimately its undisputed hegemony ended. New forces appeared in western culture and a great transition occurred. We turn now to a brief review of some traditions which stem from the post-medieval era and which are of significance to our own times.

TRADITIONS OF THE MODERN WORLD

The breakup of the feudal system and the great transition movement of which it was a part brought new forces and new ideas to the west. Under the feudal pattern of society Europe had been a patchwork of petty political states, the power of kings was limited, and more often than not the real political power lay in the hands of the warlike lesser nobility. The emotional attachments of men were to their own communities, their own feudal lord, and, under the aegis of the Universal Church, to the Christian community. The horizons of medieval man were restricted. He seldom went far beyond the locality in which he was born and whatever glimpses he had of any other life was that of the next world portrayed by the parish priest. He seldom thought of himself as a Frenchman or a German or an Englishman, and if he ever did, the thought meant little to him. He could not read, and even if he had been able he would not have read his native tongue but Latin, the great universal language which all literate men used for communication and scholarship.

The social structure he knew was rigidly stratified. Most men were bound to the soil in serfdom. And from the lowest serf to the most powerful noble, all men were bound in the feudal network of responsibilities. To rise from one social class to another was unknown, and social, economic, or political equality was unthought. By and large, the economic life of medieval man was restricted to the locality. The manor was self-sufficient, or nearly so. Economic production occurred in the vineyards, fields, and shops of the manor, and what was produced was consumed by the inhabitants. Trade and commerce with distant localities played but a small part. Money was scarce and no Christian could lend it at interest, for usury was forbidden in the canon law.

Whatever one may think of the lot of medieval man, it must be agreed that if life for most people was hard and the fruits of it scanty, yet there was a kind of security and regularity to life that can come only when beliefs and ideals are widely—and by the mass of people unthinkingly—held. The middle ages were not the time of cultural stagnation they have sometimes been thought, but compared with the modern age they seem a time when much of life was settled and secure. There was above all the security offered by the Universal Church in which all communicants could find refuge from an often hard and resistant world. By the beginning of the 15th century the great transition movement was well underway. The events attending it are far too complicated even to be outlined here, but out of it developed four great traditions that were to determine in large measure the mind of the modern American. These traditions are nationalism, democracy, capitalism, and science—all unknown, at least as we understand them, in the ancient and medieval worlds—and all of them challenges in one way or another to the old traditions.

Nationalism

Though its roots lie far back in history, nationalism is itself a tradition of the modern world. It is compounded of two ingredients: nationality, the consciousness of belonging to some defined group with certain common attributes, and patriotism, the love for and attachment to the land in which one lives. These sentiments are very old. They are seen in the ancient Hebrew tribes who thought of themselves as different from all other peoples and who set themselves as the chosen people apart from the Gentiles. So too with the Greek who thought of himself as superior in all respects to the barbarians.

There is no absolute set of conditions which are necessary for the emergence of nationalities. Some common conditions which are influential are a common language, a common body of tradition, and a common religion. However, there are well-defined nationalities today which do not meet these criteria. More than anything else nationality is a state of mind, a feeling of belonging to a group based on some common ties, ties which may vary from one group to another, but which lay strong claim to the allegiance of the individual.

Patriotism, the other factor in modern nationalism, is primarily an emotional attachment to one's locality, an emotion which was common even in ancient times. For example, the patriotism of the Greeks tended to be local. The Greek's attachment was not so much to all that was Greek but to his own city—to Athens or Sparta or Corinth. In highly developed political units, even in the ancient world, the tendency is strong to place patriotism above all other loyalties and to submerge oneself in the honor and destiny of the state.

Modern nationalism goes far beyond the simple patriotism of earlier periods, for only in the modern world has the idea been accepted that *it is not only the right but the historic destiny of every nationality to form its own national state.* This is modern nationalism, the tradition which perhaps more than any other determines the political pattern of the contemporary world. The essence of nationalism is the claim of the national state to the primary allegiance of all members of a nationality, and history indicates that this claim of primary allegiance is never relinquished. Nationalities may be submerged in great empires, as indeed they frequently have been, but more often than not repression only serves to fan the flame of patriotism.

International organizations may be formed, and indeed two of them have existed in this century, but there is as yet no visible evidence that any modern state will willingly surrender one shred of its national sovereignty. To be sure, states have surrendered part or all of their sovereignty as the result of threat or outright conquest, but this is invariably viewed as a calamity. Furthermore internationalism is not, strictly speaking, the antithesis of nationalism. Internationalism presupposes the existence of national states, and though to some people internationalism may imply the surrender of a measure of sovereignty, the world has yet to see such a surrender occur voluntarily.

The character of modern nationalism is perhaps seen most clearly in its opposition to other traditions which also compete for the primary allegiance of men. Nationalism has frequently been in conflict with the church, which historically has functioned as a great universal institution seeking to realize the doctrine of the reconciliation of classes, the brotherhood of all men, and their union in the Fatherhood of God. The conflict has sometimes been overt, more often, perhaps, somewhat concealed. A common effort to solve the problem has been to combine church and state completely, as for example in Spain under the Franco government. Another way has been to separate church and state legally, guaranteeing religious freedom for individuals, prohibiting the use of taxes for support of churches, but in no way compromising the rights of the state to the allegiance of its citizens. The United States is an example of this policy, and though the United States has shown it to be workable, there have always been complicated problems, some of which have not as yet been solved. Another approach has been that of ruthless suppression of the church, the seizure of church property, and liquidation of the clergy. The best example of this kind of effort of a national state to deal with the challenge of organized religion is, of course, the Soviet Union.

In those states in which religion plays an important part in social life the strategy has usually been to identify the destiny of the state with the will of God. Each nation always considers its cause the just cause and the name of God is invoked to help make the right prevail. The cross and the flag advance together, and the enemies of the state become the enemies of the Deity. No other institution, excepting perhaps the church, has understood symbol and ceremony so well or used them so effectively to appeal to the emotions of men as has the national state. As the cross is the symbol of Christianity and the Star of David the symbol of Judaism, so the flag is the symbol of the national state. There is music which is sacred to the state: hymns and anthems, and above all, martial music. Each nation has its roll of martyrs and saints. The state maintains sacred places which people journey long distances to visit.

And just as excommunication is the most awful punishment the Church can visit on the heretic, so banishment—loss of citizenship—is the supreme penalty of the national state. Many men have shown that they would prefer death to this punishment, for to be without national citizenship to most men is a living death.

The amount of freedom a state grants to its nationals is usually in direct proportion to the degree of threat it is undergoing. The threat may be internal or external—or both. In times when domestic and international events are relatively tranquil the state, particularly if it has a liberal and democratic tradition, will enlarge and preserve the area of civil liberties. Citizens will feel generally free to speak and publish within wide bounds. Due legal processes will be followed more or less scrupulously and there will be a minimum of police spying on the activities of citizens. Teachers will be free to teach and sometimes they may even teach, without being molested, doctrines that some conservative citizens think are utterly subversive of the state.

But let the threat of internal uprising or invasion from without appear and this picture changes quickly. The area of freedom contracts and civil liberties are curtailed. Censorship is established over the press and other media of communication. Freedom of expression is narrowed, sometimes to the vanishing point. Official, quasi-official, and even private committees, commissions, and investigating bodies are formed whose fundamental purpose is to root out treason and insure orthodoxy.

The schools are among the first to feel the effects of these measures. There is scarcely any group within a nation of whose loyalties the state is more jealous than that of teachers. Complete political orthodoxy is demanded. Textbooks are scanned for material that might be thought threatening to the state. Teachers are required to sign special oaths of allegiance to the state and not infrequently these contain a disclaimer in which the signer attests that he is not a member of subversive organizations. The teacher is expected to infuse his teaching with the spirit of patriotism and to defend and glorify the institutions of the nation.

The emergence of free, compulsory education so closely parallels the development of nationalism that some historians have thought that the development of universal education is more closely associated with the development of modern nationalism than with any other cultural development.[6] The role the school has played most consistently in the modern world is that of an instrument of the national state. It has

[6] Carleton J. H. Hayes, *Essays on Nationalism*, New York: The Macmillan Company, 1926, pp. 80–82.

PHILOSOPHY OF AMERICAN EDUCATION

been the key agent in the preservation and propagation of the national heritage. It has proved itself, as Napoleon wrote in 1805, the most strategic of political institutions.

> Of all political questions, that [of education] is perhaps the most important . . . If the child is not taught from infancy that he ought to be a republican or a monarchist or a freethinker, the state will not constitute a nation; it will rest on uncertain and shifting foundations; and it will be constantly exposed to disorder and change.[7]

Nationalism has challenged the old traditions at every point. It has competed actively, and more often than not successfully, for the primary allegiance of men. It has sought to supersede the ancient Christian doctrine of the reconciliation of classes and the brotherhood of men which knows no boundaries of race, nationality, or geography. It has not united mankind but only nationalities. Modern nationalism has challenged the Greek idea that it is reason that binds men in community life, for nationalism's real appeal is to the emotions of men—not their reason. It is a glorification of the nationality, of blood and soil and tradition. Perhaps more than at any other point the challenge of nationalism has been felt most deeply by the church over the question of the education of children. For ages, the church held stubbornly to the principle that above all else education is its prerogative, and the oldest segment of Christendom still holds tenaciously to this doctrine. In most western countries—and most certainly in America—the national state has clearly won the day in the struggle to control the schools. Our schools are public and presumably secular. They are operated by the state in the interest of the state and this holds true even in a country with as decentralized a system as our own.

Capitalism

Coincident with the rise of nationalism and closely related to it, capitalism appeared after the break up of the feudal system and the medieval world. Primarily the term capitalism refers to a certain kind of economic system which is different in many respects from earlier forms of economy. Ultimately capitalism is more than a system of economy. It is, in a sense, a philosophical system involving well defined ideas about human nature, the existence and operation of natural law, and the source and character of values. This system of thought has had

[7] Quoted in Edward H. Reisner, *Education and Nationalism Since 1789*, New York: The Macmillan Company, 1922, p. 12.

profound influence on the shaping of the American mind and many of the values Americans hold are closely related to it.

As an institution, capitalism is built on the doctrine that the purpose of the economic system is to enable individuals to acquire wealth—primarily, monetary wealth. This idea contrasts with pre-capitalistic ideas of economy in which the individual as producer or consumer was the focus of economic effort. Under capitalism the purpose of the economy is not primarily to produce goods and services in terms of the needs of consumers, but to acquire wealth in the form of profits. There are no discernible limits to this profit-seeking activity. It is common knowledge that individuals will continue to work long after they have amassed more wealth than they or their immediate families could possibly consume in a lifetime. The motive for this activity surely is not that of making a living—even a sumptuous one—for oneself and one's family; the motive must be that of acquiring wealth for its own sake.

If this is true of individuals, consider what it means for the corporation—the fundamental unit of modern capitalism. The corporation is not a person with needs for food and clothing and other commodities. The corporation exists to make profits and this "need" for profit making is unlimited. A corporate enterprise is never satiated, regardless of the amount of profit it succeeds in making.

As a system, capitalism involves certain definite ideas concerning human nature, particularly human motivation. Just as, according to classic capitalistic doctrine, competition is the life of trade, so competition is also the basic motive for human behavior. Life is a continuous struggle for acquisition and supremacy. In this struggle the strong and self-reliant survive and the weak and ineffectual lose out. This is the law of nature.[8]

Capitalistic doctrine relies heavily on the concept of natural law as a rationale. Just as physical nature is governed by the inexorable operation of natural law, so also is the economic system.[9] The law of supply and demand, for example, is no more an invention of the human mind than is the law of gravity. It is true that we can ignore the operation of natural law or attempt to interfere with its operation, but we always

[8] When this attitude was combined with Darwin's evolutionary thesis of the "survival of the fittest" in the latter part of the nineteenth century, the idea of "Social Darwinism" emerged. A definitive work on the influence of this development in America is: Richard Hofstadter, *Social Darwinism in American Thought*, rev. ed., Boston: The Beacon Press, 1955.

[9] See as an example: Fred G. Clark and Richard S. Rimanoczy, "The Master Blueprint" in A. G. Heinsohn, Jr. (ed.) *Anthology of Conservative Writing in the United States: 1932–1960*, Chicago: Henry Regnery Company, 1962, p. 386 ff.

suffer the consequences of our folly. A man can ignore the law of gravity by jumping off a cliff but in so doing he does not violate the law, he illustrates its workings.

Similarly, a government can interfere with the natural operations of the market by price fixing or other operations of this kind. But the consequences that follow on this interference with nature can be as calamitous as those that befall the man who jumps off the cliff. What is needed therefore is a hands-off attitude by the state. The only legitimate function of the government is to exert police power to keep the market free. The economic system is rational, lawful, and predictable so long as it is allowed to function without interference. And so, too, is the economic activity of human beings so long as they are given freedom to act in the market. This, in fact, becomes the fundamental concept of freedom espoused under capitalism. Without freedom to acquire and hold wealth and property there is no real freedom for the individual. Hence, almost by definition, no society organized along socialist lines, or any other form of collectivism, can ever be a free society, nor can individuals within such a society experience freedom in its true sense. One reason for this is, of course, that lack of economic freedom is a basic violation of human nature. By nature man is a competitive and acquisitive creature. His basic motives stem from his desire for self-preservation and self-interest. His major effort is to preserve himself in the unending economic struggle. To the extent that government or other institutions interfere in this struggle, to that extent does government subvert the fundamental pattern of the nature of man. Man's freedom is destroyed, or, at the very least, is gravely compromised.

Now it follows from this that the basic human virtues are thrift, personal industry, self-reliance, and prudence. The corresponding evils are profligacy, sloth, and reliance on charity—in short, all forms of economic irresponsibility and improvidence. The ethical ideal is individualism as rugged as possible. A favorite ethical symbol of American society has long been the man of humble origins—preferably one born in a log cabin or, in later days, in a modest cottage on the wrong side of the railroad tracks—who by his own efforts fought his way to wealth and the power and prestige that wealth brings.

This is not necessarily the bloodless doctrine of selfishness and economic savagery that some radical thinkers have tried to make it out. Under capitalism there is not necessarily a lack of concern for social and human welfare. The capitalistic tradition insists that the interests of society will always advance best when natural law is allowed to operate without interference. There will be more goods and services produced, distribution of the fruits of production will be more widespread and more even. The increase of wealth in the form of capital obtained from profits will redound to the advantage of the whole community in terms of a higher standard of living and all the blessings that follow on economic prosperity. When the economic system is allowed to take its natural course, it is a self-correcting operation. If evils appear, as for example over-production of some commodity, the system has a built-in mechanism to correct this fault.

Likewise, the welfare of the individual is most advanced under the capitalistic system. Man is free to express those fundamental virtues of humanity: intelligence, industry, self-reliance, and to reap the rewards they bring. He is free from the arbitrary controls of government over his economic activity. He is allowed to acquire as much as he can through his own efforts and to use this wealth as he sees fit. He is not penalized by the government for exercising his initiative and labor. Only as man experiences this fundamental economic freedom can he expect to have those political and social freedoms he so much desires.

The motives of men are many and varied. Some crave power and fame, some desire to do good works through philanthropy, but all such aims as these are necessarily dependent on the fundamental aim, that of profit making. Unless a man in his economic activity is successful, i.e., unless he makes a profit, he cannot hope to do good works or achieve power or fame. The drive to acquire, therefore, remains the basic motive under the system of capitalism.

Although the beginnings of capitalism may be traced to the 13th century, its period of vigorous growth began in the 17th century with the growing power of the middle class. Plainly, there was much in this new development that was at odds with the old traditions. For one thing, capitalism glorified the useful and practical. It attributed honor to productive work, and where the classic Greek had seen such activity as slavish and servile, the capitalist saw useful work as among the highest forms of human activity.

In the beginning, the spirit of capitalism was plainly hostile to certain old and deep-seated Christian principles. Avarice had long since been declared by the church to be a serious sin. The scriptures advise that the love of money is the root of all evil. Jesus Himself had said that it is as hard for a rich man to find the Kingdom of God as it is for a camel to go through the eye of a needle. Christianity had ordinarily looked upon poverty as being associated with individual sanctity and spiritual purity, an attribute that was harmonious with the notion of the elevation of the spirit through subjugation of the flesh. Certainly it has been a common practice for monastic orders to require their members to take the vow of poverty. Moreover, the medieval church had forbidden Christians to lend money at interest. Added to this was the plain fact that under the emerging capitalistic system man was to be regarded mainly as an element in the productive process. Human labor was a commodity subject to the natural laws of the market. If, in a surplus labor market, men were deprived of gainful employment this might be a regrettable thing but it was caused by the inexorable laws of nature. Obviously it is only a short step from this belief that the pursuit of economic gain is a law of nature to the identification of profit seeking with the will of God and success in the market as a sign of divine favor.

It was, in fact, Puritanism that supplied the rationale for a philosophy that in the end deserted the older Christian attitudes toward economic life. This process began in England in the 17th century and its effects were shortly felt in the New World as English Puritans began their colonization. The Puritan ethic, in brief, centered around the sanctification of work. The primary duty of Christians is the love and service of God. Faith is the primary obligation, but God is served through good works, and good works in the Puritan mind came to be interpreted not as labors done in penance for sin but useful and productive work—i.e., *economic activity*. Tawney quotes from a remarkable Puritan tract entitled *The Trademan's Calling, being a Discourse concerning the Nature, Necessity, Choice, etc. of a Calling in General,* published in 1684 by a minister, one Richard Steele:

> God doth call every man and woman . . . to serve him in some peculiar employment in this world, both for their own and the common good . . . The Great Governour of the world hath appointed to every man his proper post and province, and let him be never so active out of his sphere, he will be at a great loss, if he do not keep his own vineyard and mind his own business.[10]

In such a scheme of things poverty is surely no virtue nor any sign of sanctity. To be poor and destitute is to be a nuisance to society but it also is a breach of ethics. In fact, destitution may very well be a punishment for the sin of idleness. The poor can be seen now, not as unfor-

---

[10] Quoted in R. H. Tawney, *Religion and the Rise of Capitalism,* New York: The New American Library of World Literature; a Mentor Book, copyright 1926 by Harcourt Brace, p. 200. These sentiments offer an interesting contrast to certain ideas of the Founder of Christianity: "Consider the ravens: for they neither sow nor reap; which neither have storehouse nor barn; and God feedeth them; how much more are ye better than the fowls?" (Luke 12:24)

tunate victims of a system of economy, but rather victims of their own idleness and sloth. Charity, the virtue which the older Christianity had held in such reverence, must be re-interpreted. Charity seen as the giving of alms only weakens the individual and compounds the problem. He must be made to work, not only for the sake of society but for his own soul's salvation. This attitude towards the plight of the losers in the economic struggle linked itself naturally with the prevailing economic idea of human labor as a commodity of the market subject to the natural laws of economics. It was manifested in the exploitation of human beings under the early factory system, the growth of urban slums, and all the misery associated with early industrialism.

So far as America is concerned, historians are all but unanimous in the belief that no tradition could have been more appropriate for a people faced with the prospect of exploiting a new and boundlessly rich continent. The union of *laissez faire* economics and Puritan morality which sanctified productive work, making it second in ethical importance only to faith in the divine, is fundamental in the American mind. This tradition has supported those characteristically American virtues of industry, thrift, and aggressive individualism.

Great modifications have been made in the structure of capitalism since its early period and many of the evils associated with it have been eliminated, but much of the classic thesis is so engrained in the American mind that for many it has become a philosophy, as well as a conception of economics. Throughout our entire national history American schools have been called upon to promote the Puritan-capitalistic virtues and they have always responded. The schools have been expected to advocate the virtues of capitalistic economics and denigrate other conceptions of economic organization, and this they have done with conspicuous success. Among other things, American education has always been seen as a means for the individual to "get ahead," to rise above his economic and social origins. Americans are as fond of statistics which purport to show the financial advantages of prolonged schooling as they are of the belief in unlimited social and occupational mobility.[11]

Democracy

There is perhaps no word in the language that has more emotional impact on Americans nor one which is more difficult to define than

[11] See: Theodore W. Schultz, *The Economic Value of Education*, New York: Columbia University Press, 1963.

the word "democracy." It means all things to all Americans and commonly we use it to justify our actions in numerous fields and to legitimize our most diverse ambitions and desires. Its commonest significance is probably political. We think of democracy as rule by all the people rather than by an elite based on wealth, power, and blood. We tend to identify the term with certain political institutions and processes, as for example, universal suffrage, the secret ballot, representative government, majority rule. In American society we customarily identify democracy with certain economic institutions and processes, most notably economic individualism, free competition in the market, absence, or relative absence, of government interference in economic affairs. Probably to a majority of Americans democracy is as indissolubly linked with nationalism as it is with capitalism. American democracy is American nationalism and American capitalism and it is all but impossible for the average American to conceive of one apart from the other. The reason for this identification of democracy with capitalism and nationalism are to considerable degree historical. The three developments occurred together and were intertwined in the complex of cultural changes which have occurred in the post-medieval world.

The tracing of the myriad connections between these traditions is a task that cannot be attempted here. For reasons of economy of space and hopefully, of clarity, let us state initially that democracy, as idea and ideal, is ultimately a moral or ethical thesis. Its historical development has been long and often erratic. As an ideal it is a product of experience in many areas of cultural life: politics, economics, law, philosophy, religion, and education.

One key element in the conception of democracy is equality; the principle that all men are in some fashion equal. The important question is, of course, in what specific respects are men equal? And the only tenable answer to such a question seems to be that men are equal in the ethical sense. Common observation indicates that men are far from equal biologically and intellectually. What does a tradition of moral equality really mean? A common answer is that moral equality means that the human personality is of intrinsic worth. This is a notion that began early in western cultural experience and which found expression in both the great traditions of antiquity, but particularly in the Hebraic-Christian tradition. In this tradition all men are conceived as morally equal in the sight of God, and though on this earth there may be distinctions of wealth, and birth, and power, ultimately these will be as nothing when each man stands before the Seat of Judgment to account for his stewardship. The idea slowly developed that man possesses certain natural rights that cannot be abrogated. They cannot be abrogated because they have been given by God, and what God has given no man can rightfully take away. Human rights, therefore, depend ultimately on supernatural sanction. The dignity of man is the endowment of the creator, and the moral imperative is, as Kant said, "to treat humanity in every case as an end, never as a means only."

The doctrine of inalienable natural rights enjoys wide acceptance at the conceptual level in American society. Probably a majority of Americans still accept the eighteenth century idea of human rights as endowments of the Creator and believe, as did the author of the *Declaration of Independence*, that human rights originate with God. But among those who find it impossible to accept the supernatural account, there is also deep devotion to the idea of moral equality. Those who hold to this view most often seek to justify their belief on naturalistic grounds, citing cultural experience as the origin of and justification for their belief.

Our difficulties do not so much stem from lack of verbal agreement on the ethical thesis, rather they originate from attempts to express the ideal of equality in specific areas of social life. What, for example, does equality mean in political life? Does it mean the right to vote, to run for office, to advocate overthrow of the government, to contribute money to political parties or particular candidates for office? Does it mean literacy qualifications for voting or property qualifications or both? Is there a real relationship between political democracy and economic democracy?

And, for that matter, can equality in political rights exist apart from equality in economic affairs? What does economic democracy mean— if it means anything? Does it mean the same thing under conditions of industrial society that it meant to the eighteenth-century free-holder living on a farm he had carved out of the wilderness with his own hands? What do we mean when we speak of "equality of economic opportunity?" Should property rights take precedence over human rights or vice versa; or is the distinction valid anyway?

What is meant by "equality of educational opportunity?" To some it refers primarily to school finance and the operations of government to distribute equally the public funds available for the support of schools. To others it means that public institutions will not be segregated on racial, religious, or other arbitrary lines. A common sentiment is that every child and young person shall have the opportunity to as many years of schooling as he can profit by, but related to this idea is the nagging question of whether this means fourteen to eighteen years for some people and six or eight for others. We have long puzzled over the problem of whether equality of education means that everybody in the school shall receive exactly the same treatment with respect to curriculum and teaching, or whether programs and methods should vary with individual abilities and preferences.

Perhaps the most difficult question of all relates to the relation of "freedom" and "equality," both key words in most people's conception of the democratic ethic. These terms may appear easily accommodated under a single concept, but when we attempt to determine what they mean in specific circumstances of social activity the task is not easy. For instance given a scheme of economy in which freedom of competition is a basic principle, what happens to equality? Given a system of schooling in which academic competition is dominant, and what happens to equality? We need ask ourselves only a few questions of this kind to see how complicated the interpretation of these terms really is.

Though problems of interpretation and implementation are numerous and perplexing, the American mind clings resolutely to the ideal of democracy. As we have already observed, to most citizens American democracy means American capitalism and American nationalism. These traditions are the "Big Three" of contemporary culture, and to most of us any one of them could not exist in the absence of the other two. Be this as it may, it does not require much discernment to see that among these traditions, so closely linked by history, there are basic conflicts. Perhaps the most momentous of these is the conflict between the rugged individualism, which is so much a part of the tradition of American capitalism, and the democratic doctrine of ethical equality. This conflict involves, for one thing, the knotty question of the virtues of cooperation as opposed to competition in various aspects of social life. This question is by no means confined to economic theory, for one of the persistent questions, both of pedagogical theory and school practice, is the extent to which competition shall be exploited in the life of the school and to what extent cooperation should be the dominant value. Thus, such a commonplace issue as competitive school marking becomes entwined in the mind of antagonists and protagonists of the system, and invariably in the end each side will appeal to the "argument from democracy."

Although we have always been unsure whether democracy means freedom for the individual to act, with a minimum of interference from government or other authority, or whether the ultimate values lie in shared effort and a high degree of cooperation, this problem has increased in gravity in the present century. There can be little doubt that the democratic ethic places a high value on individual liberties and rights, nor is there much question but that democracy implies diversity in social life rather than a high level of uniformity. Still, the meaning of these ideas for contemporary life is obscure in many aspects. How much diversity in beliefs, habits, tastes, and loyalties can a democratic state tolerate and still maintain its national integrity in the face of external ideological and military threat?

A conception of education that has been with us throughout our national history is that the purpose of education is the enlightenment of men and the school is not in the service of any social class or institution of society. Yet how can such an idea be accommodated to our equally fervent convictions concerning, for example, nationalism? Academic freedom is a problem only in societies that subscribe in some measure to the doctrine of education as enlightenment, as opposed to indoctrination. In authoritarian societies it is not a problem because there the term itself has no meaning. But for the democratic society the question is: What are the limits of freedom to teach and to learn? How are they to be determined? And by whom? Can we place any limits at all and still preserve the ideal?

Historically, the advance of democracy has paralleled the development of public education in America. From the beginning of our history statesmen have maintained that the existence of a free democratic society necessitates a system of public education, open and free to all and dedicated to enlightenment. We can be sure that all but a handful of Americans today subscribe to these abstract sentiments. The real problem is to determine what the abstractions mean in operational terms, for it is here that our manifold controversies begin.

Science

The intellectual tradition that more than any other distinguishes the modern mind from that of the classic or medieval outlook is experimental science. We cannot pause here for more than a passing note on older conceptions of science: the preoccupation of the ancients with qualitative as opposed to quantitative relationships in most fields of inquiry; their tendency to explain the behavior of natural phenomena by means of internal factors: "forces," "urges" and "nature"; the insistence—even in the most elaborate cosmologies—on making the earth the center of the universe; the elevation of deductive reasoning over induction; and, at the same time, a naive faith in sensory data that seems almost pathetic to us of a later time. If we should look for the single element that distinguishes modern science from the older efforts to unravel the secrets of nature we will find it in the method that employs *hypothesis and experiment* as the foundation of method. There will be much more to say about scientific method and its influence on philosophical and educational developments in subsequent chapters. Our interest at this point is in a brief survey of the major components of the tradition and the relation of these principles to the other strands in the fabric of modern culture.[12]

Modern science is characterized first of all by *empiricism* and *naturalism*. By this we mean that science finds both its subject matter and its method within the natural process. Empiricism is the doctrine that all knowledge originates in sense experience and is ultimately reducible to sensory experience. On the negative side, it is a denial that there are any universal or necessary truths which hold independently of experience; that ideas are innate; or that men possess any faculty or power of "right reason" that automatically enables them to distinguish truth from opinion or error. A fundamental tenet of empiricism is, therefore, that *the limits of human knowledge are the limits of human experience.* Whatever lies outside the scope of experience, therefore, by definition lies outside the possibility of our knowledge. Moreover, empiricism implies that our knowledge, being a product of our experience, is a result of actions or operations which are consciously designed to test certain ideas or hypotheses that we develop.

These ideas about the nature and origin of knowledge are linked in turn with certain doctrines about the world and the reality that surrounds us. Naturalism, briefly, is the doctrine that the world does not depend for its existence and operation on any supernatural force of any kind, that the processes of the universe are not the product of any predetermined conscious design, and that nature is not moving towards any final or ultimate end. Naturalism involves also the principle that any or all the processes of nature are explainable in terms of the system of nature itself, and therefore all phenomena are explainable ultimately in purely natural terms without importing any force or entity, which, by definition, is outside of and independent of the world process.

A basic assumption of science is that nature is a continuous system, that there are no sudden breaks or dichotomies and that all allegedly

[12] Those who at this point desire to pursue the character of modern scientific philosophy further may wish to consult: *The Rise of Scientific Philosophy* by Hans Reichenbach, Berkeley and Los Angeles: The University of California Press, 1951.

absolute distinctions such as inorganic *and* organic; animate *and* inanimate, soul *and* body are unwarranted. The principle of continuity in nature postulates differences that are of degree rather than kind and explains the emergence of novelties and unique qualities in terms of the processes of nature—as, for example, natural selection. There is the further principle that all events are caused. That is, they depend for their occurrence on some antecedent state of affairs. And we understand, of course, that this state of affairs we call "cause" always has a material basis and is itself a part of the world process. This eliminates all allegedly "miraculous" happenings that are supposed to be the result of some kind of supernatural intervention in the natural process. It also eliminates the possibility of any events being self-caused or spontaneous.[13] If the cause-effect relation does hold throughout nature, then we can assume with confidence that whenever the same causal conditions are present the same results will follow. And this, in turn, implies the possibility that all events in the natural order are ultimately predictable and theoretically, at least, controllable. It is important to understand that this generalization applies to *all* events, not merely to that class of events with which physical scientists concern themselves.

The regularities of nature have always impressed mankind, and a common way of generalizing the idea of cosmic regularity and predictability is through the concept of natural law, a point to which some attention has already been given in connection with the doctrines of capitalism.[14] The view of natural law which was most amenable to the older science and to the prevailing religious climate was that natural laws are prior to and independent of the particular events that are governed by them. Given this notion, it is possible to achieve a kind of rapprochement between physics and theology. Under this view we can conceive of the physical universe as a great mechanism designed and executed by an omniscient and omnipotent Creator. This great cosmic machine is governed by a complex system of natural laws that regulate

---

13 Some students of scientific philosophy have maintained that *chance* is a real force in the world and that therefore the occurrence of some events is fortuitous, i.e., *uncaused* in the precise sense in which the term is defined above. One interesting discussion of this idea occurs in an essay by Charles Sanders Peirce called, "The Doctrine of Necessity Examined." This essay may be found in various editions of Peirce's collected works.

14 The term "natural law" is used in more than one sense and it is important to distinguish among them. As it is used in the present context the term refers to those laws to which the behavior of the phenomena of nature conform. Sometimes these are referred to as "the laws of nature." Another important sense in which the term is used involves an ethical concept. There is a natural law that is a part of the structure of nature itself and determines the rightness or wrongness of human actions. In this sense, the natural law is identical with the moral law.

every aspect of its working, including as we have already seen, the operations of the economic system. The universe, therefore, is logical in its structure and function and, therefore, potentially knowable. The purpose of science is to discover the universal laws that govern all things and express them in precise (i.e., mathematical) terms.[15]

As brilliant and useful as it was scientifically, and as comfortable as it came to be theologically, this view of natural law is no longer held by scientists. The prevailing view today is that what we call natural laws are really generalizations observers have made about the behavior of phenomena; these laws represent, in effect, *descriptions* of observed behavior. These descriptions are not final, and certainly they are not necessarily conclusive. Above all, they are not themselves causes. The law of gravity is not the *cause* of man's falling to the ground when he trips. Rather, the law of gravity is a description of the behavior of bodies (in this case the man and the earth) with respect to each other under certain conditions. As a law its power lies in its generality, that is, in the fact that we can account for all known instances by means of it and predict with accuracy events which have not as yet occurred.

Thus, the tradition of experimental science rests on a thorough-going naturalism and its method is firmly anchored in the thesis of empiricism. Modern science is not engaged in any quest for certainty. It does not promise any "ultimate truth" and, in fact, finds such an idea hampering to its efforts. Science recognizes only one method of proof and that is the appeal to experience, i.e., to *controlled experiment*.

No other element in modern culture has offered such challenge to the older traditions. Science has not only transformed the intellectual structure of the west, it has also transformed our civilization physically. Technology and industrialism, the practical fruits of scientific method, have created a new culture, a pattern of society which is completely different from any the world has seen before. And, as we have already had occasion to note, much of the upheaval in this great movement of cultural transition results from the conflict of scientific and pre-scientific traditions.

Modern man is proud of the achievements of scientific method; he enjoys the fruits of technology, yet he often displays a dogged reluctance to give up his favored place in the universe—a universe which was cre-

---

[15] This is the great world system of Sir Isaac Newton. There are countless discussions of Newton's achievements and of the character and influence of eighteenth century cosmology. A particularly useful discussion is found in E. A. Burtt, *The Metaphysical Foundations of Modern Science*, Garden City, New York: Doubleday and Company, Inc., 1954. (The book was published originally in 1924 by the Humanities Press.)

ated largely by speculative philosophy and theology, not by science. The mind of modern man is divided between a world of certainty and stability, a world in which value has a secure place and individual salvation can be achieved. And over against this is a world which is contingent and in many respects as yet unpredictable. Science confronts man with a universe that exhibits no concern for human welfare, in which there is no discernible cosmic plan, but only the impersonal forces of matter and energy at work. Modern man is not sure in which of these worlds he lives; he prefers the former, but try as he will, he finds it increasingly difficult to believe that such a world really exists.

Perhaps most of all, contemporary man finds it difficult to accept the image of himself that science reveals. In the eyes of science he is no longer a creature half of earth and half of heaven whose welfare is the main concern of an Ultimate Creator. He finds himself portrayed as a natural organism, subject to the same necessities of the natural process as any other animal. He sees himself distinguished from other creatures only by certain kinds of behavior which in turn depend on physiological structures, particularly the central nervous system. He learns that the only destiny man has is that which he works out for himself, and even this is determined in its major aspects by cultural forces over which he has but little if any control. Modern man may not like this portrait of himself any better than he likes the cosmology of modern science. But he is confronted with it, and this confrontation is irrevocable.

The scientific tradition challenges the older traditions at virtually every turn. In place of the Greek appeal to reason, it insists on the appeal to experience. Modern science finds no grounds for the ancient dualism of mind and body, whether we interpret this dualism in Christian or in classic terms. Many people are finding it increasingly difficult to believe that the whole Hebraic-Christian account of the process of creation, the idea of providential purpose as the governing force in the world, and divine revelation as the ultimate source of truth, really find any sanction in the scientific tradition, though the most heroic intellectual efforts have been expanded to find some way of reconciliation.

This clash of traditions has made modern education itself a house divided. Even though we may wish to pretend otherwise, the fact is that in our schools, the humanistic studies, whose roots are nourished in the older traditions, are now arrayed in a desperate struggle for survival against the aggressive advance of the scientific disciplines. No amount of log-rolling and forced compromising in campus curriculum committees seems likely to alter the situation significantly.

A TAXONOMY OF CONFLICT

This rapid survey of traditions in western culture and American society will serve at least to reveal some of the origins and the manifold nature of the conflicts that attend this period of cultural transition. There is no important aspect of social life that remains unaffected by this clash of traditions. One way to dramatize the situation is to classify these conflicts under certain categories, and thus to portray both the breadth and the depth of current disagreement and confusion. Perhaps the crucial character of the situation can be made clearest if the conflicting issues are put in the form of alternatives.

In considering the following classifications, the reader should bear in mind that the purpose of the taxonomy is to emphasize and, in a sense, to dramatize the range and variety of conflicting ideas in contemporary society. Each of the educational traditions we will examine in this book treats in some way the ideas classified in the categories below. As we shall see, however, spokesmen for various traditions do not necessarily maintain the strict consistency that may seem to be implied in this listing. One of the major purposes of the chapters that follow is one of determining how these ideas are treated in various philosophical contexts and the impact these interpretations have on conceptions of educational policy.

Category I: Cosmology

Are we to assume that the ultimate explanation for the existence and operation of the physical universe is found in the supernatural? Further, are we to proceed on the assumption that behind the processes of nature there is a plan or design, even though at present we may not comprehend very fully the nature of this plan? Is the totality of all things the result of a purposeful act of creation, granting that the true nature of this act does not necessarily coincide with descriptions of it in various religious documents?

OR

Are we to believe that the cosmos is not the product of any act of creation in any intelligible meaning of that term but rather that it has *evolved* and this evolution is independent of any force or entity that ultimately is outside the cosmic totality? Must we accept, then, that the emergence of our own planet, and the system of which it is but a minor part, was fortuitous, that there was no necessity that it be what it actually is but that it might very well have been something else or not have existed at all? And must we then agree that the regularities and contingencies of nature are whatever they are in themselves and bear no necessary relation to the hopes and aspirations of the human species?

Category II: Human Nature

Is man himself a special object of creation? Is he different in some absolute sense from every other living thing? Does human nature exhibit two (or perhaps more than two) dimensions, as for example, both a spiritual and a physical nature? And if so, are we to regard man's spiritual as higher than his physical or animal nature? Is there a common human nature in which all men share, and if so, must this not reside in some entity or attribute that is unique to man? Is it possible that this unique complex we call human nature can ever be understood in purely biological terms—even when we extend "biology" to include psychology and all the so-called behavioral sciences? And if all the evidence were available, would we not find that human nature does not change—that it is a constant? Do not the motives of man stem from within the self rather than from the mechanical stimulation of the environment? Can we not see that man—unlike other creatures, perhaps —finds direction from within himself and thus guides his aspirations and behavior toward his final end or destiny?

OR

Do we agree that man's origins are explainable only in naturalistic terms; that the emergence of the human species has occurred through a process of evolution in the same general sense that everything else in the natural world has evolved. Is not what we have called human nature really a unitary thing, and, although complex as it may be, are all instances of human behavior not reducible ultimately to biological and social causes? Is not the "original nature of man" owed primarily to social experience and hence really learned behavior? And, if so, do not all such common terms as "personality," and "selfhood" really refer to acquired behavior? Are not the motives of men chiefly social in character, stemming from the interaction between inward and outward factors, both of which are dimensions of experience? And in view of these considerations, must we not say that human nature changes as environment changes, that, aside perhaps, from a native biological structure, there is no constant pattern discernible that we can call an unalterable human nature?

Category III: Human Society

Should we agree that the ultimate society is the brotherhood of all men who owe to each other the obligations of brotherhood, and that this ideal must not be compromised by other institutions and processes? We recognize that this condition has never existed on earth as yet, but is it not the ultimate goal we should strive for? Would not the ultimate society be that in which all men are free: free of the dictates of authority, free of the pressures of institutions and conventions that stifle the self and hinder the development of self-direction, making a man a robot controlled by social pressures rather than a free creature capable of realizing and guiding his own destiny? Are men not equal? Does not the personality have intrinsic worth, and does not human dignity reside ultimately in man's own awareness of self rather than in material possessions or economic prosperity? Can the good society be other than that in which the primary concern is for human happiness and self-realization and that society in which all functions, whether they be economic, political, educational, religious, or whatever, are designed to further human welfare and well being?

OR

Must we not honestly face the fact that human nature is not perfectable in any sense and certainly not in the sense that it can be improved through tampering with social institutions, whether this be done in the name of social reform or in the name of revolution. Can we not see that the institutions and conventions of society are not the fetters that constrain men, denying them freedom, but rather that they are the very conditions that must be present if men are to be human rather than bestial? Man is not innately good; innately he is an animal, and must not this animal nature be trained and moulded and even coerced into being human? Must we not be held within the bounds of convention and custom in order that our rebellious and inherently wayward nature be controlled? Dare we risk having society governed by any except the best and wisest men; that is, by an aristocracy based on intellect and achievement, whose wisdom and judgment is far superior to that of the masses of people?

Category IV: Knowledge

Do we agree that there are various degrees or levels of knowledge and that, therefore, it is possible to make distinctions among various ways of knowing? Is sense impression anything more than a gateway through which we can come to the truth through the operation of reason? Can we equate sense experience, which treats of the immediate and the particular and the changing, with knowledge? Are there not realms of being that lie beyond the immediate foreground of experience, realms which are permanent, unchanging and far higher than the world that sense opens to us? If we reflect upon these matters must we not ultimately conclude that the highest forms of knowledge are those based on reason and faith and must we not also concede that these two ultimate sources of truth are not exclusive but complementary? For, can we not hold that rational insight, which is based on the operation of the powers of the human intellect, is reinforced by and in turn supports the truth that is revealed to us by a power that is higher and greater than any on earth? Must we not then conclude that there is a source of truth that is higher than men; that truth exists independent of its being known by man, and that the highest purpose of humanity is to discover and apprehend this truth?

OR

Must we not concede that human experience, which is the natural interaction of an organism with its external environment, sets the limits of human knowledge? And does this not imply that all knowing activity, and hence all knowledge, arises out of sense impression? If the kind of behavior we call "rational" means anything, it means the ability to relate cause and effect (means and ends) and to foresee the probable consequences of actions? Is "pure reason," therefore, anything more than the ability to establish *logical validity* among a set of propositions? If the limits of our knowledge are determined by the limits of experience, can we speak meaningfully of anything called "ultimate" or "universal" or "immutable" truth? Can there be any other criterion for the truth of an idea except that of empirical testing of it? And, therefore, if knowledge is the result of controlled operations (experiments), then can we reasonably expect that the knowledge we have can be anything more than probable? Therefore, if there is a "problem of knowledge" is this problem not concerned with increasing the probability of the truth of our ideas rather than establishing some body of universal and unchanging truth?

Category V: Education

By education do we mean the effort to free men's minds from ignorance and superstition and hence to build that human nature that every man has the potential for? Should we not, therefore, conceive education as a process of enlightenment in which the human mind is brought into clear perception of the truth? Must we not then resolutely reject all ideas of education as a means of adjusting men's behavior to some existing environment, some ideology, some single way of life? And do these considerations not indicate that the source of our ultimate educational objectives is not to be found in human society but in human nature itself and in the truth that is higher than man? And must we not also agree that education in the real sense is not the training of men for economic activity or for the mastery of narrow techniques and skills, but rather that its concern is with the great body of truth that is the accumulated treasure of mankind and whose preservation, transmission, and extension is the sacred task of every generation?

OR

Do we see the school for what it is: an institution with a specialized responsibility for inducting the young of a generation into the life of a culture? Is it not an illusion to suppose that man is born free of cultural influence and must we not conclude, therefore, that formal education is in reality a conscious means for imposing on the young certain customs, dispositions, understandings, values? Is the real question not whether education involves imposition, but rather what is imposed and with respect to what values? Can we arbitrarily divide education into what is "liberal" and therefore "higher" and what is "practical" and thereby lower, since both theoretical and practical activity are necessary in all cultures? Is it not the case that when theory is separated from action it becomes a thing in itself and ultimately is separated from the world of social reality? And is it not also true that when action is divorced from reflection and abstract thinking it becomes sterile, routine, and rigid? In our search for values to govern education should we not look to experience, to those modes of activity that have been tested in the crucible of cultural experience, rather than look to some realm of alleged universality which stands above, and hence outside, the realities of human society or the possibility of knowledge?

Any thoughtful person can extend almost indefinitely the number of questions under each of these categories. When we look at the brief "taxonomy" presented here we see the primary reason why there are in America today *philosophies* rather than *a philosophy* of education. Our task, therefore, is not the simple one of presenting a neat exposition of an American ideology of education to which all citizens agree. Rather we are faced with the prospect of making our way through a number of traditions about education, seeking to find what these varying systems of thought propose for the conduct of our schools and what these proposals in turn imply for the broader dimensions of culture.

SUMMARY

In this chapter we have considered the major historical traditions that have shaped the character of western culture and, hence, the character of the western tradition in education. Two of these traditions, the Greek and the Hebraic-Christian, had their origins in antiquity, but their influence is still powerful in the modern world. The other traditions we have considered are products of the post-medieval world.

The primary thesis that has been advanced is that the most severe conflicts in contemporary American society today are caused in large measure by conflicts among these traditions. It has also been suggested that the disputes over questions of educational policy, which are such a prominent feature of American society today, are themselves reflections of the deeper schisms created by the clash of traditions. To demonstrate the intensity of the stresses within American society, a kind of classification or taxonomy of conflict was devised. This taxonomy shows the great variations in interpretation and belief that are present in contemporary American society. One of the major purposes of the remaining chapters of this book is to demonstrate the effects these differences have on conceptions of educational policy.

The Conservative Tradition in Education

Human nature with all its infirmities and depravities is still capable of great things . . . Education makes a greater difference between man and man, than nature has made between man and brute. The virtues and powers to which men may be trained, by early education and constant discipline, are truly sublime and astonishing.

—JOHN ADAMS

Quoted in Clinton Rossiter's *Conservatism in America*, New York: Random House, (A Vintage Book), 1962, p. 111.

CHAPTER THREE

The Conservative Tradition

The first tradition in American education we will undertake to analyze in accord with the plan proposed in Chapter I is best known under the name "Essentialism." This term is thought to have been used first by Michael Demiashkevich in a book on philosophy of education published in 1935.[1] It was given its widest currency by an article published in 1938 in which there was presented a platform for a conservative reform movement in education.[2] Since that time the term has been adopted by many conservative teachers and educational theorists and is widely used in writings about the conservative tradition in American education. Conservatives apparently agree that the word expresses particularly well their basic attitude towards education and their conception of the role of the school in society.

The major task of Part II of this book is an analysis of the educational doctrines advocated by conservatives. This task will be accomplished most thoroughly if the specific analysis of educational ideas is made against a general background of the conservative tradition as it exists today. In this chapter, therefore, the main concern is with the character of modern conservatism as it is expressed in various aspects of contemporary social life.

Conservatism as a tradition stems from the eighteenth century and it is universally acknowledged that the founder was Edmund Burke, the British statesman and political philosopher. In the United States the tradition was expressed through such illustrious early Americans as John

[1] Michael Demiashkevich, *An Introduction to the Philosophy of Education,* New York: American Book Company, 1935.
[2] See William C. Bagley, "An Essentialist's Platform for the Advancement of American Education," *Educational Administration and Supervision,* 24:241–256 (April, 1938).

Adams, Alexander Hamilton, and James Madison. The *Federalist Papers* are considered to be perhaps the purest American expression of political and social conservatism. The two-volume work, *Democracy in America*, by Alexis deTocqueville, the noted French political observer and philosopher, is viewed by conservatives to be the most penetrating study of early American society and is often cited along with Burke's work as being an unusually fertile source for the understanding of conservatism in America.[3]

There is an unfortunate tendency among Americans to identify conservatism exclusively with politics. This tendency is deplored by conservative intellectuals who are always quick to point out that such a limited view effectively obscures the nature of the tradition. Conservatism is not a mere body of political doctrine—and anyway conservatives typically look on bodies of doctrine with grave suspicion. Conservatism is more an attitude toward life—a certain view of the world. The conservative sees the world through a frame of reference and his interpretation of the great matters of society in any generation is influenced by his regard for the continuity of tradition, his resistance to uncontrolled social change, and his profound distrust of all utopian reform movements that are based allegedly on reason.

The conservative tradition is expressed most clearly in the great areas of political and social life, to be sure. It is expressed in ideas about politics, religion, education, economics; as a tradition it is more than any of these and in fact, more than their sum-total. Our present concern is with the way the conservative tradition is expressed in education practice in America, but this cannot be our sole concern. The conservative himself knows that education is never independent of other institutions and that it is inseparably linked to political, economic, and religious tradition. Before we turn directly to educational theory, we will give some attention to the general character of the conservative tradition.

THE RESURGENCE OF CONSERVATISM

Ever since the end of World War II there has been increasing evidence of a resurgence of conservative sentiment in the United States.

---

[3] In his study of the conservative tradition in America, Mr. Clinton Rossiter has made a careful distinction between Burkean conservatism and the indigenous American tradition which owes considerable to Burke but which also has developed its own character. See his *Conservatism in America*, 2nd ed., New York: Vintage Books, 1962, particularly Chapters 2 and 7.

Some observers, for example, profess to find a definite turn to the right in political affairs at every level of political life. They find that as a people our attention increasingly has been directed away from internal affairs and from a preoccupation with social and economic reform that was characteristic of our society in the third and fourth decades of this century. It is sometimes said that our concern for civil liberties has diminished and our attention is focused on the necessity to preserve our historic way of life in the face of an imminent possibility of external military as well as ideological threat. Various observers point to the emergence of groups of the "extreme right" whose interests are primarily political and whose convictions are highly conservative.

There are, of course, various ways of accounting for this alteration in the political complexion of America and of assaying the significance these events may have for the future. These political matters lie largely outside the scope of this book and will not be included in our analysis. It is worth noting, however, that at least some of the ultra-conservative groups and individuals have on occasion had considerable to say about education and the need for reform in the schools.[4]

Observers of the current scene also report a corresponding growth of conservatism among theologians. This movement has taken American religion in the general direction of a return to orthodoxy, a reassertion of the doctrine of original sin and the inherent weakness of human nature. Whether the increase in church membership that began in the fifth decade of the century can be regarded as evidence of a significant reawakening of religious interest is still a matter of debate. There can be little doubt, however, that at mid-century, organized religion has shown a definite turn away from interest in affairs that are primarily economic and social and in the direction of concern for matters of personal morality, self-realization, and ultimate spiritual salvation.

Other evidence for the resurgence of the conservative spirit in America is to be found among students in colleges and universities throughout the country. For the first time in many years students in considerable numbers have banded themselves together in societies whose avowed purpose is to propagate conservative ideas and to participate in conservative reform movements. These groups are partly, but by no means exclusively, political in their character and sentiments. Some of these younger conservatives, in fact, maintain that neither of the major political parties in the United States has an acceptable political orienta-

[4] For a review of contemporary political extremism in the U.S., including groups of extreme conservatives, see: *The Journal of Social Issues*, Vol. 19, No. 2 (April, 1963).

tion. Some young conservatives have stated that they have little faith in the abilities or convictions of leading political figures who call themselves conservatives.[5]

Much of the argument of these younger conservatives appears to stem from their rebellion against the alleged curtailment of individual liberties by the state in general and educational institutions in particular. (Whether some of their arguments and proposals for non-academic reform fit into the general pattern of conservative thought is a matter worth pondering.) Another kind of charge heard frequently on college campuses is that faculties, by and large, are converts to doctrinaire liberalism and that this point of view is propagated in classrooms at the expense of conservative views. The name of a leading organization of these young people, "Young Americans for Freedom," expresses about as well as anything the spirit of anti-statism that seems to be typical of a resurgent conservatism among the young.

Certainly one area in which there is unmistakable evidence of a great resurgence of conservative doctrine is in the general field of education. This resurgence began shortly after the end of World War II and has grown steadily ever since that time. Its effects have been felt at every level of the American school system. Rarely, if ever, has the American controversy over educational policy been more heated or more bitter than in the years since the end of the war. In fact, to find a comparable period of such intense and acrimonious debate over education it is probably necessary to go back more than a century to the period in which Americans struggled to found a public system of schools and secure tax support for universal schooling.

The resurgence of orthodoxy in conservative educational thought began with a polemical movement of awesome proportions. This reaction was in large measure against the alleged excesses of the progressive doctrine that, in the judgment of conservatives, had perverted the American educational system almost beyond hope of recovery. The polemic was directed primarily against the acknowledged leaders of the progressive movement, institutions for the preparation of teachers, and state agencies for the certification of teachers. As is usually the case with polemic, much of the language has been not only bitter but vituperative.[6]

[5] For a brief survey see: "Campus Conservatives," an article by Robert D. Novak in *The Wall Street Journal* for November 30, 1961. For an extended treatment by a conservative see: M. Stanton Evans, *The Revolt on the Campus*, Chicago: Henry Regnery Company, 1961.
[6] The volume of polemical literature by conservative critics is so great that even a listing of it is far beyond the possible scope of this book. For an interesting

While conservative critics have been all but unanimous in placing the blame for what they consider the dire state of education on the shoulders of schools and colleges of education and professors of education, their attitudes toward the teachers in the schools have been mixed. Some have held forthrightly that much of the fault can be attributed to class-room teachers who themselves have abdicated their historic duties, lowered standards in the classroom, and substituted for rigorous education a program of juvenile entertainment.[7]

There are others, however, who have portrayed teachers as captives of school administrators and certification authorities, aided and abetted by professors of education, who force them against their will and better judgment to cheapen and degrade the educational process. Those who argue from this position have held that the salvation of the school system depends on breaking the stranglehold the "educationists" have maintained on American education for nearly half a century. Once the great conspiracy has been broken, teachers can feel themselves free once again to give their students a genuine education.[8]

It would be possible to prolong indefinitely this presentation of the conservative's objections to the state of things in contemporary American education as he perceives it. In the interests of economy a few propositions are stated here that summarize passably well the conservative view of the need for a return to educational tradition.

1. Americans have largely lost sight of the true purpose of education, which is intellectual training. We tend to confuse education with all kinds of social, psychological, and vocational services that are often lumped together under the rubric of "life adjustment."

2. The rigor of our educational programs and teaching methods has been declining steadily for several decades. This is true in some measure of every level of the school system from the kindergarten to the university, but the condition is particularly acute in the elementary and secondary schools.

sample of a biting critique of American education by a leading figure of the new conservatism see: Russell Kirk, *Prospects for Conservatives*, Chicago: Henry Regnery Company, 1956, Chapter III. One of the earlier polemical articles that attracted wide attention and seems to have set the general tone for the many that were yet to come is: Harry J. Fuller, "The Emperor's New Clothes, or Prius Dementat," *The Scientific Monthly*, January, 1951, pp. 32–41.

[7] See for example: Bernard Iddings Bell, *Crisis in Education*, New York: McGraw-Hill Book Company, 1949, Chapter 3 and *passim*.

[8] See: Albert Lynd, *Quackery in the Public Schools*, Boston: Little, Brown and Company, 1950.

3. We have failed to provide for the education of our brightest children because instruction has been pitched at the level of the mediocre student and the ablest have been systematically deprived in the name of "equality" and "democracy."

4. The curriculums of our schools have been diluted by the introduction of courses consisting largely of "life adjustment" trivia and these worthless substitutes have crowded out the historic disciplines that are the core of a true education. Even the brightest students, seeking an easy way out, elect the easy courses and neglect the basic intellectual program.

5. Intellectual achievement has declined steadily among American students. Not only is their achievement inferior to that of American students of two or three generations ago,[9] it is also inferior to that of students in every major European country.[10]

6. The schools are failing to meet their obligations to American youth and to American society. They are not only failing in the intellectual task, they are also failing in their responsibility to transmit those values that are the basis of the American tradition. The ancient norms for personal morality are systematically ignored in our classrooms, and teachers no longer transmit the basic American virtues of self-sufficiency, free enterprise, self-direction, and respect for tradition.

The resurgence of conservatism in educational theory is an important episode in the philosophy of American education, but it should be seen for what it is—one historical episode in the development of the conservative tradition. The events that combine to make up this episode are patterned primarily around the threat posed by another tradition in the earlier decades of the century. Thus, much that has been written about education in recent times by conservatives has been directed against the influence of progressivism.

However interesting the present great educational controversy may be, the important matter for consideration here is not so much what conservatives are against as the basic principles they espouse so firmly and defend so resolutely. What, we may ask ourselves, is it that characterizes the conservative mind insofar as educational theory is con-

[9] The actual number of generations since the golden age of American education is uncertain, although it is possible to infer the existence of such a period from some conservative writing.

[10] See, for example: Hyman G. Rickover, *Swiss Schools and Ours: Why Theirs Are Better*, Boston: Atlantic—Little, Brown, 1962.

cerned? What is it that distinguishes the conservative from those of other persuasions?

To answer this question even briefly we must consider the major components of the conservative tradition and the part these play in determining the frame of reference through which the conservative mind views education and other matters of high moment.

CULTURAL COMPONENTS OF ESSENTIALISM

In any historical period, all traditions are products of a common culture. The differences among them stem from the emphases and interpretations that are placed on various elements in the cultural pattern. The conservative tradition is primarily a product of the post-medieval world. It represents for one thing the effort to reconcile important historic elements of antique culture with certain others of the modern world and to present this reconciliation as an integral tradition. Similarly, essentialism, as the conservative educational ideology, also represents the effort to amalgamate into one synthesis the educational ideals both of the ancient and modern worlds. Many of the tensions that exist within the tradition of conservatism today originate in this effort to combine two world views within a common ideology.

The conservative tradition in America is built primarily on four great components of modern culture discussed in Chapter II: capitalism, nationalism, democracy, and science. But the key to the understanding of the conservative tradition, and hence of the educational ideology of essentialism, lies in apprehending the part these elements play in conservatism and the interpretations placed on them by conservatives. Attention will be given, therefore, to the meaning these key concepts have for the conservative mind.

Supernaturalism, Religion and Human Nature

The conservative tradition rests ultimately on the belief in the existence of a supernatural creator who is responsible for the existence of the world and the course of events that make up its history. Although there are various sectarian and doctrinal differences about the details of this cosmology, the fact of an ultimate source of power and authority that transcends nature is a central thesis of this tradition. Mr. Russell

Kirk, one of the most noted of the new conservatives, has indicated that this belief is fundamental in the conservative mind.[11]

The conservative links ethics and morality closely to religion and the idea is very common within the tradition that any system of ethics worthy of the name ultimately must be anchored in religious sanctions. Politics, as the conservative understands that term, are ultimately concerned with value and, therefore, in the conservative mind there is an indissoluble relation between religion and politics.[12]

The conservative finds a close relation also between the ultimate fact of a supernatural creator and the nature of man. The conservative view of human nature reveals a curious combination of outright pessimism and a carefully guarded optimism. The pessimism derives from the conservative acceptance of the Christian doctrine of original sin, which Mr. Peter Viereck has said all conservatives accept, either in the literal sense or metaphorically.[13] The concern of the conservative is to disown the doctrine of human perfectability, historically associated with the liberal tradition, and to emphasize the need for control through tradition of a human nature that is wayward, capricious, and often given to evil thoughts and deeds. This sharp strain of pessimism about human nature runs as a major theme through the conservative tradition. Traditional institutions of religion and society, we are assured, are not intolerable curbs to the free development of human nature nor are they as Rousseau called them "the chains that bind men." Rather these products of tradition are what makes human nature possible. They make us men rather than beasts, and they must be preserved. This same pessimism about human nature flows copiously into conservative educational theory. The authors of a survey of the San Francisco Public Schools, for example, observe that "few children want to do anything difficult without a little prodding or stimulation."[14] A constant warning note pervades the literature of essentialism that even the best high school students will take easy courses instead of courses with intellectual rigor, unless school authorities are constantly alert.

The guarded optimism of the conservative stems from his belief that if the continuity of tradition can be maintained, every generation

[11] Russell Kirk, *Prospects for Conservatives*, Chicago: Henry Regnery Company, 1956, p. 37.
[12] *Ibid.*, p. 37.
[13] Peter Viereck, *Conservatism from John Adams to Churchill*, Princeton, New Jersey: D. Van Nostrand Company, Inc., 1956, pp. 13–14.
[14] *Report of the San Francisco Curriculum Survey Committee: Prepared for the Board of Education, San Francisco Unified School District*, April 1, 1960. Published jointly by the University of California at Berkeley and by Stanford University.

will have a source of wisdom to which it can turn for guidance. As a tradition, conservatism insists that in the ordinary affairs of life men should be free to exercise their own judgment and to profit from their own initiative and energy. But beyond the ordinary matters of daily life, the conservative has little faith in either the wisdom or judgment of an individual—or even of a whole generation. Kirk has said, echoing Edmund Burke, ". . . in matters beyond the scope of material endeavor and the present moment, the individual tends to be foolish, but the species is wise; therefore, we rely in great matters upon the wisdom of our ancestors."[15] The optimism of the conservative, therefore, derives not from his faith in human nature, but from his faith in the accumulated wisdom of all the generations that is available to guide men of any generation through their own perplexities and crises, if they will only take advantage of it.

The ultimate thesis of the modern conservative (at least of those conservatives who understand conservatism) is identical with that originally propounded by Edmund Burke, the greatest of them all.[16] Burke's conservatism stems from his belief that a great *compact* exists among the generations. Under this compact no single generation has the right to uproot and destroy the existing pattern of society, whether this be done by revolution or by non-violent doctrinaire social reform movements. To uproot institutions and ways of life is a breach of faith both with the generations that are gone and those that are yet to come. This is the ultimate immorality and the road to social chaos.

Small wonder, then, that conservatives reserve some of their strongest wrath and most bitter language for the progressive movement in American education, for as the conservative sees it, this doctrinaire reform movement almost succeeded in less than half a century in destroying our historic conceptions of the school and the very purpose of education itself.

To the conservative mind the great fact of life is the existence of an ultimate power that transcends nature and is responsible for the existence and operations of the natural world. The workings of this ultimate power are made manifest in history, and history itself is, as Mr. Kirk has said, "the record of Providential purpose." This same Providence

---

[15] Kirk, *op. cit.*, p. 38.

[16] The modern conservative always cites Burke as the founder of the tradition and regards Burke's *Reflections on the Revolution in France* as the seminal source of conservative ideals. Viereck has observed that any person can tell whether his own instincts are conservative or liberal by his reactions to the great debate between Burke and Tom Paine. See Viereck's *Conservatism*, p. 13.

has created human nature in such a fashion that men display elements both of good and evil in their common nature. To the extent that this human nature can be improved (the conservative will have none of the idea that it can be perfected), this improvement must stem from within the individual himself as an act of his own will.[17]

The conservative reserves his undying enmity for any idea that advances social reform as a means for betterment or perfection of man's nature. As he sees it, the chance we have for improving the human prospect is to maintain tradition, to keep inviolate the great contract among the generations, to rely for guidance on the wisdom of our ancestors, and to avoid doctrinaire reform proposals in any form. To the conservative, education, when it is conceived as intellectual and moral discipline, and when it is dedicated to preserving and transmitting the essential core of tradition, has an important part to play. The conservative would have us understand that the purpose of education is to preserve and transmit and, as Mr. William Buckley has said:

> Conservatism is the tacit acknowledgement that all that is finally important in human experience is behind us; that the crucial explorations have been undertaken, and that it is given to men to know what are the great truths that emerged from them. Whatever is to come cannot outweigh the importance to man of what has gone before.[18]

Capitalism and the Conservative Tradition

The conservative mind as it has developed in America tends to identify capitalism as one of the main components of the conservative tradition. Capitalism is all but synonymous with such ideas as "free enterprise," "individual initiative," "the sanctity of property," "the American standard of living" and "freedom." As was noted in an earlier chapter, Americans typically do not discriminate among American capitalistic economics, American nationalism, and American interpretations of democracy. To the majority of us any one of these great traditions could not be maintained in the absence of the others.

This interpretation may be seen in the way Americans view politics— and particularly the way in which they classify politicians. Although the tendency is irksome to some conservative intellectuals, it is common in this country for politicians to be classed as conservatives if they adhere, at least verbally, to *laissez faire* economic sentiments, emphasize

---

[17] See for example: Kirk, *op. cit.*, p. 37.
[18] William F. Buckley, Jr., *Up From Liberalism*, New York: Hillman Periodicals, Inc., 1959, p. 172.

free enterprise and individual initiative, deplore high taxes, and excoriate "government planning." An even more simple-minded kind of interpretation makes all conservatives members of the Republican Party and all liberals members of the Democratic Party.

The failure to discriminate between genuine conservatism and what Mr. Peter Viereck has called "a petrified right-wing of atomistic *laissez faire* liberalism" has been the subject of considerable dismayed comment by the intellectuals of conservative thought. To be sure, the conservative regards the sanctity of the "right of property" as of pre-eminent importance because he maintains it is property that makes individual freedom possible. Similarly, both the intellectual and the common garden-variety of conservative defend private economic enterprise staunchly because, in their judgment, it is the only workable system for satisfying economic needs. More than this, the conservative holds free enterprise to be the only system of economic life under which men can be truly free.[19] It is with the profit motive and the unrestrained desire for accumulation of wealth that the conservative sometimes finds difficulty. Conservatism regards inherited wealth and the state of mind it fosters as one of the bulwarks of tradition and cultural stability, but it often views with grave suspicion the influence of new wealth and the cultural rootlessness of those who possess it. To most conservatives, plutocracy is not the most desirable form of government—though they may think it no worse and perhaps far better than many liberal interpretations of democracy. Part of the disenchantment with capitalism that sometimes crops up in conservative writing may be owed to the indissoluble relation between capitalism and the industrial revolution.

The thoughtful conservative is amply aware of the disruptive effect that industrialism has had on the traditional pattern of western culture. As a conservative, he is dedicated to preserving cultural stability and the ethical ideals of honor and responsibility and justice as he conceives these. But the task in these days has become enormous. The urbaniza-

[19] See for example: Kirk, *op. cit.*, p. 35, also in the same volume, Chapter VI. In this chapter Mr. Kirk writes eloquently against the idea that production, consumption and profit making are the ends of human life. He says rather that the purpose of production is to provide enough goods so that men may have leisure for intellectual and other truly human pursuits. Profit making, therefore, under this view, is a means, not an end. But, in free enterprise capitalism, profit making *must* be the prime motive for economic activity because without profits there is no opportunity for leisure or any kind of good works.

A briefer treatment of the same subject by an economist will be found in Harold B. Wess, "We Can't Have Freedom Without Capitalism" in A. G. Heinsohn, ed., *Anthology of Conservative Writing in the United States, 1932–1960*, Chicago: Henry Regnery Company, 1962, pp. 374–377.

tion of the population; the decline of agriculture, always a strong conservative influence; the growth of a great culturally-rootless proletariat; the constant proliferation of a "new rich" class; increasing demands for all kinds of social services at state expense combine to disrupt the continuity of tradition, to alter the settled order of society, and ultimately, in the conservative's opinion, to promote the rule of the mob. The task of the modern conservative is to find ways to preserve the traditional ideas in a society grown more corporate and integrated.[20]

And yet, though there are certain nagging doubts among conservatives over economics and the character of capitalism in modern life, underneath these differences runs a common theme of agreement. Viereck, after considering the differences, concludes:

> The diversity of conservative attitudes is shown by the fact that popular parlance in America calls two opposite groups 'conservative': (1) The efficient modernism, cash-nexus selfishness, and atomistic society of the plutocrats; (2) The inefficient medievalism, anti-plutocratic idealism, and organic society of Coleridge, Carlyle, Newman, Ruskin. Yet both usages of 'conservatism' have a partly unifying common denominator: both distrust the masses, prefer an established elitist authority, and distrust the abstract radical blueprints of utopians and of statists.[21]

Just as conservatism in general has lent its strongest support for the maintenance of a capitalistic system of economics—though not always without some reservation—so essentialism, as the conservative approach to education, has also thrown its influence in this direction. There can be little question that in so doing the school has met the expectations and desires of the majority of Americans. Throughout much of the history of our educational system the system of capitalistic economics has been under criticism and often the direct threat of alternate systems ranging through variant forms of socialism to communism. An important part of the appeal to Americans for support of public education has always been that the school is a line of first defense against the incursions of alien economic doctrines.[22] By and large, a strict surveillance has

[20] An interesting example of the gravity this problem has for conservatives can be found in William F. Buckley, *op. cit.*, p. 208 ff.

[21] Viereck, *op. cit.*, p. 41.

[22] An interesting and important historical study of the attitudes of American educational leaders towards the role of the school in promoting economic orthodoxy is: Merle Curti, *The Social Ideas of American Educators*, rev. ed., Patterson, New Jersey: Littlefield, Adams & Company, 1959. Chapter 6 is particularly pertinent on this point. Originally this book was the tenth volume of the Report of the American Historical Commission on the Social Studies in the Schools. The report was first published by Charles Scribners' Sons in 1935.

been maintained over teachers to make certain that their economic ideas are orthodox, and one of the happy hunting grounds for those concerned with rooting out subversion has been the textbooks used in the schools. Sometimes even the slightest deviation from conservative economic theory discovered in a high school textbook has been sufficient cause for a thorough investigation of the schools in a community.[23]

There is reason to believe that the American people have, by and large, expected their schools to transmit such beliefs as these: (1) that an economic system based on free economic enterprise is the only system in which individual liberty can be enjoyed; (2) that the American standard of living is the highest of any society in history and this is attributable to our free-enterprise capitalism; (3) that the right to private property can be guaranteed only under capitalism; (4) that the government at any level should not interfere actively with the free operation of the market but act only in the role of umpire to see that the rules are obeyed; (5) that all alternate theories of economic organization are alien, inefficient, and tyrannous. Anyone who doubts that the schools have discharged their obligation to keep and maintain our orthodox economic tradition may find some assurance that he is in error if he will only take the trouble to examine a few current history textbooks studied by American students.

Nationalism and the Conservative Tradition

The idea was developed in Chapter II that nationalism, the tradition that holds that the primary allegiance of men belongs to the national state, is the most potent political force in the world today. By and large the conservative tradition is dedicated to the preservation of American nationalism and essentialist educational doctrine conceives an important responsibility of the school to be that of fostering the spirit of national patriotism. Conservatives are not completely in accord in their attitudes toward nationalism and the part it should play in contemporary life. Contemporary conservative thought in this respect ranges from an intense insistence on retaining jealously every aspect of national sovereignty—an attitude that approaches the pre-World War II

---

[23] A valuable summary of a heated controversy over social studies textbooks that occurred in the '40s will be found in: S. Alexander Rippa, "The Textbook Controversy and the Free Enterprise Campaign, 1940–41," *History of Education Journal*, 9:49–58 (Spring, 1958). For a first-hand contact with conservative ideas on "the textbook menace" see: E. Merrill Root, "The Quicksands of the Mind" and Rene A. Wormser, "Foundations and Radicalism in Education" both published in A. G. Heinsohn, Jr., ed., *op. cit.*

"isolation"—to an attitude of acceptance of internationalism involving membership in the United Nations, national contributions to the aid of foreign nations that are friendly to the United States, and even participation in such international agencies as UNESCO. About every shade of opinion is represented along the continuum and the strains generated by these differences within the tradition are often critical.

Part of the reason for these differences, as Viereck[24] has observed, are undoubtedly historical. In the course of its history the tradition has vacillated between nationalism and internationalism, depending on the immediate course of events. Conservatives, following Burke, regarded nationalism as a tradition that should be preserved, but many of them were aware that other revered traditions—especially Christianity—in the end are not in complete harmony with nationalism and stand the chance of being sacrificed on the altar of chauvinism.[25]

Another reason for differences among conservatives in this area stems from the conservative's deep-dyed suspicion of all doctrinaire reform movements and "social blueprints." To the conservative far too many of the proposals for mitigating and controlling the influence of nationalism in the contemporary world have about them an aura of reform and doctrinaire utopianism. Some conservatives have, in fact, professed disenchantment with the United Nations, partly on grounds of its alleged ineffectiveness and partly because of the fear of loss of national sovereignty.

Even when these differences of opinions and emphasis are taken into account, the general picture that remains is one in which the conservative tradition today staunchly upholds American nationalism, resists the infringement on national sovereignty by any kind of supranational organization, and lays on the schools the obligation to support, first of all, national loyalties.

In the schools, dominated as they are by essentialist ideas, some of the same uncertainty prevails over the question of American nationalism that was noted among conservatives as a group. Community attitudes vary widely. Some communities actively support, for example, teaching in the schools about the United Nations, the study of materials supplied by UNESCO, and an emphasis on internationalism in the teaching of

[24] Viereck, *op. cit.*, p. 22.
[25] Viereck points out that historically conservatives tended toward internationalism from 1789–1848 and toward nationalism after 1870. The end of World War II has brought a return of internationalism—particularly to European conservatives. The prime motive is the desire for mutual protection against communism which originally, at least, was international in its appeal.

history. Other communities merely tolerate such activity by the schools, and a lesser number have flatly banned it. A constant pressure for a nationalistic and patriotic slant in the teaching of the social studies comes from various patriotic societies. It is likely that no school system in the country is free from this pressure, though it is stronger in some than in others and varies somewhat with events on the national and international scene and on the character of leadership in the various societies themselves.[26]

In the long run the activities of these groups are probably superfluous because the programs of American schools have always been geared to the propagation of nationalism and there can be little doubt that the schools have met the expectations of Americans in this respect. Various studies of the content of American textbooks show these books to be highly supportive of the idea of unlimited national sovereignty, the superiority of the "American way," and the essential rightness of American foreign policy. There is also to be found in these texts the close relation between capitalism, nationalism, and democracy mentioned earlier and the effort to mend the breach between nationalism and religion by identifying the destiny of the nation with the will of the Creator.

Thus, although periodically various groups conduct vigilante investigations of textbooks and make extravagant charges about the deviation of the schools from nationalistic norms, there is no trustworthy evidence that the schools by and large have ever subverted what is surely the will of the populace in this regard. The same thing can be said about the allegiance of teachers. In spite of allegations about the national loyalties of teachers, nobody has ever turned up even a handful of professional teachers who could be classed as subversive of American nationalism. In spite of this, the "hunt" still goes on in communities throughout the nation and various forms of "loyalty oaths" are common.

Democracy and the Conservative Tradition

The third great tradition in American society is *democracy*, a term of manifold meaning, and one that various groups interpret to fit their own purposes. Many of the bitter doctrinal differences between contemporary conservatives and liberals can be traced to differing interpretations of this strategic term. Even within the conservative tradition

[26] For a summary of the activities of super-patriotic groups see: Richard Schmuck and Mark Chesler, "On Super-Patriotism: A Definition and Analysis," *Journal of Social Issues*, 19:31–50 (April, 1963).

itself there are to be found grave differences of opinion about its meaning.[27]

There appears to be agreement among conservatives that the fundamental significance of the word democracy is a moral one and that this moral conception is rooted in traditional religion, particularly the Hebraic-Christian tradition. Belief in the intrinsic worth of the human being and the equality of all men before their maker, is in harmony with the basic conservative view.[28] The difficulty the conservative finds is that these sentiments have often been exploited by doctrinaire reformers in the effort to achieve social results that are clearly out of harmony with conservative ideals. Further, those ideals of inherent personal worth have often been transformed in American society, lacking, as it does, the feudal background of European countries, into a kind of primitive egalitarianism that conservatives[29] have warned against since the very beginnings of our national history. Today one of the major charges in conservative criticism of contemporary education is that this misconceived egalitarianism has so infected our schools that the superior student is condemned to an unending mediocrity in education and this in the name of equality.

The conservative will argue that all men have the right to live in freedom and justice and that this right, being given by God, is inalienable. But at the same time, he warns sternly that most of us, particularly those of liberal persuasions, talk too much of "rights" and too little of *duty*. Part of the reason for modern decadence, in the opinion of the conservative, lies in the failure of men today to respond to the call of duty and to recognize that only as men understand and accept the responsibilities that go with their station in life and their obligation to tradition will they realize the right to freedom and justice. It is the profound conviction of many conservatives today that public education has all but failed completely to instill a sense of duty and obligation in the young. These young people, products of the social atomism of doctrinaire liberalism that stresses rights and ignores obligation, are rootless, wayward, and committed to nothing but their own desires. Out of this infection grow the ugly sores of juvenile delinquency and adult irresponsibility, improvidence, and crime.

In the field of politics the conservative is greatly concerned to make

[27] For a summary of the historical development of these differences among conservatives see: Viereck, *op. cit.*, Chapters 14, 15, and 16.
[28] See Rossiter, *op. cit.*, pp. 23–24.
[29] Important among these are John Adams, Hamilton, Madison, and the Frenchman, Alexis deTocqueville.

clear his interpretation of the word democracy. Democracy means literally, of course, rule by the people as distinct from rule by an elite class based on wealth, blood, or power. The conservative holds the deepest suspicion of democracy when that term is interpreted as the mere counting of noses to determine which way the winds of passion are blowing the mob on any particular issue of the moment.[30] Historically, conservatives simply did not believe political democracy would work and they opposed the extension of the suffrage at every turn. The fact is that universal suffrage is still to be achieved in the United States today. Perhaps in no other area (with the possible exception of educational theory) is the conservative's distrust of the masses seen more clearly than in politics. Conservatives are prone to remind us as often as possible that our form of government is a *republic*, not a democracy.[31] They are often critical of the schools for not making this distinction clear to students and for promoting a kind of mindless egalitarianism in the classroom.

To the conservative the maintenance of social order and tranquility is possible only when tradition is maintained and transmitted. The obligation for this rests always on the superior class in society, that is, the social class whose status is based on inherited wealth, superior education, and superior breeding. This is the stratum in society from which wise leadership must come, for, except in unusual cases, only in this level of society is to be found that respect for tradition and social order that are the ingredients of wise and competent leadership.

The American conservative is not apologetic about the idea of "aristocracy," though for strategic reasons he may sometimes avoid use of the term. This tradition frankly holds that society should be governed by its wisest and best men—John Adams' "natural and actual aristocracy." Burke's eloquence on the "unbought grace of life"[32] is quoted frequently by modern conservatives as they argue against the domination of political

---

[30] Mr. William Buckley has reserved some of his sharpest barbs for those who identify democracy with egalitarian nose counting. See his section on "The Liberal: His Root Assumptions," *op. cit.*, p. 132 ff.

[31] This has been a favorite theme of Mr. Barry Goldwater. See his *The Conscience of a Conservative*, Victor Publishing Company, Inc., 1960, Chapter 2. Mr. William F. Buckley has also attacked the glorification of democracy by liberals, saying among other things that, "the persistent misuse of the word democracy reflects either an ignorance of its ontological emptiness; or . . . the pathetic attempt to endow it with substantive meaning." Buckley, *op. cit.*, p. 135. But the classic statement of this attitude is to be found in Irving Babbitt's *Democracy and Leadership*, Boston: Houghton Mifflin and Company, 1924, pp. 243–247.

[32] Edmund Burke, *Reflections on the Revolution in France*, Indianapolis: The Bobbs-Merrill Company, Inc., The Liberal Arts Press, Inc., 1955, p. 85 ff.

life by the rootless masses, the degradation of morals, taste, and manners in modern society and the lack of a sense of obligation that characterizes a large portion of the American population.[33]

Thus, to the conservative mind, democracy, when that term means a regard for justice and order in society, when it indicates the opportunity for men to exercise their natural talents and enjoy the fruits of their efforts, when it protects all men in their right to property, and when it avoids the social leveling based on the idea that "all men are equal," which the conservative says they manifestly are not, then the concept is one of the precious elements in the tradition of the west. But when this same term is used by the conjurors of radicalism and liberalism to create such illusions as the elimination of social classes and distinctions in society; the cheap egalitarian doctrine that one man's opinions (and hence his vote) are as good as any other's; the perverse educational doctrine that all men have the same right to education and therefore should have the same kind of education; the advocacy that "human rights" take precedence over property rights; then the conservative rebels— as indeed many have—against the unending ritualistic recitation of the word.

To the conservative the tradition of democracy, properly conceived, is along with the accompanying historical developments of nationalism and capitalism, one of the foundation stones of modern culture. Just as he may reject nationalism in its exaggerated chauvinistic form, and the excesses of *laissez faire* capitalism, so he rejects the libertarian interpretation of democracy that at the very best, he thinks, can mean only rule by the mob and at the very worst, social dissolution, chaos, and ultimately tyranny.

Science, Scientific Method, and the Conservative Mind

It was remarked in Chapter II that experimental science is the cultural element that most clearly differentiates the modern from the medieval mind. Note has also been made of the fact that acceleration of cultural transition in our time owes more to the development of science than to any other single event or class of events. It has also been noted that science has served to question the older traditions at virtually every turn. This condition has posed the most severe challenge to the conservatism

---

[33] Burke did not believe in the "natural aristocracy" advocated by Adams, Jefferson, and other Americans. Viereck points out that this is a fundamental difference between American and European conservatism. Certainly the idea of an aristocracy of nature—rather than of blood and wealth—has important connection with ideas about occupational and social mobility and hence, with ideas about education.

of our time because conservatism is the tradition that faces the necessity of cementing into one synthesis modern experimental science, together with its tremendous intellectual achievements, and the traditional religious transcendentalism that has come down to us from antiquity and which the conservative regards as the most precious part of tradition.

That this has always been a major problem in the post-medieval world is well known, and the reality is that the questions involved grow more crucial with each generation. One way in which the conservative tradition seeks to deal with the problem is to insist that the alleged conflict between the naturalism of science and the supernaturalism of religion is not genuine and that no informed person will waste his time any longer arguing about the incompatibility of the two.

For example, when Sir Julian Huxley spoke at a convocation at the University of Chicago, convened in recognition of the centennial of Darwin's *Origin of Species*, he observed that in the evolutionary pattern of thought, there is no place for ideas about supernatural forces affecting the course of events in nature.[34] This observation promptly evoked a host of indignant protests from various clergymen and theologians. A common theme in these protests was that Sir Julian was hopelessly out of fashion in his ideas, which, in truth, would do more credit to a village atheist than to a distinguished biologist. The egregious error on Huxley's part lay, according to these spokesmen, in his failure to perceive that God can create through evolution and therefore there is no necessary contradiction between religious and evolutionary theory.

This approach differs significantly from other beliefs of a more fundamentalist character. These are based largely on a literal interpretation of the Bible, particularly the first chapter of Genesis with its account of a specific and deliberate act of creation. It is mostly because of the influence of this fundamentalist interpretation that laws have been passed forbidding the teaching of organic evolution in the schools. The most celebrated of these laws is the statute in the State of Tennessee under which John Scopes was tried and convicted in the famous Scopes Trial of the 1920s.

So long as the kind of mechanical model of the universe furnished by the Newtonian hypothesis obtained, the task of accommodating physics to theology, while not simple, seemed at least possible. In terms of this model it is possible to speak of a "first cause" in the guise of a "Master Mechanic" who designs the great mechanism of nature and sets it going to run forever in strict harmony with natural law. But as has been

[34] See: *The Chicago Tribune* for November 28, 1959, part I, p. 10.

noted previously, this conception has been outmoded by the newer physics, and although the fact may be distasteful even to some physicists, the universe that is presented to us now exhibits basic traits of contingency and apparent unpredictability that cannot be ignored.[35] Manifestly, it is not a simple matter to synthesize a cosmology of this character with the supernaturalism that so many conservatives feel is necessary, not only to their tradition, but to the very survival of western culture.

Nor is it a simple affair to harmonize the empirical, experimental conception of the knowledge process, that is the essence of science, with the supernaturalism of religion. Science is built on a method of inquiry that involves a radical empiricism—the principle that the limits of human knowledge are the limits of human experience. Though science is becoming increasingly sophisticated—which is to say it is becoming increasingly precise in its treatment of data and steadily more rational in its theoretical structure—the fact remains that the ultimate appeal of science must be to experience in the form of controlled observation and experimentation.

Propositions in metaphysics and theology do not lend themselves to this mode of inquiry because by definition these propositions lie outside the scope of experience and cannot be tested experimentally. The conservative—who cannot maintain his traditional acceptance of supernaturalism if he admits only to an empirical theory of knowledge—must by necessity postulate that there are other modes of knowing and inquiry beyond the scientific. He is most apt, of course, to advance variations on either or both of the ancient conceptions that the highest truth comes through revelation or through reason.

The strains within the conservative tradition that are occasioned by the phenomenal advances of the physical sciences, the changes in modern cosmology, and the increasing domination of the curriculum by scientific studies, as opposed to the older humanities, are severe

---

[35] It is true that statements appear from time to time in the public press by scientists, some of them distinguished in their fields, about the "Ultimate Mystery" or "that unknown region which lies beyond physics." These statements are often heralded as evidence that "modern scientists believe in God." Whether one accepts this as genuine evidence or not, it must be admitted that there is a yawning gulf between these vague assertions and the well-defined and widely-accepted anthropomorphic conceptions of a Creator and a universe designed for man, which are central to the conservative tradition.

In this connection, an interesting incident occurred not long after it became apparent that travel at least in interplanetary space was more than a possibility. On January 4, 1960, the Associated Press reported a statement by Methodist Bishop G. Bromley Oxnam to the effect that in view of the certainty of interplanetary travel, we must be prepared to carry the Gospel to other parts of the universe.

enough. To these there is added a threat that conservatives apparently fear more than any other, and yet this development has originated, in part at least, within the tradition and is closely related to some important aspects of conservative educational doctrine. The condition referred to here is the application of scientific method and scientific modes of inquiry to the study of human behavior in the form of the "social sciences."

Historically, conservatism has been built on a certain conception of human nature and the analysis of this nature has been considered the proper subject matter of philosophy and theology. It is well known, for example, that until comparatively recent times psychology, which has become one of the most aggressive of the behavioral sciences, was a branch of philosophy proper and its methods of inquiry were mainly speculative. Contemporary social scientists—psychologists in particular—are not interested in studying some vague human nature but in studying the varied phenomena of *human behavior*. Modern psychology is built on the conviction that human behavior, complex though it may be, is capable of being investigated, analyzed, and understood through scientific method in the same sense that any natural phenomenon can be studied and understood. Sociology, anthropology, and economics rest on the same principle.

The course of cultural transition being what it is, this attitude has penetrated to some extent into conservative quarters and, in fact, it is not necessarily inconsistent with many deeply conservative ideas about education. To say that this scientific realism is an entering wedge that may very well split the whole conservative tradition is to underestimate the case. The conservative is going to find it difficult in this affair both to have his cake and eat it. Trite though the phrase may be, in this case it is exactly descriptive of what most conservatives would like to do—embrace both supernaturalism and science in some kind of acceptable synthesis.

A fundamental element in scientific method is the principle of uniformity; that is, whenever the same causal conditions are given, the same results will occur. So, if human behavior is a natural phenomenon, it must be assumed that it too is subject to the principle of uniformity and is explainable in terms of the same cause-effect relationship on which all science by necessity depends. If this is accepted, we find ourselves compelled to acknowledge that certain ideas about "freedom of the will" may have to be abandoned or at the very least reinterpreted. Much of the conservative tradition's conception of human nature is built around the presumption that man is free to direct his own behavior and hence is a responsible moral agent. That is to say, man can choose consciously among alternatives and his behavior is guided by his own volition rather than being determined by forces outside himself. And not only does the conservative see this as the basic element in human nature, he also hangs his whole case for personal and social morality on it.

One does not have to be an unfriendly critic of the conservative tradition to admit the crucial nature of this situation. Conservatives themselves are amply aware of it and devote careful attention to it. For example, Mr. Joseph Wood Krutch has argued eloquently against the determinism inherent in the social sciences. An important part of his argument is based on the reality of consciousness and the awareness of self as the primary fact of consciousness. The only thing we have evidence for is our own consciousness. All of our understanding proceeds from this elemental fact.[36]

Mr. Krutch, following the sentiment of many conservatives, attacks the ideas that human nature can be understood in purely scientific terms and that ethical analysis can be nothing other than scientific inquiry. He asks whether "we should again believe that what a Shakespeare has to say about human nature and conduct is likely to be as true as, and rather more important than, what the summarizer of ten thousand questionnaires can tell us."[37] Mr. Krutch, along with many conservatives, considers such a question strictly rhetorical.

Probably the strongest objection most people have to the conception of determinism applied to human behavior is the fatal effect such an idea is believed to have for moral responsibility and the very idea of a system of ethics. Manifestly, if the course of behavior in any human being is determined by antecedent events over which he has no control, it seems idle to talk about his being responsible for what he does. And it would follow that all criminal law—as well as all moral exhortation in home, school and church—is based on impossible premises. This is what Mr. Krutch battles against in the book mentioned above and it is indeed a matter of gravest concern to the whole tradition of conservatism.

Two other objections to determinism that are often found in the literature of conservatism are: (1) the fact that physics—often thought

[36] Joseph Wood Krutch, *The Measure of Man*, New York: Grosset & Dunlap (Grosset's Universal Library Series), 1953. Particularly see Chapter 6: "The Stubborn Fact of Consciousness."
[37] *Ibid.*, pp. 231–232.

of as the most deterministic of the sciences—has found that in the case of sub-atomic particles behavior seems to be indeterminate, random, and hence unpredictable. Therefore, at least at present, it is not possible to postulate any strict cause-effect relation throughout nature; (2) Another common objection is that we cannot ignore the persistent and compelling feeling within ourselves that we do have freedom to choose among alternatives. The objector to determinism argues that we cannot rightfully ignore either the scientific evidence or the conviction of common sense and personal experience.[38]

We will have occasion to return in another context to the problem of determinism as well as additional problems related to the conflict of modern science with other traditions. Our purpose here has not been to treat these matters exhaustively, but to indicate the severe problem the conservative tradition faces in a world in which scientific modes of thought are advancing steadily—and often at the expense of the older beliefs.

SUMMARY: THE CULTURAL COMPONENTS OF CONSERVATISM

This chapter has presented a discussion of the major traditions that have gone into the making of contemporary conservatism. Conservatism has been seen as an emergent of post-medieval western culture. Its historical roots are aristocratic and the tradition still shows ample evidence of this origin. In America conservatism has developed somewhat differently from the way it has in Europe, but the American conservative like his European counterpart, is faced with the formidable intellectual task of reconciling such modern traditions as capitalism, democracy, nationalism, and science with the older traditions of supernaturalism. The task has not been easy and, in the case of science, at least, is likely to get harder.

But the American conservative also faces the task of relating the American belief in free, universal schooling to a tradition which still exhibits more than a trace of aristocratic distrust of (and sometimes outright contempt for) the common people. Although in the course of events the European conservative may well be confronted with the same necessity, he has thus far escaped a full confrontation. This is not the case in America. The American people have long been committed

[38] Stimulating discussions on both sides of the determinism question are presented in: Sidney Hook, ed., *Determinism and Freedom in the Age of Modern Science*, New York: Collier Books, Crowell-Collier Publishing Company, 1961.

to the idea of universal schooling and there is no reason to believe that they will necessarily remain content with a limit of twelve years. The real challenge that faces this tradition, therefore, is the necessity for formulating an educational policy that can embrace in a workable synthesis the divergent cultural elements that make up conservatism and thus facilitate the expression of conservative ideals in the schools of our society.

CHAPTER FOUR

Essentialism:

The Conservative Tradition

in Education

In this chapter we turn to specific ideas conservatives have about education and about the school as an institution. As we have already said, there are different levels at which educational ideas can be studied. They can be considered in their practical sense as proposals for the day by day operation of the school. They can also be studied in terms of their implications and relations with other ideas. In this book we will treat educational ideas in both ways, but in the present chapter we will be concerned with ideas about educational practice in the immediate and practical sense.

It has been indicated in the preceding chapter that the conservative mind has its own perceptions of the nature and importance of education. The conservative believes the schools exist to perform certain functions in society and not to perform others. He believes that certain subject matters are worthy to be taught in the schools and some are not. He believes that there are certain traditional values that the school should cherish and transmit, and he does not believe that the school should attempt to maintain neutrality with respect to questions of value. He believes, further, that the school plays a certain role in society, that there are certain traditional relationships between the school and other institutions. Needless to say, he believes these relationships should be retained in substantially unaltered form.

It is these practical matters that will occupy our attention at this point. In subsequent chapters the conservative views on education will be examined in a broader context and with reference to their connections with other kinds of ideas. With respect to what follows, we should remember that the conservative tradition is an old tradition and in the course of its development certain differences of opinion and emphasis have developed. It is not possible to show that all conservatives agree exactly on all issues concerning educational policy, nor would conservatives think such complete agreement necessarily desirable. What we can show is that there are certain strategic ideas on which there is agreement among conservatives in educational theory. This agreement has been sufficient to bind conservatives together in a united front on educational principles, although there are significant differences among them on certain detailed issues.

THE THESIS OF ESSENTIALISM

The educational ideology of essentialism is based on four general propositions, each of which is concerned with one of the elements to be found in any educational theory: the purpose of formal education; the nature of the curriculum; the function of teaching and the role of the teacher; and the purposes of the school in society. The convictions of the essentialist on these matters taken together define accurately the character of this tradition. Each of the four propositions will be examined in some detail and illustrative examples will be cited from the writings of essentialists and from school practices.

It is almost certain that many who may read this chapter will recognize that what is said is really a brief description of the kind of educational experience they themselves have had since the time they first entered school. In fact, many may feel that the account is no more than a repetition of what "everybody" knows and believes about what schools should do. Reactions of this kind simply testify to the enormous influence this tradition has, and always has had, on American conceptions of formal education.

The Purposes of Education

According to essentialists, the purpose of education is the transmission of certain elements of the cultural heritage whose importance is so great that they cannot be neglected. From the standpoint of the individual, the purpose of education is to help him achieve intellectual discipline. Stated briefly, the essentialist thesis about the aims of education is intellectual training for the individual achieved through rigorous application of the mind to the historic subject matters. This process the essentialist maintains, and *only* this, is worthy to be called the purpose of education.

The purpose of the school as intellectual discipline is a thesis all essentialists accept. There is, however, some difference of opinion among them about whether the school has any other responsibilities for children and youth. One group maintains that the school's responsibility is for intellectual training and for nothing else. They insist that while there are other kinds of services needed by children and youth, these matters, important as they may be, are not the concern of the school and the school should not dissipate its energies in attempting tasks that historically have belonged with the family, the church, and the community at large. The school as an institution is concerned with the life of the mind, and the program of the school should be devoted to the cultivation of intellectual life. Plainly this cannot be done if the high purposes of education are diluted with all kinds of social services and other diversionary activities.[1]

Another group of conservatives, probably much larger than the first group, takes a somewhat more extended view of the school's responsibility. Members of this group would concede that the school has some stake in the physical and emotional well-being of the young child and that child guidance in such areas is a valid responsibility of the teacher as well as of the school as an institution. They would concede, further, that the secondary school has some proper stake in the guidance of adolescents toward worthy personal and vocational goals. Similarly, they would allow the school some share in the social life of the adolescent and therefore permit such "extra-curricular" enterprises as athletics, musical activities, journalistic and social events. At the level of higher education a continuation and perhaps a widening of similar kinds of extra-curricular activities would be permitted and even encouraged.

It should be noted, however, that these are *concessions* in the strict sense of the word. These concessions are agreed to only so long as they are regarded and treated strictly as peripheral to the real purpose of the

[1] For an authoritative statement of the conservative thesis about the purpose of education, together with a blistering criticism of variant views see: Arthur E. Bestor, Jr., "Life Adjustment Education: A Critique," *Bulletin of the American Association of University Professors*, 38:413–441 (Autumn, 1952). See also by the same author: *Educational Wastelands*, Urbana, Illinois: University of Illinois Press, 1953, and *The Restoration of Learning*, New York: Alfred Knopf, 1955.

school. There is wide agreement among essentialists that when any subsidiary service or activity begins to interfere with the intellectual purpose of the school it should be relegated immediately to its proper subordinate place.[2]

The Nature of the Curriculum

The essentialist thesis is further reflected in the curriculum proposed for the school. It should be remembered that the conservative makes a careful distinction between curricular and extra-curricular aspects of the school program. He has no time for and little patience with such statements as: "The curriculum is the sum-total of all the experiences the school provides for students." To the conservative the curriculum is that part of the school's program that nurtures intellectual discipline.

So far as the nature of the curriculum is concerned, conservatives unite on the stand that it consists of a common core of subject matters, intellectual skills, and accepted values that are so essential they must be transmitted to all who come to school. As the conservative sees it, it is through this kind of program that the school can make its major contribution to preserving and transmitting the essential heritage of culture. Conservatives typically insist that while the transmission of knowledge, together with the resulting intellectual discipline, constitutes a major responsibility of the school, the responsibility for transmission does not end with knowledge and skill. The school must also play a major role in transmitting to succeeding generations that body of accepted values which are the core of western civilization.[3] Conservatives have often seen the upsurge in juvenile delinquency and the alleged increase in moral laxity in the population at large as evidence of what happens when the school neglects this aspect of its historic role.

In the opinion of the conservative, the education of a child begins when he first enters school and first applies himself to the basic core of essential subject matter. In the elementary school he receives instruction in reading, writing, spelling, and use of the number system. These subjects are taught largely as separate subjects or disciplines and thorough mastery is insisted on. It is agreed by most conservatives that progress of the child from one grade to another should be dependent on his mastery of the "essentials" for a given grade. As the child moves

---

[2] For a brief and explicit statement of the conservative view on this matter see: James D. Koerner, "Basic Education," *Education*, 79:372–374 (February, 1959).
[3] A spokesman for the Council for Basic Education refers to development of mind, will, and conscience as constituting the basic purposes of education. See Koerner, *op. cit.*, p. 372.

up through the grades he is introduced gradually to the substantive subjects in the curriculum: history, geography (these two often presented together as "social studies"), natural sciences, and perhaps foreign languages. Music and the fine and applied arts find a place in the curriculum but they, along with physical education, tend to be regarded by the conservative as more peripheral than essential.[4]

In the secondary school the organization and rigor of instruction should be increased according to conservative doctrine. The elementary school, if it has functioned as it should, has been a place of preparation so that the high school student may be equipped for serious application to the essential subject matters. At the high school level teaching is departmentalized according to subject matter and teachers of the various subjects should be required to have extensive preparation in the subjects they teach.

There is wide agreement among conservatives that all high school students should study a common core of subject matter organized in terms of the traditional disciplines: English, mathematics, history, science, foreign languages.[5] Although he is willing for the high school to make certain differentiations in curriculum for students of varying abilities, Dr. James B. Conant, one of the best known conservative educational theorists, insists that every student in the high school must study the common core of: four years of English, three or four years of social studies (to include American history), a senior course in American government, either algebra or general mathematics, and one year in natural science.[6] Beyond this common essential core Dr. Conant would permit the election of other subjects—rigorous academic courses for the intellectually able and vocational or quasi-vocational courses for the less talented.

Other conservatives think Conant has conceded too much and would insist that *all* students attending the high school should study the same subjects and that a substantial number not be shunted off into voca-

---

[4] For a brief and pungent statement of the conservative's conception of the education of young children see: Bernard Iddings Bell, *Crisis in Education*, New York: Whittlesey House, McGraw-Hill Book Company, 1949, Chapter 3, "Civilizing the Common Man's Children."

An interesting example of the conservative attitude towards "non-academic" subjects is seen in the *Report of the San Francisco Curriculum Survey Committee*, cited previously. The committee recommended that physical education be reduced to two or three times a week. The report makes no mention of either music or art.

[5] See: Arthur E. Bestor, "Education for Intellectual Discipline," in *Philosophies of Education*, Philip H. Phenix, ed., New York: John Wiley and Sons, 1961, p. 36 ff.

[6] James B. Conant, *The American High School Today*, New York: McGraw-Hill Book Company, 1959, pp. 47–48.

tional work. These conservatives would make no more concessions in curriculum structure than those necessitated by the range of differences in intelligence among high school students.[7]

At the level of higher education the conservative advocates a continued program of organized subject matters, organized both in terms of breadth and of specialization. Typically, an American college student, particularly in his first two years, continues a program of study that is in some ways very similar to the academic pattern of the high school. Requirements are set up to make certain that the college freshman and sophomore will take courses in all the essential subject matters. These requirements are often spoken of as "group requirements," "distribution requirements," or "general education."[8] After the period of general studies, and perhaps overlapping it somewhat, comes a period of specialization in which the student concentrates in ("majors in") a single field, sometimes with another less concentrated study in a second ("minor") field. Thus, according to conservative doctrine, when the student has completed his college course he should have mastered the common core of essential knowledge and gained expertness, relatively speaking, in a single discipline.

The conservative's basic conception of the curriculum may be summarized by saying that from the beginning of school to the end the curriculum is an ordered series of subject matters drawn from the total heritage and designed to be transmitted to all who attend school. The ideal scope and range of this common core is summarized succinctly in an excerpt from the writings of a distinguished philosopher and educational conservative:

> There is certainly a basic core of knowledge that every human person ought to know in order to live a genuinely human life as a member of the world community, of his own nation, and of the family. This should be studied by every student and should be presented at levels of increasing complexity and discipline throughout the entire curriculum. First of all, (a) the student should learn to use the basic instruments of knowledge, especially his own language. In order to understand it more clearly and objectively, he should gain some knowledge of at least one foreign

[7] Among these advocates are: Arthur Bestor and the Council for Basic Education. See as an example: Arthur E. Bestor, "Education and Its Proper Relationship to the Forces of American Society," *Daedalus*, 88:75–90 (Winter, 1959).
[8] The term "general education" makes many conservatives uneasy. The term is difficult to define, but probably no more so than "liberal education," which is a favorite word in the conservative lexicon. "General education" gained much of its initial respectability as a consequence of the famous "Harvard Report," *General Education in a Free Society*, published in 1945 by the Harvard University Press.

language as well. In addition, he should be taught the essentials of humane logic and elementary mathematics. Then (b), he should become acquainted with the methods of physics, chemistry, and biology and the basic facts so far revealed by these sciences. In the third place (c), he should study history and the sciences of man. Then (d), he should gain some familiarity with the great classics of his own and of world literature and art. Finally (e), in the later stages of this basic training, he should be introduced to philosophy and to those basic problems which arise from the attempt to integrate knowledge and practice. Here he should be shown that the world we inhabit is not pure chaos but possesses some stable structure on which certain moral principles at least may be solidly grounded. Of course there should be room for the choice of additional, peripheral subjects to train exceptional capacities, to realize special interests, and to prepare for the professions. But this central core, based on the nature of our human world, should be given to everyone.[9]

The Role of Teaching

To the conservative, education is in essence the transmission of an essential core of subject matters, skills, and values to all who come to school. The art of teaching, therefore, is above all the art of transmitting. Society's agent for this transmitting process is the teacher. It is the teacher who stands between the essential portion of the cultural heritage and the uninformed child, and it is the function of teaching to bring the two together. The joining of the two is accomplished by transmitting and instilling into the student the essential portion of the accumulated heritage. The teacher, therefore, is the efficient cause of the educational process. It is his activity that brings it about.[10]

Teachers have at their disposal various means for transmitting. The oldest of these ways, and therefore the most respected among conservatives, are lecturing—i.e., oral transmission[11]—and transmission through the printed word, particularly by means of books. The textbook has long been the instrument for transmission most used by American teachers

[9] John Wild, "Education and Human Society: A Realistic View," in *Modern Philosophies and Education*, ed., John S. Brubacher, 54th Yearbook of the National Society for the Study of Education, University of Chicago Press, 1955, pp. 34–35.
[10] "The teacher as an authority exercises a mediating, communicating function. His first duty is to gain firm ground, to have something sound and true to communicate. But this does not exhaust the matter. His next duty is really to communicate it, to see that it is presented in such a way as to take possession of the student. Even though the truth is known, if it cannot be transmitted and maintained, culture will die." *Ibid.*, p. 30.
[11] It has been said for many years that lecturing as a method of teaching has been outmoded since the invention of printing. The fact is it still is the single most widely used approach to teaching method. This is very likely true even in the elementary grades.

at all levels below the graduate school and it is by no means unknown at that level. In recent years, however, many other media for transmitting have become available and teachers are no longer bound by necessity to the spoken and written word. The development of a technology that originally appeared in the form of "audio-visual aids," has made many new approaches to transmission possible. Among the best known of the new devices are motion-picture photography, transparencies made from still photographs and designed for projection, sound recordings on disks and tape, elaborate graphic materials in the form of diagrams, charts, drawings, etc., three-dimensional models, mock-ups, and dioramas. Later developments in "educational technology" include the use of television for instructional purposes and the invention of the "teaching machine" and "programmed learning."

The technological development that has excited the most interest is the "teaching machine." Briefly, the teaching machine is a device for presenting to a learner a carefully developed program of material. The program is organized in a series of items to which the learner makes some kind of response. The sequence is gradual and continuous with no abrupt gaps or breaks between items. The learner is able to progress as fast or as slowly through a program as his abilities permit. Some machines for presenting programmed material are technologically sophisticated and are capable of adapting to the learner's responses. Programs may also be presented in book form, a technique that precludes the rigid control of sequence the machine makes possible, since there is nothing to prevent a learner's skipping around among the items if he desires to do so.

There is no particular point in discussing here the complicated technical questions presented by programmed learning. The body of literature in this field is already voluminous and increasing at a staggering rate. A major point of interest, however, for the philosophy of education is the relation of these new techniques to the conservative tradition and particularly to the conservative's conception of the role of teaching.

A favorite idea of many educators is that the advent of programmed learning and the technical devices that employ learning programs are creating a "revolution" in American education.[12] This idea has been eagerly taken up by the public press and others of the mass media. The teaching machine is being acclaimed widely as the first major innovation in teaching since the invention of printing. While some resistance

[12] This thesis has been developed by Mr. James D. Finn. He criticizes educational philosophy for lack of interest in the new technology. See his "A Walk on the Altered Side," *Phi Delta Kappan,* 44:29–34 (October, 1962).

to the idea of programmed learning and the teaching machine as a pedagogical device is raised by conservatives, the general attitude seems to be one of enthusiasm ranging from the carefully restrained to the ebullient.

Actually there seems to be little or nothing involved in programmed learning that poses any fundamental threat to the conservative tradition. The governing idea about education in this tradition is that it is the transmission of essential subject matter, skill, and values. The art of teaching is the art of transmission. Anything that will improve the effectiveness of transmission ought to be welcomed by the educational conservative, or so it would appear.

This promise of efficiency is precisely the argument advanced by most protagonists of the teaching machine. There is little or no hint or promise in the literature of programmed learning that proposes any different objectives for the educational process, or suggests that any alteration in the basic conservative thesis is indicated. In effect, what is promised is that the teaching machine will do the tasks that teachers have always done only it will do them more effectively and, above all, more economically. It has been difficult to get objective data that show genuine and significant differences in achievement between machine teaching and traditional teaching, but data have already been published that show a difference in economy of time in favor of programmed teaching.

According to conservative doctrine, the teacher has not only the task of transmitting the ordered sequences of subject matters, he also has the responsibility for transmitting a body of value concepts and building these into the behavior of the young. Insofar as the transmission of value is concerned, the teacher is expected by conservatives to accomplish this through precept and example.[13] There are numerous references throughout the literature of educational conservatism to the attributes of character teachers should possess. The conservative, of course, lays much stress on the academic scholarship of the teacher, particularly at the level of secondary and higher education, but to most conservatives scholarship is not sufficient. The teacher should embody in his own character and behavior such attributes as moral integrity, a profound sense of justice, hatred of evil in all its forms, and commitment to human betterment—as the conservative understands that term.[14]

[13] For a typical example of the conservative view of the school's role in the value enterprise see: Bernard Iddings Bell, *op. cit.*, Chapter 5.
[14] See for example: Theodore M. Greene, "A Liberal Christian Idealist Philosophy of Education," in *Modern Philosophies and Education*, pp. 111–112.

An idea common among conservatives is that there is always a close relation between rigorous intellectual discipline, moral discipline, and character development. These processes, far from being discrete and isolated from each other, are actually different facets of the same general process. A familiar argument is that a relaxation of intellectual training inevitably brings with it a relaxation of ethical discipline. In the opinion of some conservatives this can account for the slack standards of behavior they profess to find among youth today.[15]

The conservative thesis with respect to the role of teaching can be summed up by saying that teaching is essentially the transmission of a body of knowledge and values, accompanied by certain intellectual skills, to children and young people. The art of teaching is the art of transmitting efficiently and effectively those basic and essential elements of the cultural heritage that all must have. The modern teacher has at his disposal a variety of means of communication, but whatever of these he may find it appropriate to use, his task is the same as it has always been—to transmit the essential elements of the cultural heritage to his students. The teacher is the mediator between the historic accumulation of culture, and the generation which must perpetuate that accumulation.

The School in Society

Essentialism holds that the school is one of the most important institutions in modern society. There is little disposition among American educational conservatives to belittle the importance of the school or the institution of free public education.[16] The conservative sees the school as an institution in society whose purpose is the preservation and appraisal of the heritage of culture and whose mission is to give intellectual training to the young. In the judgment of the essentialist, the school has no mission to change or reform the social order but rather to preserve and refine that which exists. Conservatives as a group are highly resistant to ideas that would alter the historic character and role of the school and have called on the school to resist all efforts to change its nature. Mr. Bestor, in fact, has argued that the school occupies a relatively autonomous role in culture and can preserve its own essential historic pattern in the face of cultural change. He has maintained

---

[15] A sample of this kind of analysis will be found in: Leland Miles, "This Is an Age of Sloppiness," *Phi Delta Kappan*, 30:168 ff. (January, 1959).

[16] Certain exceptions exist but they are not numerous. Reference will be found to some exceptions in the section on "Problems of Essentialism."

further that the school has the power to alter society without the school itself being changed significantly in the process.[17]

The conservative is particularly apt to violent reaction against a thesis that educational progressivism once succeeded in advocating widely, namely that the school should take a prominent role in the reforming of society and its institutions. This thesis attracted most notice in the fourth decade of this century when the attention of Americans was directed to the internal economic and social problems attendant on the great depression. The reaction of the conservatives of that day is summed up in a quotation from the writings of a leading educational conservative:

> The school is the instrument for maintaining existing social orders and for helping to build new social orders when the public has decided on them; but it does not create them. In the same sense that society is prior to the individual, the social order is prior to the school. As a profession, we may have ambitions to do more than this—to criticize the existing order, to help build a better future, but the fact is inescapable that the school is the servant of society.[18]

Although the thesis of the school as a leader in social reform is not as prevalent as it once was, conservatives have not forgotten the threat that once was posed; some still see it as a cause for major concern.[19] As might be expected, the conservative is inclined to see the school as an institution for stability and order, and the more upset and disorganized social life may become in any period, the greater the need for the school to exert its stabilizing influence.[20] In short, the essentialist finds repugnant the idea that the school actually need mirror the chief characteristics of the society in which it exists. He thinks rather that the school should conserve and cherish the best that a culture has produced and transmit this essential heritage to succeeding generations.

The thesis of essentialism, therefore, can be summed up in four propositions that all conservatives accept with a minimum of qualification:

[17] Arthur Bestor, "Education and Its Proper Relationship to the Forces of American Society," *Daedalus*, 88:75–90 (Winter, 1959).

[18] Isaac L. Kandel, "Can the School Build a New Social Order?" *Kadelpian Review*, 12:147–152 (January, 1933). If Professor Kandel had inserted in the second sentence an additional phrase, "knowledge is prior to the knower," he would have produced the best nutshell definition of essentialism in the English language.

[19] See for example: Russell Kirk, *op. cit.*, Chapter III. Whether Mr. Kirk overestimates the influence of progressivism is not the point here. The point is that he is still reacting violently to the idea of the school as an agent of social reform, even though there is scant evidence that it plays any such role today or, in fact, ever did.

[20] See William Bagley, *Education and Emergent Man*, New York: The Ronald Press Company, 1934, pp. 154–156.

1. From the standpoint of the individual, the purpose of education is intellectual and moral discipline and these two are intimately related. From the standpoint of society, the purpose is to transmit the essential portion of the total heritage to all who come to school.
2. The curriculum of the school is an ordered series of subject matters, intellectual skills, and essential values that are to be transmitted to all who come to school.
3. Teaching is, in essence, transmitting. The art of teaching is the art of transmitting effectively and efficiently. The teacher is the active agent in the transmitting process.
4. The role of the school in society is one of preserving and transmitting the essential core of culture. As an institution the school has no call for reforming or altering the historic character of society, except as it may contribute incidentally to the ordered evolutionary process of change.

THE PRACTICAL PROBLEMS OF ESSENTIALISM

The major elements in the conservative's view of education have now been indicated. The point of view presented here is that those ideas taken together describe accurately the actual character of existing American educational practice. This is not to say that conservative ideas have enjoyed a complete domination of the practical aspects of American education for there have been other forces at work. The fact remains, however, that if one considers any of the ideas embodied in the propositions set out above and considers the idea in terms of his own experience in school, he will discover that these conservative notions describe with extreme accuracy the kind of school he attended and the kind of educational experience he had. There will be some exceptions to this since American education is pluralistic in certain respects, but these exceptions will not be numerous and they will not involve much deviation from the established conservative position.

Essentialism is the dominant *educational* tradition in America and it always has been; certainly this is true with respect to the practical matters of operating our schools. This means that essentialism is more than a related group of abstract ideas about education; it is a *living body of school practices*. Whenever any tradition is operative, that is, when it actively affects what happens in society, certain consequences ensue as the result of the practices. Over a period of time certain difficulties arise to plague protagonists of the governing tradition. These difficulties may arise because of original defects in the traditional ideas themselves; they may stem from a certain lag caused by rapid cultural change; or they may stem from lack of competence on the part of people to apply the ideas correctly. More often than not, the practical difficulties encountered by a tradition are the result of a combination of these causal factors.

So long as a body of educational doctrine remains purely conceptual —or nearly so—about the only problems involved are theoretical problems; that is, those concerned largely with coherence and consistency. Any effort to assess the practical significance of these ideas must of necessity be speculative. This, manifestly, is not the case with the tradition of essentialism. This tradition is faced with practical problems of the utmost gravity and this fact is known to essentialists quite as much as the opponents of that tradition. It is our purpose in this book to consider both practical and conceptual problems in various educational traditions. At this point we will concern ourselves with certain important practical problems of the conservative tradition in education.

The Problem of What Is Essential

This tradition is committed to the idea of a basic and irreducible core of tradition that must be transmitted by the school. To this much all conservatives in education agree. The term, "essential core," however, is not self-defining. The question that can always be addressed to essentialists is: "What is essential and how can we tell?" This is a simple question to ask, but essentialists have not always found it easy to answer.

The first impulse of the conservative is to appeal to tradition and to insist that that which is essential are those subject matters that have always, in the words of the Yale Report of 1828,[21] served to supply "the

---

[21] The Yale Report of 1828 is one of the classics of American essentialism. The air of certainty with which its pronouncements have been made; the open and frank acceptance of faculty psychology and mental discipline; the advocacy of the humanistic studies, particularly ancient languages, as the core of the curriculum, serve to differentiate it from the current essentialism which must by necessity try to find a place for the *experimental* sciences and the spirit of scientific method without sacrificing the humanities. The Yale Report has been reprinted substantially intact in: Richard Hofstadter and Wilson Smith, eds., *American Higher Education: A Documentary History*, Chicago: University of Chicago Press, 1961, Vol. I, pp. 275 ff.

discipline and furniture of the mind." Contemporary conservatives attempt to echo these sentiments, as for example, Mr. Clifton Fadiman, writing for the Council for Basic Education, refers to the essentials as those subjects that have "generative power"[22] and these sentiments are repeated in turn by other essentialists.

Only a rudimentary knowledge of the history of education suffices to show, however, that ideas about what the "generative subjects" are seem to change with time and circumstance. There was no doubt in the minds of the authors of the Yale Report of 1828 that the superior subjects in this respect are classical languages, and there is no disputing that they thought modern languages definitely inferior in their "generative power."

Contemporary essentialists, however, are more apt to recommend the study of modern languages, and more often than not, they argue for modern languages largely from utilitarian premises. This kind of utilitarian argument was profoundly distasteful to the essentialists of 1828. Mr. Arthur Bestor, for example, has indicated that debate over the relative merits of ancient and modern languages is legitimate, but he does not indicate how we can find a basis for deciding the issue.[23] In this case, the appeal to tradition is not very helpful in assisting us with an important practical matter of curriculum design.

Nor does simple appeal to tradition serve very well to assist us with a problem whose ramifications far outrun the ancient versus modern language controversy. This problem has to do with the relative merits of the scientific as opposed to the humanistic studies in the essential curriculum. A real appeal to tradition—if by that is meant an examination of the curriculum content of the nineteenth or some earlier century —will indicate that the humanistic studies, particularly philosophy, languages and literatures, should be the dominant elements in the curriculum. This means that the experimental sciences must necessarily play a lesser role in the educational program, which indeed they did through most of the last century.

[22] Council for Basic Education, *op. cit.*, p. 6.
[23] See: Arthur E. Bestor, Jr., "Life Adjustment Education: A Critique," *Bulletin of the American Association of University Professors*, 38:413–441 (Autumn, 1952), p. 437. Mr. Bestor's writings appear to favor modern languages over classical, and his argument is typical of the utilitarian arguments common in much contemporary conservatism. On the other hand, Mr. Samuel Eliot Morison, like Mr. Bestor a historian, prefers classical languages to modern for the education of youth. The reason he gives for his belief is in essence the superior "generative power" of Latin and Greek. See: Samuel Eliot Morison, *The Scholar in America*, New York: Oxford University Press, 1961, p. 30–31.

The struggle of the natural sciences, first for recognition in the curriculum, and presently for domination of it, began over a century ago. It is not really much of an exaggeration to say that in the academic world of America the humanistic studies and the sciences are locked in a final struggle for supremacy. Some aspects of this struggle are perfectly obvious to any observer; other aspects are often concealed in the cloistered recesses where curriculum committees meet to effect some kind of workable compromise for the schools.

The thing that is obvious to any observer is the enormous financial support given to natural science and the prestige the sciences, particularly the physical sciences, enjoy in the United States. An unending stream of money, much of it from public tax sources, flows into scientific and technical research and teaching in our institutions of higher learning. Many young men who traditionally would have gone into law or theology now enter the pursuit of the physical sciences. Even medicine, long the most revered scientific profession in America, reports difficulty in attracting suitable applicants, at least in the numbers that profession once enjoyed.

By and large, the funds for scholarly work and teaching in the humanities are paltry, at least in comparison with the support for science and technology. When funds are available they usually are for the teaching of modern languages or some other field of study thought to have practical value for the national defense. One writer has cited as an example a Title IV program in medieval and European history that was renewed only after the medieval part was cut out of the project.[24] The presence of large sums of money, earmarked for scientific and technological purposes, enables institutions to build larger and larger teaching and research staffs in certain departments. The fact of sheer weight of numbers, added, of course, to the high scholarly and social prestige of the sciences, has tipped the balance of curriculum control and policy making heavily in the favor of the natural sciences in an increasing number of institutions.

The burgeoning support for the sciences and the high prestige these

---

[24] R. M. Lumiansky, "Needed: A National Humanities Foundation," *Bulletin of the American Association of University Professors*, 48:236–239 (September, 1962), p. 237. This is a useful brief summary of the state of the humanistic studies in relation to the sciences together with a proposal for rectifying the situation. Two extensive studies of the influence of federal monies on the role of institutions of higher learning are: Homer D. Babbidge, Jr., and Robert M. Rosenzweig, *The Federal Interest in Higher Education*, New York: McGraw-Hill Book Company, Inc., 1962; and Harold Orlans, ed., *The Effects of Federal Programs on Higher Education*, Washington, D.C.: Brookings Institution, 1962.

studies enjoy is so obvious that anyone can see it plainly. However, there is another problem for the conservative tradition that is not so well understood—even in academic circles. This is the curriculum problem. If we recall that essentialism is committed to the principle of a common core of essential content to be transmitted to all, and if we also remember that the traditional content of this core has been the humanities, we begin to get at least some inkling of the impact the sciences have on conservative ideas of curriculum making.

Naturally, a common response is to say that in the modern world the sciences also are essential and therefore must have a place in the common core. This is the notion on which most curriculum innovators in secondary and higher education seem to proceed. It may appear simple to add to the humanities already in the essential core the physical, biological and social sciences. But if these newer subjects are to have a place something will have to give. Either the period of general education will have to be lengthened at the expense of the period of specialization, or the total time devoted to secondary and higher education will have to be increased beyond the time now allotted to them. Another possibility is that substantial portions of the humanities, considered by tradition to be essential, will have to be reclassified as nonessential. This has already happened to classical languages in United States schools to the sorrow of many conservatives.

The practical problem of compressing an increasing volume of factual material into the essential core has become staggering. One clear example of this is in the field of history. Mr. Arthur S. Bolster, discussing the problem in this field, points up the issue.[25] In 1899 a committee of the American Historical Association produced a document on the content of the high school curriculum in history. This report proposed a four-block sequence and recommended essential historical content to go into it. The report was influential in its day and had nine printings. Sixty-one years later, a distinguished historian, Mr. Carlton J. H. Hayes,[26] insists in effect that all of the content recommended as essential in 1899 be covered and in addition the *major historical developments that have occurred since then.* In the years since 1910 there have been two major world wars, a world-wide depression, the rise of revolutionary

[25] Arthur S. Bolster, "History, Historians, and the Secondary School Curriculum," *Harvard Educational Review*, 32:39–65 (Winter, 1962).
[26] See: Carlton J. H. Hayes, "European and World History," and also Ray Allen Billington, "American History," Council for Basic Education, *op. cit.*, pp. 27–61.

socialism, the virtual end of colonialism, the consolidation of industrial society, and the beginnings of the conquest of space—to name only some of the major events.

How can the conservative handle this problem of the vast increase in material—which certainly is not unique to the subject of history? He can for one thing insist that more time be spent in the study of history in the secondary school so the additional material can be covered. But when he suggests this he finds quickly that there are proponents of other subject matters who are also jealous of the time of high school students; the conceptual load in other fields is increasing also and the need for more time is felt here as well as in history. And what will we do in another sixty years when the historical load will be much greater?

It has long since occurred to some people that firm decisions simply will have to be made about what historical material is essential to the curriculum and what is not. This decision ought to be made by historians, or so it would appear, but there is a long history of efforts of this kind among historians and little has been accomplished in defining an irreducible core of material of workable proportions for the secondary curriculum. The difficulty of the curriculum problem is magnified by the pressures from other social sciences for more adequate representation in the curriculum: economics, sociology, geography, and anthropology, for example. Protagonists of these fields of study are increasingly aggressive in their claims, and it appears they are out to end the domination historians have maintained over the social studies in our schools.[27] Meantime, historians by and large resist the pruning job that is necessary for producing a tenable essential core.

Another possibility is to compress material more and more in the form of generalizations so that these generalized ideas may be transmitted without the attendant bulk of factual detail. This proposal is viewed with suspicion and often with hostility by the conservative who tends toward a deep antipathy for "survey" courses, watered-down content, and overblown generalities. It must be admitted that there will be great difficulty in persuading many essentialists that this is any solution to the problem.

[27] See for example: Leonard S. Kenworthy, "Ferment in the Social Studies," *Phi Delta Kappan*, 44:12–16 (October, 1962). Also: Richard E. Gross and Dwight W. Allen, "Time for a National Effort to Develop the Social Studies Curriculum," *Ibid.*, 44:360–365 (May, 1963).

Another suggestion, one that has been made somewhat tentatively up to now but is almost certain to be urged more strongly in the future, involves the "new technology." For example, Mr. Maxwell H. Goldberg, writing in the *College and University Bulletin*,[28] suggests that part of the conceptual load in general education can be carried by such technical devices as microfilm and various "information-retrieval" systems, teaching machines, and forms of programmed learning. Mr. Goldberg includes also the idea of popular writing that will compress and synthesize new material and express it in language that can be understood by the non-scientist. This last suggestion apparently is related to the one discussed in the paragraph immediately above.

It may be true that the new technological devices will be effective in processing information and ordering it in useful form. Yet, the avowed purpose of education in the conservative tradition is to transmit essential knowledge to the learner's nervous system (many essentialists would rather say his intellect), not to record it on microfilm. While there is some evidence that teaching machines can transmit certain kinds of material more quickly than ordinary teachers, it does not seem very likely that even these devices can hope to keep up with the increase in knowledge.

It may be observed also that the development of "information-retrieval" systems could eventually influence the design for teaching in a direction that conservatives in recent years have not been very friendly to-wards—namely, teaching designs that are built primarily around method (in the case of history, for example, historical method) rather than around the transmission of content. This is a controversial proposal, particularly because in the twentieth century conservatives have been at a loss to know how to handle the idea of mental discipline. In earlier times the tradition frankly embraced the idea of "mental gymnastics" and developed much of its program on the belief that the mind could be "strengthened" through intellectual exercise. The *Yale Report* mentioned earlier is a good example of this attitude.

This classic notion has been so discredited by contemporary psychology that many conservatives have felt compelled to give it up—although not without regret. Others, of course, adhere to it in the face of all evidence to the contrary. However, at least two historians of conservative persuasions have advanced ideas relating to the use of historical

[28] Maxwell H. Goldberg, "General Education and the Explosion of Knowledge," *College and University Bulletin*, Association for Higher Education, National Education Association, Vol. 14, No. 9 (unpaged).

method in intellectual discipline.[29] The argument is that even at the level of secondary education the student can be expected to do more than merely absorb the factual material transmitted to him. While the high school student cannot be expected to engage fully in the real historical analysis that is done at the college level, he can be introduced to the elements of historical method in both its analytic and synthetic phases. It may well be that if this direction is followed some of the emphasis on transmission of subject matter will have to be given up. A real adoption of procedures of this kind might, in fact, furnish the conservative with a criterion for deciding what is essential in the field of history. Not enough has been done with this idea for us to know what promise it holds for the solution of the essentialist's problem.[30]

Any other of the common branches in the curriculum would do as well for illustrating the difficulty of the situation for the conservative tradition. We have used the field of history as an example of the problem essentialism faces in attempting to maintain the thesis of an irreducible core of essential material in the face of the rapid accumulation of knowledge in the contemporary world. History furnishes a good example because it is easy to see that the constant accumulation of material in that area is as inevitable as the progress of time itself.

The examples of modern languages versus classical languages and the content of the curriculum in history illustrate one kind of practical problem for the conservative tradition, but these examples illustrate only the problem of selecting essential material *within fields that all conservatives find essential*. There may be plenty of controversy among conservatives about whether modern languages are more essential than classical and vice versa, but there is no controversy over whether some foreign languages are essential. There may be wide differences of opinion about what content of history is essential, but there surely are no great differences among conservatives about whether history itself is an essential of the common curriculum.

There is another class of problems, however, that derives from the question, "What is essential?" These problems are concerned with whether certain *areas of knowledge* are themselves essential. Certainly one of the most difficult of these for the conservative is whether religion

[29] See: W. Burlie Brown, *United States History: A Bridge to the World of Ideas*, a pamphlet published by the American Historical Service Center for Teachers of History. See also: Arthur Bestor, *The Restoration of Learning*, p. 437.
[30] Mr. Bolster's judgment is that neither Mr. Brown nor Mr. Bestor has as yet developed a tenable analysis. See Bolster, *loc. cit.*

is an essential element of the curriculum.[31] It has already been remarked that to the conservative mind supernatural religion is one of the most important forces in the direction of cultural stability and the maintenance of tradition. As we have seen, the conservative is inclined to think that all the important kinds of problems that face men—politics, education, ethics, etc.—are at bottom religious problems. Some conservatives even take this view of economic problems, for, according to them, the natural laws of the market in the last analysis represent the will of God in the economic sphere.[32]

In the light of these sentiments it is not surprising that many conservatives regard religion as an essential element in the program of the school. Burke himself, the great progenitor of the conservative tradition, considered much of the strength of British education—and consequently much of the strength of British society—to stem from the close relation between education and religion that obtained in his day.[33] Burke's sentiments in this matter still have their original validity, in the opinion of many contemporary conservatives.

The real issue for conservatives is that since the transmission of ethical values is an essential function of education and since, as the conservative sees it, ethics apart from religion are meaningless, it does not seem reasonable for the school arbitrarily to eliminate religious instruction from the curriculum. Bernard Iddings Bell has insisted that religion is of the utmost importance in education at all levels of the school. Similar declarations have been made by William F. Buckley and Russell Kirk. Since a substantial number of conservatives often profess a preference for European ideas of education over American, it is not surprising that there has been favorable comment on the practice in many European countries of incorporating religious instruction in the curriculum of the public schools and of using public tax monies for the support of private sectarian schools.

But the conservative, whose primary appeal is to tradition, is faced with the incontrovertible fact that one of the oldest elements in the American tradition is the separation of church and state and the encouragement of religious pluralism. These sentiments antedate even

---

[31] Another question is whether various vocational subjects are essential. American conservatives are well agreed that for the academically talented, vocational subjects are neither essential nor desirable. There are marked differences of opinion over the essential quality of these subjects for slower learners.

[32] See for example: Frank Chodarov, "The Penalty of Disregarding Natural Law," in A. G. Heinsohn, Jr., ed., *op. cit.*, pp. 392–396.

[33] Burke, *op. cit.*, p. 113 ff.

　　　　　　　　　　　　　PHILOSOPHY OF AMERICAN EDUCATION

our national history. A long series of court decisions has been necessary to interpret the meaning inherent in the First Amendment to the Constitution. While conservatives have not always been pleased with the judgments of the courts,[34] they have themselves been signally unsuccessful in developing a policy of religious instruction in the public schools that would satisfy sectarian interests and conform to legal requirements of the Constitution.

There are conservative educational spokesmen who have expressed grave doubts even about the effect of private schools in American society. Mr. James B. Conant, for example, has urged support for public schools, and particularly for the comprehensive high school, as against public assistance for private schools, a majority of which are church related. In his view, much of our success in assimilating the diverse populations that emigrated to the United States in the nineteenth century is owed to the American public school system. He still sees this system as an important stabilizing and conserving force in American society.[35] To be sure, there are numerous conservatives who do not concur in this judgment and there is evidence that the split within conservative ranks on this issue is growing wider. Apparently, it is one thing to appeal to the wisdom of our forefathers and quite another to know which of these forefathers to heed.[36] This is a pressing practical problem for educational conservatism because this tradition insists that by an appeal to tradition we can know what is essential for the curriculum of our schools.

In view of the considerations discussed above, it appears that two general observations are warranted. First, it is of great strategic importance to the conservative tradition to find some tenable method for determining what is essential in the curriculum and what is not. Granted that the problem has not always been as great as it is today, the fact remains that conservatism has never really had a trustworthy means for making these important discriminations. Too often, in fact,

---

[34] For example, there was an outpouring of protest, mostly from conservative quarters, when a 1962 decision of the United States Supreme Court made unconstitutional the reading of a "non-denominational" prayer in the public schools of New York. The prayer had been officially approved by the Regents of the State of New York. See *Engle vs. Vitale*, 82 S. Ct. 1261 (1962).

[35] James B. Conant, *Education and Liberty*, New York: Random House, Inc. (Vintage Books), 1953, p. 81 ff.

[36] For example, should the conservative heed James Madison on the religious issue? Madison was one of the great original protagonists of conservatism in America but he was also one of the doughtiest fighters for the separation of church and state. See his famous "Memorial and Remonstrance Against Religious Assessments" (1785).

conservatives have been seduced by the charm of easy answers: "tradition," "what everybody knows," "what the scholarly world knows." In a period of enormously accelerated cultural transition, characterized by overwhelming advances in natural science, "tradition" and the opinions of "the scholarly world" have not proved very definitive guides in the search for what is essential.

The second observation that can be made is that the challenge of the sciences for domination of the curriculums of the schools cannot be shrugged off or wished away. Influential conservatives admit that the humanistic studies are in retreat and have been for a substantial time.[37] And yet, as far as education is concerned, the humanities have always been the life blood of the conservative tradition. It is, of course, possible that the old conservatism is dying—a lingering death to be sure, but one that increasingly hastens to the end. It is conceivable that out of this may develop a new social and educational conservatism that substitutes for the older authority of religious and humanistic knowledge a new authority built on scientific certainties. Meantime, in America the conservative tradition in education seeks to preserve itself by a series of tactical compromises,[38] and increasingly these compromises are made on the grounds of the sciences, not on the grounds of the humanities as once was true. The ideal of Burkean conservatism is the *gentleman,* urbane, aristocratic, immersed in the humanistic studies, religious by nature, and always mindful of tradition. But if what is emerging is a new conservatism built on physical science and technology, the ideal must be that of the scientist (or perhaps the engineer) possessed by the rigors of scientific method, whose quest for certainty is not in the superstitions of religion and the vagaries of literature but in reason and experiment and control.[39] If the conservative humanist does not always rest well at night, it is small wonder.[40]

[37] See for example: Russell Kirk, *op. cit.,* p. 53 ff.
[38] One of the best descriptions of this tactical situation has been supplied by Mr. Gordon Keith Chalmers: "The central fact about the compromise of curriculum committees . . . is a gigantic intellectualist illusion which has characterized American academics for four decades: The illusion that almost every specialty which has managed to make space for itself in the catalog has philosophical rights and claims comparable to every other . . . almost every subject has a vote, and what comes out of the committee is a kind of philosophical congress in which all disciplines are represented." Gordon Keith Chalmers, "The Diverse Responsibilities of Liberal and General Education," *Current Issues in Higher Education, 1953,* Proceedings of the Eighth Annual National Conference on Higher Education, Washington, D.C.: Association for Higher Education, a department of the National Education Association, 1953. The quotation is from pp. 34–35.
[39] It is interesting to speculate that such a "new" conservatism, though certainly different from the Burkean variety, could still come close to the criteria suggested by

The Practical Problem of Mass Education

Almost any teacher or administrator in American schools will agree that the most persistent and baffling problems of education may be traced ultimately to the fact of individual differences among students. The area of these differences which is of most significance here is, of course, differences in ability to achieve. School achievement is known to be a function of many factors, but there is no denying that intelligence is one of the crucial elements in ability to master the curriculum of studies.

American education, dominated as it is by the conservative thesis, has always proceeded on the assumption that there is an irreducible core of essential material that must be transmitted to all. We have already seen that there are certain differences of opinion among conservatives over what should be in this core, but we have not been able to find evidence that essentialists are willing to give up the idea of a basic core for all students.

On the other hand, the United States is committed, and has been committed for a long time, to the principle of universal education. All states in the Union have compulsory attendance laws and all states provide opportunity for twelve years of public schooling. Virtually all children of elementary school age who are capable of profiting at all from formal instruction are in school. The American high school has never succeeded in enrolling all adolescent youth, and though estimates vary, it is certain that less than three-quarters of those who begin school actually finish twelve years. This condition, however, is viewed with grave concern and both educational and political leaders are constantly searching for an answer to the "drop-out" problem. The common ideal is that of at least twelve years of schooling for every American child.

When universal education is achieved or very nearly achieved, the school population is always highly heterogeneous. All social strata in society are represented and the distribution of intelligence in the school population approximates closely the distribution of intelligence in the general population. This is to say that in our schools there is a range in ability extending from those who are barely educable at all to

Viereck (*op. cit.*, p. 15), namely: a distrust of human nature; opposition to untested innovations; and a traditional framework to tame human nature. In such a new conservatism the fulfillment of these criteria would derive from scientific not religious-humanistic origins.

40 Particularly if he reflects on such sentiments as the following: "After the rigors of training in science, the subject content of the humanities seems hardly more difficult than a good novel." Editorial, "Science and the Humanities," *Science*, 138:1367 (December 28, 1962).

those whose capabilities are rated as "genius" on such a scale as the Stanford-Binet test of intelligence. The distribution of intelligence in the schools assumes the general shape of the well-known probability curve.

It is these two factors taken together that generate the most perplexing problems of policy and practice in American public education. On the one hand, there is the essentialist's insistence on a common core of essential subjects; on the other hand there is the brute fact that people differ greatly in their ability to learn abstract material. Since nobody at present knows how to alter significantly the genetic equipment of individuals and thus narrow the range in learning ability, and since essentialism is unwilling to make any very significant compromise in the thesis of a common core, the schools are full of what is known in the trade as "low-achievers" together with a considerable number of "non-achievers."[41] The first group consists of those who do not learn very much, and the second group is composed of those who learn little or nothing. The complaints of upper elementary teachers about the poor achievement in the primary grades, the complaints of high school teachers about the lack of preparation in the elementary schools, the complaints of college teachers about the lack of quality in high school graduates, the complaints of graduate schools about the lack of preparation of candidates for graduate study are all legendary.

The conservative tradition seeks to work out these problems within an administrative structure known as "the graded system." The graded system dates from about the middle of the nineteenth century and thus has been the prevailing mode of organization throughout most of the American period of universal public education. Most Americans, including most school personnel, cannot conceive that schools could be organized in any other way. The graded system of organization involves the classification of pupils into grades or classes. These grades correspond to chronological age—at least in the beginning—since children enter the first year of schooling at about the same age. As the theory goes, a basic core of essential material is set for each grade level and minimum standards for mastery are also established.[42] If a child is able to master the essential material during the year he is in the first

41 The trade also recognizes two groups known respectively as "under-achievers" and "over-achievers." These represent special problems that will not be treated formally in this volume.
42 American elementary teachers invariably speak of school achievement in terms of "first-grade reading," "third-grade arithmetic," "sixth-grade spelling," etc.

grade, he is transferred (i.e., "promoted") to the second grade and so on up through the school system. Theoretically, those who fail to achieve the essential core in one year will be retained in that grade until they show evidence of sufficient mastery. Promotion thus becomes the reward for achieving the minimum essentials and retention becomes a penalty for not doing so.

The implementation of this latter policy is more theoretical than real, however. Teachers and administrators, particularly in the elementary schools, are resistant to filling their classrooms with over-age pupils who learn slowly, achieve little, and are constant sources of disturbance. At least some administrators are aware that high scholastic standards in a school cannot be achieved by systematically saving up the most backward pupils and keeping them year after year. For reasons such as these, the policy of promotion based on achievement—a policy that numerous contemporary conservatives call for loudly[43]—is seldom followed strictly in practice and very likely never will be. Therefore, a great deal of administrative ingenuity has been expended in finding ways to circumvent this aspect of the graded system.[44]

As we have already observed, conservatives are amply aware of the practical problems outlined above and they have been diligent in their efforts to find a means of coping with them. The material related to these efforts is vast but thoroughly scattered through the literature. However, it is possible to discern in all this mass of material three general kinds of policy that are being advocated by contemporary conservatives. Each of these policies will now be examined.

The first recommended policy for dealing with the manifold problems of individual differences and mass education goes somewhat as follows: The lack of achievement which is so apparent today at every level of our school system is caused by the poor quality of teaching, the preoccupation of teachers with services and activities that do not contribute to intellectual training, and a lack of high standards of expectation; in short, soft pedagogy. The way out of our difficulties will be found if we will restore to instruction the rigor and thoroughness it once had and now has mostly lost. We will also need to return to a curriculum de-

[43] See for example: *The Report of the San Francisco Curriculum Survey Committee*, p. 15. "We recommend that promotion should never be automatic. A student should be promoted or passed only if he meets the minimum objectives of the grade or course."

[44] For useful summaries of promotion practices in American schools, see: *Encyclopedia of Educational Research*, 3rd ed., New York: The Macmillan Company, 1960, pp. 438–9 for elementary schools and p. 1253 for secondary schools.

signed for intellectual training and composed of those subjects that tradition has shown to have real intellectual value. But more than this, we need to reorient our basic attitudes about education. We need, in the words of Mr. Arthur Bestor to:

> . . . reaffirm our belief in the value of intellectual training to all men, whatever their occupation, whatever their background, whatever their income or their position in society. This is to retrace our steps, I grant. It is to retrace them back to that period when professional educators really believed in education and when public school leaders really believed in democracy.[45]

On one occasion Mr. Bestor vouchsafed the opinion that if we would only reconstruct our educational procedures and revitalize our curriculums and our teaching processes, we would find that ninety percent of the pupils in the schools would profit from this rigorous educational program. This proved too much for Mr. Russell Kirk, who has often quoted Mr. Bestor's writings with obvious approval. Mr. Kirk is sure the percentage is too high, though he hastens to agree that many more students would receive a real liberal education than are receiving it today.[46]

Be this as it may, many people undoubtedly find the ideas embodied in this policy persuasive. It probably is more widely accepted among parents of students than among the teachers of these students. Teachers usually have somewhat more psychological sophistication than parents have and in any event they have all faced the stark reality that there is a limit to what teaching skill and rigorous educational programs can achieve. On the other hand, it is certainly more comfortable for the patrons of schools to believe that the poor achievement of their children is the fault of the school and the teacher rather than the fault of poor genetic inheritance. Anyone whose duty it has been to listen to the complaints of school patrons will recognize the argument, "He can get it all right if you will only *make* him learn!"[47] and the

---

[45] Arthur E. Bestor, "Life Adjustment Education: A Critique," AAUP *Bulletin* (Autumn, 1952), p. 440.

[46] See: Russell Kirk, *op. cit.*, p. 69. Though Mr. Bestor's essentialism is classic and entirely beyond reproach, in this instance at least, he betrays an odor of equalitarian dogma for which any old-line conservative such as Russell Kirk has a very sharp nose. To suppose that nine-tenths of the population could ever hope to savor any of the unbought grace of life is a patent absurdity to a Burkean conservative.

[47] This policy has apparently played an important role in the operations of an elementary school program lately established in Washington, D.C. This school has been cited by essentialists as a model of what an elementary school should be. The school's program and the ideas behind it are discussed at length in: Carl F. Hansen, *The Amidon Elementary School: A Successful Demonstration in Basic Education*, Englewood Cliffs, New Jersey: Prentice-Hall, Inc., 1962.

clear implication that "the reason he doesn't learn is because he hasn't been taught right."

There are conservatives, however, who doubt that the policy outlined above can really be adequate to solve the problem of individual differences in a mass education design. The belief that such a high proportion of the population as ninety percent can cope with the abstractions of the typical essentialist core without any modification being made seems unduly optimistic. Accordingly, a second kind of policy has been advocated that goes something as follows: Let us recognize that differences in learning ability are large and cannot be ignored. Let us, therefore, adjust the organization of our school system to meet these differences. This can be done through ability grouping at all levels of the system, by differentiated curriculums in the high school, and by programs of guidance, particularly in secondary education, that will help individuals find the programs that are suited to their particular levels of ability and interest. This is the general position taken by such a well known and influential conservative as Mr. James B. Conant. It is also the policy advocated by Mr. Paul Woodring, who has been influential in conservative circles. As noted in an earlier chapter, the key to Mr. Conant's proposal is the establishment of "comprehensive secondary schools" which would offer under one roof a variety of courses and curriculums and a program of guidance that would help students find a program of study suitable to their talents.[48] A common core of essentials would be maintained but it would be scaled down considerably from the core recommended by Mr. Wild (see ante p. 86) or by Mr. Bestor and the Council for Basic Education. Beyond this common core students would enroll in courses appropriate to their abilities. Opportunities in the comprehensive high school would range from rigorous academic courses to various kinds of strictly vocational work. Ability grouping would be employed in the basic subjects to a degree seldom found in American secondary schools and admission to the academic program would be carefully controlled.[49]

Beyond the comprehensive high school Mr. Conant has advocated

[48] Conant, *The American High School Today.*
[49] Conservatives, by and large, are greatly taken with the idea of grouping by ability. Mr. Bestor has advocated it as an important part of his policy. In the Amidon Elementary School (see pp. 20–22) ability grouping is reported to be used for general classification purposes, but small ability groups within a class are discouraged. From the reading of the current literature of essentialism one might conclude that ability grouping has just been invented. Actually it has a long history and extensive studies of it have been made. For a review of the literature, see the *Encyclopedia of Educational Research,* 3rd ed., pp. 427–28 for elementary schools and p. 1267 for secondary schools.

two-year colleges that would offer terminal programs for those who desire education beyond the high school but who are not equipped for the rigors of a regular four-year college course. Instead of expanding the enrollments and programs of four-year colleges and universities he has suggested that we retract enrollment in those institutions and admit only applicants who clearly can profit by attendance and who ultimately can engage in graduate study.[50]

Another plan, similar in certain respects to the Conant plan, has been devised by Mr. Paul Woodring. This plan would involve a complete reorganization of the American school system. The number of years devoted to elementary schooling would be shortened, pupils would be permitted to advance through the grades at varying rates, ability grouping would be employed extensively. After high school the academically talented would find their way to liberal arts colleges and ultimately to graduate and professional schools. The average run of students would go to junior colleges, trade schools, or to work.[51]

Both these policies have been given a favorable hearing, but the ideas advocated by Mr. Conant have been more influential in practice. For one thing, Mr. Conant's plan would disrupt the traditional organization of the school system far less than the proposals of Mr. Woodring. Another factor is the unparalleled personal prestige enjoyed by Mr. Conant among citizens at large and among professional teachers and administrators. Although there have been serious objections from other conservatives about certain aspects of the Conant policy,[52] it is likely that Mr. Conant has been more influential in the practical aspects of educational policy than any other single individual. After all, he has assured the American people that our basic educational tradition is sound, that we need no upheaval in organization nor any untested innovations. He has shown us that all we really need do is correct certain details in our present system. Such assurances as these appeal strongly to the basic conservative strain in the American mind.

There is, however, a hard core of essentialists who find untenable both kinds of policy outlined above. Their approach to the problem posed by individual differences is fundamentally different and is what most liberals

---

[50] James B. Conant, *Education and Liberty*, New York: Vintage Books, a division of Random House, Inc., 1958, p. 57. This policy would restore the four-year college approximately to the position it held prior to World War I.

[51] For the details of Mr. Woodring's proposed reorganization see his *A Fourth of a Nation*, New York: McGraw-Hill Book Company, Inc., 1957, p. 143 ff.

[52] For instance, the Council for Basic Education has objected to including vocational courses in the high school curriculum and Russell Kirk has criticized the consolidation of school districts to create large comprehensive high schools.

and possibly many American conservatives would call "undemocratic." The difference in this approach to policy lies in challenging the very idea of universal education—at least beyond a bare minimum of common schooling. The argument goes somewhat as follows:

Why do we not admit that a substantial part of the population is simply uneducable in any real sense of the word *educate* and shape our plans accordingly? This would mean giving up the peculiarly American sentiment of equalitarianism and all the havoc it has created in American education. As Mr. Albert J. Nock[53] observed a generation ago, our educational system rests on three false premises: equality, democracy and the belief that the literate society is the good society. It follows that any theory of education derived from these false ideas is itself bound by logical necessity to be false.

Conservatives who follow this line of thought are apparently convinced that humanity is composed of three groups: a relatively small group of the talented, a larger middle stratum of moderately intelligent people who are able and willing to accept the leadership and authority of the elite, and at the lowest level a great mass of people who may with great effort be capable of simple literacy but very little beyond that. The great error of egalitarian educational ideals lies in failing to take account of these ineradicable differences. Under the spell of "democratic" ideas we attempt to educate all men as if they were all equal in ability. The only way this can be done is to keep everybody at the same level of mediocrity or worse and this, in the view of these conservatives, is what has been done in the United States. We have failed to educate our talent; in fact, we have not even provided a decent education for the middle group. In trying to educate the masses—who can't be educated anyway—we wind up educating nobody.

There is, say the proponents of this position, only one thing to do. This is to design a school system that will be increasingly selective. Perhaps we must begin with a common school to which everybody will be admitted at first.[54] But the conservative maintains that though everybody may come in the beginning, everybody does not have to stay in school long after he has learned all he can. What should happen to a

[53] The classic quality of Nock's book on education is being rediscovered by contemporary conservatives. It surely is one of the most remarkable treatises on educational theory written in this century. See: Albert J. Nock, *The Theory of Education in the United States*, New York: Harcourt, Brace, 1932.
[54] Conservatives are not always clear on this point, but given the inexorable demands of industrial society it appears likely that all must agree to a common school which will supply at least the elements of literacy.

person when he ceases to learn? The answer, though it can be expressed in various ways, is simply that he should leave the school forthwith.[55]

Whether these conservatives believe individuals should be put out of school before they have completed the common schooling of the elementary grades is mostly a matter for speculation. But there is no room for doubt about their position on secondary education. The secondary school should be selective. It should admit only those who have demonstrated their ability and willingness to do high level work. The curriculum of the high school should be uniform, it should be academically rigorous, and the very highest standards of achievement should be maintained. With arrangements such as these we could give a good education to those who are capable of being educated.[56]

Those who advocate this policy are unimpressed by such arguments as the lack of opportunity for gainful employment for youth who would be forced to terminate their schooling at an early age. A common reply to such an argument is that while the plight of many uneducable—and perhaps unemployable—youth is a difficult one, it is not really an educational problem and the school should not be called on to deal with economic and social difficulties that are not its business. To do so is only to continue the debasement of our educational system.[57]

This third policy is accepted by only a minority of American conservatives today and it is all but certain that the mass of the population rejects it as public policy. Its proposals run too much counter to the ingrained doctrine of equality in the American mind. Though proponents of selective schooling may fulminate against the misapplication of equalitarian doctrine in deciding who shall be educated, their message is not really given a sympathetic hearing by the masses. In spite of all the talk about European models for our school system, there is as yet scant evidence that Americans are ready to move in the direction of a truly selective secondary school.[58]

[55] This is the thesis stated with clarity and conviction by Caspar D. Green. See: "What Shall We Do with the Dullards?" *The Atlantic Monthly*, 197:72–74 (May, 1956).

[56] See for example: J. N. D. Bush, "My Credo: Humanist Critic," *Kenyon Review*, 13:81–92; and Harold L. Clapp, "Some Lessons from Swiss Education," *Modern Age*, 2:10–17.

[57] See: Caspar D. Green, *loc. cit.*

[58] Advocacy of a policy of rigorous selection of students for secondary schools has already created dissension in the ranks of the Council for Basic Education. According to an Associated Press release for October 26, 1963, Admiral Hyman G. Rickover, as a featured speaker at the annual meeting of the Council, advocated substantially the policy outlined here. In a discussion that followed, his ideas were criticized, in some respects quite severely, by such stalwarts of essentialism as Arthur Bestor and Carl F. Hansen.

And yet, it may be premature to discount completely the chances of the third policy. Equalitarianism, as commonly understood, may be workable in public education under conditions of early industrialism, but this is not necessarily to say that it is workable under a truly integrated technological society in which the need for semi-skilled human labor is not very great and the real demand is for intensive, specialized scientific and technological training. Equalitarian doctrine to the contrary notwithstanding, nobody knows today how to transmit specialized, sophisticated scientific and technological knowledge and skill to the mass of people, no matter how they may be grouped for instruction in the school. It can be argued that the real need of a mature technological society is a relatively small group of scientists and technologists—a scientific and technological elite.[59] It is the primary business of education to sort out potential members of this elite and educate them for their responsibilities. The schooling of the rest of a generation may be a troublesome necessity, but it is not the real educational problem, and the rudimentary schooling of the masses should never be permitted to interfere with the *education* of those who are capable of being *educated*.

These three kinds of policy for dealing with the problems of individual differences and mass education in contemporary society illustrate the practical difficulties essentialism faces in interpreting its basic conservative principles in terms of workable policies for the conduct of our schools. Adherents of the tradition of conservatism are badly split over this question, and it is not possible to discern with clarity which, if any, of the three policies outlined above will become the dominant mode of organization in our public schools.

The Practical Problems of Retention and Transfer

There is one other problem of major significance that should be given consideration before we leave the present subject. This practical question is posed by two considerations known to psychologists as "retention" and "transfer of learning." The first term refers to the *perpetua-*

[59] Mr. Paul Woodring, in commenting on certain ideas of Admiral Hyman G. Rickover, has said that such a policy would not result in an elite, since everybody has the same chance in the beginning. If this is so, it involves an unusual sense of the term "elite." Under this view, Plato's philosopher-kings would not constitute an elite either, since Plato was careful to point out that every child in the Republic had a chance *in the beginning.* See: *Saturday Review*, 45:86–7 (October 20, 1962). For a summary of Rickover's views on educational matters see: "Admiral Rickover on American Education," *The Journal of Teacher Education*, 10:3–27 (September, 1959).

tion in subsequent experience of material learned at some prior time. The second term refers to the *application* of learned material in subsequent experience. The processes of remembering and using learned material are generally thought of as psychological rather than philosophical matters of concern. However, the phenomena of retention and transfer of knowledge are at the bottom of certain difficult problems facing the conservative tradition in education, and hence they merit some attention in the present context.

The conservative tradition in education is built on the belief that the true purpose of education is the transmission of selected portions of certain organized subject matters. Much of the work of the teacher, according to essentialist doctrine, must necessarily be devoted to the transmission of facts. This fundamental principle is also expressed in the essentialist idea of the curriculum as an ordered series of subject matters to be transmitted by teachers and "absorbed" by pupils.

To be sure, essentialists regularly point out that students should be expected to do more with factual material than merely commit it to memory, but in the last analysis, it is always the fact-learning aspect of education that gets the emphasis in essentialist writing. In the case of young children, for example, the Council for Basic Education has compared the factual learning of young children to a squirrel who gathers up nuts and stores them away against the coming winter.[60] Thus, the child in his early years at school gathers and stores away nuggets of factual material against the day that he will need them in his affairs. In this sense, elementary schooling is a preparation for and an anticipation of secondary education and beyond that, adulthood.

In the secondary school the transmission of organized facts becomes more inclusive and more rigorous. The conceptual load becomes greater and greater as the student is expected to study a wider variety of subject matters and some of these subjects in greater depth. At the college level the same process determines the general character of the teaching design —the transmission of subject matters in increasing scope and depth. In the mind of the conservative the purpose at every level is for something that is to come later. Elementary school is preparatory for secondary education; the secondary school prepares for college; the college prepares for graduate school; and the graduate school prepares for adult life. Since very few survive the process through the graduate school, each educational level in the system prepares both for "life" and for the

[60] *CBE Bulletin*, Vol. 2, No. 7, Washington, D.C.: The Council for Basic Education (February, 1958).

next school level above. One thing is certain: to the conservative, education is first of all a *process of preparation.*

Over and against this conception of education as transmission and preparation are certain facts that are known both to common sense and to psychology. One of these facts is that a great deal of what is learned under the formal conditions provided in schools is forgotten very quickly. Anyone who has had formal schooling can test this for himself. In fact, all one need do is consider what his chances would be of passing an examination over material he had studied even as short a time as six months previously. Unless he had kept practicing on the material in the interim, the chances are not very good for a satisfactory performance on an examination.[61] Students simply assume that they will forget a major part of the factual content of any course they take. Their instructors apparently make the same assumption.[62]

When an essentialist is asked about this state of affairs he is constrained to admit that a great deal of factual material is lost—he can hardly maintain anything else. But a typical reply to the question, "What is left after the transmitted material is lost in such large amount?" is typically, "What is left is intellectual discipline!" Before we analyze this answer it will be useful to consider briefly another dimension of the problem.

A fundamental presumption of essentialist educational doctrine is that what is learned at one time in school will be available at some future time —either in subsequent school experience or in the broader affairs of life. Clearly, this availability will depend on whether the learning is retained. If the learner forgets it, it will not be available to him. But there is even more to the presumption than this for apparently there is also the belief that if the material is retained *it will necessarily be transferrable to novel situations.*

Contemporary psychological investigations do not lend much comfort to this presumption. The phenomena involved in the transfer of learning are complicated and some of them obscure, but our present state of understanding is sufficient to show that merely having learned some

[61] Almost any text in general psychology or educational psychology contains material on remembering and forgetting, theoretical explanations for these phenomena, etc. A psychological discussion of these matters is outside the scope of this book.
[62] For instance, if a high school student takes a year's course in chemistry as a junior and then takes the College Entrance Board Examinations in that year as a kind of "trial run," he is permitted to have his score in chemistry made his official record of achievement in that subject. Thus, the tacit admission is made that if the student waited until his senior year to take the examination he would have forgotten a very considerable part of what he had learned about chemistry the year before.

fact or principle by no means guarantees that this learning will function in some situation that is greatly unlike the conditions under which the original learning took place. If the conservative seeks to hang his case on this presumption, he may well find it a slender reed.

Now we consider the question, "What is left over?" The conservative answers "What is left over is intellectual discipline." What does this mean? As has been noted earlier in this chapter, it is really very hard to know what it means. It would appear that what the essentialist is saying is that by virtue of "applying the mind" to the essential subject matters something happens to the processes of the mind. They become in some fashion more rigorous and effective. It is said, for example, that a disciplined mind is one that can operate efficiently in any situation[63] and this by virtue of intellectual training.

This kind of explanation could be taken as an application of the classic Aristotelian conception of mind where the intellect is conceived as an aggregate of specific powers. Or by a real stretch of the imagination it could be construed to mean the development of the kind of processes of inquiry advocated by John Dewey and the progressivists.[64] What the essentialist really means remains enigmatic. If the intent is to attach Aristotelian psychology to conservative pedagogy, that is one thing. But it is difficult to adopt Aristotle's psychology in isolation from his biology and metaphysics, and probably there are few contemporary conservatives who care to be counted as full-fledged Aristotelians. It is even more difficult to believe that what essentialists intend is something of the kind of thing Dewey spoke of when he advocated an educational program directed towards developing in pupils the scientific attitude, increasing skill in problem solving, and emphasizing functional use of factual material in inquiry. For one thing, conservatives consistently deplore Dewey's emphasis on method instead of on formal teaching of content; for another, Dewey's name is simply anathema among contemporary conservatives.

It is fair to say that the problems of retention and transfer remain among the most difficult practical problems of modern essentialism.

---

[63] See for example: Arthur Bestor, "Education for Intellectual Discipline," in Philip H. Phenix, ed., *Philosophies of Education*, New York: John Wiley & Sons, Inc., 1961, p. 37 ff. When he comes down to explaining this idea, Mr. Bestor mentions only that a disciplined mind will "analyze" a situation not "merely adjust to it." *Analysis* is the only mental function he mentions specifically in this discussion. Since this idea is such an important one in essentialist educational theory — and, in fact, in all educational theory — it seems a pity that we cannot have a more searching and definitive analysis than this.

[64] Both these interpretations are complex and will be discussed at length in their proper places in subsequent chapters.

This tradition typically has sought to solve its basic problems by organizational means: ability grouping, multiple curricula, acceleration for the gifted, and so on. The problem of retaining and applying learning, however, does not appear to be capable of resolution by organizational manipulation. The conservative will have to look for other means than changes in administrative policies, but as yet he has accomplished very little in this respect.

There are other practical problems of essentialism that could well be discussed, but those that have received attention are perhaps sufficient to show the crucial character these problems have for this tradition.[65] It does not seem rash to say that in considerable measure the future of the tradition depends on the ability of its adherents to find workable solutions to these problems. The analyses presented here indicate that essentialism, at least as yet, has not been able to develop such policies.

PHILOSOPHICAL REQUIREMENTS FOR A CONSISTENT AND COHERENT ESSENTIALISM

We have seen that essentialism is a body of doctrine about the purposes and means of education. We have also seen that essentialism in education has a close, organic relationship with the general tradition of political and social conservatism. The general structure of modern conservatism has been outlined in Chapter III. In the present chapter we have examined the conservative thesis with respect to education, and in addition we have analyzed in some detail certain important practical problems in education that confront this tradition.

We come now to the final question of whether essentialism as a body of ideas about education can properly be considered a *philosophy* of education. As we noted earlier, there are various definitions of philosophy available. Whatever definition one may wish to accept for himself, it is likely that there are certain fundamental requirements on which there is wide agreement.

One of these is the requirement of internal coherence. This means that the ideas that make up our beliefs in any field must be in harmony with each other. For example, the ideas we hold about teaching method

---

[65] The reader may wish to try analyzing for himself essentialist conceptions of such practical policy problems as: academic freedom, the preparation of teachers, and financial support for education (including, of course, the question of federal financial aid).

should be consonant with our ideas about the nature of the curriculum. These ideas, in turn, should be harmonious with the way the purposes of education are conceived. Much of the popular thinking about education that goes on in any historical period fails to meet the criteria of coherence and consistency. Since most folk wisdom about educational matters is based on rule of thumb and on uncritical acceptance of previous experience, it should be no surprise that much of this folk wisdom is based on questionable premises and that often it is shot through with incoherences and logical contradictions.

It goes without saying that the modern conservative does not want his position on educational matters to be considered little if anything more than an aggregate of miscellaneous notions about schools and teaching. The conservative not only believes his ideas are the right ideas and that they should guide our educational efforts, he also believes that his ideas form a coherent and consistent way of looking at the process of education. A great many modern essentialists also like to believe that their ideas on education are consistent with the major elements in the general conservative tradition. Our business in the next two chapters is to ascertain whether this is true, and on what grounds the essentialist argues his case.

There are at least three major elements in the tradition of essentialism that must be investigated. These matters are not primarily educational in character, but they are closely allied with certain aspects of the essentialist position on educational principles. The position taken here is that a clear and convincing explanation must be forthcoming from conservatives if their educational doctrines are to meet the criteria of coherence and consistency. The concluding sections of this chapter, therefore, are devoted to the analysis of three issues whose satisfactory resolution must be accomplished if essentialism is to be regarded as a coherent and consistent body of ideas about education.

Certainty in Knowledge and Truth

One cannot read the literature of modern educational conservatism without being impressed with the air of certainty that attends its pronouncements. The essentialist rarely is tentative in his argument. One almost never finds him saying that there are different ways of looking at a problem or a situation or entertaining the notion that there are possible alternative answers to important questions. This air of certainty seems often to have bred a kind of arrogance among conservatives and it is only fair to point this out. Any person can test this statement for himself by reading such diverse works as Mr. Albert

Lynd's *Quackery in the Public Schools*,[66] *The Monthly Bulletin* of the Council for Basic Education, or such a scholarly philosophical essay on education as Mr. John Wild's "Education and Human Society: A Realistic View."[67]

Whether the conservative is entitled to the superior attitude he displays so frequently in contemporary writing is a tangential question that need not concern us here. However, there is a question that must be of concern and it is this: *What is the source of this air of certainty that pervades essentialist thinking on educational issues?* What is it that makes the conservative so sure that he is right?

Let it be remembered that a basic proposition of all conservative thought on education is the existence of a central body of essential knowledge that must be transmitted to all who come to school. Surely this must be a body of *truth* for it is exceedingly difficult to think of the essentialist upholding the wholesale transmission of error. Involved also in this position is the belief that education is a preparation for adult life, and it apparently follows that the essentialist knows, or thinks he knows, what essential truths are necessary for such preparation.[68] Moreover, the essentialist must believe that truth has some kind of constancy sufficient to ensure us that what is taught in childhood and adolescence will be both true and usable in adulthood.

When an educational theorist talks this way he is talking about more than educational theory. Underneath his statements about the curriculum and the processes of schooling we may properly suspect there is a conviction concerning some ultimate source of certainty and dependability for our knowledge.[69] This is to say that the conservative apparently subscribes to *some* conception of knowledge that gives him assurance that our judgments are capable of being true, that the *certainty* of truth is at least potentially possible, and this with respect to some objective and trustworthy criterion of validity. If the conservative can make a strong case for such a conception of knowledge, we

[66] Boston: Little, Brown & Company, 1953.

[67] *Modern Philosophies and Education*, pp. 17–56.

[68] Mr. Arthur Bestor's attempts to handle this issue are always interesting because he seems not quite sure whether to argue from the intrinsic or the instrumental values of essential knowledge. In a source cited earlier (Phenix, ed., *op. cit.*, p. 39), Mr. Bestor insists that nine-tenths of what is essential "will always be relatively unchanging." The term "relatively" perhaps provides a convenient escape hatch.

[69] One of the most revealing passages in the *Report of the San Francisco Curriculum Survey Committee* occurs in a discussion of the teaching of reading in the elementary school. It is as follows: "Quite apart from the practical advantage of being infinitely more effective, phonics has an immense pedagogical advantage over look-say: it encourages the child to think rather than to guess. Nothing is more essential to clear, logical habits of mind, particularly in the formative years than the faith that the universe is rational and orderly." pp. 20–21.

are constrained to admit that he has strengthened the support for his tradition. If, on the other hand, he fails to develop a convincing demonstration, his cause will necessarily suffer considerably. This situation must be studied in depth.

The Certainty of Values

The question of value is the second crucial element in the conservative case. As we have already seen, one of the most important functions of the school, according to educational conservatives, is the transmission of certain traditional values to the young. The conservative is certain that there is a body of value and that the school has a proper role in conserving and transmitting this body of truth. One does not have to search far in the literature of conservatism to find that these values are eternal, that they do not change with time or circumstance, and that they can be known to be ultimate in their importance.

The air of certainty with which the conservative presents this view leads us to speculate that he believes in some principle that gives his conception of value standards and value judgments the character—or at least the potential character—of certainty. Such a principle surely would eliminate various kinds of relativism, that is, ideas that standards for value change with changes in culture and therefore any given set of standards can apply only in a certain cultural context. There is a strong implication in conservative writing that some *source* exists that can provide authoritative answers for our value problems. If such a source does exist, we can see why it is the conservative does not feel apologetic about transmitting value concepts to children and youth, or even on occasion imposing them. The conservative finds it difficult to understand why, when the truth is known, it should not be transmitted to the uninformed.

We can say again, therefore, that if conservatism can sustain its case for a source of immutable values, its position on the ethical aspects of education is strong. If a case cannot be made to stand, the tradition will suffer accordingly.

The Individual and Society

This third philosophical requirement for a systematic and coherent conservatism is somewhat different from the two already indicated. In it we are concerned with the very old problem of the relation of the individual to society. This question is of importance to conservatism because in this tradition there are two strains of thought that sometimes seem contradictory of each other. As we know, conservatism has always stressed the importance of conserving existing institutions and patterns in society. The conservative insists that we must maintain a slow and gradual rate of social change. A basic belief in this tradition is that the individual owes his primary allegiance to the existing order and its institutions and the conservative shows bitter hostility to those who would institute abrupt change through revolution or doctrinaire reform movements.

When we consider this major theme of conservatism we may be tempted to believe that, to the conservative, society itself is the main consideration and the individual must fit himself without serious protest to the requirements of the social pattern. If so, this would seem to be primarily a process of individual conformity and adjustment.

There is, however, another major theme in the conservative tradition. This is the idea that the integrity and self-identification of the individual must be maintained. Much attention has been given by modern conservatives to this aspect of their tradition. In fact, a great deal of their antistatism has been argued from the point of view that the modern collectivistic state, with all its promises of social welfare, ultimately will engulf the individual and he will become lost in the faceless crowd. Similarly, there has been bitter criticism by essentialists against contemporary schools. These schools, critics say, are designed only for adjustment of the individual to the group. The net effort of such schooling is to destroy, or even prevent the development of individualism and self-identity.

Admittedly, there seems to be some element of paradox involved in these two major themes of the conservative tradition but we do not at this point know whether this apparent paradox is genuine. We need, therefore, to explore the problem of the conservative theory of society in which the individual can maintain his own identity and selfhood and at the same time render his primary respect and allegiance to a pattern of society that is built on tradition and a scarcely perceptible rate of change. An account that will successfully reconcile the individual and society—at the expense of neither—will be a strategic success for this tradition, providing, of course, that such an account is possible.

SUMMARY

This chapter has been about essentialism as the conservative view of education. Its purpose has been to describe the major tenets of conservative doctrine in education, to examine important recommendations for educational practice advocated by conservatives, and to consider certain important practical problems that face this tradition. The design throughout this chapter has been practical, and yet as we close we find ourselves confronted by certain questions that go far beyond the confines of educational practice. This is inevitable for, as was pointed out in Chapter I, if we are obstinate in our efforts to think clearly about the problems of education, we will find ourselves thinking about many things in addition to the practical side of educational affairs.

Our next step in the study of the conservative tradition must be to search for possible answers to the questions that have just been posed. We will have to search in the domain of philosophy for whatever answers there may be, and no one would support this statement more strongly than a conservative. The conservative tradition rests much of its case on such ideas as the certainty of truth, the certainty of value, the validity of tradition, and the integrity of the individual. If we are really to understand the conservative tradition we must understand the basic support for these principles.

This aspect of the task of understanding the conservative position is more complicated today than it was in an earlier time. This more complicated situation is the result of cultural transition that in turn has wrought important changes in conservatism. The fact is that in our effort to find answers to the questions we have identified we must look in two directions. First, we must turn to the philosophical tradition of idealism, a tradition that long has colored the perceptions of social, political, and educational conservatives, and hence has a close historical connection with the conservative tradition.

Our search, however, cannot cease there, although if we had been making this analysis a century ago we might well have found our answers within idealism. In the present we must look not only in metaphysical idealism but also in another philosophical direction—that of realism. While to many contemporary conservatives idealism still can account most fully for the requirements of coherence and consistency in educational theory, there is a growing number of social and educational conservatives who simply cannot accept the idealistic account of philosophy. These conservatives, whose influence undoubtedly is growing stronger, are inclined to look to certain doctrines of philosophical realism to support their ideas.

In the next chapter we will address ourselves to a study of the great philosophical tradition of idealism. Our purpose is not, of course, a complete explication of this intricate and variegated system of thought.

Instead we will be concerned with certain major themes in idealistic philosophy and the connection these have for conservative educational ideas.

Following our encounter with idealism, we will turn attention in Chapter VI to realism and the import some conservatives find in that tradition for their beliefs about education.

CHAPTER FIVE

Philosophical Idealism

and the Conservative Tradition

Our purpose in this chapter is to investigate certain connections between idealism, an old and highly revered tradition in western philosophy, and the conservative tradition in American education. We have no interest here in attempting to maintain the thesis that essentialist ideas about education are logical conclusions from some set of *a priori* principles of idealist philosophy. It is possible that some conservative educational theorists do believe that their educational philosophy represents a series of deductions from certain principles of metaphysical idealism. Be this as it may, we have already raised the question of whether this position actually is tenable.

Whatever else it may be, essentialism is a living body of educational doctrines and practices. In this sense it has a history of development stretching back to the break-up of the medieval world. Essentialism represents the effort to develop an approach to education that can satisfy the requirements of the new historic age that succeeded the medieval era. Every important cultural component of post-renaissance culture has entered into the making of the essentialist tradition: democracy, capitalism, nationalism, experimental science. We have seen that the stresses and strains this tradition has suffered over its long history have been engendered in no small part by conflicts among the leading traditions of modern culture and, in addition, the conflicts between such modern traditions as capitalism and nationalism and the older but still powerful traditions of antiquity. We have also seen that certain of the crucial practical problems faced by essentialism in the modern

PHILOSOPHY OF AMERICAN EDUCATION

world are occasioned by conflicting patterns of tradition and value in contemporary culture.

Having said this, we should also say that ideas about education do not develop in a cultural vacuum. Men's perceptions of any aspect of social life are conditioned by their total background of experience. How a man views the question of the need for public education, the objectives the school should seek to attain, or the way in which the school should approach its tasks is inevitably affected by other opinions he holds. A person who believes that the ultimate end of human life is eternal salvation is likely to see the function of the school in a different light from the person who subscribes to a naturalistic view of man and his place in the world. We are not saying at this point that one of these viewpoints is necessarily right and one necessarily wrong. We are saying that two people with different conceptions of human nature and human destiny are likely to see the role of the school in somewhat different lights.

At this point it may be useful to consider a fundamental distinction, a distinction that will be important for much that follows in this book. The distinction involves the difference between the *causes* by reason of which any person holds a belief and the *grounds* on which this belief is held. *Causes* and *grounds* for belief are genuinely different factors and it is important to recognize the difference.

The *causes* for a person's beliefs refer to those experiences and associations that have led him to accept certain ideas and reject others. Hence, the causes for beliefs are cultural; that is, they are primarily sociological and psychological. A man may be a Republican in politics because all members of his family have always been members of that party, because he comes from a section of the country in which that party has overwhelming dominance, and because all the people with whom he associated are members of that party and it is in that sense the only socially approved political affiliation.

These factors are genuine *causes* which have determined this man's beliefs in Republicanism, and they are, as we have said, primarily sociological and psychological. However, though we may understand the causes for his political belief, it is also important to know on what *grounds* his belief in Republican political doctrine can be substantiated. Here we are confronted by the necessity for *evidence* that will support the validity of a belief in Republican political doctrine. *Grounds* for belief involve evidence and the logical treatment of evidence. Thus, a man may adhere to the Republican Party because it favors private economic enterprise, minimum interference in local affairs by the federal government, and lower taxes on private property and incomes. These matters are offered as *grounds* for the superiority of this body of political doctrine over others.

Sometimes, perhaps often in the case of many individuals, causes take precedence over grounds. People may cling with great tenacity to some political or religious or educational view without ever giving serious attention to the evidence on which the validity of these views is alleged to rest. Such people as these are not much interested in evidence or logical analysis of their beliefs. In fact, they are often gravely threatened by objective analysis of their cherished convictions.

This distinction between cause and ground is important to our study of the relation between philosophical idealism and the conservative tradition in education. We will be concerned partly with the causes for the influence of idealism on conservative thought and partly with the grounds for the validity of their influence. It is important to our purpose here to study both of these factors. Before we can make this assessment, however, we must first understand something of the basic structure of philosophical idealism.

IDEALISM AS A PHILOSOPHY

Idealism is one of the oldest philosophical traditions of the west; certainly, it is one of the most revered. It is common for adherents of this tradition to trace their philosophical ancestry back to Plato and to regard the illustrious Greek as the greatest idealist of them all. Any intellectual tradition with a history as long and complicated as that of idealism is bound to be marvelously complex and intricate. It is far beyond the scope of this book to trace all the developments and variations this tradition has undergone over the years. Rather we will concern ourselves with those variations on the idealistic theme which have a definite relation to the conservative tradition in education. Before we can develop these variations we must first present the general theme around which this tradition has developed.

THE BASIC THESIS OF IDEALISM

It has often been maintained that all the great systems of philosophical thought that have come into existence are at heart developments

124 PHILOSOPHY OF AMERICAN EDUCATION

and elaborations of certain common elements of human experience. In the case of idealism the common experience that has been expanded into a philosophical system is that of the awareness of self. This awareness of the irreducibility of our own consciousness is a universal experience among human beings, and according to idealists, at least, it is the most significant fact of individual experience.

The great French philosopher Descartes (1596–1650) pointed out in his *Meditations on the First Philosophy* that a man may doubt everything that he has hitherto accepted as a matter of course. A man may doubt that the elements of physical nature exist; he may doubt that God is divinely good or that He has created the world; a man may, in fact, doubt that his own body—his own arms and legs—exists. But there is one thing that no man can doubt, no matter what effort he makes. *He cannot doubt that he, himself, exists.* Awareness of his own existence is the irreducible element in the experience of every man. As Descartes points out, "I am" is a true proposition everytime I express it or conceive it in my mind. And, although I may succeed in doubting the existence of everything else, one thing is certain, everytime I think, *I exist.* The primary and ultimate fact of my experience is that what is real in me is mind and consciousness. It is not my physical body of members and organs that is necessarily real, for it is possible to believe my body does not exist. The ultimate reality in my experience is my *mind.* It alone can be known to be real. The famous Cartesian argument was summed up in the sentence, "*Cogito, ergo sum*"—"I think, therefore, I am."

Now the argument is that idealism, as a systematic philosophy, is the elaboration and systematization of this basic proposition that mind is the primary and irreducible fact of individual experience. One part of the basic thesis of all idealism is that mind is prior; that when we seek for that which is ultimate in the world, when we push back behind the veil of immediate sense experience we will find that that which is ultimate in the whole universe is of the nature of mind or spirit (the two words are interchangeable in most discussions of idealism)—just as it is mind that is ultimate in the inner world of personal experience. This idea may be expressed in the conception that is central to idealism: *the principle of the priority of consciousness.*

From this central principle of idealism we may come to certain conclusions that are of importance to the understanding of the tradition. First, we may conclude that if mind is prior in the sense that it is the ultimate reality, then material things either do not exist at all, or if they do exist, they in some way depend for their existence on mind.

At this point in the analysis we do not as yet know what the nature of the relationship is between mind and matter and, in fact, different forms of idealistic philosophy explain this relationship in somewhat different ways. However, given the basic postulate of the priority of consciousness, we can infer properly that if mind is prior then it is in some sense the *cause* for the existence of other things and for the character of that world of things and events that we encounter in our ordinary experience.

This first inference serves to illustrate the function that idealism as a philosophical tradition has played in the intellectual history of western culture. Idealism has always been conceived as the ancient and implacable enemy of all forms of materialism. There are various forms of philosophical materialism but the basic tenet of all these is that that which is ultimately and irreducibly real in the universe is *matter*. This materialistic thesis idealists flatly reject. For one thing, they are fond of saying, "How can we conceive that mind which is active and dynamic and creative could have come from mere material stuff which is inert and lifeless?" Another question idealists often ask—and one we will give attention to a little later—is how a universe that is nothing but matter in motion could possibly have a place in it for value and for those concerns that have always engaged the highest efforts of mankind.

A second important inference that may be drawn from the principle of the priority of consciousness concerns the character of the ultimately real. We know from our own experience that the fact of consciousness gives us certain powers or functions. We know for one thing that as conscious beings, we are capable of *rational thought and knowledge*. We know that one of the attributes of self is rationality and since ultimate reality is of the nature of mind we can say with logical certainty that one of the traits of the ultimate Reality must be reason—the powers of cognition and of logical thought.

We can also know from an examination of our own self-experience that as conscious beings we have the power of *volition*. One of the facts of individual experience is the fundamental realization that we are free to choose among alternatives. Our behavior is self-directed and is not merely a response to the pressures of a material environment. In fact, we have the distinct impression that through the effort of our will we can rise above the pressures of the environment and seek the good, even when this seeking is the harder path to follow. Therefore, in view of these convictions, which every person has or can gain from an examination of his own experience, we can know that one of the fundamental attributes of reality is *will*—the power of volition.

Beyond this, our personal experience also reveals that we are endowed with the potential of creativity. We know that, potentially at least, we are creatures of imagination and vision. The strongest drive to action that we experience in our own lives is the urge to self-realization—the drive not only to preserve ourselves, but *to realize ourselves.* This creative dynamic activity of self-realization, even though it may be realized imperfectly, is a fundamental aspect of personal experience, and no man can deny this honestly.

We now are in a position to state the propositions that make up the metaphysical thesis of idealism. The idealist sees these propositions as *logical* inferences from certain personal experiences and convictions that are certain and undeniable. He therefore tends to believe that these propositions constitute *evidence,* that is *grounds,* for the validity of the metaphysical thesis of idealism.[1]

THE RELATIONSHIP OF MIND AND MATTER

We have examined the idealistic thesis concerning metaphysics and have discovered that by this account mind is *the* reality in individual experience and that in some fashion those things we call "material" and which we encounter in our experience are dependent on mind for their character and for their very existence. We have not as yet discovered, however, what the precise nature of this relationship is. In order to pursue this matter it will be necessary to give attention to a second great philosophical aspect of idealism: its theory of knowledge.

From the point of view of technical philosophy, epistemology is the central idea in idealism. Although idealism has important things to say about metaphysics and about axiology, as a system it probably must stand or fall as a theory of knowledge. As is often pointed out, a more nearly correct name for this tradition would be "ideaism" since it is the role of *ideas* that plays such an important part in it. The "l" has been added to the term, presumably for purposes of euphony. To understand something of the epistemological thesis of idealism we must turn to

---

[1] An important discussion of what idealists consider *grounds* for accepting idealism will be found in: Herman H. Horne, "An Idealistic Philosophy of Education," in John S. Brubacher, ed., *Philosophies of Education,* Forty-first Yearbook of the National Society for the Study of Education, Bloomington, Illinois: Public School Publishing Company, 1942, p. 141 ff.

some of the early architects of modern idealism. An important part of the story begins with the work of the seventeenth century philosopher John Locke (1632–1714).

Locke fell heir to certain philosophical problems that Descartes left to the modern world. In his analysis, which we have already mentioned briefly, Descartes had concluded that there are two kinds of "substance" in the world and these two kinds are absolutely distinct from each other.[2] These two substances are *body* and *mind*. Everything that exists is either one or the other of these. We have already seen that Descartes believed that the mind could have certain knowledge of its own character and workings—and idealists have followed this idea ever since. But Descartes also believed that through certain operations, which he called "intuition," the mind could also know of the existence of material substance. Thus, Descartes set the problem of knowledge that Locke—and countless epistemologists since him—have grappled with. According to this view, knowing involves three elements: a subject (knower), an object (the known), and some kind of relation that is established between subject and object. An illustrative diagram would be something like this:

$$\text{Subject} \longleftarrow \text{Cognitive} \quad \text{Object}$$
$$(\text{Knower}) \qquad \text{Relationship} \quad (\text{Known})$$

Locke set himself the task of studying the relationship that exists between the knower and the object which is known in any act of cognition. First off, Locke flatly denied a theory about knowledge that is at least as old as Plato. This is the thesis that ideas are innate in an individual and need only to be brought to consciousness to be known. Locke mustered various kinds of evidence against the notion that we are born with our ideas and concluded that this ancient and influential theory was false. In place of the theory of innate ideas Locke advanced the idea that all of our knowledge originates in sense perception and our ideas are products of our sensory experience. Locke used the analogy of the mind as a kind of blank tablet on which experience writes, and the sum total of this writing is the sum total of a man's knowledge of the external world.[3]

Our knowledge of the external world, then, comes to us in the form of *ideas* that are induced in some way in the mind, by the external

[2] Mind and matter are the only *created* substances. Descartes also accepted another reality, God, which is uncreated and the idea of which is innate in man.

[3] Locke's "tabula rasa" analogy to the mind was not entirely a happy one for this implies rather definitely a passive role for mind. Actually, as will be seen a little later, Locke conceived of mind also as an active, dynamic principle.

object of our perception. What the mind knows is ideas of things. Only ideas exist in the mind (obviously physical substances cannot) and ideas can exist only as they are in some mind. In terms of the diagram already presented, that which mediates between subject and object is *idea*. Our knowledge of the physical world, therefore, is *represented* in the mind in the form of ideas. In this sense we never know the material world directly but only in terms of our ideas of it.

We now need to take account of the way Locke thought ideas are formed. We recall that he held that all our ideas begin in some sensory experience in which sense data come into our consciousness through our sensory organs. In this respect the mind is passive in that it is the recipient of sense data, but the important function of the mind is its *activity*. In a sense, the mind is like a machine that processes sensory material. As soon as material is fed into the machine it begins its operations.

The sense data that come to us by way of our eyes and ears, and noses, and touch are known as *simple ideas*. Locke considered that there are four classes of these and that every iota of our knowledge derives from these simple ideas. But in addition to its capacity to receive simple ideas, the mind has reflective and associative powers, for it can combine and recombine simple ideas into various complex ideas by such operations as comparing, combining, and separating simple ideas. In this general way, Locke sought to explain how all our knowledge originates in sense experience and how every idea we may have ultimately is reducible to sense perception. The ideas that mediate between our own minds and the objects in the external world derive from certain qualities in objects and these qualities are *represented* in our minds.

Locke thought it necessary to distinguish between two kinds of qualities associated with objects. He divided them into the class of *primary qualities* and the class of *secondary qualities*. In his view it is the primary qualities that are "real" in the sense that they inhere in objects. Locke classified these as: extension, shape, solidity, and rest or motion. Thus, any object such as a chair or table occupies a certain amount of space, it has a certain form or shape, it is solid, and is at rest. These primary qualities are *in the object* and when these qualities are known by the mind, the mind apprehends the reality of these qualities. If I apprehend the idea of quadrangularity in a table I am apprehending a real quality of that object.

There is a difference between these "bedrock" primary qualities and other kinds of qualities that we are aware are associated with objects. In

Locke's view, such qualities as tastes, odors, tactile sensations, and sounds are examples of *secondary qualities*. Secondary qualities exist because the primary qualities in objects *have the power to induce them in the mind*. The quality of redness, therefore, does not exist independently in some object; redness exists only in some *mind*. When no mind is present no quality of redness can exist. The reason such a quality as redness ever exists is that some objects, through their primary qualities, have the power to induce certain sensations in the mind. We now know, as Locke did not, that redness involves radiation of a certain frequency impinging on the retina of the eye. But Locke's point is that while redness may be the product of "swift motion" (radiation), redness is not the same thing as swift motion. Redness exists only as it is induced in some mind by the primary quality of motion and in no other way. Exactly the same thing may be said for all other secondary qualities. If we were to make a diagram of Locke's analysis it would appear thus:

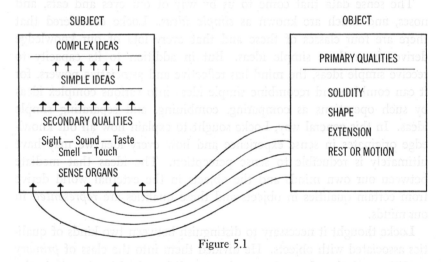

Figure 5.1

If we reflect a little on these elements of Locke's analysis we see that he actually did not subscribe to the principle of the priority of consciousness, which we have identified as being a basic doctrine of idealism. Locke's conception of the cognitive situation is one in which there is a knower and something that is known. As he conceived it, that which is known exists independently of the knower and is the source of his ideas. Locke was unwilling to conceive of external objects as merely collections or clusters of qualities. He thought it necessary that there be something to hold these qualities together, just as there must be something that unites the activities and functions of the soul. Following the example of Descartes and others before him, Locke called these unifying *principles* substance and his metaphysics is not really very different from Descartes'. Thus, there is material substance and spiritual substance; physical bodies and immaterial minds.

Evidently Locke was not aware that his theories of ideas as objects of knowledge were thoroughly subjective. His view was that knowledge is real only insofar as our ideas correspond with the reality of things. But if the mind can know only ideas, how can it ever know whether its ideas correspond to things as they actually are in themselves? The fact seems to be that Locke did not attach much importance to this problem; at least he paid little attention to it. Another difficulty that tends to be glossed over in his analysis lies in the meaning of the term "substance". This is one of those slippery philosophic terms that can be interpreted in many ways, and Locke was unusually vague about its significance. It is clear, however, that he subscribed to the idea that the two primary substances—spiritual and material—are independent of each other and the existence of either one does not depend on the other.

One point of great interest to our purpose here is the distinction Locke made between primary and secondary qualities. We recall that he had classified some qualities as existing only in the mind (the secondary qualities) and some qualities as existing independently of mind (the primary qualities). With the perspective we now have on history, we can see that sooner or later someone was bound to raise the sticky question of how such a neat distinction as Locke had made could be sustained. We can also anticipate that embarrassing questions were bound to be raised about the term "substance" that Locke had used in such a vague and undefined way. He had distinguished between the qualities of an object and something called "substance" that acts as a kind of sub-stratum and in some ways unites qualities. It is perfectly reasonable to raise the question of how the mind knows anything about "substance" if that term is defined as something other than simply the sum of its qualities.

As a matter of historical fact, questions of this kind were raised, and one of the most influential questioners of certain aspects of the Lockean analysis of knowledge was George Berkeley (1685–1753), a British cleric and one of the seminal sources in the development of modern idealism. In our search for understanding of the principle of the priority of consciousness we turn now to certain ideas developed by this great idealist.

BERKELEY'S ANALYSIS

Berkeley's analysis of the problem of knowledge is one of the most provocative and intriguing epistemological analyses in western philosophy. In the present context we will be content to indicate only the main lines of it, since our primary concern is to understand the principles of the priority of consciousness and not to present a full explication of Berkeley's theory of knowledge. We will examine briefly four arguments that Berkeley advocated in his analysis.

His first argument is that we can never get outside our own experience and thus it is impossible for us to conceive of anything that is outside our experience; anything, that is, that is independent of our consciousness. To speak of our conceiving some object that is outside our experience is contradictory for it amounts to saying that we are able to conceive of something that we are not able to conceive of.[4]

The second argument deals with the idea of *substance* that Locke had treated so vaguely. Berkeley's argument was that if substance (matter) is held to be anything beyond the qualities that are alleged to characterize it, then there is no way in which we can know anything about it. Even by Locke's definition of knowledge, matter is not an idea and if it is not an idea it cannot be known. It is perfectly possible to conceive of objects in terms of their qualities, and the addition of this vague notion of substance adds nothing to our understanding of the process of knowledge. We would be better off to get rid of the term.[5]

The third argument, and a crucial one, relates to Locke's distinction between primary and secondary qualities. Berkeley agreed that what Locke had called secondary qualities exist only when they are in some mind, but he raised the question of why the same thing should not be said of the primary qualities. If, as in the second argument, we rid ourselves of the vague idea of "substance," we arrive at the view that what common sense calls objects are simply groups of qualities. Locke had shown that secondary (i.e., sensory) qualities could not exist apart from primary qualities, and since objects are simply clusters of qualities, the sensible conclusion would seem to be that all qualities are *sensory* and that there are no *hard* primary qualities distinguishable from sense qualities. And, therefore, our ideas do not refer to something apart from consciousness.[6]

[4] This argument is developed by Berkeley in *Of the Principles of Human Knowledge*, Part I.
[5] *Ibid*. See also the first of the "Three Dialogues Between Hylas and Philonous."
[6] *Ibid*.

The fourth argument is one that modern idealists rarely tire of citing. This argument revolves around the question of how the mind can ever know anything that is absolutely unlike itself—as matter is by definition. The only meaningful conception of knowledge is that only ideas can enter into consciousness and become objects of knowledge.[7]

Underlying these arguments is Berkeley's belief that all ideas are specific and particular. There are no such things as "general" ideas, which, by definition, must be abstractions. He agrees that it is possible for us to divide things up in our thoughts—we can think of our arms and legs apart from our bodies, for example. But the fact remains that we cannot conceive anything except that of which we have perceptions. Sensations and objects are the same thing, and it makes no sense to speak of abstracting one from the other.[8]

There are certain implications of these arguments that we must take note of. First of all, since what we call objects are simply groupings of qualities, and since qualities cannot exist apart from some mind, it follows that objects do not exist apart from perception. A necessary condition for the existence of any object is, therefore, that it be perceived. Or to put it in Berkeley's famous words, "Esse est percipi." It should be noted that Berkeley is not arguing about the reality of the world; what he is arguing is that the world *is not material* and that it does not exist independently of consciousness.

A second implication is that there are only two kinds of things that exist—ideas and minds (spirits, Berkeley called them). It is completely impossible for us to know of the existence of anything other than these two. Minds (spirits) are "active, indivisible substances" and ideas are "fleeting, dependent beings" that must rely for their existence on their being in some mind. What Berkeley had done was to substitute for the material world of common sense a world composed of ideas and a world, therefore, that depends for its existence on mind. And here indeed is the principle of the priority of consciousness! This priority of mind that he had so ingeniously demonstrated—and of which the exposition here is only a pale shadow—decisively put an end to all materialism, at least to the satisfaction of George Berkeley.

Yet, there are other questions that must be asked, for common sense finds it difficult to believe that the hard, concrete world of experience consists only of clusters of sensory qualities that depend for their very being on their being perceived. Is it possible to believe that the world in which I live is only a projection of my own mind? Do I create my

[7] See the third of the "Dialogues Between Hylas and Philonous."
[8] See *Of the Principles of Human Knowledge.*

own world through my own conscious processes? Since, according to Berkeley's own arguments, I can never get outside my own consciousness, how can I know that other minds exist? For that matter, how can I know even that God exists?

If we are resolute in pushing these questions as far as they will go, we arrive at the ultimate in subjectivity—solipsism. Solipsism is the doctrine that only the individual mind exists and that all else in its experience is a creation of that mind. This doctrine is one of the most intriguing ideas in philosophy and one that is extremely resistant to *logical* disproof. It is also one that few philosophers, including Berkeley, have cared to profess seriously.

Berkeley sought to escape the dead-end of solipsism by positing, in addition to a plurality of ideas, a plurality of minds. So when, for example, I go to sleep there are still other perceiving minds that keep objects in existence. And yet this does not seem to be sufficient, for suppose that all men should go to sleep at once (or lapse into some form of unconsciousness). Would the entire universe then cease to exist? Along with this is another question. Ideas are in themselves passive (it is mind that is active) yet there must be some force that produces ideas and changes and organizes them into the coherent pattern we call the world. What is this force? It cannot be matter, for that has already been shown not to exist. There can be only one answer— the force must be of the nature of mind and this is the all-encompassing mind—the mind of God! In Berkeley's own words:

> There is, therefore, some other Mind wherein they [ideas] exist; during the intervals between the times of my perceiving them: as likewise they did before my birth, and would do after my supposed annihilation and, as the same is true with regard to all other finite created spirits, it necessarily follows that there is an *omnipresent eternal Mind*, which knows and comprehends all things, and exhibits them to our view in such a manner, and according to such rules, as He Himself hath ordained, and are by us termed the laws of nature.[9]

Thus, by this stroke Berkeley saved himself (and presumably the rest of us) from solipsism and at the same time produced a proof for the existence of God in his judgment, at least, that is the most powerful argument conceivable. Berkeley thought he had destroyed materialism and atheism, those twin devils that stand always in opposition to the

[9] George Berkeley, "Three Dialogues Between Hylas and Philonous," in *Berkeley: Essays, Principles, Dialogues,* ed., Mary W. Calkins, New York: Charles Scribner's Sons, 1929, pp. 300–301.

spirituality and freedom of man, and he (in the person of Philonous) proclaims in the second dialogue:

> You may now, without any laborious search into the sciences, without any subtlety of reason, or tedious length of discourse, oppose and baffle the most strenuous advocate for Atheism . . . Let any one of those abettors of impiety but look into his own thoughts, and there try if he can conceive . . . how anything at all, either sensible or imaginable, can exist independent of a Mind . . .[10]

Berkeley seems to have overstated his case, for some three hundred years later materialism and atheism still flourish. The significant thing Berkeley did do was point the way toward the development of the great systems of absolute idealism that dominated the intellectual life of the west through much of the nineteenth century and which are of the greatest importance to our purpose here.

TWO INTERPRETATIONS OF THE PRIORITY OF CONSCIOUSNESS

There are two strains of idealism in Berkeley's thought—and therefore two interpretations of the priority of consciousness are present. In the earlier part of his work, Berkeley's orientation was around the *individual mind* and the interpretation here is that consciousness is prior because it is the mind of the individual that creates the coherent reality he as an individual experiences. This interpretation of the priority of mind is perfectly tenable—given, of course, the grounds on which it is derived. This conception of the relation of mind and matter is one in which ideas take the place of "matter" and the objects of our knowledge are ideas, which are themselves products of our own conscious processes.

But in his flight from solipsism Berkeley introduced another interpretation of the principle of the priority of consciousness. In order to account for the continuing existence of a common world of experience he introduced the idea of a Universal Mind which is the source of all ideas and which orders and introduces to our minds those ideas we experience. Here the principle of the priority of consciousness becomes the idea that the ultimately real is an Absolute Mind that is the source of all Reality. In this view we can believe in the existence of a real world and at the same time believe that the ultimate source of this

[10] *Ibid.*, pp. 277–8.

world is spiritual. In this sense, Berkeley pointed out the way to a philosophy that would satisfy both the hardheadedness of common sense, in its belief in an objective reality, and the deep-seated conviction that the spiritual is higher and more important and hence "more real." In this way, as has often been pointed out, idealism satisfies both the heart and the mind.

ABSOLUTE IDEALISM

We are ready now to consider certain of the leading ideas involved in absolute idealism and to investigate their relationship to the conservative tradition in education. The great names in the history of absolute idealism are Johann Gotleib Fichte (1762–1814), Friedrich Wilhelm von Schelling (1775–1854), and Georg Wilhelm Friedrich Hegel (1780–1831)—all German philosophers and all in part the intellectual heirs of the great Immanuel Kant (1724–1804). There is wide agreement that Kant is the greatest name in the history of modern western philosophy, but his critical and somewhat eclectic, approach to philosophy is of less direct importance to our purpose here than the great system builders—Fichte, Schelling, and Hegel.[11]

Our purpose is not that of examining in detail the philosophical systems of these three men. It is rather to survey the general architecture of absolute idealism as an important tradition in philosophy and to examine the effects it often has on men's minds as they consider the problems of education. Accordingly, we will give some attention to the metaphysical, the epistemological, and the ethical dimensions of this approach to philosophy.

Absolute idealism is built around the idea that mind is prior in the cosmic sense. As we have seen, this is the general idea Berkeley advanced in his efforts to escape the complete subjectivism toward which his earlier analysis unerringly pointed. In the hands of absolute idealism, reality is one unified whole and this whole is of the nature of mind or spirit. The attributes that characterize this Absolute Mind are those that we know intimately in our own experience: reason, volition, cre-

---

11 Kant's connection with absolute idealism lies largely in his derivation of the forms or "categories" of thought which made knowledge possible. Some writers on the relation of idealism and education take Kant as their chief example. It is the thesis of this book that the conservative educator owes far more directly to the Hegelians and other absolute idealists than to Kant.

ativity. The "objective" world that we know in our own experience—the world of things and events—is itself a concrete manifestation of the Absolute Mind as it develops to higher and higher (and endless) levels of self-realization.

Mind is not a static, finished substance. Mind is in a real sense a process. And in that Mind that is ultimate in its perfection the processes proceed in accordance with a dynamic and logically perfect pattern. With Hegel this logic was that of the dialectic in which the resolution of opposites is achieved by their transformation in a synthesis that is novel and yet is a product of that out of which it emerged. The famous Hegelian triad of thesis, antithesis, and synthesis is complex, and to many students of philosophy it is an impenetrable metaphysical thicket. Whatever other purpose it may serve, it is one way of accounting for a basic belief of idealists that everything that exists is part of an ultimate Unity and that what may appear on the partial view to be contraries (in the logical sense) are actually in process of being transformed into a higher synthesis. This synthesis then becomes a new thesis, is amalgamated with its own contrary (anti-thesis), and a new synthesis emerges and so on and on forever in this Great Consciousness that is all-inclusive.

The world as we know it is one concrete manifestation of this cosmic logical process. And what we call history is the objective process of self-realization of the Absolute. In this sense reality (which is itself a process) is *rational and orderly*. The events that make up the world in which we live are not the product of some fortuitous set of circumstances. Every event that occurs must necessarily occur. Every event has a purpose because it is a part of a vast logical system, and every event, no matter how inconsequential it may appear, has meaning because it is a part of this vast process whose innermost character is that of regularity and logical order. Within the conscious process of the Absolute there is no internal contradiction. Just as in all truly logical systems, mathematics for example, all propositions are coherent with each other and all have meaning because of their membership in the system.

In Absolute Idealism we are not talking merely of analytical systems such as mathematics, we are talking about the whole process of the cosmos. History in its development displays the same characteristics as geometry. Everything follows necessarily, every event has meaning because every event is related to every other event, and the whole process proceeds towards higher and higher levels of realization. This is Hegel's theory of history; the theory that history is a concrete manifestation of an all-including Conscious Process that had no beginning and will have no end, and which proceeds for no other purpose outside itself.

Thus, in its metaphysical thesis, absolute idealism interprets the principle of the priority of consciousness as meaning that the concrete world of things and events is a product of the conscious processes of the Absolute Mind. The process we call history is rational and orderly because it is the product of a Supreme Reason in which rationality and orderliness function in complete perfection. Even before we examine other dimensions of absolute idealism we can anticipate the moral dictum that is implicit in this metaphysics: *"Whatever is, is right!"* For if history is the process of unfolding of a Great Idea, and if every event in this process follows as a matter of logical necessity, then whatever is at any moment must be right—*in the ethical sense.*

The outline of metaphysics sketched above is more Hegelian than anything else. In it reality is conceived as a process of consciousness that incorporates all existence within itself. In this sense it may seem impersonal, even aloof, from the temporal order of things. Many idealists—particularly Americans—have sought to endow the Absolute with a more personalistic character. As we said earlier in this discussion idealism can be thought of as the magnification and elaboration of the individual's conviction that the ultimate in personal experience is the reality of self. All we need do to personalize the Absolute is to conceive it not as an aloof process of logical development, but as a Self with all the attributes of selfhood that we know in our own experience. As we have already said, those qualities that can be attributed only to self—never to matter—are thought, will, and creativity. Thus we can project our own consciousness of self and conceive that that which is the ultimately Real is a great Self—an Absolute Self, the cause and ground for all existence.

And having said this we now realize that we as individuals and as finite selves bear a special relationship to the Ultimate Reality, for we as human selves share with the Absolute Self those attributes that make It what It is. We are, as idealists rarely tire of saying, "the universe writ small." The universe is a self—an all-inclusive self. It is *macrocosm,* reality in its totality. The human self is in a sense a miniature, though a necessarily imperfect,[12] counterpart of this Ultimate Self. The human self is the universe in *microcosm* and this relationship gives man a unique and exhalted position in the scheme of things.

[12] Imperfect for reasons that will be considered shortly.

The Absolute Self is the embodiment of perfection in every conceivable sense of that word, and its perfection inheres in its complete unity. In our own finite existence we are impelled to strive for apprehension of those supreme value concepts of Truth, Goodness, and Beauty, and in some measure we are able to apprehend these, though always partially and therefore imperfectly. Through reason we can anticipate that that which is only partial and incomplete with us is complete and perfect in the Absolute. In the Mind of the Ultimate there exist in pure essential form those universal conceptions of Truth and Goodness and Beauty. In the Absolute there is no trace of error, no evil, no ugliness. Value has objective reference—it is real, for it exists in pure conceptual form in the Absolute Mind. But disvalue has no objective reality. Error, evil, ugliness have no ideational counterpart in the mind of the Ultimate Self, and hence these have no real character.

If we take all these ideas and combine them into a general scheme we come out with the kind of cosmology that profoundly influenced the American intellectual climate of the nineteenth century and whose influence in this century is still substantial. If we were to make a diagram of this cosmic scheme of things it would look something as follows:

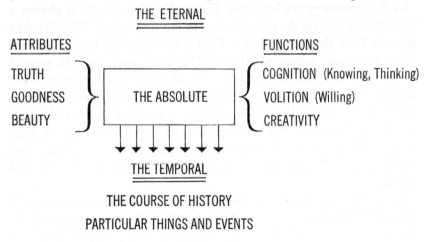

THE ETERNAL

ATTRIBUTES   FUNCTIONS

TRUTH   COGNITION (Knowing, Thinking)
GOODNESS   THE ABSOLUTE   VOLITION (Willing)
BEAUTY   CREATIVITY

THE TEMPORAL

THE COURSE OF HISTORY
PARTICULAR THINGS AND EVENTS

Figure 5.2

This diagram portrays the Absolute as mind or spirit, characterized by the ultimate perfection embodied in the great essences of value, making itself manifest through cognition, volition, and its creative powers in a historical process that unifies all persons, all things, all events in an unending stream of history. In this historical process man is the highest manifestation of the Absolute Mind.

To one who encounters these ideas for the first time they have an element of strangeness, and yet most people find there is something about them that has a familiar ring. Idealism is a tradition in philosophy and the doctrines that make up this tradition can be argued on purely philosophical grounds. If idealism is a tenable philosophical position, it can be advanced and defended entirely on metaphysical, epistemological, and axiological grounds. And yet in the history of idealism few of its protagonists have cared to confine themselves to purely philosophical ideas and arguments.

Much of the enormous influence idealism exerted in its heyday was undoubtedly owed to its close affiliation with Christian religious doctrine, particularly Christian Protestant doctrine. Without exception every great American exponent of absolute idealism has found an organic connection between the philosophy of idealism and the basic tenets of the Hebraic-Christian view of the world and of man. It is the amalgamation with religious doctrine that gives this philosophy the ring of familiarity to its major ideas.

In the cosmology we have just discussed we need only to change a few terms to convert the metaphysical to the theological. The Absolute becomes God, the eternal Spirit. God is not material, but all material things are manifestations of His will, His intelligence, and His creative power. The mind of God encompasses all creation—all that is or has been or ever will be. God is omniscient, He is omnipotent, He is rational. He has made Himself manifest in a world of things and events and the processes of this world reflect the rational nature of their Author. History is, as religious idealists point out, "a record of Providential purpose,"[13] and the whole of reality is rational, orderly, and unified.

The religious conception of human nature is all but synonymous with that which idealism presents. Man is the highest expression of the creative power of God. Man was deliberately created in the image of his Maker and he shares some of the same attributes that characterize God himself. Like God, man is a spiritual being, though unlike Him man is also a creature of flesh and this aspect of his being is in time, while God's entire being is outside time. The universe that God created was formed with man's life and destiny foremost in mind. The created world, which is a manifestation of the Divine Intelligence, is a kind of

[13] See ante, p. 65.

stage on which the human drama of self-realization takes place and in which man seeks to unite himself with the Ultimate. There is nothing fixed in the nature of things that stands between man and his realization of his highest desires. The world itself is friendly to man, and ideals have an objective reality in the nature of things.

There is little need to go further in this recital, partly because these things have already been said in an earlier chapter and partly because most of us have been taught these ideas from earliest childhood. The immediate purpose for repeating them here is to illustrate the close connection that exists between absolute idealism and many versions of the Hebraic-Christian cosmology.

THE PROBLEM OF EVIL

To a great many Americans what has been outlined briefly in preceding pages constitutes philosophy in its grandest and most compelling form. They think that beside the grandeur of Absolute Idealism other systems of thought, particularly those that have experimental science as their central core, present a pale and lifeless, even a humanless, character. Much of the appeal of idealism is undoubtedly owing to its assurance that the highest reality of the universe is spiritual in nature, that man as a conscious self is in his own nature a creature of spirit, and that the world and the total process which is its history is a manifestation of an Ultimate Mind.

Yet these convictions, as appealing and important as they are, are plagued by one of the great problems of speculative philosophy: the question of the origin and existence of evil in the world. The problem of evil is a crucial issue for idealism because this philosophy maintains that the entire created world (including man) is the conscious product of an Ultimate Spirit in which there is no objective existence of error, evil or ugliness. The problem lies in explaining why it is that this world, itself a product of supreme goodness, should contain so much within itself that is evil and ugly. Why is it that human nature, which shares the same attributes with the Absolute, should be wayward and capricious, prone to evil and error? Why should it be that, in the words of Russell Kirk, human nature has "a character of mingled good and evil"? The source of man's goodness is clear enough in idealism; how are we to account for the evil?

This problem is often put another way, a way that makes its crucial aspect more apparent to many people. If God is benevolent, He must desire to avert suffering. If He is omnipotent, He is able to avert it. But there is a great deal of suffering in the world and we must conclude, therefore, that either God is not benevolent or He is not omnipotent. In this case we are presented with a logical dilemma. Regardless of which of the two alternatives we choose we necessarily diminish God's nature. Is there a way out of this dilemma for the religious idealist?

The crucial character of the problem of evil has always been apparent to the adherents of idealism and they have given the most careful attention to it. Efforts to find some satisfactory way of resolving this difficulty have occupied the time of major figures in the tradition from Plato, who was concerned with it throughout most of his life, to contemporary representatives of idealism in philosophy and religion. Since this problem is of so much importance in idealism we will examine some of the answers that have been developed in response to it.

A very famous attack on the problem of evil was developed by Plato and has often been employed by idealists. The essence of this argument is our failure to discriminate clearly between the apparent and the real. Because of this failure we fall into the error of attributing the character of reality to events that actually are only appearances. As we said at the beginning of this chapter, idealists are fond of claiming Plato as the great progenitor of the idealistic tradition and many recognize him as the greatest of the objective idealists. Platonism is a system of objective idealism and certainly it is a very great one, but there are important differences between Platonic idealism and the absolute idealism we have been examining here.

In Plato's system the Real is composed of Universals—ideas that exist independently of their being known by any mind. These Platonic *forms*, as they are usually called in English, are universal and unchanging. They may be known, at least in part, by a properly developed human *intellect*, but they are not known through the senses. What we call the "world"—that is, the environment that is known to us in sense experience—depends in some fashion on the forms for its character and existence, but what the precise nature of this relationship is was never made completely clear by Plato.[14]

At any rate, for Plato reality is the forms, and the phenomena of sensory experience are only appearances—poor copies or shadows of

[14] The relation of the universal to the particular was one of the important points of disagreement between Plato and his great pupil, Aristotle.

reality. For example, there is a *form* Man that is the universal concept of man in his essence. There are also *individual* men. Now Tom, Dick, and Harry as individuals owe their natures in some way to the form or idea Man, but their individual natures for some reason do not mirror completely the idea (or ideal) of man. The mistake we make lies in concluding that human nature in essence is mean and nasty, at least in some respects, because we detect a certain amount of meanness and nastiness in such particular men as Tom, Dick, and Harry. If we go on to generalize that *human nature* is mean and nasty we make the error of confusing the appearance (individuals such as Tom, Dick, and Harry) with the real which is the form MAN.

But, it is often objected, experience demonstrates that there *are* meanness and nastiness in individual men. The answer is that while this may *appear* to be true, the fact is that these evils of meanness and nastiness are not objectively real. They represent failures of men to realize completely the form in which they participate. This inability of ours to perceive the difference between appearance and reality leads us to the incorrect conclusion that evil (in this case the evil in human nature) is objectively real. Actually what we call evil is the failure to achieve the good. According to Plato, this lack in human nature is caused by ignorance. When men know what the right is they will regulate their behavior accordingly. No man wills to do evil.

This example of the attempt to settle the problem can be extended to all instances of what we interpret to be evil. The central point is that evil has no objective reality. What we interpret as evil is in reality the failure to realize the good.[15] Many idealists consider this argument a very weighty one and often cite variations on it in their discussions of the problem.[16] It should be said, however, that there are also those who fail to see that it constitutes any solution at all to the problem. Whether the misery and suffering and wrong-doing men undergo is called appearance or whether it is called reality, the hard fact is that men still are afflicted with evil and error and assailed from every side

[15] Plato found difficult the problem of whether base and ugly things have corresponding forms (i.e., whether they are "real"). The problem is considered in the dialogue "Parmenides" but there Plato did not come to a conclusion about the matter. However, the great neo-Platonist, Plotinus, did not hedge on the question. He stated plainly that there are no forms of evil and ugly things and what these appearances represent are lacks of true being. This is substantially the point made above and one that has wide acceptance among idealists.

[16] For an example of an argument by a modern idealist along these general lines see: William E. Hocking, *The Meaning of God in Human Experience*, New Haven: Yale University Press, 1928.

with all manner of ugliness, and all this in a world that idealists claim is the product of an Ultimate Perfection.

Another kind of argument familiar in the literature of idealism is the argument that proceeds from the assumption that men have free will. In consequence of their freedom of choice men do on occasion choose evil. Even so, we should understand that what evil does exist is not characteristic of the whole of reality but only exists in the human mind. Further, since evil exists only as it is in some mind, men may conquer it by putting it out of mind. When this is done evil no longer has any existence; consequently, it is not real.[17]

Those who remain unconvinced by this kind of solution point out that freedom to choose does not necessarily mean that the choice must be between good and evil, for it is possible to conceive of freedom to choose among competing goods. Moreover, to say that men are free to choose between good and evil does not explain how evil got into the world in the first place so that it might be chosen voluntarily. And further, a substantial part of the human misery in this world comes from natural catastrophe—earthquake, flood, plague, etc.—and these emphatically do exist somewhere outside the mind and cannot be made non-existent by an act of mental negation.

Still another assault on the problem involves the argument that the presence of evil serves to enhance the good that characterizes the world. Thus, we cannot appreciate a good dinner unless we are hungry, though in many circumstances we interpret hunger as an evil. In such a case the evil (hunger) enhances and causes us to appreciate more fully the good (dinner). Without the presence of hunger our food would be unappetizing and our eating without enjoyment. The hub of this argument is that in making this world, the Creator has put into it enough evil to make us appreciate and cherish the good he has put there in greater amount. Whether this makes evil real or not is difficult to determine from the argument, but presumably it does. It could be argued that the "facts" on which this argument is based can be subjected to a different kind of interpretation. It may be as reasonable to argue that this world is really the work of an omnipotent and malevolent spirit whose nature is the essence of evil and who has put just enough good into his handiwork to make us appreciate the evil![18]

17 It should be pointed out that this undoubtedly is the basis for much of the moralizing that is done in schools, homes and other institutions. The child is exhorted to "put evil thoughts out of his mind" and when he does he himself will not be evil.
18 This reversal of the argument has been advanced by Bertrand Russell in his discussion of the problem of evil with respect to the philosophy of Leibnitz. See

There is one other argument we should examine before we leave this aspect of idealism. This approach is in part a variation on the appearance-reality theme. In this case we are advised that what we interpret as evil is really evil only to the limited grasp of finite minds. Evil is not a problem in the infinite mind of God. As the saying goes, "The Lord moves in mysterious ways his wonders to perform." Some of the works of God are incomprehensible to man and always will be. Man in his finite existence can never hope to see the whole scheme of things— the "big picture." However, by an act of faith we can believe that if our minds could encompass the whole of reality we would realize that what we have mistakenly interpreted as evil is part of that which is supremely good. This, however, is not an argument in the logical sense but an exhortation to faith, and it may very well be that these sentiments that are expressed so poignantly in the *Book of Job* really are the idealist's resolution of the problem of evil. At any rate, and in spite of the problem of evil, idealism clings resolutely to the doctrine that "all things work together for the glory of an external spiritual life, despite appearances."[19]

We have presented here the commonest answers to the problem of evil. Whether any one of these, or all of them taken together, constitute a genuine solution to the problem must be left to the judgment of the reader. The judgment should be made in the full realization that absolute idealism as a system may very well stand or fall on the adequacy of its solution of this problem.[20]

CERTAINTY OF TRUTH AND VALUE

At this point we should perhaps remind ourselves that the real object of our search in this chapter is to find the sources of certainty that play

---

Russell's, *A History of Western Philosophy*, New York: Simon and Schuster, 1945, p. 590. Other writers have pointed out that a great deal of philosophical energy has been expended on the problem of evil but very little on the problem of good. Why should the presence of evil be a problem and the presence of good not? Clearly, among idealists, this is not considered a significant question.
[19] Ralph Barton Perry, *Present Philosophical Tendencies*, New York: Longmans, Green and Company, 1912, p. 188.
[20] The doctrine of *meliorism* has not been considered here because the author of this book has difficulty in understanding how it can be a solution to the problem of evil. Meliorism is the doctrine that although there is evil in the world, the world itself is capable of improvement. Social meliorism is appropriate in the context of such a philosophy as the experimentalism of John Dewey, but the real problem in idealism is to account for the fact that there *is* evil in the world in the first place.

an important part in the conservative tradition. For an important segment of modern conservatism the source of certainty is to be found in the tradition of absolute idealism and the key to it is the idealistic doctrine of the priority of consciousness. This doctrine we have already examined at some length.

In the first place, we are assured by the idealist that the reality we encounter in our own experience is the product of an Ultimate Intelligence, and that the world in its essential character is rational and orderly. This, the idealist thinks, means that our knowledge of the world has the potential of being certain, at least in some respects. This latter qualification has to be made because idealists must necessarily admit that there is a certain "slippage" between the ideal and the actual. How this discrepancy is explained depends on how the problem of evil (and, therefore, the problem of error) is explained. Nevertheless, the idealist assures us there is an objective body of Truth, and even finite minds are capable of apprehending it, though not necessarily in its entirety.

For the idealist knowing is always a creative, constructive act. The data that originate in sense experience are combined and interpreted and formed into intelligible ideas. In this sense, what the mind actually does is to construct the object of its own knowledge. The question now becomes one of knowing what the criterion for Truth is: Granted that it is the creative power of mind that accounts for our knowledge, how are we to know when the ideas we hold are true and when they are not true? How are we able to distinguish between truth and error?

To this question the idealist has a considered answer. We know our ideas are true, he says, *when they are in harmony with the already existing and accepted body of truth.* In other words, the criterion for truth is *consistency* and idealists often point out that consistency, being a logical criterion, is the most rigorous standard possible.[21] In fact, idealists may point out that the most rigorous body of truth in existence is mathematics and the criterion of truth for any mathematical proposition is its consistency with the whole body of mathematical knowledge. What, the idealist asks, can be more certain than truth established through logical coherence?

[21] Kant and some contemporary idealists have spoken of two criteria: correspondence and coherence. The term "correspondence" in this respect refers to the correspondence of an idea *with the accepted body of truth.* The term "coherence" used in the body of the text in this book includes both "correspondence" as just defined and coherence in the logical sense. Correspondence is an important term in realistic epistemologies and should not be confused with the way idealists use it in their discussions of truth.

PHILOSOPHY OF AMERICAN EDUCATION

Critics of idealism have pointed out that while it is true that coherence is the criterion for truth *in an analytic system such as mathematics,* it is a criterion only for formal validity—since that is the only form of validity possible in an analytic system. If all knowledge were like pure mathematics, then coherence would be the only necessary criterion (and the only possible one). But much of our concern with knowledge is not with those forms that are purely analytical as in mathematical and logical systems. Our main concerns are those that involve facts, as in common sense and scientific experience. It is in these areas that critics find coherence an insufficient criterion.

However, the idealist can point out that what is overlooked by these critics is the principle that all existence is itself rational and orderly— that the world of experience, being itself a rational product of an Ultimate Reason, does exhibit in macrocosm the formal properties of a logical system and hence, the criterion of coherence is entirely proper. It must be admitted that error does sometimes occur in human knowledge. The corpus of knowledge does have to be revised periodically. Theories in science, once accepted as true, have had to be abandoned. Historians find it necessary to "correct" history, and so on. What this shows, according to idealism, is that finite human nature is on occasion fallible and so, even with the rigor of logical coherence, we sometimes mistake error for truth. When we drop one idea for another it is because the latter meets better the criterion of consistency. Our efforts are in the direction of closer and closer approximations to the Truth. Though we may never reach the ultimate apprehension of all Truth, we can come nearer and nearer to it.

We are now in a position to state in propositional form the thesis of idealism concerning knowledge and truth:

a. The universe is rational and orderly and, therefore, intelligible.

b. There is an objective body of Truth that has its origin and existence in the Absolute Mind and which can be known, at least in part, by the human mind.

c. The act of knowing is essentially an act of reconstructing the data of awareness into intelligible ideas and systems of ideas.

d. The criterion for the truth of an idea is coherence; that is, an idea is true when it is consistent with the existing and accepted body of truth.

We can see now that idealism has an answer for the first question that motivated our search: There *is* a source of certainty for our knowledge. The universe *is* rational and orderly. There *is* an objective body of

Truth. The human mind *is* capable of knowing this Truth; though finite minds can never grasp all Truth in its entirety, they are capable of closer and closer approximations to it. There *is* a criterion that enables us to distinguish truth from falsity. Thus, we can say that if one of the requirements of a consistent essentialism is the assurance that there is a body of objective Truth and that it is capable of being known, then the tradition of idealism can fulfill this requirement.

The next question is whether idealism can extend the same assurance of certainty concerning our value judgments. Essentialism sees the role of education as involving not only the transmission of knowledge, but also the transmission of value. Surely no more cogent question can be asked than whether there are objective values that hold for all men in all times and which can be transmitted by the teacher with full confidence in their certainty.

There are various strains in the idealistic tradition that converge to form the ethical thesis, which many idealists think is the single greatest element in their philosophical tradition. First of all, we should remember that in the eyes of idealists human behavior is inherently purposive. As they see it, behavior is not merely the responses to external stimuli, as psychological behaviorists would have it. Rather, there is within the human self an inherent urge for self-realization; the basic motivation for behavior, therefore, lies within the self and is not external to it. The fact that man is a purposive creature means also that he is a *valuing* creature. He cannot escape the necessity of placing value (or disvalue) on the things and events he encounters in his experience. The whole of history portrays the continuing efforts of man to gain a firmer and more valid grasp of the Good.

Secondly, if men are to make judgments about value, they must have some standards by means of which particular things can be judged as good or not good. These norms should be comprehensive and they should be dependable. As we have already seen, the idealist is certain that such norms do exist and that, in fact, they characterize Reality itself. There are ultimate essences of the supreme values of Truth, Goodness, and Beauty. In our world of experience we see these great Ideas embodied in concrete form in things and events. Though it must be admitted that these values are never perfectly expressed in this world, nevertheless we can through reason know that in that which is ultimate they exist in pure essential form and they serve as the ideals toward which we strive, even though our best efforts may only be approximations.

In the third place, we have a rigorous criterion for assessing the truth of our value judgments. This criterion is that of coherence, which as we have already seen, is the criterion by which we assess the validity of all our judgments. If those judgments we make that have value significance are consistent with our own most reliable value experience, and if they are coherent with the body of value judgments that are the collective product of human experience, then we can rest assured of their truth and their dependability.

It follows, of course, that the good life for man is the life in which value concepts are apprehended intellectually and in which they are expressed in personal conduct. Hence, both understanding and acting are involved, but the essence of goodness in our conduct is that actions be guided by knowledge. So in response to the second question, we can say that from the standpoint of idealism there *is* a source of certainty for value standards. There *is* a criterion for distinguishing good from evil. There *is* a way of knowing what the good life is for man. And all these taken together can give assurance that education must be concerned with transmitting tried and tested values both as standards in conceptual form, and as expressions of these concepts in behavior.

THE INDIVIDUAL AND SOCIETY

We turn now to the third requirement of a consistent and coherent conservative position in educational philosophy. This requirement involves the relationship of the individual to society, and it is an important question in essentialism because the conservative tradition emphasizes both the necessity for individuals to support and conform to the existing order in society and the need for personal freedom and self-realization. As we have remarked before, on the surface, at least, there does appear to be an element of paradox in the conservative position on these matters. Our purpose now is to see whether these two aspects of conservative thought are capable of harmonious resolution.

This problem of the relation of the individual to society has always been one of the important issues in social and political philosophy. It is also an important problem in educational theory because the school has a major responsibility in establishing whatever relation is to be established between individuals and the greater social group. Sometimes schools are criticized for promoting an excessive conformity in students and thereby teaching them that adjustment to existing society is the greatest good. On the other hand, schools are also criticized for permitting excessive individual freedom which, it is said, amounts to little more than social anarchy and which permits a generation to grow up without restraint or direction.[22] The problem is often stated in such terms as these: which comes first (or should come first) the interests of the individual or the interests of society? Which has priority? the rights of society or the rights of individuals? Should education find its orientation around the needs of the individual or the needs of society?

To the idealist these distinctions between the individual and society are unwarranted and the key to the understanding of idealism's position on this problem is the idea of *unity*, which, as we have seen, is a fundamental element in the idealistic tradition. The point is that every particular thing that exists (and this includes human selves) is part of a total, all-embracing unity. The meaning that anything has is a consequence of its membership in a total system. This is in the same sense that the meaning of any proposition in a logical system is dependent on the system of which it is a part. Away from this context a proposition has no function or meaning at all.

Something similar can be said about individual persons. Realization of self is the most important thing in human life; it is literally a sacred right. But this realization can be achieved and selfhood realized only as the individual is able to relate himself progressively to that which is greater than he. If man isolates himself from the greater unity, if he is unwilling or unable to amalgamate himself with it, then like a proposition stripped of its context; he has no real identity. His life has no point to it—it is nothing.

An important idea that is involved here is the so-called *organic conception of society*. There are various ways of conceiving the nature of society. One way is to see it as an aggregation of individuals who live and work together on the basis of an agreement or contract. If the agreement becomes undesirable for some reason it is the right of individuals to abrogate or modify it. This conception of the state is extremely distasteful to idealists, who often speak of it as "atomistic." The true nature of society is seen by idealists as being *organic*. This is to say that a society displays the same kind of internal unity that characterizes a living organism. Living things are composed of various parts and members—arms, legs, head, torso, etc. Ultimately a living thing is composed of chemical elements arranged in various combina-

22 Conservatives have from time to time launched both kinds of criticism against the progressive school.

tions. But, the idealist points out, a living thing is far more than a collection of discrete bodily members. Surely it is far more than an aggregation of chemical elements. The idealist's point is often expressed in the familiar saying that "the whole is greater than the sum of its parts."

For example, the human body is a vastly complex organization of physiological members, but each of these members has identity and function only because it is a part of a larger system. If through some circumstance any member of the body is separated from the total organic unity, it immediately loses both its character and its function, and in a short time, its very existence. Similarly when one organ of the body is diseased, the whole organism is affected adversely. When a man has a "sick" liver, we have more on our hands than a sick liver; we have a sick man.

Now, as the idealist sees it, the organic unity of society is exactly analogous to the unity of an organism. Society in the large sense is composed of lesser unities—which may be compared to the various members of the body. Among these are such institutions as family, community, school, church, nation and so on. Each of these units of society has its meaning and function because it is part of a larger unity, which as we have already seen, ultimately is the complete unity of the Absolute. If one part of the social body becomes "sick" the total organism suffers. Whenever an institution, the church or the school, for example, misfunctions, the totality of society suffers. In this way societies become sick in the same sense that individual organisms become sick. The only way by which the social organism can regain its health is through the restoration of a harmonious relationship among its constituent parts.

There is another dimension to these matters that is of considerable importance to our present purpose. As idealists commonly see it, society not only exhibits attributes of organic unity, *it also exhibits attributes of personality or selfhood.* Even common speech is shot through with the belief that personal attributes are possessed by social organisms. For example, we often speak of "school spirit" and most schools employ various methods of stimulating it. What is "school spirit?" Is it simply the sum total of the individual "spirits" of the persons who make up the school? Or does it mean that the school is an entity that has the power to possess spirit? It seems likely that if the term "school spirit" has any real meaning it can be only in this second sense. Now, what kind of things are capable of exhibiting spirit? Certainly inanimate things are not, and just as surely, things that are without consciousness are not. The idealist's conclusion is that the school as an institution is a self and like any self it is possible to predicate spirit of it. A school, it is true, is composed of individual teachers and students, but as an institution it is more than a mere collection of people, just as an organism is more than the arithmetical sum of its various parts.

We now see that the school as a self is a greater and more inclusive unity than the individual student in the school. But, the idealist may ask, what sense does it make to set the student off and over against the school? How can we speak meaningfully of the welfare of the student as opposed in some way to the welfare of the school? If the school did not exist students would not exist, because to be a student means to be a part of a school, in the same sense that a finger is a finger only when it is part of a hand—and ultimately a part of a total organism. Schools exist, in part at least, to enable students to realize the potential of their own selfhood, but an individual achieves this only when he identifies himself and his interests with the self that is greater than he is. Only as the individual is able to achieve this self-transcendence and identification with higher and more inclusive levels of unity can he achieve his own self-realization. The interests of the school are the interests of the individual and one cannot be set off separately against the other. The process of self-realization, then, involves the progressive identification of the individual with more and more inclusive levels of unity. This process is illustrated by Figure 5.3.

The realization of self is a continuous process that begins with the birth of the individual. The innermost of the concentric circles in the diagram represents the individual, who at birth is completely self-centered, interested only in his own needs and desires and their fulfillment. His first encounter with an entity greater than himself occurs in his earliest experiences in the family. The family is a self and this selfhood is greater and more inclusive than the members who make up the institution. Consequently, the first necessary act of self-transcendence and identification of the young child is in the family. Contemporary psychologists agree on the crucial nature of this early experience. Those individuals who through some unfortunate circumstances are unable to achieve this first identification are sorely hampered throughout their lives and may well find it difficult, if not impossible, to make subsequent adjustments.

As the child grows and matures and his environment broadens, he is called upon to identify himself with greater levels of unity. After the family comes the school and the church and the community, each more

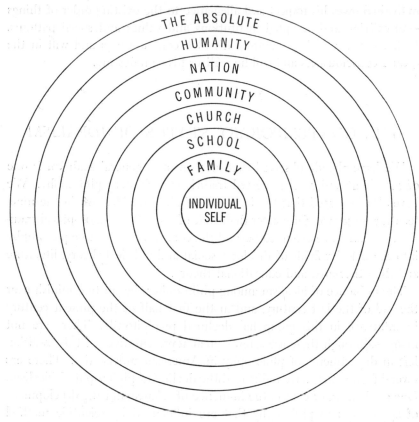

Figure 5.3

Figure 5.3 NOTE: There is some variation in the interpretation of the progression of unity. This diagram shows the church as more inclusive than the school. This interpretation would be agreeable to some idealists and not to others. The diagram is intended to be illustrative and not definitive of every possible position.

inclusive of reality and each institution a self. Beyond these institutions is the nation, which in the modern world encompasses all of them and in which the individual realizes his own selfhood through the identification process. Beyond the nation lies the greater unity of humanity and beyond that the all-embracing unity of the Absolute Mind, which to most idealists is the mind of God. Thus, the end toward which the whole process of self-realization moves is the identification of the individual with the totality of all existence. In this process he finds his own selfhood.

Thus, the paradox we spoke of earlier turns out, according to idealists, to be an illusion. The doctrine of the interest of the individual in opposition to the interest of society involves a false dichotomy. The individual owes his respect and allegiance to the existing order of things —to existing and accepted institutions and values and social patterns. In the very act of incorporating his own consciousness and will in the greater consciousness and will he realizes his own destiny.

THE CONTEMPORARY STATUS OF IDEALISM

We have already observed that idealism as a general tradition is one of the oldest and most respected traditions in western philosophy. We have also indicated that the influence of absolute idealism in the nineteenth century was far greater than that of any other philosophical tradition. Its influence extended beyond the confines of academic philosophy into the broader fields of theology, social and political theory, literature and the other arts, and educational theory.

The influence of idealism among philosophers began to diminish near the end of the last century, and in the first half of the present century its influence in this group has declined precipitously. There are not many—although there are a few—great representatives of this tradition left in departments of philosophy in American universities. There are several factors that have influenced the decline of philosophical idealism. One of them is, of course, the influence of science and the development of approaches to philosophy that are influenced by scientific method and that are concerned with kinds of problems with which idealism does not ordinarily concern itself.

A second factor is that there is very little current interest among philosophers in system building. The essence of such a great speculative tradition in philosophy as idealism is its effort to develop an all-encompassing theoretical structure in which the whole of reality is patterned according to some cosmic design. Contemporary philosophy, however, is mainly concerned with problems of analyses and criticism. While, in the eyes of idealists and other system builders, this must give philosophy a more mundane role than it has had traditionally, most contemporary philosophers insist that the critical and analytical function is the most important contribution philosophy has to offer today. In their judgment, idealism is really a matter of interest only in the history of philosophy.

It is reasonable to ask, therefore, why so much attention has been given to idealism here if it actually is a matter of little interest among contemporary philosophers. The answer is that although this tradition has lost much of its influence among philosophers, it is far from being without effect in certain other quarters. In fact, the stronghold of idealism in higher education today is undoubtedly in various departments of the humanistic studies. The scholars and teachers in these departments are not primarily philosophers, but important aspects of the studies they pursue are closely related to philosophical ideas. For one thing, there are many humanistic scholars who are profoundly disturbed by the concepts of human nature that are emerging from the work of behavioral scientists. There are also many of them who take exception to ideas about knowledge, truth, and value that have been influenced by scientific method.

These scholars and teachers believe that there is more to the nature of reality and more to human nature and destiny than has been or ever will be revealed by the scientific approach. Many of them believe that the road to complete cultural dissolution is paved with the positivism, ethical relativism, and the psychological behaviorism that have been fostered by science—and also in no small measure by much contemporary philosophy. It is natural, therefore, that persons with this attitude should continue to hold with philosophical ideas that stress the transcendent character of human selfhood, the objectivity of truth—particularly ethical truth—and the fundamental regularity and rationality of the cosmos. To them it is only in a world of the kind portrayed by idealism that the human drama has meaning, and only in this kind of world can the highest aspirations of man have any chance of being realized.

Since the tradition of idealism is still influential in affecting the perceptions of many people in the field of education, it is important that certain specific aspects of this tradition and their relation to the educational enterprise be understood clearly. The remainder of this chapter is devoted to a summary of certain specific and crucial relationships between idealism and conservative ideas about education.

THE EMPHASIS ON THE SPIRITUAL

The educational conservative whose views are colored by philosophical idealism sees education as one means by which individuals realize their own selfhood. In this sense, education is a spiritual undertaking and its task, along with the task of religion, is the most important and exalted responsibility in society. As the idealist sees it, the highest values are those of the spirit; the highest achievements are those of the intellect;

the highest motives of man are those that arise from within the self. The purpose of education should be the inspiration of the individual to realize himself through a progressive identification with that which is supremely real.

To the idealist this means that the irreducible core of the curriculum must be the humanistic studies, for the greatest achievements of the human spirit are the great literary and artistic works of all mankind. It is through our intellectual apprehension of and our own identification with these supreme products of the human spirit that we can achieve the unity of our finite selves with the Ultimate. There is no other source in which we can see so clearly the nobility of human nature portrayed and to witness the struggle of all mankind to apprehend the supreme ethical values.[23]

In this century, as we have already noted, the natural sciences have assumed a greatly increased status in society and in the schools. Although to many idealists this is not a happy state of affairs, they have been forced to make compromises with it. In the field of the physical sciences this has not been easy, but it has been even more difficult for the idealist to accept the influence of science in those fields that deal with human nature and behavior. One common example of this is the typical dissatisfaction of a substantial number of conservatives with psychological measurement, which is, of course, the effort to apply quantitative methods to the study of certain aspects of human behavior. Several kinds of objection have been urged against the "scientific movement" in education, not all of them by idealists.

A major reservation held by the idealist concerns the behavioristic conception of human nature that underlies much of the effort to apply quantitative methods to the study of human nature. To the idealist, man is a spiritual being and the mainspring of his behavior lies within the self. Human actions cannot be interpreted as mere reactions to external stimuli, for man is possessed of will and this will is free. Human behavior can be guided by conscious choice and decision. Man is a moral being and is impelled by an inner working to pursue and realize the good. The idealist argues, therefore, that the presence of free will negates any idea that human behavior is determined in any complete sense by events external to the person. Man is, or at least he can be, "the captain of his soul." This freedom of the will and the attendant indeterminism means to many idealists that psychological measurement

---

[23] For an impassioned statement of this thesis see: "The Problem of the Mind," Chapter III in Kirk, *op. cit.* Particularly important statements are on pages 54 and 55.

(and the uses to which it is put) is in the last analysis a fraud, and more than that, it is a dangerous fraud. The real enemies of the human spirit and of true human education are determinism and materialism and, as the idealist sees it, both of these are assumptions of psychological and educational measurement. What is involved here is not merely the question of the technological adequacy of various psychological instruments of measure. The point is that in the estimation of the idealist *there are vast areas of human experience that are incapable ever of being "measured" by psychological instruments and these areas are the most important of all in human life.*

An important example of the development of this thesis will be found in a book by Mr. Joseph Wood Krutch, a distinguished literary critic, teacher, and scholar.[24] Mr. Krutch's thesis is in essence that the modern "science of human behavior" has steadily denigrated human nature to a point at which we have all but lost the chance to restore it to its rightful position of honor and dignity. We have about lost our sense of what the measure of man really is, and, it may be said parenthetically, the status of the curriculums in our schools shows this plainly. Mr. Krutch argues his thesis from the principle of the priority of consciousness and one important conclusion, partly stated and partly implied, is that the humanistic studies should constitute the central core of the curriculum.[25] The great literary heritage is more the measure of man than anything else can ever be.

THE CERTAINTY OF TRUTH

To the educational conservative the school is an institution whose purpose is the preservation, refinement, and transmission of a body of essential truth. The conservative has never been able to understand the diffidence some teachers exhibit over the question of teaching the truth as if it were *the truth*. This is particularly true of the conservative whose views are tempered by philosophical idealism. As we have seen, the idealist is committed to the belief that there is a body of truth, that this truth can be known, and that it must be transmitted to the young. As an idealist, he is inclined to think that the most important repository of the eternal verities, as they are known to man, are to be found in great

[24] Joseph Wood Krutch, *The Measure of Man*, New York: Grosset and Dunlap (Grosset's Universal Library), 1953.
[25] See: *Ibid.*, Chapter 11.

literary and other humanistic sources. And, as we have already seen, the idealist holds the humanistic studies to be the most important of the essentials, for the truth that is portrayed in these sources is superior and more complete than any to be found anywhere.[26]

As was pointed out in an earlier chapter, the conservative has mixed feelings about the ability of the individual to mind his own affairs. He is inclined to think that in the ordinary affairs of life the individual ought to be free to act on his own initiative and responsibility. It is in the important matters that the conservative believes the individual to be incompetent to make unguided decisions. And, as we have already seen, the conservative believes that in matters of great importance we must be guided by tradition—by the wisdom of our ancestors. Here is one point on which the general conservative tradition and the philosophical tradition of idealism coincide. The conservative tells us that our ideas and actions should always be judged in the light of tradition, which is another way of saying that our ideas are worthy *if they are in harmony with the accumulated wisdom of all the generations.* The idealist tells us that the test for the truth of an idea is *its coherence with the body of existing and accepted truth.* Now this body of existing and accepted truth can be nothing other than the wisdom of our ancestors, about which social conservatives say so much.

It seems clear, therefore, (at least to conservatives) that the responsibility of the school must be to transmit the essential portions of this heritage of tradition to all who come to school. There must be no exceptions because every individual must regulate his conduct in accordance with tradition and the wisdom of our ancestors. Unless he knows what the enduring truths are, unless he has grasped the essential truths, a man is adrift and without any landmarks to guide him. The idealist believes that the truth exists and that it has objective reality. He also believes that the human mind is capable of distinguishing between truth and error, and since it is tradition that furnishes the basis for evaluation of our own ideas, tradition must be perpetuated and passed unblemished from one generation to another. This is the responsibility of education.

THE PRIMACY OF VALUE

It has been said that the real purpose of philosophical idealism is to make the world safe for value. To the idealist the value enterprise is

[26] See for example: *Ibid.,* p. 231 ff.

the most important quest in human life—and in philosophy. There is agreement among idealists that, with the possible exception of religion, education is more intimately involved in the value enterprise than any other activity of social life. The teacher is a moral agent in the most fundamental sense of that term, for he is the transmitter of truth, and truth always has moral dimensions. In one sense, any scheme for education is a moral enterprise because the effort to educate is the effort to help an individual become what he would not otherwise be. To the idealist there are objective and well-defined criteria for value and these criteria define the moral dimensions of education. If there were not objective criteria for value in the ultimate sense, then men would not encounter manifestations of value in their individual experience.

This is one point at which the idealist thinks the insufficiencies of science are readily apparent. Science, he points out, may in many instances indicate to us ways of realizing our objectives, but it is entirely outside possibility for science to tell us what objectives we *ought* to seek to realize. Moreover, although there is an ultimate reference for value, the manifestation of value in human life is not automatic. If men are to apprehend values and incorporate them in their own lives, they must make an effort. As in the case of any idea, value concepts must be recreated by the individual and become a part of his own self. In the last analysis, only the individual can do this for himself, but he can be helped in the process—or hindered. As we have already seen, this process comes about through the progressive self-identification of the individual with greater dimensions of unity and ultimately with the Absolute Spirit, which is God.

The role of the school is to assist the individual in his apprehension and incorporation of value in his life. The school is not alone in this responsibility, for clearly the family and the church and ultimately the total human community also share in the process. The thing that distinguishes the school's responsibility is that it is the only institution in society whose primary purpose is intellectual development of the individual. Other institutions have some responsibility for the intellectual development of the young, but only in the school is this a primary responsibility.[27]

The intellectual enterprise, however, is not distinct from the moral. Man is a unity—a spiritual unity. Both intellect and will are aspects of

[27] See for example: Theodore M. Greene, "A Liberal Christian Idealist Philosophy of Education," in J. S. Brubacher, ed., *Modern Philosophies and Education*, Fifty-fourth Yearbook of the National Society for the Study of Education, Chicago: University of Chicago Press, 1955, pp. 115–117.

his nature. The school as curator of the great intellectual heritage of mankind is thereby also a potent force in the moral life of man, for the school preserves and transmits the great literary heritage whose very essence is ethical.

To the idealist the highest things in life are those of the spirit—the intellectual and moral achievements of man. As he sees it, human life can have meaning only in a world which is itself meaningful, which is itself a product of an Ultimate Reason, and whose very nature is ethical.

SUMMARY

This in its general outline is the case the conservative makes for education when he views it from the standpoint of philosophical idealism, which, in fact, a substantial number of conservatives still do. The basic argument of idealism is the priority of consciousness and closely allied to this is the argument that the nature of the world is such that man's highest aspirations are capable of realization. Both of these arguments have been considered at some length in this chapter.

Our purpose has been to see whether idealism as a philosophic tradition can provide answers to certain strategic questions posed by the educational tradition of essentialism. It should be left to the reader to judge whether idealism's answers to these questions are adequate. Even so, it should be said that to a substantial number of educational conservatives today idealism still provides the most trustworthy and dependable answers to the fundamental questions of education policy.

CHAPTER SIX

Realistic Philosophy

and the Conservative Tradition

In the preceding chapter we surveyed the tradition of philosophical idealism and noted some of the relations of this tradition with conservative educational theory and practice. In a number of instances it was remarked that absolute idealism had a powerful influence on the intellectual life of the nineteenth century and that this influence underwent a marked decline, the decline setting in about the turn of the century.

It was pointed out in the discussion of idealism that, in the judgment of its adherents, idealism supplies answers to certain questions that are strategic to educational conservatism. To those who find it possible to accept the basic outline of idealism, the answers this philosophy gives are adequate to furnish essentialism with the coherence and consistency it must have if it is to constitute a systematic theory of education. In an earlier period of American education it was possible for a majority of those who were thoughtful about questions of educational philosophy to view these problems in the broader context of idealism. In the present day, however, this is no longer the case. There is still a substantial number of people who find idealistic principles the best standpoint from which to analyze the persistent problems of education, but the size and the influence of this group diminishes steadily. This process has been going on throughout the present century and idealism consequently has lost much of its influence on educational thought.

The decline of idealism, beginning around the turn of the century, was attended by the resurgence of one old philosophical tradition that had been greatly in eclipse and also by the appearance of what was essentially a new tradition in philosophy, one to which America was to make the major contribution. The first of these was the old and distinguished tradition of philosophical realism. The second was the newer tradition of pragmatism. Both of them attained importance in this historical period and initially, at least, both of them were protests against the domination of idealism.

We will reserve our discussion of pragmatism for a later chapter, since it is closely linked with the educational tradition of progressivism. In this chapter we will investigate some of the basic doctrines of realistic philosophy and observe how these doctrines have come to be related to basic ideas in education. We will be concerned particularly to find whether realism can provide adequate answers for the strategic questions in educational essentialism that we have already dealt with in idealism and whether these answers from realistic philosophy are more in harmony with the modern temper.

THE RESURGENCE OF REALISTIC PHILOSOPHY

In his account of the development of realism in American philosophy William P. Montague[1] describes the philosophical scene in America at the end of the nineteenth century. Idealism was fully in control of departments of philosophy in the leading universities. Scholastic realism was given little or no attention, presumably because of its close link with Catholic theology. American idealism had gone through two periods of development. The first was the transcendentalism of Emerson, Alcott, and others of the New England group. This had given way to the more or less orthodox Hegelianism whose distinguished advocates were William T. Harris and the "St. Louis School." There had been rumblings on the philosophical front for some time and in the first decade of the new century the battle finally broke out.

In essence, the issue around which this battle developed was the speculative, system-building character of idealism as opposed to the emphasis on common sense and the belief in science that had been in many ways characteristic of realism even in antiquity. As might be expected, the insurgents against philosophical idealism were younger

[1] William P. Montague, "The Story of American Realism," in Dagobert D. Runes, ed., *Living Schools of Philosophy*, Ames, Iowa: Littlefield, Adams & Company, 1958.

men and their interests lay more in the direction of logic, science, and scientific method than in the familiar idealistic direction of metaphysical speculation. They had many bones to pick with the idealists, but a main source of their dissatisfaction lay in the cavalier attitude idealism had taken toward science and the achievements of scientific method. As they saw it, a new realism was to lead the way to a return to common sense and to a realization of the importance of science in the modern world and in modern philosophy.

In 1910 six of the insurgents formed themselves into a kind of alliance to which they gave the name "The New Realists."[2] The philosophical program they advocated is usually referred to as neo-realism or the new-realism. Their philosophical position was most fully presented in a book published in 1912 to which they gave the title, *The New Realism.*[3]

There was an important area of agreement among the new realists, but, perhaps since they were philosophers, they did not always remain within that area and in consequence many differences of opinion developed among them. In the preparation of their position they agreed on several matters which they called postulates. These postulates show evidence of the temper of the new realism and are worth noting here. One of these was the idea that, following the example of scientists, philosophers should work together rather than in splendid isolation (as idealists were often wont to do).[4] In the second place, philosophers should behave like scientists by dividing up the problems and working on them one at a time rather than trying to wrap up everything in one grand synthesis (as idealists also had often tried to do). Thus, in the first two postulates the new realists were proposing to model their philosophical inquiries along the same general lines scientists use in their investigations. This was quite in accord with the intellectual outlook of this group.

The remaining three postulates were really propositions in ontology and epistemology and formed the basis of the brand of realism advocated by this group. One of these postulates was to the effect that at least some of the particular things we encounter in experience exist apart from our consciousness. This clearly is a denial of the priority of consciousness and, hence, of idealism, for as we have seen, idealism holds that

[2] The original six of the New Realists were: R. B. Perry, E. B. Holt, W. T. Marvin, E. G. Spaulding, W. B. Pitkin, and W. P. Montague.
[3] Edwin B. Holt and associates, *The New Realism, Cooperative Studies in Philosophy,* New York: The Macmillan Company, 1912.
[4] According to Montague, the new realists did not live up to this very fully.

the existence of any object presupposes the existence of a subject (knower).

Another postulate stated that at least some of the essences (that is, universal ideas) that we encounter in our experiences also exist when we are not aware of them. This principle of the independent reality of universal ideas came from Plato and his theory of the independent existence of the forms.

The last of the postulates was that at least some of the particular things and some of the universal ideas are known directly by the mind and not through some intervening mental state or other construction of the mind. This proposition also is a denial of idealism for idealistic philosophy maintains that the object of knowledge is idea and therefore what is known is in some sense a construct of consciousness.

THE BASIC THESES OF REALISM

We are now in a position to state the two fundamental propositions of realistic philosophy. These propositions have the same importance in realism that the principle of the priority of consciousness has in modern idealism. The first of these propositions is usually called the "principle of independence." This is primarily a proposition about ontology, but it has close relationship with a theory of knowledge. *The principle of independence is that there exists a world of things and events and relations among these things and events, and this world is not dependent for its existence and character on its being known.* This belief in an independently existing reality, whose character is not affected by its being known, squares both with common sense and with science—at least in the opinion of the realist it does.

Like idealism, realism is a very old tradition with its main roots in certain portions of the classic tradition. Typically, realists like to claim Aristotle as the great progenitor of their tradition and, as we have seen, they tend to interpret at least part of Plato's doctrine as being realistic (i.e., the independent reality of forms). As we have already observed in the case of idealism, when a philosophical tradition is as old as realism is, and when it has attracted as many great minds to its doctrines as realism has done, then we can expect that there will be areas of disagreement, differences in emphasis, variant interpretations of the same questions, and different conclusions from the same evidence. These conditions are as descriptive of realism as they are of idealism. And yet, for all these manifold differences, there is a common rallying point for realists—the principle of independence. It is difficult to see how anyone could profess philosophical realism without acceptance of the principle of a world that exists apart from consciousness and does not owe its essential character to its being known.

The second basic thesis of realism concerns our knowledge of this independent world and the processes by which we gain knowledge of it. This thesis may be stated somewhat as follows: *The world is capable of being known, at least in part, as it is in itself.* This epistemological principle was partly stated and partly implied in the last postulate of the new realists mentioned above. Here again the realist emphasizes that this doctrine is in consonance with common sense. Our fundamental common sense conviction is that what we know is something outside our own conscious processes and that we know it directly.

It is one thing to insist that we can know the world as it is in itself, even when this statement includes the qualifications "at least in part," and quite another thing to demonstrate how it is accomplished. This question about the nature of the knowledge process is a crucial one in modern realism[5] and it was a question over which a great deal of controversy has developed among the realists of the present century. We will now consider some of the ways realists have interpreted the knowledge process.

The new realists, who it will be recalled were the original group of insurgents, maintained that there is no fundamental dualism of mind *and* matter as Descartes and Locke and others had maintained. They insisted that in any act of knowing the objects of our knowledge are *presented directly in consciousness* and there is no intervening mental construct or mental state and none is needed to account for our knowledge of the external world. We can know this world directly and as it is in its real character. This idea may be interpreted to mean that when any object is present to my consciousness the qualities that are a part of this object are identical with the qualities that are in my consciousness. This kind of direct realism presupposes a conception of mind that is different in important respects from those we have encountered heretofore.

For example, a common view of mind is that it is in some sense within the organism. Our sense organs convey stimuli from objects to our

[5] The classical Aristotelian and the Thomistic analysis of the problem is discussed in the context of the perennial philosophy. See Chapter X.

minds, and these sense data then furnish the raw material for the cognitive processes of the mind. This, as we have seen, is essentially the conception of mind that Locke advocated and around which his theory of knowledge was developed. A theory of knowledge of this kind involves a basic dualism: There are some things called minds and some things that are matter, and these two kinds of things are absolutely different in character. This is the Cartesian dualism we encountered in the preceding chapter. Both common sense and much philosophy simply assume that the mind is within the knower and the object of his knowing is external to his mind.

Locke was a realist, at least in metaphysics, for he maintained that the primary qualities and the underlying substance are independently real. He also located consciousness and its operations with the knower. Actually, it is possible to subscribe to a mind-body dualism of this kind without doing violence to the principle of independence. Initially, at least, all this principle states is that objects (some, at least) exist independently of their being known. While the principle postulates a world which partly is material in nature, it does not necessarily exclude the existence of mind or consciousness. One way to interpret this is to think of mind as *in* certain organisms and material objects as external to these organisms and their conscious processes. This was Locke's position.

The new realists, however, were opposed to a dualism of this kind. As they saw it, what this kind of interpretation leads to is a "copy" theory of cognition. Thus, under this view, when any object is present to my consciousness there is in my mind a more or less perfect copy or representation of it. This the new realists saw as a chief pitfall of idealism, for how are we ever to break out of the "pictures" that are in our minds and know that they really represent objects in the real world? The new realists thought the worst that can come from this is subjectivism and about the best we can hope from it is scepticism.

To escape the dualistic pitfall the new realists developed another theory of mind. This theory for many people is not easy to grasp. The reason for this difficulty is not so much in the complexity of the idea— certainly it is no more complex than Locke's or Berkeley's—but in the common sense acceptance of the mind as being *in* the organism and the object of knowledge *in* the external environment. In order to grasp the essential notions of mind as the new realism developed them, we have to make a kind of reorientation of our common sense beliefs about mind.

For one thing, according to the new realists, mind is not located in the body in the sense that it is *in* the cerebral cortex or the central nervous system or any other specific physiological system. To be sure, mind requires some structure—a nervous system, for example—in order to function, just as walking requires some structure (legs). But just as walking is not the same thing as legs, neither is mind the same thing as the central nervous system. This analogy may also illustrate the new realist's idea that consciousness is a *process* (in this sense walking is also a process). It is one of the processes that go on in nature and the essence of it is the establishment of a certain kind of *relation* between an organism and various objects in its environment. Sensory organs operating at any given time reveal a kind of cross-section of reality and the particular cross-section that is revealed is the result of the selection made by the central nervous system of the perceiving organism. Now, as is frequently pointed out, this conception is the view that mind is not simply within the organism, it is also out in the environment with the objects of its awareness.[6] This conception of the unity of mind and object has led to the often quoted observation that idealism had reduced everything to mind but the new realism had reduced mind to everything!

What has been set down here is only the barest statement of a theory of knowledge developed within the new realism and accepted by some —but not all—of the original founders of the movement. However, even in this scanty treatment there are implicit certain ideas that can be of great importance to our investigation of the relation between modern realism and the conservative theory of education. In the first place, the cross-sectional theory of consciousness eliminates the dualism between subject and object that has haunted philosophy virtually since its beginning. If the epistemological monism advocated by this theory can be made to stick, we are relieved of dealing with a number of problems that history has shown to be extremely resistant to solution. In the second place, under this theory it can be explained how it is that our awareness is of an independently existing reality and not merely of the self-made furniture of our own minds. In the third place—and this is the point of greatest immediate significance for our purpose—it is possible to interpret this presentative realism in behavioristic terms and relate it to certain important developments in scientific psychology that were going on simultaneously with the development of the new realism. We will now give some attention to this third point.

One member of the new realists besides Holt who advocated a behavioristic interpretation of consciousness was Ralph Barton Perry. The general position Holt and Perry took was that in any instance of aware-

[6] Edwin B. Holt is credited with the original formulation of the "cross-sectional" theory of mind.

ness our actual consciousness of an object *is a specific response we make to that object*.[7] This idea of knowing as responding, while familiar to all today who have the slightest acquaintance with modern psychology, throws on the theory of knowledge a light that is very different from the usual philosophical treatment of this problem.

It will be recalled that in our study of idealism we portrayed the knowledge situation by a simple diagram:

Subject   Cognitive   Object
(Knower) ← Relationship   (Known)

The problem of knowledge is to describe the kind of relation that is established between subject and object in the cognitive relationship. We now know from our previous analysis that according to idealism the relationships between subject and object are *internal* and therefore unified. It is by this means that idealism ultimately is able to explain the unity of subject and object. But we also know that such an explanation cannot do for the realist. The principle of independence indicates that at least some relations are external.[8] This means that objects can enter into new kinds of relations without losing their original character. We know also, in terms of the idea of the new realists, that objects are *presented* in consciousness and there is no intervening mental state needed to account for awareness.

Now suppose we should take the same diagram above and merely alter the names given to the two elements. We need only refer to the object as the "stimulus" and the subject as the "response" and we have $S \to R$ which will be recognized immediately as the basic pattern of all behavioristic psychology—granted, of course, that different variations can be developed on this original theme. This conception may be summed up by an excerpt from Perry's presentation.

> We . . . find that consciousness is a species of function, exercised by an organism. The organism is correlated with an environment, from which it evolved, and on which it acts. Consciousness is a selective response to a pre-existing and independently existing environment. There must be something to be responded to if there is to be any response. The spatial and temporal distribution of bodies in its field of action, and the more abstract logical and mathematical relationships which this field contains,

[7] For an exposition of Perry's argument, see the chapter "A Realistic Theory of Mind," in his *Present Philosophical Tendencies,* New York: Longmans, Green and Company, 1912.
[8] See: Perry, *op. cit.,* p. 319 ff.

determine the possible objects of consciousness. The actual objects of consciousness are selected from this manifold of possibilities in obedience to the various exigencies of life.[9]

Not all the new realists found this form of behaviorism acceptable. Montague, in the article mentioned above, specifically rejected as wrong the view of both Holt and Perry and his essay includes a short criticism of the behavioristic interpretation of the realistic theory of knowledge. Various rifts continued to occur, not only within the new realist group but also among other realists who had not allied themselves with the original new realists. Probably the most important development in this respect was the emergence of a group whose members called themselves "critical realists." Members of this group could not agree with various aspects of the new realism—particularly with its various theories of knowledge. In 1920 this group published a book, *Essays in Critical Realism*.[10]

The critical realists rejected the epistemological monism of neo-realism and returned to the dualism of subject and object. In order to account for the relation of subject and object in cognition this form of realism introduced the idea of essences that mediate between the knower and the known and also the idea that objects are *represented* in consciousness rather than being presented directly, as the new realists had maintained.

Critical realism was an important development in twentieth century philosophy and it claimed some of the ablest philosophical minds of the earlier part of the century. However, our concern here is not with the history of philosophy but with the relation of a resurgent realism with the conservative theory of education. It is difficult to find any direct influence of the critical realists on educational theory, although there well may have been certain indirect influences. Since evidence for any direct connection is lacking, we will not concern ourselves with the analyses of critical realism.

Our main concern in the rest of this chapter will be with the development in this century of what may be called "scientific realism" and with an assessment of the influence this philosophical position has on educational theory. Our thesis is that the new realism of the earlier part of the century played an important part in subsequent development of

[9] See: *op. cit.*, pp. 322–23.
[10] Durant Drake, ed., New York: The Macmillan Company, 1920. The original critical realist group was composed of: Durant Drake, Arthur O. Lovejoy, James B. Pratt, Arthur K. Rogers, Roy W. Sellars, Charles A. Strong, and George Santayana.

a realistic philosophical doctrine that finds much of its substance in the physical sciences. Some evidence in support of this has already been presented, particularly in the behavioristic interpretation of cognition advanced by some of the new realists. We will have more to say about the connection between scientific realism and psychological behaviorism, but before we pass to that we should make certain additional observations about the scientific realism of the present century.[11]

In the first place, scientific realism tends to be naturalistic in its ontology. In this sense, naturalism means that the cosmos exists in and of itself and that no supernatural power or force of any kind is necessary to account for either the existence of the natural world or its operation. Reality, then, means the sum total of all things and events that exist in space and time and whatever regularities occur are parts of the system and not imposed from without. The term naturalism, however, is not synonymous with materialism, although the two terms are sometimes used interchangeably in common speech. As a doctrine, materialism represents the effort to reduce everything to matter and to posit some ultimate irreducible substance as the basis for all reality. It is perhaps possible to say that all materialists are naturalists, but it is not necessarily true that all naturalists are materialists.

In the second place, scientific realism holds that the most dependable knowledge is scientific knowledge—that is, knowledge established by the techniques and processes of scientific method. The purpose of inquiry is to uncover the real character of the processes of nature, the laws that govern the relations of things and events. In this sense, facts exist prior to and independent of their being known. To know the truth means literally to *dis*cover it, that is, to reveal something that is already there. We will have more to say about the realistic account of truth a little later. In the meantime, we will take a further look at the relation of realism to psychological behaviorism for it is in this area that realism has had a significant impact on the conservative tradition in education.

[11] Another kind of development in realism has occurred in this century. This is the movement in which Mr. John Wild of Harvard University has taken the primary leadership. The most definite statement by the group participating in this movement is to be found in Wild, ed., *The Return to Reason*, Chicago: Henry Regnery Company, 1953. A full discussion of this form of realism will be postponed until the chapter on perennialism. Mr. Wild has had considerable to say that indicates his agreement with essentialism on various practical matters of education (see ante, pp. 86–87). But Wild's interpretation of realistic philosophy, which presumably is related to his theories of education, represents a return to a more orthodox Aristotelian realism, which seems to the present author, at least, to be better discussed along with other theories that take their direction from classical sources.

PSYCHOLOGICAL BEHAVIORISM

The first great achievements of science were largely in the area of the physical sciences. Sophisticated application of the processes of empirical observation and experimentation to the phenomena of human behavior did not occur in any significant degree until the latter part of the nineteenth century. Many of the controversies in educational theory, and much of the internal stress in the conservative tradition itself, may be traced to the development of such behavioral sciences as psychology and sociology. The important developments in these fields have occurred mostly in the present century.

Historically, psychology has been regarded as one of the branches of philosophy. The methods employed by various philosophers who have concerned themselves with human nature and human conduct (this includes most of the important ones) involved mostly speculation and introspection, usually combined with common sense observations that sometimes were acute. Since speculative thought necessarily starts with some *a priori* principles, much that went on under the name of psychology was really a product of deductive logical analysis. Another approach was the effort to arrive at certain general principles through introspection and logical induction. The familiar philosophical terms of reason, mind, will, cognition, etc., provided the basic categories of psychological investigation. The dominance of absolute idealism in the nineteenth century determined in large measure the character of psychological investigation.[12]

Our concern here is not with the history of psychology and it will be sufficient to note that at the same time the new realists were busily clearing away the metaphysical and epistemological lumber left by idealism, some psychologists were engaged in a similar task in their domain. One of the most noted of these psychologists was Edward L. Thorndike.[13]

---

[12] An interesting example of this may be found in Josiah Royce's *Outlines of Psychology*, New York: The Macmillan Company, 1904. Royce was one of the greatest of American idealists. In the editor's introduction to Royce's book, Nicholas Murray Butler listed what he conceived to be noteworthy problems in psychology: "How and by what warrant do I pass from a knowledge of my own mental states to a knowledge and interpretation of the mental states of others? What are the primary evidences of mind? Into what and how few simplest units can my own complex mental states be broken up? What are the processes of mental growth and development, and what laws govern them?" (p. xxvi)

[13] Thorndike is chosen as the example here partly because of his eminence as a psychologist and partly because of his influence on educational theory and practice in America. It can perhaps be argued that there were other psychologists equal in

Thorndike's interests lay in experimental work and were conditioned by the changing climate in psychology. Traditionally, the subject matter of psychology was considered to be *mind*, its structure and functions, but under the influence of scientific methodology psychologists more and more were coming to think that the real subject matter of psychology must be *behavior*.[14] So long as psychologists deal with "mind" they are practically driven to introspection as their basic method. Mind cannot be observed—some say it cannot even be defined. The "contents" of mind, by definition, are private and subjective. On the other hand, *behavior* is objective and observable. If it is both public and observable it may perhaps be capable of measurement, perhaps predictable, and ultimately even controllable. At least, it is capable of being studied objectively and experimentally. Ideas of this kind were stimulating psychologists in their experimental work with animal and human subjects. Thorndike's early work was with animal subjects and his invention of the "puzzle box" to study animal behavior is regarded as one of the important contributions to psychological technique.

At this point we may note certain agreements—or at least similarities—between leading ideas in the philosophy of the new realists and in the developing behavioristic psychology. A passage from one of Thorndike's books in which he summarized his position will serve as a point of departure:

All human activity is *reactivity*. For every action there is a definite incentive or cause. Activity is not the result of a sort of spontaneous combustion; it is the response to stimulation. The total state of affairs by which a man is at any time influenced is called the *stimulus* or *situation* and whatever action results—attention, perception, thought, feeling, emotion, glandular secretion, or muscular movement—is called the *reaction* or the *response*.[15]

If we compare this statement cited above with that of Ralph Barton Perry, making some allowance for the differences of vocabulary among philosophers and psychologists, we find similarities with respect to the following points:

---

stature to Thorndike during the early decades of the century. It is, however, difficult to argue that any of them had the impact on education that he has had.

[14] For an excellent discussion of the development and present status of behaviorism see: B. F. Skinner, "Behaviorism at Fifty," *Science*, 140:951–8 (May 31, 1963). In this article Mr. Skinner identifies behaviorism as a *philosophy of science* concerned with psychological method and subject matter.

[15] Edward L. Thorndike and A. I. Gates, *Elementary Principles of Education*, New York: The Macmillan Company, 1930, p. 62. Italics are in the original.

1. Behavior is a process of reacting to stimuli. (Those functions called "consciousness," "awareness," etc. are behaviors.)
2. The presence of a stimulus presupposes the existence of some objective environmental state of affairs.
3. Behavior is always caused; it is never spontaneous (i.e., "un-caused").
4. The character of the response is a function of the nature of the stimulus field (the "situation").

Now in consideration of these ideas we see that what the psychologist calls *learning* and what the philosopher calls *knowing* are held to be *responses* of the organism to an objective environmental condition. One of the concerns of the new realism was to emphasize the independence of this external reality from any of the processes of consciousness, while to the psychologists this principle was more or less axiomatic. Whether we adopt the psychological or the philosophical term, the process of learning *or* the process of knowing is a process of reacting to stimulation. Every mental act from the most primitive and elementary to the most complex and sophisticated can be explained in terms of the basic $S \rightarrow R$ pattern. Learning (knowing) is the formation of bonds or connections between specific stimuli and specific responses. This theory is summed up by Thorndike in the following passage:

> I read the facts which psychologists report about adjustment, configurations, drives, integrations, purposes, tensions, and the like, and all of these facts seem to me to be reducible, so far as concerns their powers to influence the course of thought or feeling or action, to connections and readiness. Learning is connecting. The mind is man's connection system. Purposes are as mechanical in their nature and action as anything else is.[16]

Other examples of the similarity between behaviorism in psychology and in the new realism could be cited; however, we have perhaps seen enough for our present purpose. We are not attempting to show that the resurgence of realistic philosophy was the *cause* of the development of psychological behaviorism, nor that such developments in psychology were the *cause* of the revival of interest in philosophical realism. The most defensible thesis would seem to be that both these developments in intellectual life were the result of the increasing and diversified influence of science on cultural life. Given the progress science had made in the physical realm and the far-reaching changes in outlook it had engendered, it was all but inevitable that sooner or later its influence would

[16] Edward L. Thorndike, *Human Learning*, New York: The Century Company, 1931, p. 122.

be felt with full force in the fields that deal with human behavior. Though formidable road blocks were thrown up periodically by idealistic philosophers and by theology, in retrospect it seems clear that none of these barriers could have been sufficient to keep scientific method out of a consideration of the nature of man.

We have seen some evidence of a close resemblance between psychological behaviorism and that interpretation of neo-realism advocated by Holt and Perry. However, as we have also seen, not all the new realists agreed with the behavioristic interpretation of consciousness, and some of the early twentieth century realists did not agree with the epistemological monism that the new realists advocated. However, it can be argued that the whole intellectual climate of a resurgent realism really worked in favor of the development of scientific philosophy. All approaches to psychology that make use of scientific method are in some measure behavioristic—at least in their methodology. This is not to say that there are no real differences among the various "schools" of contemporary psychology for assuredly there are. All these "schools," however, find agreement that the subject matter of psychological investigation is *behavior* and that the methods used in studying behavior should be empirical. It is submitted that such an approach to the phenomena of human behavior will not flourish in a cultural setting that is dominated by idealistic conceptions of mind and self. We have historical evidence that when the cultural focus is on the transcendent and supernatural, psychology—if it can be said to exist at all under such conditions—will find its area of interest in those aspects of human nature that are alleged to be transcendent and supernatural. Certainly this was the case with idealism in the nineteenth century.

In Chapter II it was pointed out that one of the fundamental presuppositions of science is the principle of uniformity; that is, whenever the same antecedent conditions are given, the same results will occur. In the present time it is widely acknowledged that such a presupposition is fundamental in the natural sciences. If human psychology is to be a natural science, it must operate within the general canons of scientific method. It must be naturalistic in its orientation; it must be empirical in its methodology; and it must subscribe to the principle of uniformity.

It is submitted that the resurgence of realism in philosophy was generally beneficent to these developments. The principle of independence does not necessarily imply naturalism, although it certainly can be consistent with a naturalistic outlook. A presentative theory of knowledge does not necessarily imply behaviorism, though this theory can be (and was) interpreted in behavioristic terms by some realists. In addition, there is another strain in realistic philosophy that can be traced far back into its history and which is of importance to our analysis. This is the emphasis that realism places on regularity and lawfulness. We will now give some attention to this matter.

THE EMPHASIS ON REGULARITY AND LAWFULNESS

Men have always been impressed by the fact that in many respects nature exhibits regularity in its working. The earth always moves in the same direction on its axis; the sun always rises in the east and disappears in the west; water always flows downhill; unsupported objects always fall toward the center of the earth; and so on and on for all the observed regularities that even ordinary experience reveals. This awareness of the lawfulness of nature is common to all men, whatever philosophy they may profess, or, for that matter, whether they profess any at all.

There are at least two kinds of intellectual challenge inherent in the observed regularities of nature. One of these challenges is scientific—the challenge to observe, and classify, and express these regularities in unequivocal (preferably mathematical) terms. When this has been done we can speak of them as the *laws of nature*. These laws are very powerful intellectual tools because they enable us to make predictions of events before these events actually occur. If we can predict, we may well be in a position to exert control over events—at least in some measure. And so, we can list the primary concerns of science as observing, analyzing, classifying, quantifying, predicting, experimenting.

As we have already observed, the intellectual enterprise we call science depends on the principle of uniformity. Unless this principle holds, it seems idle to speak of the possibility of accurate prediction of future events—which, of course, must always be done on the basis of what has been learned from past experience. We may take passing note that the uniformities of nature have always tended to impress those with a predilection for philosophical realism. This was true even with the classic realism of Aristotle in a time when scientific method, as we understand that term, was unknown. Aristotle himself was a great observer and classifier of natural phenomena and his studies in natural science ranged from astronomy to zoology. The working scientist today, of course, is apt to take the principle of uniformity as an axiom and to spend very little time speculating on its ultimate significance in cosmology.

The second challenge inherent in our awareness of the regularities of nature is philosophical. Men are inclined to speculate on what the meaning of natural regularity is for our total grasp of the cosmos. They consider such questions as: Is nature in and of itself characterized by uniformity, regularity, and dependability? Do the orderliness and regularity that characterize events in physical nature also extend to other kinds of phenomena; as for example, individual human behavior or the behavior of men living in social groups? Are there universal laws that govern human behavior in the same sense that the laws of physics govern the behavior of physical bodies or economic laws govern the operations of the market? Behaviorists in psychology are inclined to answer such questions in the affirmative, although they may differ with each other over many details. Under this view, the purpose of psychological science is to discover the laws that govern various aspects of human behavior and to state them in the same general terms as physicists state physical laws. Although psychology is a young science, compared, for example, with physics, it will become a mature science as it uncovers and quantifies the laws of human behavior. When this has been achieved to a reasonable degree, we can expect to develop a technology for behavior control and utilization comparable to the technology we have already achieved for using physical forces for cultural ends. This will be educational technology in the broadest sense.

As we have already indicated, there are today people who find sufficient evidence to believe that we are now in a position to construct an educational technology based on the achievements of scientific psychology. In fact, there are many who maintain that significant achievements—programmed learning, for example—have already been accomplished. This is often held to presage a great revolutionary movement in educational practice. It is also often pointed out that similar advances in the understanding of emotional behavior are being made and the control of these processes by chemical and other means is a certainty. For the first time in human history, it is said, men see the possibility (as distinguished from the desirability) of a society in which wrong-doing need not exist and in which truth and justice can prevail. Men have always dreamed of such a utopia, but only in recent years has the

possibility of achieving it seemed reasonable. Thorndike himself foresaw the possibility in the first decade of the century:

> A complete science of psychology would tell every fact about everyone's
> intellect and character and behavior, would tell the cause of every change
> in human nature, would tell the result which every educational force . . .
> would have. It would aid us to use human beings for the world's welfare
> with the same surety of result that we now have when we use falling
> bodies or chemical elements. In proportion as we get such a science we
> shall become masters of our own souls as we are now masters of heat
> and light. Progress towards such a science is being made.[17]

A few years later another famous behaviorist proclaimed:

> . . . Give me a
> dozen healthy infants, well-formed, and my own specified world to bring
> them up in and I'll guarantee to take anyone at random and train him
> to become any type of specialist I might select—doctor, lawyer, artist,
> merchant-chief, and yes, even beggar-man and thief, regardless of his
> talents, penchants, tendencies, abilities, vocations, and race of his an-
> cestors. I am going beyond my facts and I admit it, but so have the
> advocates of the contrary and they have been doing it for many thousands
> of years. Please note that when this experiment is made I am to be
> allowed to specify the way the children are to be brought up and the
> type of world they have to live in.[18]

With the continued development of psychological science, the conviction has become stronger that the good society, brought about by
psychological science and technology, can be a reality any time we are
willing to give the behavioral scientist the degree of control he needs.
The most famous contemporary exponent of this idea is Mr. B. F.
Skinner, whose novel, *Walden Two*,[19] describes a utopia which has been
achieved by scientific management of children's behavior from a very
early age. This book has excited the most diverse reactions in its readers,
ranging from complete acceptance to what can only be described as
utter revulsion.

[17] Edward L. Thorndike, "The Contribution of Psychology to Education," *Journal
of Educational Psychology*, 1:6 (January, 1910).
[18] John B. Watson, *Behaviorism*, New York: W. W. Norton and Company, 1924,
p. 82. In his article, "Behaviorism at Fifty," B. F. Skinner credits Watson with
the first statement that psychology should be viewed as a science of behavior.
Skinner acknowledges the importance of Thorndike's contributions but insists that
he remained a "mentalist."
[19] B. F. Skinner, *Walden Two*, New York: The Macmillan Company, 1948. This
book was the main target of Mr. Joseph Wood Krutch's *The Measure of Man*,
see ante, p. 78.

It is interesting to speculate that an inhabitant of another part of the universe visiting this planet and observing the varied reactions to the proposals of the behavioral scientists would be puzzled. He might well wonder why so many people resist the idea of improving individual and social life by careful scientific control of behavior. Why do we resist the idea of utopia, which, we are assured, is no longer a dream but a potential reality? Our imaginary observer would not have to inquire very far to learn that there is more to the objections than the argument that the behavioral scientists are overstating their case—that they do not really know enough as yet to establish Walden Two or any other allegedly utopian society.

The real objection is to the very idea that human behavior *should be* manipulated in such manner. We would be forced to explain to our visitor, if he could not ferret it out for himself, that some of our oldest traditions about man eliminate the possibility of his being managed and shaped like an ingot of iron or a lump of clay. And we should have to advise him that these same traditions would brand the ambitions of the scientists as the ultimate immorality—worse even than slavery, which at least was only able to dominate man's physical body, not his spirit. In other words, the real objection is ethical, not scientific, and a very significant element in the whole controversy is over the question of determinism as this applies to human nature.[20]

HUMAN NATURE

There is nothing new about the idea that the original nature of man needs to be altered and shaped in desirable directions by external forces. Certainly most, if not all, systems of formal education and most child-rearing practices are designed on the assumption that the behavior of human beings can be managed by exerting certain causal forces on the behavior of children. Although many people insist that there is more to education than training, there are not many who would argue that education does not involve training in some form. To train a child means to alter his "natural" behavior by causing him to react in certain

---

[20] A book of great interest on the problem of determinism is: Sidney Hook, ed., *Determinism and Freedom in the Age of Modern Science*, New York: Collier Books, 1961. See also: Sidney Hook, "Moral Freedom in a Determined World," in his *The Quest for Being*, New York: Dell Publishing Company, Inc., 1963, p. 26 ff.

ways to given stimuli and by fixing these responses through appropriate reinforcement.

Over against this doctrine is another, also well known in the history of education, that holds education is fundamentally the unfolding of a design that is inherent in the organism. The most famous advocate of this position was Rousseau, who held that education should be "negative" in the sense that the growing child should be shielded from unfavorable environmental influences and left to develop "according to nature." Another famous advocate of these sentiments was Froebel, who conceived the development of the child to be analogous to the growth of a plant which needs no "training" but only a favorable environment in which to unfold its inherent nature. Hence, Froebel called his institution "Kindergarten." Both Rousseau and Froebel maintained that human nature is inherently good, at least in the beginning, and the evil that enters into man's nature is the result of evil environmental influences of various kinds.

We have already seen enough to know that this conception of human nature is not acceptable in the general tradition of social conservatism, that it is rejected by contemporary educational essentialism, and that it is out of harmony with behavioristic psychology and the scientific realism discussed in this chapter. There are some differences, however, over the basic reasons for the common objections.

Social conservatives, in the original tradition of Burke, are more apt to object on theological and metaphysical grounds than on scientific grounds, believing as they do that a total conception of human nature is revealed by theology and philosophy. The literature of contemporary essentialism contains both philosophical-theological and scientific arguments. Those essentialists who are affected by scientific realism, of course, advance scientific arguments against the doctrines of the original goodness of human nature and human development as unfolding of an inherent pattern.

Behaviorists in psychology by and large agree that the "original nature of man" is insufficient and must be developed along desirable lines which ultimately are determined by society. Ideas about the character of this original nature have changed over the years. Thorndike, for example, held the view that original nature is a complex of inherited tendencies, instincts, and capacities that are capable of being investigated and described objectively. A considerable amount of his early work was devoted to this effort and he came eventually to the conclusion that the purpose of education is the modification of this original human nature—to make it better.[21] He wished to be very clear that the original nature of man could not be conceived as right:

> The original tendencies of man have not been right, are not right, and probably never will be right. By them alone few of the best wants in human life would have been felt and fewer still satisfied . . . Man is thus eternally altering himself to suit himself. His nature is not right in his own eyes. Only one thing in it, indeed, is unreservedly good, the power to make it better. This power, the power of learning or modification in favor of the satisfying, the capacity represented by the law of effect, is the essential principle of reason and right in the world.[22]

Since Thorndike's time, behaviorists have modified their ideas about the character of man's original nature, but they agree by and large that the educational problem is the alteration of this original nature through environmental means. A major difference between the earlier and the later behaviorism is that the latter conceives original nature to be more plastic and less determined by inherited instinctive patterns. This position is seen in extreme form in the reference from J. B. Watson cited earlier in this chapter.[23] Mr. Skinner does not go as far as Watson in discounting the importance of inherited factors. In *Walden Two* the point is made that even though the children have all had the same environment since birth, the range of intelligence quotients within the 10-year age group is about the same as in the general population. Thus, environment can work only with the physical structure that nature provides and cannot go beyond the limits provided by inheritance.

Regardless of scientific differences on the "nature-nurture" question, behavioristic psychologists agree that the original nature of any individual (or of man in general) is not "right" in the sense that it is insufficient for social life or for the preservation of the species, much less for achievement of the cultural refinements that constitute civilization. This original nature must be modified and, of course, in all cultures this always has been done in some way. Before the advent of behavioral science these ways have generally been crude and ineffective, based usually on rule of thumb, folk wisdom, and superstition.

In the *Republic* Plato proposes that a just society is one in which each person does what he is fitted to do and does not interfere with the

---

[21] Edward L. Thorndike, *Educational Psychology: Briefer Course*, New York: Teachers College, Columbia University, 1927, p. 3.
[22] *Ibid.*, p. 124. Thorndike's views here are reminiscent of an observation by Thomas Hobbes, seventeenth century materialist philosopher, that in the "natural condition" the life of man is "solitary, poor, nasty, brutish, and short."
[23] See also: Watson, *op. cit.*, Chapter V and VI.

work of others. He developed an elaborate plan for modifying the original nature of the citizens of the Republic so this condition might be achieved. His insight was good enough to indicate that the way to achieve this is through careful environmental control, but there is much about the details of his scheme that today appears crude and unimaginative. There is good reason to think that the Republic would never have worked, even if Plato's scheme had ever been put to action.

It was not until the advent of behavioral science that men have claimed to know how to modify the original nature of man with precision and efficiency. It is possible that we now could create the Republic, if scientists could be given the control they would require and provided, of course, that we actually want something like that utopia. Now the fact is that conservatives have often held the Republic up as a kind of model for what a good society would be. They have admired the Spartan austerity on which it was modeled; they have agreed with the rigid class structure inherent in it; they have, of course, thought it a supreme example of a state governed by the wisest and best men. Now that something like this is within our grasp—or so we are told—many conservatives draw back in consternation.

Apparently, it is one thing to accept application of behavioral science in the form of programmed material for a book or a teaching machine (which many, but not all, essentialists do) and something else to subscribe to plans for a really comprehensive control and development of human nature through scientific means. Thus, one of the points of real stress for contemporary essentialism lies in competing conceptions of the nature of man. This tradition, that developed originally out of prescientific conceptions of human nature, now finds itself attempting to embrace the humanism of the older conservatism with the behaviorism of the scientific realists. In this respect, at least, essentialism is a house divided.

TRUTH AS CORRESPONDENCE

It will be recalled that one of the requirements for a consistent and coherent essentialism is a conception of truth that assures us that our ideas potentially are capable of being judged true or false in terms of some dependable criterion. Such a criterion will enable us to transmit only true ideas in the schools, or at least will assure a minimum of error. Knowledge of such a criterion will also enable us to transmit to students a method for discriminating between truth and error themselves, thus helping to make their own intellectual processes more rigorous.

We have already seen that idealism offers for such a criterion the principle of coherence. Our ideas are true to the extent that they are consistent with the body of truth already existing and accepted. The idealist thinks that coherence is the most rigorous method of proof possible, particularly since it is the method of mathematics, the most rigorous of all systems of knowledge.

The realist, while agreeing that coherence has a part to play in scientific and even in common sense knowledge, does not think it can be the final criterion for truth. If all knowledge were like pure mathematics, in which all relations are internal (that is, within the system) then coherence would be the ultimate and only criterion for truth. But we now know that realists do not agree that all knowledge is like pure mathematics. The principle of independence implies directly that some relations are external. Both common sense and science deal with matters in which external relations predominate. Therefore, coherence is inadequate to help us distinguish between the truth and falsity of ideas outside of purely logical systems.

Accordingly, realism advocates a criterion for truth that respects the external character of relations and gives our judgments a character of objectivity and precision that, according to realists, is not possible with any other method. The criterion offered by realistic philosophies is that of *correspondence*. This means that any idea (proposition) we may hold is true to the extent *that it corresponds with the reality to which it refers*. Thus, an idea A, which I hold to be true and which is about some fact B, is true if the idea, A, corresponds to the fact, B. The realist insists that this is what our common sense tells us, anyway. If I believe that there is the sum of $2.87 in the sugar bowl on the top shelf of the pantry, this belief is true if the sugar bowl really does contain that amount. If it contains more or less than that amount, the idea is false. It may be, of course, that I would like to think that the sugar bowl contains $2,000.00 but what I wish does not affect the actual contents in any way. The principle of independence, along with ordinary common sense, tells us that what is actually in that sugar bowl has nothing to do with what I think about it or what I desire.

It is possible that I do not know how much money is in the sugar bowl. I may have been putting money in and taking it out without keeping account of the transactions, or other members of the family may have been doing the same. Whatever sum is actually in the bowl is *a fact* and it is a fact whether anybody knows how much is in the bowl. I may believe (or estimate) that the actual sum is $2.87 but there is only one way of knowing whether this belief is true and that, as anyone over the age of three knows, is to determine *the fact* of the contents of the sugar bowl—in this case to count the money.

Now, if we substitute the universe for the sugar bowl and the substantial entities of the universe for the coins in the sugar bowl, we have the same kind of situation, only on the largest possible scale. The truths of common sense and the truths of science must be established in the same way we established whether our belief about the contents of the sugar bowl was true or false. For example, some scientists may accept the hypothesis that living organisms exist on the planet Mars and this hypothesis may be consistent with certain data that are believed to be reliable. Thus, coherence lends credibility to the hypothesis, but it does not establish it as true or false. The only way the hypothesis can be validated is to determine whether it squares with the reality on Mars. If it is *a fact* that organic life exists on Mars then the hypothesis is true; if it is not a fact, then the hypothesis lacks correspondence with the reality to which it refers and is therefore false. Knowing, then, is the uncovering of the realities (facts) that exist independently of their being known and truth is a property ideas have when they correspond to the realities to which they refer.

In thinking about this we must be sure to understand that: 1) *Facts* are not true or false. They are what they are, and what they are has nothing to do with whether anybody knows what they are. 2) Truth can only be a property of judgments (propositions, ideas). 3) The correspondence is established between the judgment and the fact. The realist, by and large, is willing to let the argument rest at this point. As he sees it, correspondence is a rigorous, objective criterion that squares with common sense and scientific experience. It is applicable in any kind of intellectual enterprise in which the rigorous testing of propositions is involved. It enables us to know what is true and what is false, and thus to act accordingly.

We should take note, however, that the idea of correspondence as the criterion for truth is not immune to criticism. There are several kinds of criticism possible, but perhaps the most telling one is that originally advanced by Aristotle. We will use the money in the sugar bowl to illustrate this objection. My judgment that there is $2.87 in the sugar bowl is true if it corresponds to the fact that there is that amount of money in the bowl. Either I know how much money is in the bowl or I do not know it. If I do know that there is $2.87 in the bowl, then what point is there in my making a judgment about what I already know to be a fact? On the other hand, if I do not know how much money is in the sugar bowl, how can I possibly know whether my idea corresponds to the actual fact?

There is, of course, a common sense answer to this that occurs immediately. If I don't know how much money is in the bowl, why don't I go look to see? But this suggestion inserts something into the argument for correspondence that was not there originally. Namely, the suggestion is that certain operations are necessary in order to validate the judgment. In this case the indicated operations are going to the sugar bowl and counting the money. Without these operations our judgment is either redundant or it is indeterminate.

Some critics of the correspondence theory think this is a serious objection. It may seem only common sense to say in the example above, go count the money in the sugar bowl, but there are other kinds of judgments that do not fit this simple factual matter and, presumably, correspondence is the criterion for the truth of all cognitive statements. If I say that penicillin is a more effective drug than castor oil for treating pneumonia, how does the principle of correspondence hold here? With what must I establish correspondence in order to validate this judgment? What an example of this kind shows, say various critics of the criterion of correspondence, is that correspondence if it is a useful criterion at all, is useful only in certain kinds of cases and realists are overstating the case badly when they hold it to be the universal test of truth.

Adherents of the theory, of course, hold that in spite of such objections the criterion of correspondence satisfies the demands of common sense and the more rigorous demands of science and philosophy. It is based on the realistic doctrine that we can know the world as it is in its own nature and the ideas we have about the world are true when they correspond to the facts of the world.

THE PROBLEM OF VALUE

When we come to the way in which realists look at the problem of value we find a variety of approaches. It is completely impossible to state *the* realist position on value, for there is a considerable variety of opinion on this matter. In this section we will examine briefly the most important realistic theories of value and consider these with respect to various aspects of the conservative tradition in education.

Perhaps the oldest, and certainly one of the most important realist conceptions of the source of value is the view that goes somewhat as follows: Just as the processes of nature are governed by universal laws, so is there also a lawfulness inherent in human nature. The law that governs the development of man demands that certain conditions be supplied so that the common human nature in which we all share may be realized. Now the conditions that are necessary for the completion of human nature are the same for all men and, in the words of one of the most distinguished advocates of this view:

> The invariable, universal pattern of action, individual as well as social, required for the completion of human nature is called *the moral law* or *natural law*. By self-observation every individual has some minimal knowledge of it. By disciplined study of human nature and the events of history, this knowledge may be increased and clarified. Such knowledge is the only trustworthy guide for human action.[24]

Under this view, ethics, which is the philosophy of value applied to human conduct, is built on objective foundations. What is right for man and what man needs in order to realize his nature is not a matter of vague speculation or opinion. By the use of our powers of observation and reason we can know what human nature is and what is needed to complete it. We can *know* that there is a natural (moral) law in the same sense that there are laws of physics. And just as physics is the only reliable knowledge for guiding human action in its dealings with physical nature, so knowledge of the moral law is the only dependable guide for action in dealing with human nature.

It is important to note that such a view as this can be held only by those who accept the basic realistic theses: a) The existence of a world independent of consciousness; b) The fact that we can know the world as it is in its essential nature. In this respect Wild's ethical theory is as consistent with his realism as anything can be. The natural law is a *moral imperative*. It tells us what must be. But it is an imperative that is grounded in objective existence, and although idealists (Kant is the leading example) may also speak of a moral imperative, they are unable to demonstrate that such an imperative is grounded on objective knowledge of the nature of things, or so the realist thinks.

[24] John Wild, "Education and Human Society: A Realistic View," in Brubacher, ed., *op. cit.*, p. 18. Mr. Wild's views are elaborated more fully in his *Introduction to Realist Philosophy*, New York: Harper and Brothers, 1948.

However, Wild's realism—and hence his ethical theory—represents, as we observed earlier, a return to the orthodox realism of Aristotle and the classic tradition. Ultimately, it rests on a view of nature that is essentially teleological in character. This means that all existences move toward some final fulfillment that is inherent in their natures, and it is in this way that the regularities of the laws of nature operate. The teleological aspect of Wild's realism puts it out of harmony with much of contemporary science and with those varieties of realism that are closely related to modern science. Scientists attempt resolutely to eliminate teleological concepts from their inquiries and particularly to eliminate any trace of the notion that the processes of nature are explained by some predetermined final end. We will have occasion to return to this classical conception of nature and ethics in the chapter on the perennial philosophy, a body of thought in which it plays a leading part. In the meantime we will consider some other approaches of realists to the theory of ethics.[25]

One of the most influential contributions to ethical theory in this century was the work of George E. Moore. Moore was a British philosopher and, along with Bertrand Russell, a member of the British group of new realists that flourished about the same time as its American counterpart and whose philosophic interests were similar in some respects to those of the American group. Moore's most famous contribution to ethical philosophy is his book, *Principia Ethica*[26], in which he analyzes the meaning of the term "good," criticizes certain traditional interpretations of that term, and discusses the practical impact of ethical theory for human conduct.

The most important aspect of Moore's analysis is his contention that "good" in the intrinsic sense, is a simple, indefinable quality. In Moore's opinion, good is like a color. He points out that yellow, as a color, is a quality that is simple and incapable of being reduced by analysis to anything else. A person who has never known the color yellow cannot have explained to him what that color is because it is a

[25] Mr. Wild has specifically denied that the theory of natural law depends on a teleological conception of nature. See his *Plato's Modern Enemies and the Theory of Natural Law*, Chicago: University of Chicago Press, 1953, Chapter 3 and specifically p. 72 ff. We will leave it to the reader to make his own judgment on the merits of opposing views. A common meaning of the term "teleological" is that events in nature are explained in terms of their results, not of their antecedent causes. The difference between mechanism and teleology is that the former explains events in terms of "efficient causes" and the latter explains them in terms of "final causes."

[26] Cambridge University Press, first published in 1903. Citations here are to the paperback edition published in 1959.

simple notion incapable of definition. Yellow is simply a quality that can be predicated of some objects and that is all anybody can say about it. In the same way, good is also a simple irreducible quality that can be predicated of some objects and it, too, is indefinable and incapable of analysis. Thus, some objects have goodness among the qualities they possess and some do not. There is nothing in Moore's theory that rules out our recognizing objects that possess good as one of their qualities, but their possession of goodness does not depend on our liking or desiring these objects.[27]

Moore's analysis was directed against two kinds of ethical theory, both of which have a long history. The first of these is what is generally called "naturalistic" ethics. Naturalistic ethical theories invariably involve the effort to reduce good to something else, particularly something that is open to study by empirical method. Moore mentions specifically in this connection: 1) The very old idea that good is equatable with pleasure (hedonism); 2) That good is the same as what is "natural" (as in Rousseau, for example); and 3) The notion that that which is more highly evolved in the process of evolution is good (as in Herbert Spencer). All of these approaches to ethical theory are, in the opinion of Moore, examples of "the naturalistic fallacy." All of them are fallacious because their advocates have confused the question of what the term *good* means with the entirely different question of what things *possess good as a quality*. The first of these is the ethical question and the second is a scientific question. If there really is a subject matter called ethics, then the two questions are genuinely different and it is a fallacy to try to make them identical.[28]

The second target of Moore's criticism was the approach to ethical theory that he calls "metaphysical." Metaphysical ethics are built on the belief that good is equatable with that which is "ultimately real." By definition, metaphysical, as a term, refers to something that lies outside the natural order and, if knowable at all, must be known by logical deduction from some *a priori* principle, since it cannot be known by ordinary sensory processes. Further, in order to know what good is we must first know what is ultimately real. Here, Moore points out, the metaphysical approach to ethics also falls into the naturalistic fallacy because what is being maintained is that the question, "What is real?" has some necessary connection with, "What is good?"[29] And, in

[27] *Ibid.*, pp. 7–8.
[28] *Ibid.*, Chapter II.
[29] *Ibid.*, pp. 113–114.

Moore's view, it is as much a fallacy to attempt to analyze good in terms of metaphysical concepts of being as it is for naturalistic philosophers to define good as pleasure.

Beyond this, Moore points out that the metaphysical approach to ethics presupposes that there is only one source of good in the world. If this is true, and if its implications are followed resolutely, we are faced with the conclusion that human effort has nothing to do with the good that exists. However, most ethical systems in some way involve the idea that human action can be (and should be) a force for bringing about good in the world. If this is true, then there is some other source of good besides the metaphysical *a priori*, and this is contradictory of the original thesis that the source of good lies beyond nature. Moore also points out that metaphysics may possibly be of use to us in practical ethics, for it might help us answer the question, "What ought we do?" But, he notes, all the help it can give us here is to aid us in estimating what the future effects of our proposed action will likely be; what metaphysics cannot do is tell us whether these anticipated consequences are good or bad in themselves.

Perhaps we have seen enough of Moore's ideas to understand how effectively his doctrine of good as simple and indefinable cuts at both the metaphysical and naturalistic approaches to ethical theory. Moore's analysis can properly be called a radical break with conventional ethical theory and the *Principia* paved the way for much of the modern analytical approach to ethical theory.

However, when Moore comes to consider the question of practical ethics, we find him taking a much more subdued and traditional approach. He observes that the question with which practical ethics deals is, "What ought we do?" And he insists that this question should be distinguished carefully from the questions, "What is good in itself?" and, "What things are good in themselves?" When we consider the question, "What ought we do?" we should understand that the answer must involve some connection between means and ends. Certain actions must be undertaken to bring about certain results. The answer Moore gives to the question, "What actions should we take?" is that we should do that which promises that the total result of our action will be the best it is possible to achieve.[30] In fact, Moore asserts that all moral laws, so called, are really statements that such and such an act will have good consequences. Moreover, he maintains that there are no moral laws that are self-evident and therefore knowable directly by

[30] *Ibid.*, p. 146 ff.

some intuitive process. All ethical judgments of a practical nature involve a causal relation and are capable of being studied empirically. Therefore, there is something more involved than direct, intuitive apprehension.

Moore points out that there is no way in which we can be absolutely sure that any of our actions will be the best. This is because our knowledge of the causal connections between means and ends is never sufficient to enable us to predict with certainty. In light of this, we may ask, is it possible to develop any rules which, if followed, will usually help us select the best course of conduct and thereby produce the most good?

Moore thinks it is possible to lay down certain rules to guide conduct, so long as we recognize that these rules do not promise certainty but only probability. He thinks the origins of these rules are social in character and that they can be applied profitably only in a cultural context in which they are appropriate. They cannot be universal in character and therefore must be acknowledged as relative to a given social context. Moore thinks the rules should be those that common sense indicates to be usually productive of good and, in addition, those rules that have acquired legal status in society. Moore, in fact, recommends that we adhere to existing custom, even if in some instances we regard it as bad.[31] The probability is that, in the long run, acting in accord with established custom will be most productive of good. Ultimately, of course, the choice of action must be left up to individuals. Moore advises that we will generally choose wisely if we strive for lesser goods in which we have a strong interest rather than for some greater good in which we have no real stake; if we choose that which affects our own interests strongly rather than that which has a wider influence (egoism is a better guide than altruism, he says); and if we strive for goods that can be realized in some immediate time rather than in some remote future. Moore is not impressed by the argument that such advice is advocacy of mere expedience. There is no final distinction between duty and expedience, anyway, for any course of action, whether we call it duty or expedience, can be tested only by the question, "Will it have the best possible effects?"[32]

The contrast between the radical character of Moore's conception of good as a simple, unanalyzable quality and the traditional character of

[31] *Ibid.*, p. 164. Compare this statement with the general stand of the conservative tradition.
[32] *Ibid.*, p. 168.

his practical ethics is striking. It should be pointed out that there is little in his practical ethics that poses any threat to the conservative tradition and a good deal that supports it. True, his attacks on both naturalism and idealism in ethical theory have proved disruptive in those traditions, but when he comes down to cases of practical conduct Moore's advice seems to be supportive of existing institutions and ways of life. The cultural relativism inherent in his practical ethics may be disturbing, particularly to idealists, but it is hard to see how this aspect of his ethical position really poses a threat to cultural conservatism.

We will conclude this section on ethical theory by considering another approach developed by realistic philosophers of this century. This approach is built around the idea that *value is a function of desire or interest*. This means simply that if I desire a thing, that is, have need of it, that thing thereby acquires value. What invests it with value is the fact that I desire it. This principle is often stated concisely as follows: "Value is any object of interest." One of the chief American proponents of this theory is the realist Ralph Barton Perry, whose work we have already had occasion to consider. The analysis presented here is derived primarily from his work.

In the first place, Perry reminds us that there are two basic doctrines of realistic philosophy that must be taken into account in thinking about value theory and he attributes what he calls G. E. Moore's basic error to Moore's misconception of realistic doctrine. These realistic principles are: 1) Consciousness is a kind of relation into which objects can enter without losing their independence or their essential character. This indicates that something can be desired by me without having its original nature altered, but the new relationship it acquires by being an object of my conscious interest or desire invests it with value. Hence, says Perry, it is correct to suppose that the nature of a thing is independent of its possessing value, but it is not correct to suppose that the value any given thing possesses is independent of consciousness.[33] 2) Realism maintains that a proposition is independent of its being judged. If I desire some particular thing, the proposition "I desire A" is, according to Perry, independent of any judgment I or anybody else may make about it. The upshot of the matter is that whenever values exist it is because they stand in relation to some interest.[34]

These considerations of realistic philosophy point to the character of *moral* value. Problems of moral value occur because the relations of

[33] Perry, *op. cit.*, p. 332.
[34] *Ibid.*, p. 333.

interest are complex and often conflicting. In analyzing moral values two ideas must be introduced. These are: 1) rightness and 2) comparative goodness.[35]

When it is necessary to act in order to fulfill an interest, the action that is *right* in these circumstances is that action that is *appropriate*—that is, the action that secures the desired results. Rightness, in this sense, refers to intelligent apprehension of the relation of ends and means, but a right action in this sense is not necessarily a moral action. The moral question arises when there is a conflict of interest.

According to Perry, an act may be right when it helps to fulfill one interest, but it may also be wrong if it detracts from the realization of another interest, and so we have the theory of comparative goodness which is outlined in Perry's own words as follows:

> Now just as an act may be both right and wrong in that it conduces to the fulfillment of one interest and the detriment of another; so it may be doubly right in that it conduces to the fulfillment of two interests . . . If the fulfillment of one interest is good, the fulfillment of two is better; and the fulfillment of all interests is best. Similarly, if the act which conduces to goodness is right, the act that conduces to more goodness is more right, and the act which conduces to most goodness is most right. Morality, then, is *such performance as under the circumstances, and in view of all the interests affected, conduces to most goodness.*[36]

Beyond this, Perry points out that it is possible that various acts may all contribute to the same maximum goodness, and when this is the case, they are all morally right. In addition, and Perry calls this the most important single conclusion, *all values are absolute.* By this is meant that all values are completely independent of any opinion. If I desire something, my desiring it is *a fact* that cannot be changed by any amount of opinion about the matter. In that sense it is absolute.

We may make substantially the same observation about Perry's value theory as we made about that of G. E. Moore; that is, the difference between Perry's radical assertion that a value is any object of interest and the comparatively conservative conception of valuation as the determination of comparative goodness. Perry's value theory, like Moore's, is a slashing attack on traditional conceptions of value—particularly those of idealism. And while the relativism inherent in Perry's position has often been excoriated by moral idealists, it is interesting that Perry, like Moore, is able in the end to assure us that values are absolute in

[35] *Ibid.*, pp. 333–334.
[36] *Ibid.*, p. 334.

character because they are what they are in themselves and are independent of any judgment about them. Thus, Perry's position is capable of satisfying the hankering of the social conservative for absolute value but who at the same time is unable to accept either the metaphysical account furnished by absolute idealism or the teleological character of the classic tradition.

SUMMARY

In this chapter certain ideas of contemporary realistic philosophy have been examined. Our primary intent has been to show that the resurgence of realism in the philosophy of this century has had an effect on the character of the conservative tradition, and more specifically on educational essentialism. It is not an intention here to argue that there is some logical connection between philosophical realism and cultural and educational conservatism such that the latter is necessarily implied by the former. On the other hand, it has been argued at various points in the chapter that the rise of modern realism has made it possible for conservatives to account for certain ideas that are fundamental to a consistent social conservatism and hence to a systematic body of educational doctrines. These ideas are chiefly those relating to certainty in knowledge and in value judgments and the relation of the individual to society. It is submitted that philosophical realism can be made to render answers to the problem of certainty that are more in accord with the temper of many contemporary conservatives, particularly those who are influenced intellectually by natural science.

It seems almost superfluous to say that the current drive to make mathematics and the sciences the dominant subjects in the school curriculum would not have occurred in a society in which the cultural focus was mainly on the transcendent and metaphysical. Modern realism has advertised itself widely as the return to common sense and to science. There is good reason to think that, in education at least, it has had effects of this kind, although it must be admitted that common sense is not always an easy term to define.

Commentators have often pointed out that realism is the philosophy that reveals to us the independent existence of an external world to which we must adapt and on whose terms we must learn to live. Realism assures us that we can know this world as it is in itself and our knowledge of it is the most trustworthy guide to action. The body of truth that generations of rational beings have won by their intellectual effort is the funded capital of culture. The purpose of education is to transmit the truth as it exists to the ignorant and uninformed. We must face up, says the realist, to the stern reality of an external world that is not of our own making. In these days the stern realities that confront us are the threat of alien ideological and military aggression. Persons whose basic instincts are realistic, although their philosophical position may not always be explicit, are present these days in large numbers to insist that education must concern itself chiefly, if not exclusively, with scientific and technological studies.

This condition, as we have already observed, is creating profound changes in the historic character of educational conservatism. And yet, there is still much to bind essentialists in a common front. The controversies over the specific content of the curriculum may often be bitter and frustrating, but conservatism clings resolutely—almost to a man— to the propositions that the purpose of education is the transmission of the essential subject matters, that the art of teaching is the art of transmitting, and that the school is a chief agent of cultural conservation.

PART THREE

The Liberal Protest

*Let us admit the case of the conservative: if we once
start thinking no one can guarantee where we shall
come out, except that many objects, ends and institutions are doomed. Every thinker puts some portion
of an apparently stable world in peril and no one can
wholly predict what will emerge in its place.*

—JOHN DEWEY

From "Characters and Events," quoted in *Intelligence in the Modern World: John Dewey's Philosophy* (Ed. Joseph Ratner), New York: The Modern Library, 1939, p. vi.

CHAPTER SEVEN

Progressivism:

The Liberal Protest

The remainder of this book is devoted to the study of certain traditions in educational theory that are in some way protests against the fundamental character of educational conservatism and its domination of practical educational affairs in America. The major thesis that has been advanced is that essentialism, the conservative tradition in education, has dominated educational practice in this country throughout our national history. It has been pointed out in some detail that the character of the conservative tradition has changed in certain important respects, largely because of the acceleration of cultural change in the present century. That there are severe stresses within conservatism is no secret, and in previous chapters some of the important sources of these strains have been discussed. Our conclusion is, however, that in spite of numerous disruptive conditions, the conservative tradition in education has been able to consolidate its position into one of great strength.

In the course of its history essentialism has had to withstand the impact of certain protest movements, some of which have been potent enough to pose severe threats to educational conservatism. There is not much doubt that the most severe threat to which essentialism has been subjected thus far was that posed by a tradition in education commonly called *progressivism*. In fact, it has been pointed out in an earlier chapter that much of the literature of essentialism published since the end of World War II has been devoted to continuing violent reactions against the threat progressivism once posed. It is our contention, however, that in spite of the great strength the progressive tradition was able to muster at an earlier time in this century, the conservative tradition in education has emerged substantially intact. Whether progressivism or something akin to it may again in some future time pose a new threat is an interesting speculative matter.

Our immediate concern is to analyze the progressive tradition, giving attention to the general social orientation of this tradition, its major educational ideas and the relation of these ideas to underlying philosophical issues. We will begin by considering the general nature of social liberalism and the relation this tradition bears to ideas about education.

THE LIBERAL TRADITION IN AMERICA

Liberalism, as a social and political tradition, resists any rigorous definition and none will be attempted here. Rather we will attempt to describe various aspects of this tradition and at strategic points contrast it with social conservatism. As is the case with all historical traditions, the character of liberalism has changed with the years and in response to the pressures of cultural transition.

The origins of liberalism lie mainly in the eighteenth century and the development of this tradition is closely related to the rise of the middle class. Even before the beginning of the eighteenth century John Locke, the great English philosopher we have already had occasion to mention, had advanced the basic theses of political liberalism. In brief, these theses deny the divine right of kings to govern as they see fit, and substitute instead the idea that society is in reality a contract between citizens and their government. The terms of this contract are that the government is delegated certain power and authority and in return government must protect the natural rights of citizens. These natural rights, according to Locke and numerous political liberals since his time, are life, liberty and property.

Originally, liberalism was a protest movement against the arbitrary interference of institutions, particularly church and state, in the affairs of citizens. Liberalism was a call for men to be free to pursue their own affairs unmolested and to enjoy the civil liberties that are the rights of all. Early in its history, however, the main stream of liberalism split into two branches. One branch was that form of liberal thought whose main emphasis was on freedom in economic activity. The general outlines of this development have already been discussed in Chapter II. In essence, the doctrines of *laissez-faire* capitalism formed the basic core around which economic liberalism formed itself. The major ideas here were the existence of natural economic law, the basic motives in human nature as the desire for personal gain, and the belief that individuals are capable of managing their own affairs and should be left alone.

This stream of liberal thought had more influence in England than on the continent and the rugged individualism that is inherent in it has had a great effect on the American character, a point we have already made. The classic intellectual work of this early economic liberalism was Adam Smith's *The Wealth of Nations.* This branch of liberalism became closely related to the development of industrial capitalism and, therefore, is associated historically with the various social and political problems that have emerged from industrial society.

The other branch into which the main stream of liberal thought divided is often spoken of as social and humanitarian liberalism. This branch of the liberal tradition owes more to French political philosophy than to British. Inherent in the social and humanitarian liberalism of the eighteenth century is a concern for the welfare of the common people, expressed, for example, by Rousseau in his idea that the state rests on the general will of all the people, not merely on that of property owners. This tradition emphasized the idea of natural rights but insisted that the rights to life, liberty, and property do not exhaust the list of natural rights. To these must be added the right of the individual to the pursuit of happiness—a phrase that ultimately was to be incorporated in the American *Declaration of Independence.* Even in its earliest period the weight of this stream of liberalism was thrown in the direction of social and political reform that would better the condition of the mass of people.

Although the two components of liberal thought had a common historical source, the differences between them grew constantly greater and by the early decades of the nineteenth century grave conflicts had developed between them. These conflicts were primarily associated with the poor condition of the common people under the early factory system. Humanitarian liberals launched bitter protests against the exploitation of human beings in factories, the employment of young children and women in the most onerous and dangerous occupations, and the cancerous growth of urban slums. These liberals denied the thesis that human labor is an economic commodity, subject only to the laws of the market, and their demands for social reform grew in volume.

It is with humanitarian liberalism that we are concerned in this part of the present volume. The basic idea that will be developed in this chapter is that the protest movement in education we call progressivism was one of the historical emergents of the tradition of humanitarian liberalism. Our first task in developing this thesis will be to examine some distinguishing characteristics of this tradition and to contrast them at certain points with the ideas of conservatism.

In considering the general character of the American liberal tradition we should first note the emphasis on experience and on an experimental attitude toward social institutions and social ideals. In part, at least, contemporary liberals are in this respect heirs of the rationalism of the eighteenth century. Briefly, the liberal attitude is that no set of ideals, no constellation of institutions, is so hallowed by tradition that it should stand outside the possibility of critical scrutiny and, if necessary, substantial alteration. Institutions exist to serve human welfare, and when they fail to do so they should be changed or abolished. Tradition is not the only criterion of value for assessing the worth of institutions. The real test of their worth is how they serve human beings.

This experimental attitude is linked to an abiding faith in the potential power of human intelligence. The call of social liberalism is for men to face up resolutely to the problems of their own times and to employ intelligence, the most powerful means at their disposal, to build a better society and a better life for all of a generation. There are differing attitudes towards religion to be found among liberals, but even among those who are devout adherents to some religious body, this same orientation to the here and now keeps breaking through. As in the old "Wobbly" song, there may be "pie in the sky by and by" but the liberal believes typically that our business is here in this world, with the problems and injustices that infest it. And if the Creator did endow every man with certain inalienable rights, it is the business of society to see that in every generation, men secure the full enjoyment of these rights. The liberal, therefore, is more concerned with human rights than with property rights. He is generally in agreement that the right to hold property is an important matter, but when the case comes down to whether the rights of property or the rights of men shall prevail, the liberal typically casts his lot with man and insists that human welfare must come first.

It is not difficult to see that sentiments of this kind imply in some respects a very different attitude towards human nature from that which we discovered in the conservative tradition. In fact, throughout its history the liberal tradition has been noted for the essentially optimistic view it has of the nature of man. It is perhaps unnecessary to say that this has always been one of the sore points between conservatives and liberals. Whereas the conservative has maintained that, except in the common affairs of life, the judgment of the individual is not to be trusted, the liberal has insisted that intelligence is sufficiently distributed in the population that all men, when sufficiently nurtured by education, are capable of making the wise decisions necessary to self-government. The conservative has never been very sanguine about popular rule, preferring to think that society should be governed by its wisest and most able men, and more often than not arguing for the education of an elite governing class.

Although the belief of Condorcet and other liberals of the eighteenth century that the possible extent of human progress is unlimited has been tempered somewhat in contemporary liberalism, still there is more than a little of this attitude left. The modern liberal still believes with Rousseau that human nature in its original state is essentially good (or at the very least, is not contaminated by original evil).[1] If evil is not inherent in human nature, then it must stem from the environment, and particularly from the social environment. Immoral society produces immoral men, and the elimination of evil from human nature must necessarily involve the reform and reconstruction of social institutions.

These considerations provide the grounds for the deepest controversies between liberal and conservative forces. We have already seen that the conservative rejects any notion of the perfectability of human nature. To the extent that he believes human nature is capable of any improvement he believes this must come largely from within the individual. Thus, religion, moral exhortation, and perhaps the influence of great literature can bring about the necessary "inner working." So, from the standpoint of conservatism the focus of morality is within man, and a man with the will to do it can raise the quality of his own life above that of the environment. We have already seen how idealism can be employed to contribute strong philosophical support to this view of man and his nature.

There is a far different view of man implicit in the liberal's approach to human society and the problems of bettering human life. Under this view, human behavior is a product of both internal and external factors. The quality of human life is partly a product of what is within

---

[1] It will be remembered that Viereck has said that the idea of original sin, taken either figuratively or literally, is one criterion for distinguishing the conservative from the liberal.

man, but it is also a product of the social environment in which men live. The liberal cannot agree with the basic conservative presumption of an inherent evil in man. To liberalism human nature is originally good (or, at least, neutral). It may be that we can do little to change the inherited part of human nature but *we can control the environment in which this nature develops.*

Now this leads, of course, to the ground that liberals and conservatives have contested for years—the need for consciously designed liberal reform movements. We have already seen the general contempt a thorough-going conservative has for what he usually refers to as "doctrinaire liberal reform." To him, "do-gooding" reforms sponsored by private groups are bad enough, the real tragedy comes when liberals call for government to intervene on the side of social reform. As we noted earlier, essentialists even today are reacting violently to the idea that the school itself should be a force for effecting far-reaching social changes.

To these basic differences over the nature of man and the efficacy of social reform in improving human life, we may add some lesser but still important issues. For one thing, liberalism customarily has viewed cultural pluralism as the condition of a healthy society. This means that a good society will not only *tolerate* differences of opinion and belief, it will actually *encourage* them. Liberalism historically has opposed resolutely various authoritarian schemes for enforcing conformity in personal and political life.

The liberal, moreover, is not impressed with conservative claims that it is the conservative tradition which promotes individual freedom and variety in social life. No tradition, the liberal is inclined to think, that stresses the adherence of the individual to the existing order of things and that conceives the realization of self as coming through the identification of the individual with the greater unity of society, is in any position to talk seriously about promoting individuality and social pluralism. In the estimation of some liberals, the basic educational doctrines of the conservative tradition are plain evidence for this conclusion. The typical curriculum with its essential core that all must study, the inflexible requirements and standards that are always involved, and a methodology that is designed for transmitting subject matter, appears to the liberal unlikely to do much besides promote intellectual and social conformity.

Another source of difference between the two traditions lies in the area of civil liberties and their preservation. The differences here are not of the stark black and white character they are sometimes taken to be for, after all, the liberal has no private option on the idea of inalienable rights. Liberals, however, may point out that the real issue is not the acceptance of high-level abstractions but the concrete support of individual rights when these are threatened in specific cases. Thus, the liberal will submit that it is one thing to talk in lofty generalizations about intellectual freedom and another thing to defend the schools of a given community against book banning by a group that justifies its actions in the name of social morality and protection of children against subversion.[2]

As has already been pointed out, there are considerable practical differences among conservatives on the question of civil liberties and there are also differences among liberals. Historical evidence does seem sufficient to support the generalization that liberalism, as a tradition, has supported the idea of basic civil liberties and the guarantee of these liberties in law.

In Chapter III, which deals with the conservative tradition, some brief comments were made on the relation of that tradition to the great cultural components of supernaturalism, capitalism, nationalism, democracy, and science. By way of a summary of the liberal tradition, the same thing will now be done here.

Supernaturalism and Human Nature

As noted previously, liberal attitudes toward organized religion and religious doctrines vary considerably, and it is by no means possible to point to *the* liberal position in this area. There are still traces of the eighteenth century age of reason left in the liberal mind and not a little of the deism that colored the philosophy of a man such as Jefferson. The range of religious belief within the tradition is from the reasonably orthodox acceptance of the supernatural basis of religion to out and out naturalism.[3] The effects of cultural transition have left their marks on the liberal as well as the conservative tradition in this respect.

There have been efforts within the liberal tradition to reconcile supernaturalism and naturalism. We have already seen that some conservatives have tried the same thing. Liberals have more often than not stressed the ethic of the Hebraic-Christian tradition more than they

---

[2] Perhaps substantially the same thing can be said about similar issues; e.g., loyalty oaths for teachers, the fifth amendment to the Constitution, the separation of church and state and religious liberty, etc.

[3] For example, two outstanding spokesmen for social liberalism in the 1930's were Dr. John Haynes Holmes, Minister of the Community Church in New York City, and John Dewey. There was a wide area of agreement between the social views of Holmes and Dewey, but a very considerable difference in their views on religion.

have the supernatural basis of that ethic, and many of them believe there is a close connection between the Hebraic-Christian tradition and the ethical ideals of modern democracy.

Thus, some of the same doubts and confusions concerning supernatural religion that beset the conservative tradition also are present in modern liberalism. There are, however, certain differences between the two traditions with respect to supernaturalism and the nature of man that are of importance. In the first place, the liberal tends to be more tolerant in matters of religion than does his conservative counterpart. This means the liberal typically will hold that the right *not* to adhere to any religion is as firmly grounded as the right to preference among religious creeds. Secondly, the liberal defends that part of the first amendment to the Constitution that provides for separation of church and state, and while this may be true of some conservatives also, they are more apt to be the exception than the rule. Liberals generally have applauded decisions of the Supreme Court that have upheld the division between state and church. In the third place, liberals have not insisted that adherence to some form of supernaturalism is a necessity for personal and social ethics—although in their own personal lives many liberals may agree with this principle.

The significant thing, it would seem, is that liberalism has exhibited more concern for the condition of man here in this world. Liberals have believed that the earthly lot of man can, and should, be improved; and, by and large, they have maintained that the reform of certain aspects of the social structure is the way to get it. Liberalism has always seen popular education as an important means for the improvement of human society and human life, but it has not supported the union of public school and religious sectarianism in the process. Perhaps the outstanding characteristic of the liberal mind in its conception of human nature is its faith in the power of human intelligence and the underlying optimism about the possibility of improving the lot of mankind.

Capitalism

Many of the fierce struggles between liberals and conservatives have occurred in the economic sphere of social life. By and large, American liberalism has accepted capitalism as the basic economic pattern and has not advocated the overthrow of that system, even though on occasion this effort has been alleged by conservatives. However, in large measure the history of liberalism in America is the history of the struggle for economic reform and the betterment of the conditions of the working class. Humanitarian liberals have often found historic institutions and processes of capitalism to be laden with weaknesses and injustice, and they have insisted that there is nothing so sacred about tradition that these conditions should be allowed to persist.

By and large, however, the liberal approach to economic reform has been piecemeal and atomistic. This tradition has often displayed a nostalgic longing for an economy based on small-scale enterprise and a chance for the small businessman and the individual farmer to compete successfully in the market. Similarly, liberalism has had a close relation to the growth of trade unionism and has been involved in the struggle to have the rights of trade unions established in law. Yet another approach to economic reform has been that of the manipulation of money and credit—inflation, deflation, or stabilization, depending on the nature of conditions at a particular time. To this may be added the periodic crusades of liberals against the trusts and monopolies and their efforts to invoke the power of government against these hindrances to a free economy and the interests of common citizens.

In summation of liberals' attitudes toward capitalism, it may be said that they accept the system but with considerable reservation about many aspects of it. This tradition has always been in the forefront of campaigns to reform the institutions and processes of capitalism, but by and large, no comprehensive program has been advocated or instituted. The liberal approach to economic reform has been gradualistic, in many respects opportunistic, and generally piecemeal.[4] This tradition has seldom hesitated to invoke the power of government on the side of reform whenever this could be achieved. In so far as the school is concerned in these matters, liberals have seen it as a chief means of social mobility, enabling an individual to rise, by means of superior education, to a higher social and economic status. In the depths of the Great Depression that began in 1929 there was a movement among liberal educational theorists to make the school itself an instrument of political and economic reform. We have already noted the ferocity of the conservative reaction to such a proposal and we will examine this matter again in a subsequent chapter.

Nationalism

The sentiments of modern liberalism concerning nationalism are often as mixed as those of conservatism. Liberalism accepts the fact of a world whose basic political unit is the national state. The liberal

[4] Perhaps the most concerted effort at economic reform through the power of government occurred during the New Deal under President F. D. Roosevelt. For a discussion of the essentially opportunistic character of the New Deal economic reform movement see: Richard Hofstadter, *The Age of Reform*, New York: Vintage Books, 1960, Chapter VII and particularly p. 302 ff.

would, of course, like to see these nation-states liberal and democratic in their basic internal character and in their relations with each other. There does not seem to be much question that contemporary liberals accept the idea of national self-determination and that their vision of a world community is one of a plurality of nation-states, liberal and democratic in their orientation, and actively engaged in cooperative effort for the good of all concerned. Liberalism has tried to keep chauvinism out of American national life and usually has been suspicious of the activities of aggressively patriotic groups and societies. Liberals have often come to the defense of schools when these institutions have felt undue pressure from nationalistic groups.[5]

On the other hand, liberalism has not agitated notably for a true cosmopolitanism and has not supported the teaching of such a doctrine in the schools. In the earlier part of the century liberals supported the League of Nations as a means to international peace and security. Contemporary liberals typically support the United Nations for about the same reasons. We have pointed out before, however, that the opposite of nationalism is not internationalism because, by definition, the latter term presupposes the existence of nation-states. Contemporary liberalism has been staunch in its advocacy of international sentiments and support for the United Nations. On occasion it has appeared to favor some relinquishing of national sovereignty (at least many conservatives think it has) in order that the power of the United Nations might be increased. While liberals are certainly more willing to discuss the need and advisability of such relinquishment, there is little evidence to indicate that such policies have made significant headway.

There can be little doubt, however, that liberalism has supported the idea that the schools should foster internationalist ideas and propagate them among students. Liberals have supported the activities of UNESCO and recommended the use of materials from that organization as a means for international understanding. They have sought to temper the irrationalism and chauvinism that are apparently inherent in much of modern nationalism and to interpret to the young the idea that patriotism is devotion to the good of the total community and not the paranoid intolerance of everything that lies outside the immediate interest of the national state.

[5] Although it was written a decade before World War II, contemporary liberals are in general agreement with John Dewey's estimation of the strengths and weaknesses of modern nationalism. See his *Characters and Events*, New York: Henry Holt and Company, Inc., 1929, pp. 798–803.

Democracy

There is no concept in contemporary American thought that has a closer relation to modern liberalism than the idea of democracy. Conceptually, at least, contemporary liberals agree that at heart democracy is an ethical concept and that when the equality of all men is asserted the assertion concerns their moral equality. It must be admitted that in making decisions about what moral equality means in particular and concrete cases the contemporary liberal finds problems as thorny as those of his conservative counterpart. A case in point is the question of what equality of opportunity means in the educational sense. We have already seen that this problem causes severe strains and disruptions in modern educational conservatism. It often serves the same purpose among those of liberal persuasion. Typically, the liberal has worked for legislation and other formal guarantees for free schooling—tax support for education, free schooling for all for at least twelve years, compulsory attendance laws, free textbooks, and so on. More often than not, liberals have been in the forefront of the battle to extend the scope of the curriculum so that the needs and interests of a diversified school population might be served, but it is more difficult to make broad generalizations here. The presence of various kinds of practical and vocational subjects in the curriculum is far from being altogether the work of educational liberals, and, in fact, many of them do not view highly vocational courses with approval.

On the broader social and political scale the contemporary liberal approaches the problems of society in much the same fashion as he approaches educational problems. This is to say he is apt to stress its formal, political phases, particularly universal suffrage, representative government, legal protection of civil liberties, and the rights of minority groups. There is no question that these are necessary ingredients for the realization of a democratic way of life. There is some question, however, whether these outward forms are sufficient for the purpose. Such an important spokesman for the liberal tradition as John Dewey often pointed this out and attempted to infuse a deeper understanding of the democratic ethic into his liberal associates. Even though liberalism has often found the problems of realizing political democracy in an age of industrial society exceedingly difficult, this tradition has battled resolutely to retain and improve the basic parliamentary institutions of popular government, to encourage pluralism and diversity in social life, to emphasize individual freedom in social action, and to put the needs of men above the sanctity of tradition.

To the adherents of every tradition with which this book deals education is an important enterprise, but to American liberalism it comes close to being a sacred word. Much of the battle in the nineteenth century to establish a system of free, universal education was fought under the banners of political liberalism and the leaders of the forces were middle-class intellectuals, perhaps best typified in that era by Horace Mann. It was out of the great resurgence of political and social liberalism that began in the last decade of the nineteenth century that the progressive protest against the domination of essentialism emerged. Before we consider the conditions out of which this protest movement developed, we must give some attention to the relation of experimental science to contemporary liberalism.

Science, Scientific Method, and the Liberal Mind

Since the attitudes of modern liberals toward supernatural religious doctrines display considerable variation, this tradition has not escaped the effects of the impact of scientific achievement on the traditions of religion. In many cases the effects of the contradictory influence of science has troubled the liberal in the same way it has troubled his conservative counterpart. But, when this has been said, the fact remains that the liberal tradition has often been more hospitable to the scientific enterprise, has been more willing to accept the deeper implications of science for various areas of experience, and, more than any other tradition, has recognized the possibilities for educational method that are inherent in scientific method.

It may well be that an important reason for these attitudes is historical, that, in fact, the effects of the eighteenth century Enlightenment still have a potent influence in this tradition. We have already observed that one characteristic that distinguishes the liberal from the conservative is the effort of the former to maintain an experimental attitude toward social institutions and modes of social life. The liberal, often to the disgust of conservatives, is more apt to appeal to empirical evidence and to evaluate social policies on the basis of objective evidence rather than on the basis of tradition. At its best, this approach has been a conscious effort to apply the canons of scientific method to the study of social problems and the formulation of social policy.

Adherents to the liberal tradition have often echoed Francis Bacon's famous dictum that "knowledge is power." And they have believed, as Bacon believed, that the knowledge that yields power is scientific knowledge. It is true that presently there is considerable disenchantment among liberal elements about the power of military destruction that the scientific enterprise has made possible, but much of this disenchantment is with technology and social policy and not with experimental science itself. The liberal would hold that the threat of total annihilation is of our own making and that it results from our own misuse of modern technology and our own failure to apply the method of intelligence to political affairs with the same dedication we have employed it in creating the engines of military destruction.

One of the major theses that will be developed in the chapters immediately following is that progressivism in education, as a facet of American liberalism, represented the effort to achieve a new humanism built on the achievements and potentialities of experimental science and the power inherent in scientific method. At a time when the program of the schools was dominated by the conservative tradition, liberals were agitating in favor of a larger place for the scientific studies in the curriculum and John Dewey, as an outstanding example, was experimenting with a scientific program for children in the Laboratory School at the University of Chicago.

While some liberals have been troubled by the radical naturalism that is inherent in experimental science, this tradition, certainly more than conservatism, has been willing to face the consequences of an out and out naturalistic interpretation of human nature. John Dewey, who is recognized above all others as the philosopher of modern liberalism and of educational progressivism, built his whole philosophical structure on a thorough-going naturalism. One of the major tasks of Chapter IX will be an analysis of the effects of experimental naturalism on psychology, epistemology, and ethics and the impact these matters have for a unified theory of education.

THE RESURGENCE OF AMERICAN LIBERALISM AND THE DEVELOPMENT OF PROGRESSIVISM IN EDUCATION

We have already noted in other contexts that progressivism in education developed as a protest movement against essentialism and its domination of American education. It has also been indicated that the protest lodged against the conservative tradition in education was part of a larger liberal reform movement that had powerful effects on the course of events in America from the turn of the century to the beginning of World War II. It is beyond the scope of this book to present in any detail the nature of this age of reform or to recount the twists and turns that the progressive movement in education took in its development.

In this section we will confine our attention to the systematic theoretical aspect of the liberal protest in educational theory. It should be understood that many times there was a great, and often a complete gap between the actions of educational progressives and the theoretical constructs to which they presumably were dedicated. Progressive education, as an historic reality, was a movement of vast and untidy proportions. It was eclectic in its origins, in some of its aspects incurably romantic and even sentimental about childhood, and self-contradictory on numerous theoretical points. The thing the progressives had in common, and which was sufficient to hold them together for four decades, was a profound distaste for the traditional school and for many aspects of the society that supported that school. Sometimes—and this is often the case with protest movements—it was easier to tell what the progressives were against than what they were for. Fortunately, we now have available an admirable study of the historical reality of the progressive protest and the many variant forms it took. Any student who seriously wishes to grasp the historic character of the liberal protest should apply himself to Mr. Lawrence A. Cremin's *The Transformation of the School*.[6]

In the present context we can make only the briefest comments about the origins of the progressive protest. Perhaps it will be sufficient to observe that the reform movement of the earlier part of the present century was in large measure a revolt of humanitarian liberals against some very unfavorable aspects of industrial culture. Among these were the appalling conditions of urban living in the earlier part of the industrial era, the submersion of humanity in the emerging factory system, the increasingly arbitrary division of labor and leisure, and all the tawdriness and uniformity that flowed from it. This revolt of the liberals was in considerable part the effort to re-establish under different cultural conditions the ideals of moral equality and individual worth which Americans have held as an important part of their heritage.

Much of the energy of the liberal reformers was directed toward economic and political reform. The familiar liberal thesis that the improvement of the human prospect inevitably involves social reforms

---

[6] New York: Alfred A. Knopf, 1961. Another briefer but useful source is Oscar Handlin, *John Dewey's Challenge to Education*, New York: Harper & Brothers, 1959.

PHILOSOPHY OF AMERICAN EDUCATION

of far reaching significance was everywhere to be heard. These reformers were a motley lot, ranging from "free-silverites" and "greenbackers" to trade unionists, settlement house workers and agitators for female suffrage. The battles they fought were many and varied and their total forces were never coordinated, but one conviction held them together: there was something rotten in the state of things in America and it needed to be cleaned out. The liberals had nurtured a dream, based in large part on the promises of the eighteenth century, and the gritty reality in which they found themselves revolted them.[7]

One aspect of this gritty reality against which liberal elements revolted was the American system of public education. We have already remarked that to the liberal mind of America, education comes near to being a sacred word. Liberal elements had battled through most of the nineteenth century to establish and support a system of free schools, a system that was to be the very life-blood of American democracy. They had fought the tight-fisted burghers of a score of states for a tax on property and they had battled with the "interests." By the last decade of the century they had very nearly achieved at least the outward form of a system of universal schooling, ranging from the primary grades through the high school. These things had been done in large measure under the spell of the eighteenth century belief that the school is an agent of popular enlightenment and that only an enlightened people can be free. Now as the century drew to its close they looked about them, and what did they see?

In a remarkable series of articles published in a New York magazine, *The Forum*, in 1892 and 1893, Joseph Mayer Rice told them what they would see if they would take the trouble to look at their schools. Rice was a pediatrician who had become interested enough in educational theory to spend two years of study on that subject in German universities. When he returned to the States he agreed to do a study of American schools for *The Forum*.

In the course of this study he toured the country, visiting more than a score of cities, talking with hundreds of teachers and parents, and attending school board meetings wherever he could. What he found in his travels was profoundly shocking to the liberals. In his articles he portrayed a school system shot through with the worst kind of ward-heeling politics, political corruption in appointments of teachers and administrators, and an atmosphere in the schools so deadly to the intel-

[7] Hofstadter's *The Age of Reform*, cited above, is a valuable source of information on the general social context out of which educational progressivism developed.

lectual enterprise that it was enough to shock even a hardened journalistic muckraker.[8]

Rice found some signs of hope, but they were few and far between. He was most attracted by the work of Col. Francis Parker at the Cook County Normal School in Chicago where he reported an educational program for children could be found that involved a broad curriculum of studies and teachers of competence and enthusiasm. But aside from this and a few other places the picture was uniform and black. The temptation here is to describe the authoritarianism, the mechanical uniformity, the sterility of method and content as reported by Rice but in the interests of space we will let a brief summary by Mr. Handlin suffice:

> The realm of the classroom in the 1890's was totally set off from the experience of the child who inhabited it. The teachers' lessons encrusted by habit, the seats arranged in formal rows, and the rigid etiquette of behavior all emphasized the difference between school and life. Hence learning consisted of the tedious memorization of data without a meaning immediately clear to the pupil.[9]

Even where innovations from European reformers had found their way into the schools these new approaches had succumbed quickly to the formalism of the prevailing tradition:

> When some years ago a little boy entered the elementary school, he conceived in his heart a curse upon beans and busy work, which had by that time invaded the midlands, even the hinterlands of the United States . . . Little did the boy suspect as he sat long hours before his simple rows of beans and corn, that in one book there were '62 pages of busy work devices to occupy heads and hands from September to June.'[10]

The protest of liberal elements against the prevailing state of education at the turn of the century had a number of facets. These may be summarized somewhat as follows:

1. Liberals had seen education as a necessity for a free people and they had envisioned the school always in the vanguard of social progress, an institution always close to the people and always in the

---

[8] For a more complete account of Rice's findings see: Cremin, op. cit., Chapter I. The articles in The Forum later were published in book form as The Public School System of the United States (1893). Those familiar with the history of educational research will remember Rice as the author of the article, "The Futility of the Spelling Grind," one of the first empirical studies of the relation of achievement to the amount of time invested in isolated drill. The 1960 edition of the Encyclopedia of Educational Research still lists Rice's article in the bibliography on spelling.
[9] Handlin, op. cit., p. 42.
[10] Thomas Woody in: National Society for the Study of Education, Thirty-third Yearbook, Bloomington, Illinois: Public School Publishing Company, 1934, p. 31.

mainstream of social life. But the reality was an institution that had walled itself off from society and become a kind of separate universe in itself. Thus, to the liberal perception, the social role played by the school was essentially negative—a perverse kind of conservatism whose total effect was blind perpetuation of the *status quo.*

2. The exalted American tradition, and one for which liberalism always had a strong affinity, that the school is the cradle of liberty, the institution in which the young can learn the meaning of democracy and freedom, had been completely abrogated by the prevailing conservatism. Instead of being a place in which children could learn the basic elements of democratic social life, and not only by precept *but also by example,* the educational reality was an institution authoritarian to its core and based on the most coercive and even brutal discipline.

3. The ideal of a school as a source of popular enlightenment has always been close to the heart of the American liberal. But as he looked about him, perhaps under the guidance of Dr. Rice's *Forum* articles, he saw an educational process grown dull and mechanical beyond belief. The curriculum was a dreary lockstep of dessicated subject matters. The chief teaching methods were repetitive drill and endless recitation of half-understood facts. Individual differences were ignored as much as possible, and the graded system, which had already received virtually universal acceptance in urban schools, only served to increase the emphasis on uniformity.

These, then, were the kinds of conditions the liberals were protesting against. They were protesting against the idea of education as primarily transmission of subject matter; against the authoritarian character of an institution whose major role should be the extension of democratic ideals; and against the failure of the school to act as a means of social betterment for the masses. Much of this protest was emotional and sometimes ill-informed, at least in the beginning; for many, of course, it was never anything else. But these protests came from the heart of American liberalism and the trend of the times was such that people were disposed to listen.

Meantime, as the school boy sat over his rows of corn and beans or pursued the "spelling grind" Dr. Rice had excoriated so thoroughly, certain events were shaping themselves so that out of this resurgence of liberal sentiment would grow a protest against the reigning conservatism that would be more than emotional—a philosophical protest that would rock essentialism as it had never been rocked before. This part of the story begins when a young professor of philosophy left his post at the University of Michigan and went to Chicago to assume his duties as Chairman of the Department of Philosophy in the new university there.

THE GROWTH OF PROGRESSIVISM

Not all the dissatisfaction and disillusionment over education were centered in New York City and there were other sources of protest besides the articles of Dr. Rice. The city of Chicago itself was one of the major centers of the reform movement, and representatives of virtually every one of the liberal reform groups were congregated there. This city was already experiencing a storm of protests from liberal elements over the state of the public schools and an ad-hoc citizens' committee composed of some of Chicago's most distinguished liberals had been formed to investigate the character of the city's public education.[11]

In one of his *Forum* articles Rice had made a blistering attack on the Chicago schools and had extolled Col. Parker's work at the Cook County Normal School as being one of the bright spots in an otherwise dreary picture. In so doing, Rice had touched an exposed nerve, for a major storm center of the educational controversy in Chicago was Col. Parker himself. Parker, who had been an outstanding school administrator in Quincy, Massachusetts, had come to the Cook County Normal School with the reputation of a leading educational reformer. He had not been there long before he was locked in mortal combat with the Cook County Board of Commissioners, which controlled the budget of his institution and whose members' views on education were decidedly conservative. The local press was full of intelligence about Parker's annual batterings of the Cook County Board, and the citizenry were fairly well divided into two opposing groups: the pro-Parkerites and the anti-Parkerites. It was in this heady atmosphere of controversy and reform that the young professor, lately come from the chairmanship of philosophy at Michigan, was to begin his work of providing the liberal re-

11 Among the committee members were Jane Addams and Marshall Field. Various other committees and commissions were formed to deal with educational problems in this reform period. For a panorama of the situation in Chicago in the '90s see: Robert L. McCaul, "Dewey's Chicago," *The School Review*, 67:258–286 (Summer, 1959).

form movement in America with the means for a systematic philosophical attack on the conservative tradition and all its works; most notably, its educational works.

John Dewey was thirty-five years old when he went to the University of Chicago as chairman of the department of philosophy, psychology, and education. He was born in 1859 in Burlington, Vermont where he grew up and attended the state university. Subsequently he studied at the Johns Hopkins University where he came under the tutelage of Professor George Sylvester Morris and by whom he was introduced to Hegelian idealism, the dominant philosophical influence of that time. At Hopkins he also heard lectures by G. Stanley Hall, who founded the child-study movement, and Charles Sanders Peirce, who gave pragmatic philosophy its original title.

After he had finished his doctoral studies, Dewey accepted an invitation from G. S. Morris, who had gone to the University of Michigan as head of the philosophy department, to come to that institution as an instructor in philosophy. Accordingly, Dewey came to Ann Arbor where he was to remain for a decade, excepting one year when he was lured away by the University of Minnesota. During his last five years at Michigan he did not teach any courses in educational theory nor did he publish anything of significance in that field.[12]

The situation at Chicago offered unusual opportunity for Dewey to expand his philosophical activities to include work in educational theory. We have already noted that the whole atmosphere of the city was one of protest and reform and there was strong dissatisfaction with the status of the schools. More than this, William Rainey Harper, president of the university, was himself deeply interested in the problems of public education and the improvement of the schools and was extending the services and facilities of the university for conferences, study groups, and public meetings on educational questions.[13] And, of course, Dewey had the opportunity to build a department that would reflect his own ideas

[12] Dewey would never authorize a comprehensive biography of himself and steadfastly refused to write an autobiography. Important sources of information about his life and career are: "Biography of John Dewey" by his daughter, Jane M. Dewey in Paul Schilpp, ed., The Philosophy of John Dewey, Chicago and Evanston: Northwestern University, 1939; "From Absolutism to Experimentalism" in G. P. Adams and William P. Montague, eds., Contemporary American Philosophy, New York: The Macmillan Company, 1930, Vol. 2; Max Eastman, "John Dewey," The Atlantic Monthly, 168:671–685 (December, 1941). An interesting account of his career at the University of Michigan is: Willinda Savage, The Evolution of John Dewey's Philosophy of Experimentalism as Developed at the University of Michigan (Unpublished doctoral dissertation, University of Michigan, 1950).
[13] See: McCaul, op. cit., pp. 262–3.

on the role of philosophy as an intellectual discipline and its relation to cultural affairs.

There seems to be good reason to think that while Dewey did not teach any courses in education at Michigan, his studies in philosophy and psychology had strongly influenced his ideas about education and the need for reform of the schools. Admittedly, this is partly conjecture, but there is also evidence for it in Dewey's own writings. In one instance, he wrote that the ideas that led to the founding of the Laboratory School at Chicago originated in philosophy and psychology and owed far more to those fields than to "educational experience or precedent."[14]

Once in Chicago, Dewey aligned himself on the side of the pro-Parkerites. He attended meetings and conferences on educational issues and took an active role in the controversy that developed over the transferal of the Cook County Normal School to the Chicago Board of Education. On this issue, Parker, strongly supported by militant liberals, won a decisive victory. The Cook County Normal became a part of the Chicago Public School System and thus was enabled to play an important role in the educational reform movement.

THE FOUNDING OF THE LABORATORY SCHOOL

One of the decisive events in the history of the progressive movement in education was the founding by Dewey and his associates of the Laboratory School at the University of Chicago.[15] This school was founded in 1896, two years after Dewey's arrival at the University, and is important in the history of education for a number of reasons. In the first place, the decision to found an experimental school illustrates the conviction that permeates Dewey's philosophy that ideas, even though they may appear to stand to reason, can be tested and their meaning clarified only as they are given concrete application and the results are noted. Dewey had developed certain ideas about the conduct of the educational

14 John Dewey, "The Theory of the Chicago Experiment," Appendix II in Katherine C. Mayhew and Anna C. Edwards, *The Dewey School*, New York: D. Appleton-Century Company, 1936, p. 464.

15 Two major sources of information concerning the Dewey Laboratory School are: Katherine C. Mayhew and Anna C. Edwards, *Ibid.*; and Melvin C. Baker, *Foundations of John Dewey's Educational Theory*, New York: Columbia University, Kings Crown Press, 1955. I am indebted to these sources for my exposition of the program of the Dewey School.

process and certain proposals for the reform of the schools, but he believed that these ideas needed to be tested and clarified and the only way this could be done was by applying them in a school situation.

It obviously was idle to think of testing new ideas in the existing public schools and while Col. Parker's school was a vigorous institution, Dewey did not believe it would serve the purpose of testing his own ideas for educational reform. Therefore, the decision was made to found another school which was to be a laboratory for educational experimentation.

A second reason for the importance of the Laboratory School is that it, far more than any other school bearing the name "progressive," was a concrete example of what education would be like if Dewey's ideas were faithfully and intelligently applied in practice. The Laboratory School was an institution for young children and, hence, through the study of extant documents we can get a fairly clear picture of an elementary school that operated on Dewey's basic principles. What secondary education would be if it had ever felt the real impact of Dewey's philosophy is for the most part purely and simply a speculative matter and will remain such until someone undertakes to put his ideas to work in a secondary school—a possibility that at present seems remote.

A third reason for the historic importance of the Laboratory School was the way in which its founders sought to meet the major criticisms liberals were making of American public education. The first of these, it will be remembered, was the allegation by liberal elements that the existing schools were basically undemocratic in their structure and internal relationships. In shaping the organization of the school, Dewey and his associates sought to find a way between the rigid authoritarianism against which liberals were reacting and the loose, *laissez faire* romanticism which was an inevitable reaction against the educational lockstep and which was already creeping into the progressive movement. The fundamental idea in the Laboratory School was that the school should itself be a community simplified and purified, to be sure, in order to match the developmental stage of its pupils. As a community it would give children a chance to live and work day by day in a social setting that exemplified the basic tenets of democracy.

Organization and Administration of the Laboratory School

It was recognized from the beginning that a democratic community requires leadership and that social order is a necessity in any satisfactory social life. The problem here was not to react blindly against the excesses of authoritarianism by abandoning social structure and social order, but rather to reinterpret the source and character of these in a genuinely democratic mode of social life.

Accordingly, careful attention was given to the interpersonal relationships in the school. The most important of these relations are those among children in the school and between children and their teachers. Apparently, Dewey and his co-workers had already learned that democracy in the life of a school is all of a piece—an institution is either democratic from top to bottom or it is not democratic at all. It is hopeless to suppose that democratic modes of life can exist in the schoolroom while the administration of education remains autocratic and repressive. There was plenty of evidence available for this conclusion to be found by even a cursory examination of the existing system.

A fundamental meaning of the term *community* is *shared effort*. In a democratic community the work of the group and the responsibility for it is shared by all participants and basic policies and plans are the product of all. The fact is often overlooked that democracy, more than any other mode of social life, lays the heaviest obligations on its members. In some respects, it is always easier to follow the dictates of authority and thus escape the necessity for making decisions and shouldering the responsibility for them, but, as Dewey thought, this is no way to educate the prospective citizens of a society whose cherished belief is in political democracy. Since active participation in policy making is not only crucial in democratic social life, as well as being exceedingly difficult to learn, it seemed to those in the Laboratory School that it is important to get about it as early as possible, and this means as soon as the child comes to school.

It was for such reasons as these that the Dewey school placed great emphasis on the participation of pupils in planning activities and procedures in their school. Children were encouraged to participate in planning activities and in evaluating the results obtained. It is well to emphasize that the idea was *participation* by pupils in planning, not turning over to pupils the responsibility for curriculum making. The business of the teacher was to guide the process, exercising the authority he had as a natural consequence of the role he played as the representative of adult society.

To say that this emphasis on pupil participation was a radical departure from accepted practice in 1896 is to understate the case badly. The idea of the participation of pupils in formulating activities is well known today, at least as an idea, and "pupil-teacher planning" has become one of the bromides against which conservatives erupt periodically. But in the Laboratory School the reasons for it were understood clearly and, in fact, the whole curricular structure depended on it, as will be seen presently.

The same emphasis that was placed on shared effort among pupils also extended to members of the teaching staff. The most painstaking efforts were made to keep the channels of communication open among faculty members and the prevailing practice of dictating content and teaching method from the top of the organizational hierarchy apparently was unknown in this school. There is evidence that Dewey believed that qualified teachers are capable of knowing what needs to be done in the educational enterprise and of knowing how to accomplish it. He saw no need for the kind of supervision of teachers that was common in those days (and by no means unknown in these) and which consisted largely of prescription and inspection.

This is not to say, however, that there were no recognizable lines of responsibility and authority in the school's organization. Dewey had seen how teachers under the prevailing conservatism in the schools misused their authority, but he never questioned the authority of the teacher's role. As he saw it, the business of the teacher, as the representative of the adult culture, was to assist in inducting the immature child into social life. This was not to be accomplished by imposition, as essentialists have always maintained it should be. Rather:

> The teacher is not in the school to impose certain ideas or to form certain habits in the child but is there as a member of the community to select the influences which shall affect the child and to assist him in properly responding to these influences.[16]

Likewise, Dewey never questioned the need for responsibility and authority in administration of the school, though he was bitterly critical of the hierarchical authoritarianism prevalent in the schools of that day. Administrative roles in the Laboratory School were assigned to a general supervisor, a principal, and department heads. Dewey himself was the general head of the school. Each administrative officer was responsible for certain aspects of the school's operation and hence the division was more one of responsibility than of authority. But the contributions of all members of the staff were always solicited and every

[16] John Dewey, *My Pedagogic Creed* (first published by E. L. Kellogg & Company, 1897), reprinted in *Education Today*, New York: G. P. Putnam's Sons, 1940.

effort was made to implement the idea that democracy means the participation of all in the making of policy.

It remains to be noted that the parents of children enrolled in the school were also considered members of the community and no effort was spared to involve them in the development of the school's curriculum and the experimental work being carried on. A parents' association of the Laboratory School was formed and members of the association were encouraged to participate in evaluating and developing the school's program. Some of Dewey's early publications on educational theory had their origin in materials he prepared for discussion by the parent group.

So, the organization of the school as a community of pupils, teachers, and parents, each with his own unique interest and role, and all committed to mutual effort was Dewey's solution for the increasing tendency of the school to remove itself from the mainstream of social life and to become a world apart, not only apart from the experience of the child, but from the living culture itself.

Curriculum and Instruction in the Laboratory School

From the standpoint of the organization for instruction, two major innovations were made in the Laboratory School. In the first place, the school was departmentalized, each of the departments being under the direction of a staff member who had thorough training in the field of knowledge represented in his department. Departmentalization of instruction has never been common in American elementary schools, although it has been the prevailing pattern in secondary and higher education. Elementary teachers in those days, as well as these, commonly have been expected to teach all the subject matters in the curriculum with the possible exceptions of such "special subjects" as art, music, and physical education. This traditional role of the elementary teacher has dictated a program of teacher education that necessarily stresses breadth at the expense of depth of scholarship. This fact has often provoked criticism from conservative circles, but no one has ever been able to show how elementary teachers can secure the depth of learning in a single field that most essentialists think desirable, have the generality of background necessitated by their role, and still complete their college education in the traditional four years.

Dewey's conviction was that the teacher should be so well grounded in the subject matter with which he deals that his attention should be on the student and his responses to the material. In *Democracy and Education*, written after the Laboratory School had closed, he observed:

When engaged in the direct act of teaching, the instructor needs to have subject matter at his finger's ends; his attention should be upon the attitude and response of the pupil. To understand the latter in its interplay with subject matter is his task, while the pupil's mind, naturally, should be not on itself but on the topic in hand.[17]

It was thought that one way of ensuring this degree of academic competence lay in departmentalizing the school and putting each department in the charge of a person with the necessary degree of scholarship. The school was divided into the following departments: Kindergarten, history (the social sciences), natural science and mathematics, domestic science and industries, manual training, art, music, languages (French and Latin were taught), and physical culture.

Dewey and his associates were aware of the danger of compartmentalization of subject matter inherent in a departmental organization for they had seen its effects in the secondary schools and in higher education. They believed, however, that the usual compartmentalization need not occur if lines of communication among staff members were always open and if every member of the staff played his proper role in planning for the educational experiences of the various groups of pupils. This, by necessity, involved a high degree of shared effort on the part of staff members which, as we have already observed, Dewey thought to be the very essence of social democracy.

The second major innovation in the instructional organization of the school was that it was ungraded. The graded system of organization of elementary education dates only from the middle of the nineteenth century, but even in the days of the Laboratory School the graded system had already become virtually the only mode of organization for elementary education outside the one-room schools of the rural areas. In Chapter IV we considered at some length the gravity of the administrative and instructional problems occasioned by the graded system and the concentrated efforts essentialists make to solve these problems.

In the Laboratory School these problems did not exist because the school was not graded and there were none of the familiar features of the graded system: minimum essentials for each grade, promotion from grade to grade on the basis of mastering the material deemed essential for a given grade, the effort to deal with individual differences in achievement by non-promotion and by acceleration. Children in Dewey's school were grouped for instruction according to interests and abilities

[17] John Dewey, *Democracy and Education*, New York: The Macmillan Company, 1916, p. 215.

and while these provided a rough correlation with age, there was no effort to construct the groups exclusively along chronological age lines. Flexibility in grouping was the basic principle and there were no problems of grade standards and promotions. This arrangement was in part Dewey's answer to the "educational lockstep" which was receiving bitter criticism from liberals.

Thus, the two major innovations in the organization of the school were departmentalization and a flexible, non-graded structure. There is one other feature of the school that should be mentioned in passing. This is the character of the school plant. As everybody knows, the conventional school building, which is designed to accommodate the kind of program which has always been advocated by essentialists, consists mainly of classrooms. Usually, though by no means always, there are certain auxiliary rooms: a gymnasium, an auditorium, music and/or art room, etc. Generally, these rooms are for the "special subjects" or for "extra-curricular activities." Under the traditional view, the main business of the school goes on in classrooms which are designed for the traditional methods of lecturing, reciting, and testing.

Since the methodology employed in the Laboratory School did not involve these traditional techniques of instruction, it was necessary that a different kind of school plant be arranged. The school was never housed in a proper school building. Instead, it occupied a series of buildings originally designed for other purposes. When the school began it was quite small but as the enrollment grew, it was necessary to move to larger quarters. In each instance the house and its outbuildings were adapted to the needs of the program.

The significant aspect is that all of the rooms in the building were designed for active work, not for lecturing and reciting. There was a gymnasium; manual training rooms (shop); art and textile studios; two laboratories, one for the physical sciences and one for the biological sciences; a suite of rooms for languages and social sciences. As we have already noted, each of these locations was under the supervision of a staff member with thorough training in the field. Thus, the school plant was a place for active work in all fields represented in the curriculum.[18]

18 In one of his early books, *The School and Society*, originally published by the University of Chicago Press in 1899, Dewey relates the difficulties he experienced in buying furniture and equipment for the school. After searching the school supply houses of Chicago he finally was told by one dealer that he would never find what he sought because the school furniture of that day was designed for sitting and listening, not for working.

These innovations in the design of the school plant were necessitated by the nature of the school's program, and with this observation we now come to the feature of the Dewey school which effectively differentiates it from the pedagogy of the conservative tradition and which is the most telling aspect of the liberal protest against educational essentialism. This is the conception of the nature of the curriculum. All the organizational innovations we have examined above derive from this basic departure from conservative pedagogical orthodoxy.

In order to grasp the significance of this matter we should perhaps remind ourselves first that in essentialism the curriculum is always viewed as some organized series of subject matters which are deemed essential and which are to be mastered by all who come to school. As we observed in Chapter IV, there may be disagreement among conservatives about what subjects are essential and therefore must be in the curriculum, but there is no disagreement among essentialists over the principle that what is meant by curriculum is *some* series of subject matters.

In place of this basic conservative principle, Dewey and his co-workers proposed that the curriculum should be conceived as *an ordered series of active occupations*.[19] Admittedly, it is very difficult for most of us to conceive what a school program would be like whose basic conception of curriculum is that of an organized series of active enterprises carried on by pupils under the guidance and leadership of teachers. In the pedagogy of essentialism, which has always dominated American education, the unit of instruction is "the lesson." There are different patterns of lessons, but they all involve assigning some task to be done and then checking the work of the pupils to see that they have done it. The task may be listening to a lecture by the teacher, reading a portion of a book and "learning" the contents, engaging in drill as in arithmetic or spelling, or writing some kind of assigned composition. The teacher may check the work of the pupils by oral recitation and various kinds of written tests. The pupil is "graded" in terms of his performance. It is the sequence of lessons that constitutes the curriculum of the conservative tradition.

In the Dewey school there were no lessons, no assignments as conservatives understand that term, and no examinations. *The unit of instruction was the enterprise.* An enterprise differs from a lesson in im-

[19] Dewey used the term "occupations" in describing the program of the Laboratory School. The present author is convinced that the term "enterprise" in some contexts is more descriptive of what actually went on in the school and that it has the further advantage of being relatively free of a vocational connotation. For these reasons, in my own discussion I will often use the term *enterprise*.

portant and strategic ways. For one thing an enterprise is of longer duration, when planned properly it has an inherent unity of organization, and it involves generally the union of thought and action. An enterprise involves some goal or end that those involved in it wish to attain. In order to attain this goal, certain strategies and plans must be made which promise to bring about the desired consummation. These plans must then be implemented by appropriate actions and judged for their adequacy by the way they work out.

Clearly, enterprises can be of various kinds depending on the character of the desired end. For example, there are enterprises that involve the production of some physical thing or things as in the manual arts; there are enterprises that involve inquiry and the effort to find solutions to problems and the answers to questions as in the various sciences; and there are enterprises that involve the production of objects of beauty as in literature and the fine arts. There are also enterprises that are of sufficient scope to involve all of these elements.

The problem of curriculum design in the Laboratory School involved the following points: 1) The program must be one of active work—physical and intellectual—rather than the passive absorption of subject matter. As we have seen, a major effort here was made by abandoning the lesson and substituting in its place the enterprise. 2) The sequence of enterprises that made up the educational experience of pupils should be planned around a basic unifying theme that would give an underlying unity to experiences that might otherwise be discrete and atomistic. Dewey held that the unifying force must always be the experience of the child and the basic problem of education is to ensure that the experience of the child in school builds on and illuminates the experience he has in the home and community.

However, a major technical pedagogical problem is to determine the content that should be introduced into the experience of the child while he is in school. After extensive experimentation in the early years of the school's history, the staff of the school worked out a plan by which the active enterprises carried on by pupils were developed around certain broad themes of the development of civilization. These themes, according to the report of Mayhew and Edwards, were as follows: 1) Household and social occupations (kindergarten group); 2) Progress through invention and discovery; 3) Progress through exploration and discovery; 4) Local history; 5) European backgrounds.[20]

[20] Mayhew and Edwards, op. cit. The authors give fairly extended reports of how each of these themes was developed.

Part of the rationale for this kind of program may be seen in the following quotation from an early publication by Dewey:

The primary basis of education is the child's powers at work along the same general constructive lines as those which have brought civilization into being.

The only way to make the child conscious of his social heritage is to enable him to perform those fundamental types of activity which make civilization what it is.

In the so called expressive or constructive activities is the center of correlation.

This gives the standard for the place of cooking, sewing, manual training, etc., in the school.

They are not special studies which are to be introduced over and above a lot of others in the way of relaxation or relief, or as additional accomplishments. I believe rather that they represent, as types, fundamental forms of social activity; and that it is possible and desirable that the child's introduction into the more formal subjects of the curriculum be through the medium of these constructive activities.[21]

We have now examined the salient ways in which the experimental work of the Laboratory School departed from the orthodox pedagogy of the conservative tradition. We have noted certain departures in organization of the school and we now understand that these really were necessitated by the conception of curriculum that governed the work of the school. The real challenge that the Laboratory School posed to the conservative tradition was that the curriculum must be viewed as a series of active enterprises conducted by pupils under the guidance of teachers, who themselves possess superior scholarship and keen psychological insight into the nature of childhood.

However, thus far we have considered only certain innovations introduced into educational practice by the Laboratory School staff. We have not as yet given attention to the reasons Dewey and his associates had for developing these innovations, which to the conservatives of that day (as well as this) often seemed bizarre and dangerous. In the succeeding chapter, we will give systematic attention to the educational principles developed by Dewey and other progressives, principles to which the experience in the Laboratory School contributed a great deal. Before we turn directly to this matter, we will conclude this chapter on the rise of progressivism by examining an important early statement by Dewey of his conception of the educative process.

[21] Dewey, "My Pedagogic Creed," *op. cit.*

"MY PEDAGOGIC CREED"

In the preceding section we have already referred to parts of a statement published by Dewey in 1897, the second year of operation of the Laboratory School. This little document is of the greatest importance in the history of progressivism. For one thing, it is convincing evidence that Dewey's ideas on education developed concurrently with his ideas in psychology and the various branches of philosophy and, conversely, that his educational theory is not merely a series of deductions from a pre-established pragmatic philosophy—a point that many friendly as well as unfriendly critics of Dewey have found difficult to understand.

Another reason for the importance of *My Pedagogic Creed* is that in this early statement Dewey laid down the basic lines of his educational position and, though the theses stated in this work were developed more fully and in some respects modified over the years, he never departed significantly from the basic position revealed in this early work. Only a careful reading of the original document can reveal all the nuances of the theoretical position delineated in it, but by way of introduction to a firsthand study of it we will examine its basic themes.

"What Education Is"

The document is composed of five "articles" each of which deals with a primary aspect of a theory of education. The first of these articles is concerned with what education is. In Dewey's estimation, "all education proceeds by the participation of the individual in the social consciousness of the race." This process begins with the birth of the child and in the beginning is unconscious but powerful in shaping the primary powers and dispositions of the developing child. Gradually, the child begins to share consciously in the funded intellectual and moral resources we call civilization. This developmental process is serial in character, proceeding from the gross and undifferentiated impulses of infancy to the increasingly organized responses of maturity. Thus, "the only true education comes through the stimulation of the child's powers by the demands of the social situations in which he finds himself."

There are always two sides to the educative process: the psychological and the sociological, and neither of these can safely be neglected. The psychological side provides the basis of all education, for it is the child's instincts and powers that give the starting point for the process. "Save as the efforts of the educator connect with some activity which the child is carrying on of his own initiative independent of the educator, education becomes reduced to a pressure from without."

Consideration of the sociological factor reveals that while the child has his own instincts and tendencies, the meaning of these is not known until they are translated into their social equivalents. "In order to know what a power really is we must know what its end, use, or function is, and this we cannot know save as we conceive of the individual as active in social relationships." The only tenable approach to education, particularly under the dynamic conditions of modern industrial society, consists in helping the child to realize as completely as possible the native powers he possesses. We cannot know with any certainty what society will be like even a few years from now, and it is futile to attempt to prepare the child for a specific set of future conditions. The best we can do for him is ". . . to give him command of himself . . . to train him that he will have the full and ready use of all his capacities; that his eye and ear and hand may be tools ready to command, that his judgment may be capable of grasping the conditions under which he has to work, and the executive forces be trained to act economically and efficiently."

"What the School Is"

The school is a form of community life in which a concentrated effort is made in ". . . bringing the child to share in the inherited resources of the race, and to use his own powers for social ends." Education must be conceived as a "process of living and not a preparation for future living" and the experience the child has in the school must be as real and vital to him as that of the home or the neighborhood.

The only way to secure continuity in the child's growth is to plan his school experience so that it grows gradually out of his home life and the activities he has become familiar with in the home. This background of previous experience provides the background which will give meaning to the new ideas presented in the school. A major reason for the failure of traditional education is that it does not see the school as a form of community life. The conservative tradition sees the school as a place in which certain information is transmitted and certain habits formed as a means of preparing for the future. "As a result they do not become a part of the life experience of the child and so are not truly educative."

Education has a moral dimension when it is seen as a mode of social life. Effective moral training occurs when the individual relates to others in "a unity of work and thought," and thus the child's behavior is stimulated and controlled through the life of the community. The traditional school fails to give any genuine, regular moral training because it ignores the role of the community and vests the sole responsibility for control in the teacher.

"The Subject Matter of Education"

"The social life of the child is the basis of concentration or correlation . . . social life gives the unconscious unity and the background of all his efforts and all his attainments. None of the traditional school subjects, whether taken singly or together, can furnish the true center of correlation. The traditional school errs gravely when it introduces the young child too early and too abruptly to a program of special subjects: reading, writing, geography, etc., for these are presented out of relation to social life and hence have little meaning for the child. The real business of the school is the progressive development and enrichment of the child's experience and the enhancement of his own native powers and therefore: '*Education must be conceived as a continuing reconstruction of experience; that the process and the goal of education are one and the same thing.*' "[22] Subject matters, as we usually think of them in terms of history, mathematics, literature, etc., are important as means, but they are not the ends of education and they have meaning only as they enter actively into social life.

"The Nature of Method"

"The question of method is ultimately reducible to the question of the order of development of the child's powers and interest." Thus, the order in which material is presented and the way it is treated derive from the child's own nature. In the development of the child the active side always precedes the passive, "consciousness is essentially motor or impulsive . . . and conscious states tend to project themselves in action."

Ideas result from action and are important as controls of action. It is idle to attempt to develop powers of reason and judgment apart from their role in selecting and arranging means for action. Since traditional education ignores this, the child is continuously presented with arbitrary symbols. Symbols are important means of our intellectual processes

[22] This sentence is a very famous one in Dewey's educational writings. It is one of his earliest statements that education is a process and as a process it is of far greater importance than any of its products. This is similar to Aristotle's distinction between the "art of knowledge" and its products. See ante, p. 27.

but presented in isolation, as in the traditional school, they are only "a mass of meaningless and arbitrary ideas imposed from without."

"Interests are the signs and symptoms of growing processes." A child's interests show the stage of development he has reached and indicate the stage he is about to enter. It is of the greatest importance, therefore, that the teacher give constant attention to the interests of his pupils. The point is not that interests should be indulged or that they should be repressed, for an interest is always the sign of some power and the business of the teacher is to discover this power and make arrangements for its expression and development.

"The School and Social Progress"

"Education is the fundamental method of social progress and reform." Reforms that are based on laws and legal threats or superficial modifications in society are futile. The only trustworthy means of social reconstruction lies in the adjustment, through education, of individual actions on the basis of social consciousness. This approach recognizes both the individual and the social factors and it indicates that the ideal school will reconcile individualistic and institutional ideals. ". . . thru education society can formulate its own purposes, can organize its own means and resources, and thus shape itself with definiteness and economy in the direction in which it wishes to move."

SUMMARY

In this chapter we have sketched the development of the liberal protest against the conservative domination of American society and particularly American education. This protest movement in education grew out of and was an important part of a broad resurgence of liberal sentiment and the resulting liberal reform movement, whose effects were felt in every important aspect of American life.

Major attention has been given to the work of an experimental school founded at the University of Chicago by John Dewey and his associates. This school provided a situation in which certain major ideas for the reform of education could be tested experimentally. Dewey developed these ideas, in part at least, concurrently with his work in psychology and philosophy. He regarded the school as a place in which not only practical innovations in education could be tested, but also as a means for testing psychological and philosophical ideas.

Certainly there is far more to the development of the liberal protest movement and the emergence of progressivism in education than is to be found in the work of the Laboratory School or in such early writings of Dewey as *My Pedagogic Creed*. At the same time the Dewey school was flourishing at Chicago, other schools in various parts of the country were also engaged in testing innovations in education. In many cases these schools were notably different from the Laboratory School in their programs and their conception of the objectives of education. As we observed at the beginning of this chapter, the historic reality that was progressivism in education was enormously complex and this makes easy generalizations about it impossible.

However, John Dewey is recognized universally as the major figure in the development of liberal social and political philosophy, as well as progressivist educational philosophy, in the earlier decades of this century. This recognition has always been given him by those who are friendly to his ideas as well as by those who are not. Since our primary interest in this book is the philosophy of education, in the next chapter we will engage in a systematic exposition of the salient ideas in the philosophy of educational progressivism. Most of these ideas can be attributed primarily to Dewey, though some important contributions to the philosophy of progressivism came from other sources.

CHAPTER EIGHT

John Dewey

and the Liberal Protest

in Education

In this chapter we will give systematic attention to the basic ideas that make up the ideology of progressivism in education. We have already encountered some of these ideas in *My Pedagogic Creed* which was published by Dewey during the years of the Laboratory School. Much of what will be said in this chapter relates to Dewey's thought on education as it is expressed in his voluminous writings. At the risk of becoming unbearably repetitious, we will observe again that progressivism in education was far from being a product solely of Dewey. It is our opinion, however, that Dewey's writings contain much of what was intellectually rigorous and systematic in the liberal protest against the domination of essentialism in American education and that these writings provide the best means for understanding the spirit and the content of the progressivist philosophy of education.

THE PURPOSES OF EDUCATION

We have already seen that the way an educational tradition conceives the fundamental purposes of education is an important factor in determining its conception of the character of the curriculum, the nature of educational method, and the role of the teacher. In Part II of this book we discussed the ends of education as these are conceived by conservatives. We saw the close relation between the conception of education as preparation and the conservative's views of the curriculum and teaching method.

Much of the liberal protest against essentialism stems from the conservative view that the foremost purpose of education is the perpetuation of tradition and the preparation of the immature for adulthood. The essence of Dewey's argument against the conservative thesis became apparent in his early educational writings and is clearly expressed in *My Pedagogic Creed.* In the early chapters of *Democracy and Education* he gives extended treatment to the question of how the ends of education should be conceived and criticizes certain variant views.

Dewey's argument begins with his observation that the salient fact of life is the organism's power to grow. The growth of a human being is different in important respects from that of other kinds of organisms, the chief difference being the relatively plastic nature of the child and the prolonged period of dependency that characterizes human infancy. Most animals, for example, come into the world with their potential repertory of behavior patterns already fixed by heredity. Learning in these creatures, then, is essentially that of the progressive developing and maturing of what was already present in potential. The animal learns by responding to environmental situations on the basis of instinct. Thus, experience affects the nature of animal learning but not in the same way that it affects the human being.

The human infant at birth is extraordinarily plastic in nature. By this is meant that beyond a bare minimum of what appears to be reflex (unlearned) behavior patterns, infant behavior is impulsive, that is, unformed by specific hereditary patterns and therefore capable of developing in various ways and in various directions. This initial plasticity of human nature also means that mankind has the capacity of learning from experience, that is, of becoming progressively more able to foresee the probable course of events that will ensue from some action and regulating behavior in the light of these foreseen possibilities.

The psychological mechanism by which initial native impulsive behavior is molded Dewey calls *habit.* This is a common psychological term, but it exhibits many shades of meaning. Dewey's use of the term is considerably different from that of many psychologists who use it to denote relatively simple and narrow elements of learned behavior. Dewey means by habit patterns of behavior that are far more extensive and flexible than rigid responses to specific stimuli. In his use of the word, habits are *arts*; ways of doing things.

> Habits are ways of using and incorporating the environment in which the latter has its say as surely as the former. We may borrow words from a context less technical than that of biology, and convey the same idea by saying that habits are arts. They involve skill of sensory and motor organs, cunning or craft, and objective materials. They assimilate objective energies, and eventuate in a command of environment. They require order, discipline, and manifest technique.[1]

From this we conclude that habits, as arts or learned ways of utilizing the objects and energies of the environment for conscious purposes, are the ways by which growth takes place and are also indexes of growth in the child. We can say also that, since the most important aspect of the human environment is social, habits themselves are significantly social in their origin and character. They are, in fact, the very stuff on which the continuity of social and individual experience depends. Without this capacity to preserve experience through habit, the human species could not survive. But there is also a danger that lurks always in the background, for habits have a way of becoming stiff and unyielding instead of being flexible and artistic means to furthering experience. When they become rigid they can constitute an arrest of growth.

The molding of the native, impulsive behavior of the human being into meaningful patterns of habit is what is meant by education in its broadest sense. Education, then, is a continuing process of the reconstruction of experience. This process involves the total experience of the individual and only a part of it takes place in the school. Further, the continuing process of reconstruction of experience is an aspect of growth itself and, as Dewey reasoned:

> Since growth is the characteristic of life, education is all one with growing; it has no end beyond itself. The criterion of the value of school education is the extent in which it creates a desire for continued growth and supplies means for making the desire effective in fact.[2]

This statement, occurring in Dewey's greatest contribution to educational theory, has puzzled, and frequently outraged, his readers ever since it was published. There is much in these innocent-appearing half-dozen lines that calls into question some of the most cherished convic-

[1] John Dewey, *Human Nature and Conduct*, New York: Henry Holt and Company, 1922, p. 15. This book is the most complete exposition of Dewey's psychology.
[2] *Democracy and Education*, p. 62.

tions in the western tradition; for example: Does not growth always proceed toward some final end or fulfillment? Growth is a process but a process moves toward some goal. What goal does Dewey see? His answer was always, "continued growth," but this never seemed to satisfy his critics or enlighten many of his friends. And so, inevitably, the questions came about how we can know when growth is in the right direction. The development of cancer is growth, but is *that* desirable? Becoming an increasingly expert swindler is a process of growth. Is that desirable? No, Dewey answered many times, these are not growth.[3] They are developments that stunt or destroy the possibilities for further growth. The advent of cancer heralds the end of continued growth and the death of the organism, precluding any further development. A life of crime closes important avenues of experience and stunts and perverts development. We know these things by observing the consequences sickness and crime entail. Education, as a continuing process of growth, frees impulse, keeps habit flexible and adaptable to changed circumstances, and thus provides for future development of experience.

Another criticism often urged against Dewey's conception goes somewhat as follows: Dewey has made growth the characteristic of life, and he has said further that growth has no end beyond itself. This must mean that life has no end beyond itself; in other words Dewey is really saying that life itself moves toward nothing and thus has no purpose. This kind of objection raises certain fundamental questions in the theory of value which we will not attempt to consider until we have outlined Dewey's position more fully. But, provisionally, we can say that Dewey rejects the notion that there is some *summum bonum* toward which all human striving should proceed and suggests that inflated statements about *The Meaning of Life* usually have little meaning of their own. Any human life itself has the meaning to it that the experience of the person makes possible. Meaning is not something that stands outside the life process but instead is a quality of it. The purpose of education, broadly conceived, is to make possible the widening and deepening of meaning. The end of life is synonymous with the process: to live more fully and more richly.

The process we call education, then, is the process of developing the native powers and tendencies of the child as they exist initially in impulsive form. Growth proceeds as these powers and tendencies are

[3] See for example: Dewey's *Experience and Education*, New York: The Macmillan Company, 1938, pp. 28–29.

formed into meaningful habits through their expression in an environmental context that is always social. This process has no end outside itself, since the process of growth has no end outside itself.

We will now consider some views of the objectives of education which Dewey criticized and contrasted with his own view of education as a process of growth that has no ends outside itself. Such a consideration will help us understand the protest Dewey was making against the older traditions of schooling.

He first directs attention to the idea that education is a process of preparation for some relatively distant future in the life of the child. We have already paid close attention to this notion because it is the basic working idea of essentialism. Contemporary conservatism puts the idea of education as preparation central to its educational philosophy and makes everything else subordinate to it, and this was as true in Dewey's day as it is in this. The purpose of the elementary school is preparation for the secondary school; the secondary school is preparatory for the college; the college for the graduate school. The whole process (granted, of course, that very few ever make their way through the entire gamut) is preparatory for adult life. When a child enters school at the age of five or six he is embarking on a process of preparation for something that lies in a distant future.

Dewey argues that there are insurmountable difficulties involved in this conception.[4] For one thing, an educational program based on the idea of preparation always loses the energy and motive power pupils possess in such abundance. Children live in the present, and a distant future of which they can have little or no awareness provides scant motivation for school tasks. This in turn leads to procrastination and idleness in the classroom. As the child sees it, if the future is so far off, there must be plenty of time to prepare for it, and there are so many things to do in the meantime. Thus, much time spent in school is aimless and barren of desired results.

This condition is aggravated by another element of the conservative tradition to which we have already given attention. Essentialism has always found it necessary to establish some minimum average standard —"the essentials for the grade"—as the prevailing expectation for pupils. And what began as a floor is soon found to be a ceiling. What conservative schools actually do, as Dewey saw it, is to substitute "a conventional average standard of expectation and requirement for a standard

4 See: *Democracy and Education*, Chapter V.

which concerns the specific powers of the individual . . ." And out of this comes the mediocrity that conservatives consistently deplore but which their schools systematically cultivate.

Finally, Dewey points out, it is always necessary to make use of extraneous rewards and punishments wherever the notion of education as preparation is found. The conservative school ignores or suppresses the in-born motive powers of children and in the place of this natural motivation must substitute marks, failures, praise, honor rolls, promotions, retardations, and expulsion from school. The pedagogical pendulum periodically swings from iron rule to sugar coating and back again; one as futile as the other. So long as the view prevails that education is preparation for some distant future these evils are not to be escaped.[5]

Dewey next turns attention to a conception of education as a process of unfolding of some latent potential in the child. This is one of the oldest systematic views of human growth and the development of knowledge in the individual. One form of it is found in Plato in the guise of innate ideas which are brought to consciousness by the ministrations of the teacher. A variant form appeared in the nineteenth century as an aspect of absolute idealism and received its clearest pedagogical development in the hands of Froebel. It also was a notion that played a part in the educational progressivism of Dewey's own time and to which he was strongly opposed.

The difficulty that attends the "unfolding" theory of development is at heart the same as in the "preparation" theory. While the former recognizes that development is a process of growth, it sees this process proceeding toward some ultimate perfection or final end. Growth is thus a series of "approximations to a final unchanging goal." Now the theory of preparation really is the same idea; the difference between the two lies in what the ultimate goal is thought to be. With the "preparationists" it is conceived usually as practical and vocational and with the "unfolders" it is more apt to be spiritual and ethical.

Since the goal towards which the child's nature is said to unfold is so remote, it is not only unattainable, it is also incapable of giving any real guidance to the teacher and therefore something has to be substituted for it. What usually is substituted for it is something *the*

---

[5] With respect to the observation contained in the *Report of the San Francisco Curriculum Survey Committee*, cited in Chapter IV, that: "Few children want to do anything difficult without a little prodding or a little stimulation," Dewey would undoubtedly reply that the Survey Committee is absolutely right and will continue to be right so long as education is conceived as preparation for a distant future.

teacher thinks the child should learn. So by "expert questioning" the teacher "draws out" of the child the response desired. This may satisfy the teacher, but it contributes little to the education of the child, for he has no way of knowing what the teacher really is after. Continued experience of this kind makes the pupil more and more dependent on the cues that come from the teacher; his own originality and motivation are suppressed or ignored. Dewey observes that less harm is probably done simply by telling the child whatever it is we want him to know and adds wryly, ". . . at least it remains with the child how much will stick."

The real difficulty with the unfolding theory is that it ignores the nature of experience which, as Dewey had already stated in *My Pedagogic Creed,* always involves both the inner nature of the child and the external environment in which the native powers of the child find meaningful expression. The unfolding theory concentrates on the inner nature and ignores the importance of the outer. Consequently, when this theory is acted upon in school situations its effects are found to be as bad as those of the preparation theory.

The third conception of education Dewey criticizes is education as the training of faculties or, as it is often called, "mental discipline." We have already identified this theory as one of the most persuasive pedagogical notions in the history of western education. Its history goes back at least as far as Aristotle, and it was restated in classic form by John Locke. It has always played an important role in the essentialist tradition and still remains an important influence in that tradition, despite its lack of support in experimental psychology.

Dewey begins by agreeing that the theory of mental discipline has the proper ideal in mind because it views the end products of education as "specific powers of accomplishment." In this sense, the educated person is one whose original powers are developed to the extent that he is skillful and effective in all aspects of his life and work. This is what Dewey meant when he said that habits, which are the outcomes of educative experience, are ways or arts for dealing with the environment. The difficulty with the mental discipline theory—and it is a major one in Dewey's estimation—is that it is false to the psychological facts. The origin of its major error lies in the fundamental dualism which has been characteristic of so much western philosophy and to which we have had occasion to refer in earlier chapters. This dualism, as expressed in Locke, for example, postulates an external world from which stimuli (sensations) impinge on a passive intellect. It also postulates an internal mind possessed of various powers of observation, memory, association, etc. Through the operations of these powers of the active intellect, complex ideas are constructed and these are the objects of our knowledge. As an educational theory, the task of education is the development of these specific mental powers or "faculties" through appropriate exercise.

In the first place, Dewey says, the existence of these original faculties is a pure myth. There simply are no such well-defined powers waiting to be trained. What does exist is a pool of native tendencies and impulses that take on specific and meaningful function as they are expressed in the environment and become habits. The more specific training is, the narrower and less flexible are the habits that come from it.

For another thing, this theory is in error in the way it treats subject matter, for what the character of the content used in mental training is makes little difference, so long as it provides specific training. But, Dewey points out, we want people to remember and understand and make use of learned material that will contribute to their lives and work. This point is ignored in the theory of mental discipline because this theory represents a failure to understand that the meaning of any subject matter—broad or narrow—lies in its relation to the social context in which experience goes on. Thus, although there is an important element of truth in the mental discipline approach, it turns out to be untenable because it is based on faulty psychological ideas.

In concluding this discussion of the purposes of education as they were seen by Dewey, we will give brief attention to his conception of the role aims play in the educative process. We now know that Dewey not only did not accept the notion of some ultimate aim or purpose for education, which by necessity must exist outside the process itself, but that he considered such an idea to be fatal to effective educational procedures. But, many have asked, does this mean that education has no aims, aside from the vague criterion of "continued growth?"

Dewey, of course, did not consider continuity of growth to be a vague criterion. He did agree, however, that the aims that operate *within* the educative process are important and require close attention. He observes that it is meaningless to speak of some abstract process such as education as having aims. Abstractions do not have aims but people do.[6] Educators, like people in any field of work, have certain things to accomplish, and they must work with the resources they have and in terms of the obstacles they must overcome. A teacher must formulate his aims with respect to the nature of children with whom he is working

6 *Democracy and Education*, p. 125. Chapter VIII is an extended treatment of the subject of aims in education.

and the social context in which life goes on and, as Dewey observed, the point is to have "energies work together instead of against one another." The teacher who sets up some aim without any reference either to the child's nature or the nature of society is as foolish as a farmer who sets up his aim of growing some crop without any attention to soil or climate.

In view of these matters, then, good educational aims will first of all be conceived in terms of the needs, native powers, and previous experience of the person to be educated. In the second place, an aim must be capable of giving guidance to the development of suitable method. It must function as a working idea that will guide the development of day by day operations. Dewey is strong in his belief that externally imposed aims not only are incapable of doing these things, they even prevent the teacher's using his own common sense and ingenuity. And the wisest thing a teacher can do is to be forever on his guard against aims that are allegedly general and ultimate.

THE NATURE OF THE CURRICULUM

In the preceding chapter we examined the program of the Dewey Laboratory School in some detail and we know from this study that the curriculum of that school was built around active enterprises or, as Dewey called them, active occupations. We know also that in his early writings on education Dewey had advocated an active curriculum as opposed to the passive acquisition of subject matters around which the traditional school organizes its program. In *Democracy and Education* he restated this basic thesis on curriculum organization and elaborated it more fully.

Dewey pointed out that a great many kinds of active occupations had already found their way into the curriculum to some extent in the form of the fine and applied arts. Usually this work was carried on as something "extra" to the "regular curriculum" of subject matters and more often than not such activities were employed as a means of relief from the tedium of the regular studies. Contemporary essentialism still views them mainly in this light.

As Dewey saw it:

The problem of the educator is to engage pupils in these activities in such ways that while manual skill and technical efficiency are gained and immediate satisfaction found in the work, together with preparation for later usefulness, these things shall be subordinated to *education*—that is, to intellectual results and the forming of a socialized disposition.[7]

Therefore, it is not enough to introduce active work into the school. The crucial matter is the way in which activities are used and, therefore, certain procedures are ruled out immediately. Active occupations should never be devoted merely to copying some kind of model, for this effectively prevents the employment by the pupil of his own judgment in relating means to ends—which is the intelligent factor in all enterprises. The copying of an assigned model or the meticulous following of prescribed steps is slavish, not liberating, to the child's intelligence. Further, active work should always be organized in *wholes* and, as we have seen, this was done in the Laboratory School in the form of enterprises—interest in achieving some foreseen purpose or outcome, devising plans for doing it, executing the plans, and observing the outcomes. This approach rules out isolated exercises. Whether isolated drill be with manual or intellectual tools, the results are the same. The processes lack significance for the learner because they are isolated from the purposes which alone can give them meaning.

Active occupations are sound educational devices because they work in with the active, manipulative tendencies of childhood, but their greatest educational strength is that in representing basic modes of social life they provide the necessary context out of which systematic mastery of specialized knowledge can *develop*. It is a fact of history that the great organized bodies of knowledge had their origin in and developed out of the efforts of men to cope with their basic social needs. Mathematics began with reckoning, keeping account of things, measuring, etc., and after that became the rigorous discipline we know today. The natural sciences grew out of efforts to control and utilize the natural environment for human purposes. Literature and the fine arts developed as means of expression of personal and social feeling and the effort to preserve and interpret experience. Now in a sense, this genetic development of experience, from the immediate and practical to the specialized and conceptual, through which the race has gone must be repeated by every individual and there is no true short cut. This does not mean that the child must re-create the whole of civilization but it does mean that the development of knowledge in the human being is also a genetic process and the growth of meaning in an individual's cognitive structure in this sense is necessarily of the same character as the development of knowledge in a civilization.

[7] *Democracy and Education*, p. 231.

In a passage in Chapter XIV of *Democracy and Education* Dewey describes the character of the genetic process of knowledge. This statement is often read over without its significance being appreciated. Actually, it is a major statement in his philosophy of education.

> In its first state, knowledge exists as the content of intelligent ability—power to do. This kind of subject matter or known material, is expressed in familiarity or acquaintance with things. Then this material gradually is surcharged and deepened through communicated knowledge or information. Finally, it is enlarged and worked over into rationally or logically organized material—that of the one who, relatively speaking, is expert in the subject.[8]

With respect to the first stage, Dewey points out that the knowledge that people master first and retain the longest is that of *how to do*. The first evidence we see in the behavior of young children of the growth of understanding is their increasing tendency to take the materials in the environment and use them to realize foreseen outcomes. The blocks that the child first manipulated at random become materials that are consciously shaped into a house or automobile or some other recognizable object. In this way comes acquaintance with things, their potentialities and their limitations, and this leads to the kind of wisdom that is widely recognized as being associated with the intelligent direction of life activities. "Only in education," says Dewey, "never in the life of farmer, sailor, merchant, physician, or laboratory experimenter, does knowledge mean primarily a store of information aloof from doing."[9]

Therefore, since the natural development of knowledge begins with intelligent doing, and since the manipulative, constructive activities in which children engage are pregnant with educational possibilities, Dewey insists that arts and occupations should form the first stages of the school curriculum. As we have already seen, this idea was followed in the Dewey Laboratory School.

The second stage begins early in the life of the child and overlaps and blends with the first. Learning at the human level is always social in nature. Not only does the child carry on his activities in the presence of others and with their cooperation, the very materials and ideas with which he works are social products. This social context provides the conditions necessary for communicated experience. He learns from his peers and he also learns from those adults, particularly those whose business is the welfare and development of children—parents and teachers.

[8] *Democracy and Education*, pp. 216–217.
[9] *Loc. cit.*

The enterprises in which the child is engaged provide a context in which new ideas can be communicated, ideas which illuminate and extend the meaning of knowledge already acquired.

This communication of meaning goes on throughout the life of an individual, but childhood and youth are particularly strategic in this respect. Dewey never doubted that communication is the lifeblood of education, nor did he denigrate the value of the preserved experience we call "subject matter." He did insist that certain criteria must be met if communication is to be meaningful to the pupil and thus be effective in developing his own awareness and understanding. The point is not how the communicating is done—by oral telling, by printed materials, or by the newer technological devices. There are many ways to communicate; some are old, some are new. The test any item of communicated information must meet is:

> Does it grow naturally out of some question with which the student is concerned? Does it fit into his more direct acquaintance so as to increase its efficacy and deepen its meaning? If it meets these two requirements it is educative. The amount heard or read is of no importance—the more the better, *provided* the student has a need for it and can apply it in some situation of his own.[10]

Thus, according to Dewey, the reason so much of the communication that goes on in school is fruitless is because it is done outside any context that enables the learner to relate the new material to his previous accomplishments.

The third stage in the process of the development of knowledge in the individual *emerges* as a result of his progression through the first two stages. Out of the continuum of experience that begins in childhood with familiarity with things and is expressed as intelligent ability to do, and through the communication of meanings which broaden and illuminate experience, there comes an increasing degree of organization and synthesis that represents mastery of knowledge. But this third stage is reached *only as the conditions of the first two are satisfied.*

This, says Dewey, is the natural, genetic course that the development of knowledge takes. The school can respect it and work with it, or it can ignore it and work against it, *but the school cannot change it.* This point constitutes one of Dewey's major protests against essentialism. The traditional school begins exactly end around. Instead of beginning with the native powers and tendencies of the child and seeking to shape these into increasing mastery and power, the school begins with a series

[10] *Democracy and Education, Ibid.,* p. 219.

of subject matters already organized and synthesized by somebody besides the learner. The school sees its function as that of transmitting these subject matters to the child in as intact a form as possible. External imposition of this kind is never very successful and, in fact, it is the source of most of the difficulties the traditional school has to endure and which it has never succeeded in coping with adequately.

Dewey was joined in this protest by William James, another distinguished psychologist and philosopher who played an important role in developing the basic arguments against the conservative tradition.[11] James, speaking to the teachers of Cambridge as a psychologist, advised them:

> Begin with the line of his [the child's] native interests, and offer him objects that have some immediate connection with these.
>
> Next, step by step, connect with these first objects and experiences the later objects and ideas which you wish to instill. Associate the new with the old in some natural and telling way, so that the interest, being shed along from point to point, finally suffuses the entire system of objects of thought.[12]

Thus, James also inveighed against the formalism of the education of his day and believed that the improvements in pedagogy that were so badly needed could be had by reinterpreting the teacher-learning process in the light of experimental psychology.

We now turn our attention to a second aspect of the nature of the curriculum. This aspect has to do with the part organized subject matter has to play in the educative process. We already know that Dewey did not believe that subject matters are to be transmitted directly to the young, or even that they can be. He saw the great organized subject matters as *means* for carrying on enterprises and dealing with problems successfully. As he saw it, this is the function they perform in every other area of life—except in the typical school.

Dewey disputed the belief, one that has always been a major plank in the essentialist platform, that some subject matters possess an intrinsic worth that makes them desirable regardless of any particular set of circumstances. These subjects, says the conservative, must be taught to everybody because their very nature makes them good for everybody.

---

[11] James' contributions to the development of pragmatic philosophy are considered in the next chapter.

[12] William James, *Talks to Teachers on Psychology: and to Students on some of Life's Ideals*, New York: Henry Holt and Company, 1906, pp. 95–96.

To deny this, he says, is to denigrate the greatest achievements of the human intellect. Not so, says Dewey:

> It is no reflection on the nutritive quality of beefsteak that it is not fed to infants. It is not an invidious reflection on trigonometry that we do not teach it in the first or fifth grade of school. It is not the subject *per se* that is educative or that is conducive to growth. There is no subject that is in and of itself, or without regard to the stage of growth attained by the learner, such that inherent educational value can be attributed to it . . . There is no such thing as educational value in the abstract.[13]

The value organized subject matter has lies in its instrumental potentialities. It is valuable as it enables us to deal with the perplexities and problems of our own experience for it is a bridge between the past, which is settled and secure, to the present and future which are contingent and problematic. From the standpoint of the curriculum of formal education, matters must be arranged so that pupils engage in the *use* of ideas to plan and conduct enterprises and to deal with the problems that arise within the content of these activities. It is in this way, Dewey maintained, that the native intellectual potential of the child develops. And this, of course, was one of the major ideas underlying the program of the Laboratory School.

Specifically, Dewey regarded history and geography, or what we today call in a somewhat broader sense the social studies, as the important subject matters of elementary education. As he saw it, the value of these studies lies in their enriching and liberating the more direct experience of the child. We have already seen that the occupations that are the starting point of the curriculum are themselves social in origin. Participation in these activities provides a context for meaningful communication of accomplishments already achieved by the race. The delicate pedagogical problem is to introduce these into the experience of the child so that they connect with and form a solid part of his own stock of ideas and thus become resources for understanding and assimilating new ideas.[14]

Dewey himself regarded the economic and industrial phases of history as far superior to political and military history. The economic and industrial aspects are concerned with the increasing control men have

---

[13] *Experience and Education*, pp. 45–46.
[14] The problem is more delicate than many realize and this is likely true even at the college level, where heed is virtually never given it. William James, one of the most famous of American teachers of philosophy, once observed: "I think I have seen college students unfitted forever for 'philosophy' from having taken that study up a year too soon." James, *op. cit.*, p. 149.

achieved over nature and the growth of power and liberty that have resulted. He recommends also that a major stress should be placed on intellectual history, since the progress of civilization has come about through the employment of intelligence and the great achievements of the race are not military conquests or the rise and fall of dynasties, but the inventions and discoveries that have made possible the rise of man from savagery to civilization. And, it will be recalled, this was the general theme around which the curriculum of the Laboratory School was organized.

The other subject matter that Dewey thought important in the curriculum is science. He saw a close connection between intellectual history and the history of scientific development. As has just been said, Dewey proposed that the curriculum be organized around the broad social theme of the development of civilization through progress in inventions and discoveries. The significant episode in this development was the advent and increasing perfection of scientific method. The evolution of modern science, therefore, must be a main concern in the school's program.

Dewey knew, of course, that science can be taught in a way as stereotyped as the older subjects are taught in the traditional curriculum. The view that the teaching of science is a process of transmitting information about the concepts and facts established by prior scientific inquiries leads to the same isolation of subject matter from the experience of the learner that Dewey had already criticized in connection with the older subjects in the curriculum. The description he gives of the situation in his own day is strongly reminiscent of our contemporary school:

> Pupils begin their study of science with texts in which the subject is organized into topics according to the order of the specialist. Technical concepts with their definitions, are introduced at the outset. Laws are introduced at a very early stage, with at best a few indications of the way in which they were arrived at. The pupils learn a 'science' instead of learning the scientific way of treating the familiar material of ordinary experience. The method of the advanced student dominates college teaching; the approach of the college is transferred into the high school, and so on down the line, with such omissions as may make the subject easier.[15]

[15] *Democracy and Education*, p. 257. Whether one judges Dewey's conception of the place of science in the curriculum as right or wrong, it is hard to deny that this description is an accurate account of much that exists at the present time.

Dewey had the highest possible opinion of the power of scientific method. To him the method of science is the method of intelligence *par excellence*. As we will see in the next section of this chapter, he sought to make scientific method the basis for educational methodology. The power of science derives from the basic activities of observation, reflection, and testing of ideas. The subject matter this method yields is the most dependable and trustworthy knowledge it is possible to achieve. "Both logically and educationally," he said, "science is the perfecting of knowing, its last stage."[16]

Dewey's protest against the way the essentialist approaches the teaching of science is a repetition of his protest against all education conceived primarily as transmission of information. The rigor of scientific form is what the teaching process works toward, not what it begins with. What it should begin with are the familiar phenomena encountered in the home, the garden, the fields, and woods. Experience of this kind yields the subject matter which increasingly can be treated by the rigorous methods of observation, reflection, and testing. Communicated experience plays the same role here as it does in the development of any subject matter. Out of this continuum of experience come the habits of mind and the methods of approach to problems that characterize the scientific mind.

PRINCIPLES OF METHOD

Dewey's approach to educational method was formulated during the early years at Chicago. In *My Pedagogic Creed* he stated the proposition that was to guide the later development of his ideas on pedagogical method: "I believe that the question of method is ultimately reducible to the question of the order of development of the child's powers and interests. The law for presenting and treating material is the law implicit within the child's own nature."

His protest against the methodology of essentialism is directed at the dualism of subject matter *and* learner, a conception we have already given close attention in the chapters on the conservative tradition in education. As we saw in Chapter IV, the way the essentialist sees the situation is that on the one hand there is certain essential subject matter and on the other hand the prospective learner. The methodological problem is how to bring these together. As Dewey describes it:

16 *Ibid.*, p. 256.

Subject matter then becomes a ready-made systematized classification of the facts and principles of the world of nature and man. Method then has for its province a consideration of the ways in which this antecedent subject matter may be best presented to and impressed upon the mind; or, a consideration of the ways in which the mind may be externally brought to bear upon the matter so as to facilitate its acquisition and possession.[17]

It is precisely this dualism of content *and* method that is the starting point of the quarrel between the protagonist of methods courses in the training of teachers and subject-matter specialists who have a low opinion of any alleged science of method. On the one hand, there is the assumption that methods of teaching anything can be deduced from some psychological or other scientific theories of mind without any consideration for the subject matters these methods may be applied to. On the other hand, there is the assumption that an organized subject matter has a logic inherent in it and a person who is proficient in that subject matter has all he needs to teach it to somebody else. This controversy is particularly bitter today, as the most cursory examination of the literature of essentialism will show, and ironically enough, the blame for the proliferation of isolated methods courses is often laid on progressivism and particularly on Dewey. Actually, as early as the publication of *Democracy and Education* Dewey protested not only against the pedagogical dualism of subject and method, but against the underlying philosophical dualism inherent in essentialism.[18]

To Dewey, the way out of the impasse is to reconsider the nature of the learner's experience and the parts subject matter and method play in it. The developing experience of the child is the central concern of education, but experience is a process involving both internal and external factors. Experience is always *of* something. We can make a distinction between method and the material acted upon, just as we can make a distinction between eating and food, and sometimes for technical purposes it is useful to make such a distinction. The fatal error, however, is to forget that this distinction is conceptual and not existentially real.

When we come down to it, a method is simply an effective way of using material to realize some objective. This is universally recognized, except perhaps in connection with learning in school. Under Dewey's

[17] *Ibid.*, p. 193.
[18] Both objective idealism and realism, it will be recalled, involve the dualism of mind *and* matter and these are the two philosophical traditions most closely related to essentialism.

view, method, from the standpoint of the teacher, means effective ways of utilizing the native resources present in the pupil, including the fruits of his previous experience, together with the material and social forces in the environment, in order to further the course of his intellectual development. From the standpoint of the learner, method means the way in which things and ideas are used effectively to realize some desired objective, which in itself leads on to other desired objectives. The key to understanding the true nature of method lies in grasping the nature of experience. "Experience," says Dewey, "is not a combination of mind and world, subject and object, method and subject matter, but is a single continuous interaction of a great diversity . . . of energies."[19] Here is the nub of Dewey's approach to method.

The two working ideas to be used in the formulation of educational method are *interaction and continuity* and both these concepts refer to Dewey's idea of the nature of experience. It will be recalled that in *My Pedagogic Creed* he had insisted that education, which takes place within experience, always involves two factors: the child's own native impulsive behavior and the environment in which these native powers function and which, in fact, gives them meaning. Experience, then, in its most fundamental sense, is the interaction of a living thing with the environment in which it lives and by means of which it lives. Experience is a continuum; it is serial in character. The events that make it up are not discrete and isolated, but rather succeeding events grow out of and are conditioned by antecedent events. Every experience inevitably affects the course of future experiences, sometimes for good and sometimes not.

Now what we often call "intelligence" develops within this experimental continuum. There are many definitions for this slippery word and Dewey suggested that it is better viewed as a modifier rather than a substantive. "Intelligent" behavior is that behavior that puts one in control of the environment and hence of his own experience. Our behavior is intelligent when proposed actions are determined in the light of anticipated consequences. Intelligence, therefore, signifies the ability to relate means and ends; to regulate conduct with reference to objectives desired but not yet achieved. Ability to foresee the probable course of events depends of course on the fruits of previous experience— either the fruits of direct personal experience or the communicated experience of others, and generally both of these. This, as we have already seen, is the function information (subject matter) has in experience. It

[19] *Democracy and Education*, pp. 196–197.

represents the funded capital an individual has with which to meet the necessities and perplexities that arise in his own affairs.

Experience is not necessarily educative, although one episode in some way affects the course of subsequent experience. When an experience is educative it is continuous with previous experience, resources are available for the person to deal with the situation in an intelligent (as opposed to a random) fashion. The person involved in the situation makes forward and backward connections among events; he discerns the relations between means and consequences that are operative in the situation; by reflection he decides on a course of action and, having undertaken it, now sees the results of his decision. Out of experience of this kind come changes in attitude, outlook, and behavior which, in Dewey's words, is a transformation and reconstruction of experience.

Whatever conditions favor this kind of experience are beneficial; whatever conditions hinder it are miseducative and should be avoided. Here again is Dewey's protest against the methodology of the traditional school. In his view, that school creates the separation of content from method, thinking from acting, school experience from life experience. The conservative tradition in education fails to achieve proper results because it fails to see that experience is an interactive continuum in which continuity is the key to meaningful learning. Educational method that truly respects the real nature of experience will lead to a conception of education Dewey described in this way:

> Education takes the individual while he is relatively plastic, before he has become so indurated by isolated experiences as to be rendered hopelessly empirical in his habit of mind. The attitude of childhood is naïve, wondering, experimental; the world of man and nature is new. Right methods of education preserve and perfect this attitude, and thereby short-circuit for the individual the slow progress of the race, eliminating the waste that comes from inert routine and lazy dependence on the past.[20]

In an earlier publication Dewey had described the ideal school by comparing the program of such a school with the kind of experience a child has in a good home. An ideal home involves parents who are intelligent enough to understand the nature and needs of childhood, who involve the child in the activities of the family and use these as a means for furthering the intellectual and social development of the child. This home would have facilities in which the child could engage

[20] John Dewey, *How We Think*, 2d ed., Boston: D. C. Heath and Company, 1933, p. 202.

in active work in constructing and experimenting. It would be situated in a place such that gardens and woods, and open fields would be nearby and these too, would be employed as a means for intellectual growth.[21] There are very few homes, of course, that can provide opportunities of this kind. But in Dewey's estimation an idealized home experience furnishes a proper model for what the school would be if it based its work on a correct understanding of experience and grasped the significance of this for educational method.

Educational method is the means by and through which the teacher arranges the environment so that the experience of the child continuously develops and broadens in scope and the native powers of the child are nurtured and formed into flexible and functional habits. This means that educational methodology must take account of the many-sided nature of human development: intellectual, moral and esthetic. But it is characteristic of Dewey's educational thought, as well as his general philosophical position, that experience at its best is continuous, and the moral and esthetic aspects of it are pervaded with the intellectual, for in these facets of experience there is always some element of meaning and therefore of thought. When the intellectual is arbitrarily separated from the rest of experience, says Dewey, ". . . practical activity is mechanical and routine, morals are blind and arbitrary, and esthetic appreciation is sentimental gush . . . We state emphatically *that upon its intellectual side education consists in the formation of wide-awake, careful, thorough habits of thinking.*"[22]

Therefore, in Dewey's opinion, an important problem in educational method is to discover the conditions that stimulate pupils to think. If teachers understand the psychology of thought, they will be in a position to provide the kinds of opportunity needed for the formation of the habits and attitudes involved in reflection. It is true, of course, that most theories of education in some way stress the importance of thinking and see an important role of the school as that of "teaching people how to think." Dewey's protest was never against the idea that one purpose of the school is to teach students to think. His protest, and it is a major one in his educational philosophy, was against what he considered erroneous conceptions of the role reflective thought plays in experience.

In most educational traditions, including essentialism, reflective

---

[21] See: *The School and Society*, p. 34 ff.
[22] *How We Think*, p. 78.

thought appears to be conceived either as a vague kind of psychic energy that can be turned on or off at the will of the pupil, or as some separate faculty or group of faculties that can be brought to bear through the influence of the will. In Dewey's view, both of these—and all variations on them—are false to the facts of experience.

Reflective thought is a kind of behavior people exhibit when they encounter situations that cannot be dealt with on the basis of habit. We have already seen that habit gives continuity to experience and the power to adjust to and control the environment. But the environment is never completely stable. In the experience of every person situations develop that are indeterminate and disunified. These situations, because of their existential character, are perplexing and problematic to the person involved. *They are of this problematic character because habit no longer suffices to guide behavior.* In the literal sense, *the person caught up in these circumstances does not know what to do.* Dewey illustrated the "problematic situation" in this way:

> A man traveling in an unfamiliar region comes to a branching of the road. Having no sure knowledge to fall back upon, he is brought to a standstill of hesitation and suspense. Which road is right? And how shall his perplexity be resolved? There are but two alternatives: he must either blindly and arbitrarily take his course, trusting to luck for the outcome, or he must discover grounds for the conclusion that a given road is right.[23]

In the face of the forked road, which for Dewey symbolizes all the indeterminate conditions that we encounter in our experience, we have an option. We can act blindly, trusting to chance or Providence that the decision we make will turn out; *or we can act on the basis of intelligence.* That is to say, we can regulate our behavior by reflection. The service that reflective thought offers is that of making some plan of action that promises best, so far as can be seen, to resolve the problematic and doubtful character of the situation; in terms of Dewey's example, to "choose the right fork of the road."

The data inherent in the situation itself are insufficient to yield an idea; if they were sufficient, the situation would not be problematic because habit would be adequate to guide behavior. What a person has to fall back on, therefore, is the fund of relevant knowledge that is the product of previous experience. Here again the importance of the continuity of experience is stressed. If the person does not have resources adequate for dealing with the situation intelligently, he is forced

[23] *Ibid.*, p. 13.

necessarily to some more primitive level of behavior. In Dewey's words, "confusion remains pure confusion."

> Even when a child (or a grown-up) has a problem, it is wholly futile to urge him to think when he has no prior experiences that involve some of the same conditions.[24]

One function of reflective thought, then, is that of identifying the problematic character of situations that disrupt the even flow of experience and developing possible ideas or plans for some course of action that will resolve the indeterminate and disunified character of the situation. However, in most instances we think of more than one possible course of action, which is to say that several ideas compete for acceptance and action. A major difference between impulsive behavior and behavior that is controlled by thought is that overt action is forestalled for a time so that possibilities may be evaluated in terms of relevant data and probable consequences. Our reflective thought processes enable us to choose among the possible alternatives and adopt as a course of action the plan that promises best to change the problematic and indeterminate situation. Ultimately we must act if the situation is to be altered, and if our plan works out we can know that it was adequate for the situation. By putting the idea to action we have tested it as an idea and we have found it either adequate or inadequate.

This is Dewey's analysis of the role reflective thought plays in experience. In his view, every complete act of thought involves in some measure the following steps:

1. An indeterminate situation arises. This situation disrupts the course of experience because prior experience in the form of habit is inadequate to deal with it. It is the presence of this situation that stimulates reflective behavior. When there is no disturbing state of affairs, there is no thought because habit is sufficient.

2. The person (or persons) involved perceive the situation *in its problematic character.* This is to say, they are able to structure the elements of the situation sufficiently to see what the elements in it are and what impediments must be overcome if the character of the situation is to be changed.

3. Ideas are evolved that can guide action that must be undertaken if the situation is to be changed. In this sense, *ideas are plans for acting.*

[24] *Ibid.,* pp. 15–16.

4. The ideas evolved are subjected to a process of logical elaboration which in essence is the effort to determine what outcomes can be foreseen as probably occurring if a given idea is acted upon. As a result of this operation some idea is chosen to be acted upon.
5. The operations indicated in the idea are performed. What the character of these operations is depends on the nature of the problem. They serve to change the character of the situation, and if they produce the consequences anticipated, *the idea is warranted.* In common speech, it has "paid off."[25]

There are many connections here between Dewey's analysis of thinking and his conception of educational method. The school is always concerned with the intellectual growth of its students, but it is also concerned with the ethical and esthetic phases of experience. To Dewey experience is unitary and not fragmented and the ethical and esthetic, since they too involve apprehension of meaning, are pervaded with an intellectual quality, that is to say, with thought.

Accordingly, from the standpoint of the intellectual side, the methodology of education should proceed so as to facilitate the kind of activity in school that involves problem solving through inquiry. This should begin with the child's very first experience in school. Hopefully it might have its real beginning in the home but over this, of course, the school has no real control. Within the school itself certain conditions will have to be met:

First, the activities that go on in the school must be of such character that they stimulate thought and develop in the child habits of acting on thinking. The program must be an active affair, for genuine thinking always involves action of some kind. The activities must be arranged so that pupils encounter problematic situations that arise naturally out of the work itself and are not arbitrarily imposed by the teacher.

Secondly, the school must respect the continuity of experience. The activities and materials that are introduced must mesh with the experience already had by the pupils but yet lead on to other experience that will challenge without frustrating. This, as we have already noted, Dewey regarded as one of the most delicate and difficult aspects of educational method.

[25] This formulation of a complete act of thought is one of Dewey's best known contributions to psychology and logic. The most complete treatment of it from the psychological and pedagogical standpoint is in his *How We Think.* Chapter XII in *Democracy and Education* deals with thinking in the educational process. Certain logical aspects will be considered in the next chapter.

Third, communicated knowledge (information, facts, subject matter, etc.) must be given in a relevant context if it is to have any meaning for the learner and it should be noted carefully that *the relevance is to the experience of the pupil and the situation in which he is involved,* not to the teacher's sense of logic or some organization allegedly inherent in the subject matter itself.

An important emergent of this kind of experience is a constellation of attitudes and abilities that Dewey referred to as "critical intelligence." This refers not to an attitude of destructive criticism or to the kind of easy skepticism one sometimes finds among young people; it points rather to an attitude that ideas are plans for considered action and that as ideas they are judged not by their origins or their place in tradition, but by their fruits.

Dewey did not believe that the traditional school provided the opportunities enumerated above nor did he believe that the traditional school really valued critical intelligence. In this belief he was joined by many in the progressive movement. Essentialists have always extolled the importance of thought and the development of the intellect, but Dewey protested that they did not consciously provide for it in their schools. On the other hand, the Laboratory School under his direction sought through a curriculum based on active occupations organized in the form of enterprises to provide the conditions in which the reflective powers of the child are developed through organized inquiry.

SCHOOL AND SOCIETY

As early as the publication of *My Pedagogic Creed,* Dewey had advanced the thesis that expressed his conception of the relation of the school to society: "I believe that education is the fundamental method of social progress and reform." In this statement he was stating not only his personal belief but also restating a fundamental part of the American social tradition. This sentiment cannot be attributed solely to social liberalism for it is so much a part of the American mind that many conservatives agree with it also. We grant, of course, that the liberal's interpretation of the idea may be somewhat different from that of his conservative counterpart.

Be this as it may, in advancing this proposition in 1897 Dewey assuredly was echoing the sentiments of the liberal reform group. The liberals, as we have already seen, were calling insistently for a reform of the schools that would reinstate the democratic ideal as the ethical basis for education. Dewey knew that certain ideas needed to be reinterpreted in order to make them meaningful for a society whose character had already been transformed by the industrial revolution.

Individualism has always been a cherished ideal of the American tradition and we have seen in earlier chapters that this ideal had its origins in two sources. One of these was the economic pattern of life in America in the eighteenth and earlier part of the nineteenth century. In this agrarian society there obtained a degree of economic equality that had seldom, if ever, existed before. It has been estimated that at the time of the American Revolution upwards of ninety percent of heads of family were freeholders, owning and working their own land with the assistance of their immediate families. Wealth and success were achieved largely in proportion to the ingenuity and effort of the individual. It is small wonder that observers of the early American scene were always impressed by the aggressive individualism of the American.

We have also seen that the spirit of capitalism contributed to and reinforced the spirit of individualism. Capitalism, reinforced as it was by the Protestant ethic, glorified the same qualities of independence, thrift, and individual effort. "Getting ahead" was the credo of American life and, given the basic economic pattern that obtained, occupational and social mobility were genuine realities. The schools, of course, were pervaded with this spirit of individualism and as the influence of organized education grew, the school became another important means to individual success.

The conditions that produced this "rugged individualism" were transformed by the industrial revolution and the transition to a pattern of culture focused on technology and urban living. But the old sentiments prevailed and the individualism that had found a true expression in the economic and social conditions of pre-industrial life now was expressed more and more in pressure politics and the activities of myriad groups representing special interests. Out of this condition has grown the universal plaint that has now become a major theme in literature, in psychology, and in philosophy—"the lost individual."

As Dewey saw it, the trouble stems from the effort to retain in an increasingly corporate and integrated society a conception of individuality that is the product of an age irretrievably gone. Since this effort has proved itself to be in vain, many people find no alternative except to sit in sack cloth and ashes and bewail the fate of man in the modern world.

There is an alternative, Dewey believed, that goes beyond this kind of hopelessness. The problem, he said, is to develop a new individualism that will be to the modern age what the old individualism was in its own proper time.[26] The trouble is not that modern man finds himself involved in numerous associations and relationships—far more than men have ever been involved in before. The real difficulty is that these associations do not function harmoniously and nurture the emotional and imaginative aspects of individuality. The reason they do not is because there is lack of harmony within society itself. The situation appears circular and vicious, true enough, but Dewey maintained it would yield if intelligence were brought to bear upon it. In this the school has an important role.

The school, as Dewey believed, would contribute to a new individualism by cultivating in children and young people the method of critical intelligence. To employ intelligence in one's life means to face the facts as they are and to grasp the consequences they portend. There is another aspect of acceptance and commitment, of course, and this we usually think of in terms of emotions and will. These are not separate and disconnected elements, however, and in fact any effective commitment involves intellectual acceptance or denial. The alternative to intelligence, if in truth there is one, can be little other than a kind of abject irrationalism that often becomes pathological. In view of considerations of this kind, Dewey believed that the kind of educational policies he advocated would, if intelligently put to practice in the school, help to cultivate a new individualism that would be as worthy as the older one was in its day.

But this role of the school, as important as it is, cannot be the whole story, for the school does not exist apart from the rest of society and students live in an environment more extensive than the school. This brings us again to the question of the role of the school in social change. Writing in a time when the country was still in the throes of the great depression and when the outbreak of the second World War was only two years in the future, Dewey described three possibilities: One of these is for those responsible for the schools to accede to the prevailing cultural confusion and unsettlement and simply drift with the tide.

[26] This matter is discussed in many of Dewey's writings. The most concentrated and systematic treatment of it will be found in *Individualism Old and New*, New York: Minton, Balch and Company, 1930.

Such a choice is blind and unintelligent, he pointed out, but it is a choice. A second possibility is to ally the schools with the new developments—scientific, technological and cultural—that are transforming society and help the young to develop the understanding and intellectual power that will be needed in the task of social reconstruction that lies ahead. The third alternative is for educators to adopt an intelligent conservatism and seek to make the school an agent in conserving the old order.[27]

Dewey rejected the first possibility completely, seeing in it only the seeds of social dissolution and ultimate disaster. The third he saw as an intelligent choice but one that the progress of events was making more and more untenable. He accepted the second as indicating the role the school should play. He was careful to say, however, that he was not advocating that the schools should enter the political arena and take sides there. "I am not talking about parties," he wrote, "I am talking about social forces and their movements."[28] His conviction was that the school, by developing social intelligence and awareness in individuals, could make its greatest contribution to social reconstruction.

This proposal appears to be squarely within the main stream of American liberalism, but the times were desperate and Dewey's position was a target for criticism emanating from various quarters. Part of the criticism came, of course, from the conservatives who deplored the idea that the school should be other than a conserving stabilizing force in society. We have already paid close attention to this matter and will not repeat it again.

Dewey's conception of the role of the school in social change was also criticized by others who found his liberalism inadequate for the times. In the 1930s there was considerable sentiment expressed for teachers to ally themselves with the "class struggle," as that term was understood in the Marxist-Leninist-Stalinist sense. The class concept and the irreconcilability of social classes, it was argued, would furnish the guide line for the work of the schools. Teachers must become conscious of their own class status. They must see themselves as members of the exploited working class and they must throw their weight and the weight of the schools in favor of the destruction of the old order and the establishment of the new.

[27] See: "Education and Social Change," *The Social Frontier*, 3:237 (May, 1937). This has been reprinted in: Joseph Ratner, ed., *Intelligence in the Modern World: John Dewey's Philosophy*, New York: The Modern Library, 1939, p. 691 ff.
[28] *Loc. cit.*

This proposal obviously originated outside the stream of American liberal thought and is antithetical to basic beliefs of liberalism. But other criticism came from those who were squarely in the liberal camp. Mr. George Counts, for example, who was associated with the liberal protest movement, but who was by no means friendly to the "child-centered school" espoused by many progressives, lashed out against the lack of any positive conception of social welfare within the progressive movement. As Counts saw it, the progressive schools of the '30s were dominated by upper middle class people whose liberalism was at best lukewarm and who had no grasp of the great issues of the day. In his judgment they were "romantic sentimentalists, but with a sharp eye on the main chance." These people, he said, are not competent to guide the affairs of the schools, particularly in a time of crisis.

Counts' call was for the teachers to use the power they have to influence the attitudes and beliefs of the young in definite conscious fashion and in the directing of far-reaching social reform. The old haggling over whether the school should impose on children and indoctrinate them in certain beliefs should be shelved permanently. The child is always imposed on by somebody, the real question is by whom and for what.[29]

It was against this emphasis on social reconstructionism, which was always present in the progressive movement and which received its second major emphasis in the troubled decade before the outbreak of the second great war, that conservatism exhibited perhaps its most violent reaction against progressivism. As we have already observed, this threat still seems so great to conservatives that the current literature of that tradition periodically carries polemics against the idea of the school as an agent of social reconstruction.[30]

Dewey criticized many of the proposals of the social reconstructionists. He did not question the depth or the sincerity of their liberalism, nor did he underestimate the gravity of the situation in which the country found itself. But his conception of the nature of society indicated that the school alone could never determine the direction and character of social change. The school is only one of a great number

[29] See: George S. Counts, *Dare the School Build a New Social Order?* New York: The John Day Company, Inc., Publishers, 1932.
[30] In retrospect it may seem to many people that the clarion call of the social reconstructionists was the ultimate in political naïveté but it was not so regarded at the time. A student reading Counts' *Dare the School Build a New Social Order?* today may well find the title the most radical part of the document, but in its issue for July 17, 1935, *Time* warned against the emergence of a "pedagogic party" that would give Columbia University control of the United States. By far the best account of this fascinating period in the progressive movement is in Cremin, *op. cit.*, Chapter 6.

of institutions. Education, while a necessary condition for intelligent social change, is not a sufficient condition. Schools will serve the cause of social reconstruction best if they will discharge the service they are really equipped to do and this is to help the young, through appropriate experience in school, to develop sensitivity to the great problems of the time and to cultivate the powers of critical intelligence, which alone can provide a trustworthy guide for the future.

Mention should be made of another important figure in the progressive movement who, like Counts, also found serious weaknesses within it. Boyd H. Bode, who for many years was professor of education at Ohio State University, sought to clarify certain of the key ideas current in the progressive movement, believing that popular acceptance and usage of them had obscured their meaning and converted them into empty slogans. On most of the major issues in progressivism Bode and Dewey found themselves in agreement. Bode's criticism was, for the most part, leveled against the misinterpretation of such concepts as the doctrine of interest, pupil needs, and continued growth as the purpose of the educative process.

Bode maintained that in the fourth decade of the century progressive education had reached a crossroad and was confronted with the necessity for a choice. The choice, he said, lay between "becoming the avowed exponent of democracy or becoming a set of ingenious devices for tempering the wind to the shorn lamb."[31] Genuine democracy, he maintained, must have a distinctive educational system and this system must have as its basis a psychology[32] in which knowledge and truth are seen as functions in the control of experience and an ethical theory centered around the improvement of human life through shared effort. Democracy, Bode thought, is always in conflict with absolutism in both the social and the philosophical sense. "The center of any educational program which professes to be democratic," he said, "must be the irreconcilable conflict between democracy and absolutism."

Bode's call was for the progressive movement to become more rigorous in its philosophical foundations and to face up squarely to the fact that the initial successes of the progressive schools were being undermined

[31] *Progressive Education at the Crossroads*, New York: Newson and Company, 1938, p. 26.
[32] Bode's major contribution to psychology was: *How We Learn*, Boston: D. C. Heath and Company, 1940. This volume was a revision of an earlier work, *Conflicting Psychologies of Learning*. An important contribution to educational philosophy is his *Modern Educational Theories*, New York: The Macmillan Company, 1927.

by lack of awareness of the decisive relation between social liberalism and progressive principles of education. Uncritical acceptance and lack of understanding of "education as growth," "we learn by doing," "the needs of pupils," which by the thirties had become slogans, were corrupting and weakening the progressive protest. Much of the criticism in *Crossroads* is similar to that in Dewey's *Experience and Education*. But Bode's criticism, like that of Dewey, came too late and fell on either deaf or uncomprehending ears. By the time Bode had published his discerning critique the progressive protest had about run its course. World War II was only a year away and with it the beginnings of an era of resurgent conservatism.

SUMMARY

In this chapter we have examined certain major pedagogical doctrines advanced by Dewey in his voluminous writings on educational theory. It has been maintained that his was the most authentic philosophical voice to be heard in the development of the liberal protest. There were many others, of course, who marched under the banners of social and educational liberalism, but, by and large, he was the acknowledged leader of the procession.

Dewey's educational philosophy was an organic element in his whole approach to philosophy. We have already noted in passing that his basic educational views took shape along with his ideas in logic, psychology, and ethics. Certainly the beliefs he held about educational matters cannot be considered simply as logical inferences from some predetermined ideas in logic, ethics or any other field of academic philosophy, though he found his studies in the various branches of philosophy to be fruitful sources for his ideas on education.

Since the full impact of his educational philosophy can be sensed only by understanding its relation to his position on other kinds of philosophical questions, the next chapter deals with the relation of the philosophical tradition of pragmatism to the progressive protest against essentialism and to Dewey's own formulation of educational philosophy.

A consideration of pragmatic philosophy will enable us to do for the liberal protest somewhat the same thing done in Chapters V and VI for educational essentialism. In discussing Dewey's philosophy of education we have encountered certain key ideas on which much of his case seems to hang. In this chapter we have pursued these concepts only as far as they are related immediately to some aspect of educational theory. It is more than likely, however, that the reader has already sensed that there is more to them than has met the eye in this chapter. It is our purpose now to push our inquiry further in order that we may grasp the larger significance of the ideas that are central to Dewey's philosophy of education and to the protest against essentialism.

Accordingly, in the next chapter we will consider the following concepts which have figured importantly in Dewey's educational theory but which require further elaboration: a) the nature of experience; b) the significance of meaning and the pragmatic conception of truth; c) logic as inquiry and its relation to scientific method, the nature of value, and the process of valuation; d) the ontology of pragmatism.

CHAPTER NINE

American Pragmatism

and the Liberal Protest

In an earlier chapter we observed that as the nineteenth century drew to its close two protest movements in philosophy developed. Initially, these movements were largely protests against the domination of absolute idealism over western philosophy and, in fact, its domination over much of the intellectual life of the west. One philosophical protest that developed took the form of a resurgence of philosophical realism and the emergence of a group who called themselves the New Realists. We have already considered the relation of the resurgence of realism in philosophy to the conservative tradition in education. We turn now to the other protest movement which was to have the most far-reaching effects on philosophy and on the philosophy of education. The name we will use for this philosophical tradition is pragmatism and we will first give some attention to the major contributors to this development and the context out of which pragmatic philosophy developed.

THE DEVELOPMENT OF PRAGMATISM

The major contributions to pragmatic philosophy were made by Americans and, although this philosophy is not exclusively American, it is usually thought of here as well as abroad as peculiarly American in its spirit and in its major doctrines. The great names in this tradition are those of Charles Sanders Peirce (1839–1914), William James (1842–

1910), and John Dewey (1859–1952). We have already considered some of the salient facts in Dewey's long career in philosophy and the contributions he made to the philosophy of American liberalism and to progressivism in educational theory. We have also had occasion to mention the work of James, since he too had an interest in educational theory and was himself one of the greatest of American teachers. We have not, however, given any attention to Peirce in previous chapters because his contribution to the liberal protest in education was indirect, taking the form of fundamental contributions to pragmatic philosophy rather than to educational theory. Both James and Dewey acknowledged their profound indebtedness to Peirce and considered him the original source of many of their own ideas.

Peirce, himself the son of an eminent mathematical scholar at Harvard, was thoroughly trained not only in mathematics and logic, but also in the sciences, particularly the physical sciences. He was also accomplished in philosophy and by his own account had studied Kant so thoroughly that he practically knew *The Critique of Pure Reason* by heart.[1]

In the 1870s a group of men in Cambridge were in the habit of meeting at frequent intervals to discuss philosophical questions, particularly questions concerning the impact of science and scientific method on philosophy. Peirce was a regular member of this group, as was William James. Others among the membership were Oliver Wendell Holmes, who later was to become the famed liberal justice on the United States Supreme Court, and Chauncy Wright, who was a staunch advocate of the liberal philosophy of John Stuart Mill. Members of the group called their association "The Metaphysical Club." This was supposed to be ironic because the general spirit of the group was in the direction of scientific considerations and away from metaphysical speculation. It was at meetings of this club that Peirce first presented two papers that were of great importance in the development of pragmatic philosophy. These two papers will be considered later in this chapter.[2]

Many of the same conditions were responsible for the emergence and development of pragmatism that we have already seen were involved in the resurgence of philosophical realism. A major factor was, of course, the influence of science and scientific method and particularly in the case of Dewey, the scientific revolution in biology that was initiated by the

---

[1] Justus Buchler, ed., *Philosophical Writings of Peirce*, New York: Dover Publications, Inc., Chapter I.
[2] Peirce's own account of the activities of the Metaphysical Club may be found in his paper, "Pragmatism in Retrospect: A Last Formulation." See: Buchler, ed., *op. cit.*, p. 269 ff.

publication of Darwin's *Origin of Species*. Some members of the Metaphysical Club were corresponding with Darwin and all of them were greatly interested in the impact evolutionary theory was having on science, religion and philosophy. As one historian has said, "Darwin's *Origin of Species* had come into the theological world like a plough into an ant-hill. Everywhere those thus rudely awakened from their old comfort and repose had swarmed forth angry and confused."[3] The first great disruption occurred in theology probably because the threat of organic evolutionary theory was most obvious there, but as soon became evident, the "plough" was also creating havoc in the philosophical ant-hill.

Although the scientific revolution that was set in motion by the *Origin of Species* had profound effect on all three of the founders of pragmatic philosophy, Dewey has been most explicit about the impact of biology on his own philosophical position and he, more than either Peirce or James, consciously incorporated the principles of organic evolution into his effort of what he called the reconstruction of philosophy. Dewey's estimate of the revolutionary impact of Darwinian theory on the intellectual life of the west is revealed in the following quotation:

> Doubtless the greatest dissolvent in contemporary thought of old questions, the greatest precipitant of new methods, new intentions, new problems, is the one effected by the scientific revolution that found its climax in the *Origin of Species*.[4]

We will now give some attention to the influence Dewey attributed to Darwin, particularly the effect of evolutionary theory on philosophy.

One major factor was the awareness that in the light of scientific biology man in his totality was finally brought within the natural order. The ancient dualistic conception of man that we have already encountered many times in preceding chapters could no longer hold. Man is seen now as a natural organism, only one of numerous species. He is continuous with the totality of nature and his behavior is a phenomenon of nature in the same sense that any natural event is part of the process of the natural order. Human experience, as had already been indicated in the preceding chapter, must be understood as the interaction of the hu-

---

[3] Andrew Dickson White, *A History of the Warfare of Science with Theology in Christendom* (first published in 1896), reprinted by Dover Publications, Inc., New York, New York, 1960. The quotation here is from Vol. I, p. 70. White's section on "The Final Effort of Theology" is a classic summary of the effects of Darwin's work on the intellectual life of the later part of the nineteenth century. See: Vol. I, pp. 70–88.

[4] John Dewey, *The Influence of Darwin on Philosophy*, New York: Henry Holt and Company, 1910, p. 9.

man organism with a dynamic natural and social environment. In this sense, experience is a transaction going on in nature. It is simply one among the innumerable transactions that make up the natural world, but qualitatively this form of transaction is different from other forms. The difference lies in certain attributes of human beings; attributes not possessed by other organisms, but also attributes which have originated and evolved through natural processes. These ideas will be elaborated more fully in another section of this chapter.

Far more, however, can be attributed to Darwin's influence than merely the reinterpretation of human nature in biological terms. Both Dewey and Peirce saw the need for a transformation of logic and, in fact, a complete reorientation of philosophy. Before Darwin the philosophical and scientific world was to a considerable degree still enveloped in the confines of Aristotelian logic. The logic of science rested on the idea of fixed forms or species and ultimately on the existence of a "first cause." Under this view, nature is a progressive realization of an inherent purpose and knowledge is the apprehension of that which holds all change within bounds and thus makes fixed truth possible.

In the view of the pragmatists, Darwin's work constituted the *coup de grace* for this conception of nature. The idea of a "block universe" has to be given up, said James; nature is pluralistic not monistic. Novelty is inherent in the nature of things. Chance, argued Peirce, is a genuine force in the universe. And perhaps it was all summed up best in James' cry that this is "a universe with the lid off."

Dewey saw two courses open to philosophy. One of these was to take the direction indicated by the new advances in science. If it took this course, philosophy would concern itself with the objects and methods of inquiry that originate within the natural world; its concern would be with the specific conditions and circumstances that serve to generate the problems with which men have to deal and the modes of inquiry and action that make the solution of these problems possible. The alternative he saw was to pursue the course western philosophy had customarily followed. This was to continue the historic philosophical quest for a certainty embedded in some transcendental and supernatural reality that, by definition, must lie outside the scope of human experience. In the judgment of the pragmatists, this whole course of western philosophy had been wrong, for experience reveals no ultimate certainty nor, in fact, any certainty at all.

Peirce and Dewey agreed that philosophy would become intellectually responsible when it concerned itself with problems that are capable of being studied by methods developed within experience and with conclusions that are capable of being verified by an appeal to experience. Said Dewey:

> Once admit that the sole verifiable or fruitful object of knowledge is the particular set of changes that generate the object of study together with the consequences that then flow from it, and no intelligible question can be asked about what, by assumption, lies outside.[5]

Another influence on the development of pragmatic philosophy that deserves some mention here was that of the German schools of idealism. Pragmatism was, as we have said, a protest against idealism, but it was also a kind of off-spring of that tradition. Dewey himself had been a more or less orthodox Hegelian in the earlier part of his career, having been introduced to Hegel's philosophy when he was a student of George Sylvester Morris at Johns Hopkins. Dewey never concealed his admiration for Hegel's work and on one occasion attributed to it a "greater insight and richness" than is to be found in any other philosopher, excepting, perhaps, Plato.

Hegel's appeal for Dewey lay mainly in the idea of unity, which permeates absolute idealism and which Dewey thought promised a way out of the familiar philosophical dualisms that apparently had troubled him even in his student days. He has reported his early dissatisfaction with the dualism involved in the prevailing philosophy: the separation of soul from body, self from the world, and God from nature. We have already seen some evidence of Dewey's belief that one of the fundamental defects of traditional conceptions of education lay in the dualism inherent in them. The direct influence of Hegelian philosophy on Dewey's work gradually diminished as other forces, particularly scientific method, altered his views, but the campaign against dualism, which he considered the great philosophical fallacy, continued throughout his career as a philosopher.[6]

Peirce also acknowledged his debt to German philosophy, which he has said was the first purely philosophical material he studied seriously. He had little use for the speculative system-building methodology employed in it, preferring the empirical approach of British philosophers, but he found it a "rich mine of philosophical suggestions."[7] He also

[5] *Ibid.*, p. 14. Peirce made comments in a similar vein although his language was usually more acerbic than Dewey's. See: Buchler, ed., *op. cit.*, Chapter I.
[6] Dewey's estimate of Hegelian influence on his own work will be found in: G. P. Adams and W. P. Montague, eds., *op. cit.*, Vol. II, pp. 16–19.
[7] See: Buchler, ed., *op. cit.*, p. 2.

pointed out the close relation Hegelian idealism had with pragmatism, though he rejected Hegel's effort to reduce the whole of reality to pure thought.[8]

One other influence that had much to do with the character of pragmatic philosophy should be mentioned. This is the influence that developments in scientific psychology exerted on pragmatism and the chief contributor here was William James. Dewey has said that the psychological influence that contributed most was behaviorism, and he specifically mentions J. B. Watson as the chief advocate of this approach to psychology.[9] But he also maintained that the origins of the psychological position of pragmatism lay in James' great psychological work, *Principles of Psychology*.[10]

According to Dewey, there are two strains of thought discernable in the *Principles of Psychology*. One of these is a continuation, but also a reinterpretation, of the introspective approach to psychology. In place of the atomistic approach of Locke and the other British empiricists in which ideas are built up from discrete sense data, James substituted a continuum of sensory experience that he called "the stream of consciousness."

The other theme developed by James was influenced by biology. This theme is seen clearly, said Dewey, in James' operational theory of mind: "The pursuance of future ends and the choice of means for their attainment are thus the mark and criterion of the presence of mentality in a phenomenon." Dewey's own theory of mind, which we have already seen is closely connected with his educational theory, follows this concept from the *Principles of Psychology*.

It may be said in summation that pragmatism, while in a sense developing out of idealism, also constituted a major protest against it. The chief inspiration of the pragmatists was the possibilities they saw inherent in scientific method. They saw that method not only as a means of transforming the physical structure of society, but also its power of transforming intellectual life. We now turn to a consideration of the interpretation pragmatism gives to the concepts listed at the end of the last chapter and which are strategic to this philosophical tradition.

[8] *Ibid.*, pp. 266–67.
[9] For Dewey's analysis of the development of pragmatism, including the psychological elements in it, see: "The Development of American Pragmatism" in his *Philosophy and Civilization*, New York: Minton, Balch and Company, 1931, pp. 13–35.
[10] Two vols., New York: Henry Holt & Company, Inc., 1890.

EXPERIENCE, MIND, AND MEANING

We have already considered the way in which Dewey defined experience as the process of interaction of the human being with its environment. In this interactive process two aspects are discernible: the person acts on some elements in the environment; out of this action certain consequences ensue. The person then undergoes the consequences of his action. Thus, experience is a matter of doing and undergoing in which both the individual and the environment are changed in some measure.

Now nature itself is a great complex of interactions of many and diverse kinds and one of these is experience—the interaction of a human being with the environmental media in which and by which it lives. Many of these transactions are among things that in common sense we call physical. Common sense knows, of course, that the interactions of living things with environmental conditions are different from the interactions of inanimate things. In fact, they are so different that both common sense and philosophy have often made the distinction absolute. Here is one source of the familiar dualisms we have already had occasion to consider, and here also is a point at which Darwinian theory can be seen affecting pragmatic philosophy.

Darwin's evolutionary theory postulates a continuity that persists throughout nature. Under this view there are no abrupt breaks and thus no absolute distinctions are possible. The evolution from lower and less complex forms to higher and more complex is continuous within nature. There are differences between the animate and the inanimate, but there are also similarities. Both kinds of bodies are subject to certain internal tensions set up by external conditions, and they both react so as to achieve a state of equilibrium. But the difference, according to Dewey's interpretation, lies not in the fact that a plant or other animate thing has something besides physicochemical energy, which a nugget of iron has also, but that in the plant the way in which this energy is interconnected and functions is different from that in the iron.

We know that (although we do not as yet know how) the interconnections are different because we know the consequences are different. In living things the readaptive behavior *takes place in terms of the previous history of the organism* and this is not the case with the lump of iron or any other inanimate matter. In order to distinguish the activities of living things from that of physical things, Dewey adopted the term "psychophysical." The addition of the term "psycho," however, does not represent any mystical ingredient to be added to the "physical" and thus constitute an answer to "the mystery of life." He intended it to mean simply that at this level of nature physical activity has gained additional properties, namely the ability to react selectively in terms of a continuing history. There is no dualism of psychic and physical. Empirically there are certain events marked by distinctive qualities, of which one of these is organization. We may not know now under what conditions this organization of behavior happens nor what all the consequences of it are, though assuredly we are closer to it now than when Dewey was making his naturalistic analysis of experience. But, as he saw it, the question of the origin of life is subject matter for a highly complex inquiry of science. In this inquiry no hypothesis should be ruled out arbitrarily so long as it can be tested by experimental methods, but there is one thing that must be ruled out in the beginning. What must be ruled out is any effort to explain the phenomenon of life in terms of some force from outside nature or to postulate such an outside force as the cause of changes within the evolutionary process.[11]

Thus, "animate bodies" are what they are not because they possess some transcendental factor variously called "life" or "soul," but because one of the qualities they exhibit is the continuous effort to maintain a serial pattern of behavior in the context of an environment that is always in process of change. Since environmental conditions are never stable, the organism is subjected to strains, tensions, and dislocations with reference to its relation to the environment, and the necessity arises for the organism to make certain existential changes so that the pattern of behavior may be continued. The effort of the organism is to make readjustments in its relationships to the environment and, as we have already noted in another connection, the readjustment involves changes in the organism and changes in the environment. Life, therefore, is a constant process of readaptation to a dynamic environment and experience, which is the interactive process at the human level, is a process of doing and undergoing—a matter of anticipation and consummation.

Thus, this naturalistic interpretation of experience makes possible an explanation of certain key terms without invoking transcendental forces.

By need is meant a condition of tensional distribution of energies such that the body is in a condition of uneasy or unstable equilibrium. By

11 For an extended discussion of these matters see: John Dewey, *Logic, the Theory of Inquiry*, New York: Henry Holt and Company, 1938, Chapter II. The ruling out of any extra-natural causal force in the evolutionary process, it will be recalled, was what got Sir Julian Huxley in trouble with the theologians. See ante, p. 75.

demand or effort is meant the fact that this state is manifested in movements which modify environing bodies in ways which react upon the body, so that its characteristic pattern of active equilibrium is restored. By satisfaction is meant this recovery of equilibrium pattern, consequent upon the changes of environment due to interactions with the active demands of the organism.[12]

The basis of all motivation is the effort of the organism to maintain adjustment so that its own identity may be maintained. Pleasure or self-satisfaction is not itself the motivating factor in organic activity, as various forms of hedonism maintain. Pleasure or satisfaction is the quality of the event of successful readjustment—it is the result of a process, not the goal of it.[13] Organisms are "biased" toward perpetuation of prior patterns of behavior and their readaptive efforts are directed toward that end. Empirically, sensitivity is a quality of behavior exhibited by animate bodies since they do not respond at random to environmental forces but are selective and discriminatory in their responses.

In the case of animals that have organs of locomotion and sensory organs that make possible the reception of distant stimuli, interest becomes, along with sensitivity, a realization of feeling. There is evidence for this because in the case of such organisms two kinds of activity may be observed: activity that may be distinguished as *preparatory* and that which may be identified as *consummatory*. Anticipatory activities are permeated with the anticipation of the consummation which is to come. The consummation, therefore, is not simply a fortuitous emergent of the preparatory activities; it is in Dewey's words a "funded conservation of them."[14] When consummation comes, the sensitivity of the organism is realized as *feeling*. Below the level of human structure, animals realize feeling in terms of gross states of uneasiness, comfort, vigor, exhaustion, and so on. But it is Dewey's view that even such gross bodily states serve to sum up the history of an event and that they form the threshold of mental life.

The more complex the organism, the more varied and indicative feeling becomes but, though these animals may have feelings, they do not

[12] John Dewey, *Experience and Nature*, Chicago: Open Court Publishing Company, 1925, p. 253.
[13] *Ibid.*, pp. 63–64. In this sense hedonism means the theory that all motivation can be explained in terms of desire for pleasure and the avoidance of pain. James along with Dewey criticized psychological hedonism as the explanation of motivation. James' critique will be found in the second volume of *Principles of Psychology*, p. 549 ff.
[14] *Ibid.*, p. 257.

know they have them. Activity is still psycho-physical, not mental. Psycho-physical feelings provide the threshold of mental life, but only creatures capable of having and using *meanings* are rightly described as having mental life. Thus, meaning is feeling with an added property, that of objectivity.

Meaning does not inhere in the objects and events in the environment, nor is it a peculiar property of the organism. Meaning is a quality of the interaction of organism and environment; *it is a property of behavior.* Meanings are objective—not private and subjective—because they are natural modes of interaction with objects and energies in the environment. The factor that gives meaning its objectivity, as contrasted with the essentially subjective character of feeling, is language. Meaning, since it is objectified in symbolic fashion, becomes *a sign of operations to be performed.*[15]

Since man alone is known to use language in any significant degree, it is only the human species that displays the capacity to have and use meanings in experience and hence only human beings are capable of mental life.[16] Meanings are *signs* of events and therefore are capable of being manipulated, arranged, and combined, and it is this behavior that we call reflective thought. The growth of meanings which, according to this account, occurs in and through experience, is a genetic process. It begins in the impulsive and relatively gross behavior of infancy and early childhood and grows through the medium of the experiential continuum. In the preceding chapter we considered Dewey's analysis of the genetic development of knowledge in the individual. Here we are speaking of the same thing under somewhat different terms and there is no particular gain to be made by repeating the analysis. The cognitive structure possessed by any individual is the system of meanings present in his behavior and available to him in his relationships with the social and physical environment.

We can, however, make one additional observation about the essentially biological interpretation Dewey and others in the pragmatic tradition gave to experience. What is meant by *mind* is simply the system of meanings that has developed through experience. Mind, therefore, is an *emergent* of the experiential process and in this sense it is *learned behavior.* Mind is not given; it is achieved. And the term itself does not

[15] It will be recalled that in the preceding chapter ideas were defined in similar fashion as "plans for action."
[16] Dewey maintained that though animals other than man do communicate with each other in various ways, the signaling acts of animals are generically different from human speech. *Ibid.*, p. 179.

represent a "substance" either material or immaterial. In part, as we have already seen, it is better thought of from the standpoint of language as a modifier rather than a substantive. Mind is behavior with a distinctive property and as a kind of behavior it is instrumental to adaptation to the pressures of the environment. It is, in fact, the most powerful means to survival yet to emerge from the evolutionary process. From the standpoint of physical structure, man in many ways is inferior to other species of animals, but the fact of language and the property of meaning language makes possible has given the human species a far greater power of control over the environment and a greater degree of flexibility and adaptability than any other species possesses.

A similar observation may be made about the term *self*. Under the view we have been examining here individuality or selfhood must also be an emergent of the process of experience. Only human beings are able to achieve selfhood because they are the only organisms that are capable of sharing consciously in group life. Some animals, ants and bees for example, live in highly integrated social environments but their behavior is psycho-physical, not mental. The kind of self an individual becomes depends on his genetic inheritance and on the kind of environment in which he grows up, because both of these are parts of the transaction we call experience. Society is made by men, to be sure, but men are also made by society. A man who grew up entirely apart from any human society, supposing this could actually happen, who had never acquired language, had never seen any of his kind, or been influenced by any human institution would not be a human self but a brute.[17] The physiological structure that makes possible the development of mind and self is an emergent of the evolutionary process that operates through natural selection, but the actual emergence of selfhood is the result of the individual's conscious participation in social life.

In this section we have examined the interpretation pragmatic philosophy makes of such strategic terms as experience, mind, and self. These concepts are viewed here in their biological and psychological aspects, and are completely *naturalistic* in character. The pragmatist takes experience as he finds it and attempts to analyze it as a phenomenon of

[17] A major contribution to the naturalistic conceptions of the origin of mind and self was made by George Herbert Mead (1863–1931). Mead was a colleague of Dewey at the University of Chicago and was an important figure in the development of American pragmatism. One of his major works that bears on the discussion above is: *Mind, Self, and Society*, Chicago: The University of Chicago Press, 1939. A compact anthology compiled from Mead's work is: Anselm Strauss, ed., *The Social Psychology of George Herbert Mead*, Chicago: The University of Chicago Press, 1956, in which see Part V.

nature. He does not invoke any supernatural or transcendental entities to account for human motivation, mental life, or the achievement of self, for these, he thinks, are as much a part of nature as the motion of the planets or the fall of rain on a dusty road.

Thus, for the pragmatist, the revolution in biology that was precipitated by Darwin's thesis points the way not alone to a new philosophy of human nature, but to a reconstruction and a redirection of the whole of philosophy. In Dewey's words:

> To see the organism *in* nature, the nervous system in the organism, the brain in the nervous system, the cortex in the brain is the answer to the problems which haunt philosophy. And when they are thus seen they will be seen *in*, not as marbles are in a box but as events are in history, in a moving, growing never finished process.[18]

THE LOGICAL ASPECTS OF MEANING

One of the important concepts that has appeared from time to time in the preceding section as well as in the chapter on progressivism in educational theory was the term *meaning*. We have already seen something of the significance this term has in Dewey's educational theory and we have just completed an analysis of the psychological dimensions of it as these are viewed in pragmatic philosophy. There is, however, another dimension of this strategic term and it is important that we give attention to it in order that our understanding be rounded out.

In the introduction to the present chapter reference was made to two papers Peirce presented at meetings of the Metaphysical Club. The observation was made that these two papers had a profound effect on the development of pragmatic philosophy in this country and that the ideas contained in them were greatly influential on the philosophy of Dewey and James. One of these papers bears the title, "How to Make Our Ideas Clear."[19] and is concerned with the logical aspects of meaning. We will now give some attention to the point of view Peirce developed in this paper.

He begins by demonstrating that classic logic had never succeeded in advancing any trustworthy criterion for distinguishing between clear and

---

[18] Dewey, *Experience and Nature*, p. 295.
[19] First published in *Popular Science Monthly* in 1878. Now available in *The Collected Papers of Charles Sanders Peirce*, Cambridge, Massachusetts: Harvard University Press, 1931–1935, Volume 5. This paper has been reprinted in Buchler, ed., *op. cit.*, Chapter 3. My citations are to the latter edition.

unclear concepts. It is his contention that the first lesson logic should teach is a method of making our ideas clear and, moreover, it should provide a criterion that will enable us to distinguish between the clear and the unclear conception. Briefly, Peirce's argument is that *any idea we may have can be nothing besides our grasp of its sensible effects.* The whole purpose of thought is to guide action and help us form habits, which themselves are modes of action. It appeared to Peirce, therefore, that in light of the function that thought plays and in view of the empirical character of all ideas, the following statement constitutes a maxim or rule which defines the character of meaning and at the same time provides a criterion for distinguishing meaningful concepts from those without meaning:

> Consider what effects, that might conceivably have practical bearings, we conceive the object of our conception to have. Then, our conception of these effects is the whole of our conception of the object.[20]

For example, if we let H stand for any concept, then the meaning of H, according to the pragmatic rule, are whatever consequences follow from it. If a, b, c, and d are effects that are entailed by H, then the meaning of H is a, b, c, and d. If we conceive no consequences whatever arising from H, then H has no meaning.

In applying the pragmatic rule we must always employ certain operations. In the first place, we must assume hypothetically that H is true. Secondly, we must propose that some kind of operation be performed. Third, we must anticipate that some kind of consequences must ensue as a result of the operations. It is these consequences, according to the rule, that constitute the meaning of H. In his original essay Peirce used as examples two terms *hard* and *weight*. When we say that something is "hard" we indicate that it will scratch other objects. When we say that some object has "weight" we indicate that if we remove all opposing forces the object will fall. In both these simple cases an operation is indicated (rubbing one object against another; removing support) and certain consequences ensue (appearance of scratches; falling). Thus, when we predicate hardness of some object A we mean that if A is hard it will produce scratches on other substances when it is rubbed against them and itself will not be scratched. These consequences are the meaning of the term "hard" and Peirce observes, there is no difference between a hard thing and a soft thing except as they are brought to the test.

We have seen that, according to the pragmatic rule, any concept H means whatever consequences ensue when some kind of operations are

[20] Buchler, ed., *op. cit.*, p. 31.

performed. If it is impossible to conceive of any operations and their ensuing consequences, then the term has no meaning. To this may be added the further observation that if two terms involve the same consequences, they are really the same conception expressed in different ways. Thus, if H involves as consequences a, b, c, and d and if H^1 also involves a, b, c, and d, these being identical, then H and H^1 are the same conception.

It was Peirce's opinion that the pragmatic rule would go a long way toward clearing what he considered the metaphysical rubbish out of the mansions of philosophy. In an essay published some years after "How to Make Our Ideas Clear," he said that the chief advantage to be gained from the pragmatic maxim would be that of demonstrating that most metaphysical propositions are either "meaningless gibberish" or otherwise "downright absurd." Once this rubbish is cleared away, said Peirce, what will remain are problems that can be studied by the methods of the true sciences.[21]

Anyone with the slightest acquaintance with the history of philosophy knows that there are numerous questions or problems that although they were first stated some two thousand years ago and have been puzzled over by the finest minds western civilization has produced, still remain unsettled and, in fact, show little promise of ever being settled. These problems are, of course, mostly metaphysical and theological in character. One kind of reaction to these problems is what is often called "agnostic." This is the attitude that the problems are unsettled because it is impossible to get evidence, either positive or negative, to establish truth or falsity about them. Therefore, propositions about the existence of God, for example, cannot be settled because of the impossibility of gathering evidence to support or deny the statement.

Peirce thought the pragmatic rule cut at these statements in another direction and in a different way. If the pragmatic rule is applied to such a statement it is found that the statement itself is *meaningless*. For example, if we consider the proposition, "Pixies abound in the fifth dimension," and examine this statement in the light of the pragmatic rule, we find that neither of the operations provided in the rule can be applied. If we put this statement in the hypothetical form that the rule requires and say, "If pixies abound in the fifth dimension, then what conceivable consequences follow?" we are constrained to answer that there are no operations possible that would provide any observable consequences. Therefore, the conclusion must be that this statement is

[21] See: "The Essentials of Pragmatism," in Buchler, ed., *op. cit.*, p. 251 ff.

meaningless and any debate about whether it is true or false is idle. It is generally conceded that truth or falsity cannot be predicated of meaningless statements, of which this is an example. The statement about the pixies is a perfectly proper English sentence, every word of which can be defined, but it does not meet the requirements of the pragmatic rule because it is impossible to conceive of any operations that will yield any observable consequences and, according to the rule, whatever consequences ensue is what the statement means; no consequences—no meaning. This, according to Peirce, is why there are so many "unsolved problems" in theology and metaphysics.

Peirce himself considered the heart of pragmatic philosophy to be a theory about the nature of meaning, which as we have seen, he conceived in operational terms. None of the formulations of the rule made by Peirce say anything about truth or falsity or the process of validation. Manifestly, in terms of the rule, a statement can be meaningful and still be false. If I say that water boils at 115° Farenheit at sea level, I am uttering a proposition that is capable of operational interpretation: operations can be conceived and one can anticipate what consequences can be observed. These consequences will reveal, as everyone knows, that my statement is false, but it is nevertheless meaningful.

In the same sense, there are propositions that are meaningful but whose validity is still in doubt. If I say that psychosis is caused by chemical imbalance in the body, I am making a statement whose truth or falsity is unknown at the present time. It is, however, a meaningful statement because it is possible to discern possible operations and anticipate probable consequences of these operations. For its verification, this statement involves the necessity for many complex and delicate scientific inquiries to be conducted. There is always the possibility, of course, that its truth or falsity can never be established, but this in no way affects the fact that as a statement it is meaningful. On the other hand, all statements of the kind about the pixies are meaningless now and always will be. Peirce considered most, if not all, metaphysical and theological statements to be of this kind.

Both James and Dewey were profoundly affected by Peirce's theory of meaning and his statement of the pragmatic maxim. James seized on it with his usual enthusiasm and intellectual vigor. Whatever ideas he touched had a way of being transformed and the pragmatic rule proved to be no exception. He saw pragmatic method as a means of finding a tenable middle ground between the two extremes of philosophical position which he characterized by the now famous dichotomy of "the tough minded" and "the tender minded." The tough minded were the scientific realists, the positivists, the empiricists, who among other things were materialistic, irreligious, fatalistic, and pessimistic and therefore in many ways unacceptable to James who was none of these. The tender minded alternative was, of course, idealism, particularly absolute idealism and James used such terms as intellectualistic, optimistic, religious, dogmatical and free-willist to describe this position. He believed that pragmatism offered a middle position that would be philosophically tenable; he also saw that if the new philosophy were to serve this important office it would have to be enlarged beyond the scope that Peirce, who was himself more than a little tough minded, had allowed.

What eventually happened to be the pragmatic rule in the hands of James was a reinterpretation and extension of the term "consequences" or "effects," which latter term was the one Peirce had employed in his first statement of the rule. Perhaps even more significant was James' achievement of transforming the pragmatic rule so that it became for him at least a theory of truth as well as a theory of meaning. We are going to postpone further consideration of James' contribution until we come to our discussion of the pragmatic conception of truth. This will be done in the next section of this chapter.

Dewey's philosophical thought also was much influenced by Peirce's analysis. The operationalism and the emphasis on the consequences of action became parts of his own conception of meaning and the knowledge process and particularly with respect to his conception of the relation of doing and knowing. The logical elements of the pragmatic rule worked in with and illuminated the biological and psychological interpretation of meaning we considered in the preceding section of this chapter. The influence of the pragmatic rule on pedagogical ideas, particularly those of Dewey, can be summed up in two statements:

First, if a concept is to have meaning for an individual, he must put it to work, that is, he must apply it to some state of affairs. Only in this way can he become acquainted with its consequences and hence with its relationships to other things and events. The structure of the school's curriculum must be deliberately designed to make this possible, and more than that, to encourage it. There is an inherent relation between action and knowledge, and meaning can be communicated only in a context which itself is meaningful to the learner.

Secondly, knowing is the apprehending of meaning. The object of knowledge is the consequences that occur when a concept is put to application. To know means to inquire, to change relationships, to reveal the connections between means and consequences. If there are no actions, no operations, there are no consequences, and if there are no consequences, there is no object of knowledge.

For the school program these ideas indicate the necessity for a curriculum built around active enterprises that will stimulate intellectual inquiry. This is one of the main considerations teachers must bear in mind when they make provision for activities in the classroom. Neither in the psychological nor the logical sense can mind be correctly perceived as the mere spectator of an antecedent reality, however this reality may be conceived. We have already seen that these ideas are among the most important in Dewey's conception of the educative process, and we have noted also that they played a strategic part in the experimental program of the Laboratory School.

We are now aware that the heart of pragmatism is the theory of meaning. In our discussion we have not had anything to say about the connection of the pragmatic rule with a theory of truth, except to note that James believed it denoted not only a conception of meaning but also a means of verification. Conventionally, most western epistemology has always been concerned with the question of what constitutes truth and with discovering methods by which statements may be judged to be true or false. We will now concern ourselves with the position pragmatism takes on this point and the ramifications these matters have for educational theory.

LOGIC, INQUIRY, AND THE NATURE OF TRUTH

To begin our study of this aspect of pragmatic philosophy we turn to another essay of Peirce that originally was presented at the Metaphysical Club. This paper antedated the one we have already considered and was first published in *The Scientific Monthly* in 1877. Peirce gave this paper the title, "The Fixation of Belief."[22] There is no possibility of reproducing the intriguing flavor of Peirce's exposition, and all that will be attempted here is to outline the argument Peirce advances so that its important connection with pragmatic philosophy may be grasped. Any person with a genuine interest in pragmatism will wish to savor Peirce's pungent style directly.

[22] Available in *The Collected Works of Peirce*, Vol. 5, pp. 358–87; also reprinted intact in Buchler, ed., *op. cit.*, pp. 5–22. Citations here are to Buchler's volume.

The argument begins with the statement that there is a difference between a condition of doubt and a condition of belief. Belief influences our desires and our actions and it establishes in us habits of behavior. These habits are strong or weak according to the strength or weakness of the beliefs that form them. Psychologically, a state of doubt is always irritating and uncomfortable. We resist being in this state and seek to pass beyond it to the relatively complacent and comfortable condition that belief brings. Doubt is the irritant, the stimulus, that urges us to struggle for belief. Belief, on the other hand, is not an immediate spur to action. Instead it creates in us a habit so that when the occasion arises we will act in a way determined by our belief.

The struggle to pass from a state of doubt to a state of belief Peirce calls "inquiry," noting that it is not a completely satisfactory term. Inquiry begins when doubt begins and it ends when belief is attained. The only function inquiry has, says Peirce, is to settle opinion. To be sure, people often say that merely to reach some opinion is not enough; what we really are after is a "true" opinion. This notion, however, will not stand to analysis, for as soon as a firm belief is gained, inquiry ceases and we are satisfied. Of course we like to say we are searching for beliefs that are true, but this turns out to be a tautology because we really think our beliefs are "true" anyway.[23]

Peirce next raises the question of whether under this view belief might not be attained simply by reiterating the answer to some question and resolutely ignoring anything that might be in opposition to it. If inquiry is simply the process of establishing belief, then this would appear to be the most direct method. Assuredly it is a very common way people fix belief, says Peirce, and it can be called *the method of tenacity*. He then begins the analysis of alternative methods of fixating belief which will be outlined briefly below.

When beliefs are fixed on the basis of tenacity we simply cling to some view. We have no interest in whatever evidence there may be to the contrary, or if we do have any interest, it is in ignoring or suppressing such evidence. There is no doubt, Peirce agrees, that belief maintained by tenacity can often bring peace of mind and what is often admiringly called "moral resolution." Nor should we be patronizing about people who go through life on the basis of this method of belief. What point is there in calling this method "irrational" when the people who employ it make no profession of being rational and often express doubt about the very potency of human reason?

[23] Buchler, ed., *op. cit.*, pp. 10–11.

The real difficulty with the method of tenacity is that it ultimately breaks down in practice. A person who follows this method will find sooner or later that there are other beliefs that people hold as tenaciously as he holds his own, and it is therefore inevitable that ultimately the seeds of doubt will sprout in the mind of the tenacious believer. It will occur to him that other men's beliefs may be as good as his own. Since all of us cannot go off into the wilderness and become hermits, thereby shielding our cherished beliefs from contamination, another necessity presents itself and this, says Peirce, is the problem of fixing belief in the community.[24]

We come, then, to another method of fixing belief that Peirce called *the method of authority*. To employ this method it is necessary to create some kind of authoritative institution in society. The function of this authority is to keep the desired beliefs constantly before the people and, of course, to teach them to children. All contrary ideas and negative evidence must be suppressed and people kept in ignorance of alternative possibilities. When deviants appear in society and prove to be incapable of righting their beliefs, the only course is the use of force. "A general massacre," Peirce observes, "has proved a very effective means of settling opinion in a country."

The method of authority has always been a chief means of supporting religious and political doctrines. Wherever there has been a privileged class: priesthood, aristocracy, or any group whose power rests on some body of dogma, this method will be found at work. Ultimately there is no limit to the cruelty and coercion that will be employed by the authority to maintain orthodoxy of belief.

This method, Peirce observes, is in its main effects greatly superior to emotional tenacity. History has shown that many of the works of civilization achieved under it have been impressive beyond measure. The difficulty is that in the long run it fails. It fails because all heresy cannot be kept down. Beliefs do change, though very slowly and imperceptibly, and usually the rate of change is slow enough so that the beliefs of any individual may remain virtually unchanged throughout his lifetime. To this Peirce adds the tart observation that perhaps for most people this is the best method. "If it is their highest impulse to be intellectual slaves, then slaves they ought to remain."[25] But there are always a few men who do not wish to be intellectual slaves and, since even the most tyrannous authority cannot regulate opinion on every subject, they be-

[24] *Ibid.*, pp. 12–13.
[25] *Ibid.*, p. 14.

come aware that in other places and in other times people have held opinions that are contrary to the prevailing authority. These men begin to wonder whether there is any reason to hold that the authoritative beliefs of their own time really are superior to those of other times and places. So, ultimately, these people give up the idea of fixating belief on the basis of authority and adopt another method.

This brings us to the third method which Peirce calls the *a priori*. The essence of this method is that people fix those beliefs that are in agreement with their own "reason." In a sense, this method involves a much more liberal and pluralistic approach to the formation of belief. There is a free market in ideas. Men are able to analyze and discuss their ideas and develop those beliefs they find that "stand to reason." (Peirce was careful to point out that the concern in this method is that the beliefs *stand to reason not experience.*) This method Peirce interprets as being the approach employed by speculative philosophy which typically has sought to establish beliefs that "rational" men have been inclined to accept; Plato, for example, who found it reasonable to believe ". . . that the distances of the celestial spheres from one another should be proportional to the different lengths of strings which produce harmonious chords."[26] Granted that this method in many ways is more humane and liberal than the method of authority, since it allows much more free play of instinct and habit; it also displays severe weakness when it is employed fully. In the long run, beliefs fixed on the basis of right reason turn out to be as various and subjective as personal tastes. Under this view, I may prefer monogamy over polygamy for about the same reason that I prefer oysters; is there any reason why everyone should concur in my preferred belief in monogamy? If belief is to be fixed on the basis of what is agreeable to the reason of individuals—then any substantial agreement on beliefs is impossible, and in Peirce's view the history of metaphysical philosophy is an excellent example of this fact.

What is needed to overcome the deficiencies in the *a priori* method is a basis for fixating belief that appeals to something outside the mind—something that cannot be changed by thinking and therefore something that can direct inquiry so that all men can come to agreement on the basis of evidence. This method of fixing belief, said Peirce, is precisely *the method employed by science*, which ultimately involves an appeal to experience. Experience involves both the inward activity of thought and the real things in the environment that possess the character they have

[26] *Ibid.*, p. 15.

independent of thought and are governed by laws that exist and operate apart from opinion and belief.[27] It is true that these external things affect our senses in different ways but, "any man, if he have sufficient experience and he reason enough about it, will be led to the one true conclusion."[28] Thus, scientific method can lend objectivity to our beliefs—a quality that none of the other methods is capable of yielding. Peirce took care to note that all of the methods of fixating belief have certain advantages, but he held that the most advantageous method was the scientific. The reason scientific method can be judged to be superior is that the results it yields are superior to the results obtained by other methods.

We will now give attention to some of the formal aspects of the logic of scientific method and to begin our discussion we will return to the pragmatic rule. We recall that the rule states that a conception is meaningful when it is possible to discern certain operations that can be performed and to anticipate the consequences that will ensue from these operations and are capable of being observed in some way. If we let H stand for any idea (belief) that is to be tested, then, according to the rule, we must state H in hypothetical form: If H, then a, b, c, d (where a, b, c, d, stand for operations and their ensuing consequences): but a, b, c, and d, when the operations performed are found to yield the consequences anticipated—that is, they "check out." Now what can be concluded about H? Can it be said that H is true?

In the ordinary sense of the word we cannot say that H has been shown to be "true." It is a fact that the operations performed have shown through their consequences that they bear out H, but how are we to know that a, b, c, and d exhaust all the possible operations? Even if we were to subject H to a very long sequence of operations could we ever know that we had exhausted all possibilities and therefore would be warranted in attributing unqualified truth to H? Suppose we one day found that operation x^1 failed to confirm H. What then? Peirce's answer is:

> But the scientific spirit requires a man to be at all times ready to dump his whole cartload of beliefs the moment experience is against them. The desire to learn forbids him to be perfectly cocksure that he knows already. Besides positive science can only rest on experience; and experience can never result in absolute certainty, exactitude, necessity, or universality.[29]

[27] *Ibid.*, pp. 18–19.
[28] *Loc. cit.*
[29] *Ibid.*, pp. 46–47.

Therefore, if we feel it necessary to say something about the *truth* of H, the most we can possibly say is that H is *probably true*. The whole scientific enterprise then, becomes one of increasing the probability of the adequacy of our ideas (hypotheses) and the way this is done is by increasing the number of tested inferences derived from the idea. Now, we may ask, is this true of all cognitive statements? The answer the pragmatist gives is "yes," excepting, of course, analytical statements (logical or mathematical) which are tautologies anyway and can have only formal validity. And so if we follow the logic of scientific thought, which pragmatists think is what one should do, we must give up the notion that there are some judgments that have the property of truth in the complete and unalterable sense of the word.

In his own work in pragmatic logic Dewey followed the general position stated by Peirce. Inquiry, it will be recalled, was defined by Peirce as activity that mediates between a state of doubt and the fixation of belief. Peirce had demonstrated that there are various methods of fixating belief but the way he considered most effective is that in which inquiry is identical with the method of science. Dewey joined Peirce in this conclusion and he believed, as Peirce believed, that an important need of modern philosophy was a logic of inquiry, a logic concerned with "finding out" rather than demonstrating known fact or deriving tautological statements from axioms by *a priori* methods.[30] Much of Dewey's long career in philosophy was devoted to working out a logic of inquiry, which amounted to generalizing the experimental method of science so that it might be applicable to any meaningful subject matter.

Dewey's work in logic not only paralleled his work in educational theory, it was organically related to it. In fact, in the preceding chapter we have already considered the logic of inquiry as it was formulated by Dewey in the five steps of "a complete act of thought." In this connection we considered Dewey's effort to make the method of inquiry the central element in educational method, and we also saw that the design of the curriculum in the Laboratory School followed this principle. Even though it involves a certain amount of repetition, we will review Dewey's formulation of the act of inquiry again because there are additional observations about it that need to be made.

Inquiry begins, as Peirce had said, with a state of doubt and the desire to move from doubt to belief. Dewey's interpretation of this idea is biological and behavioral. Inquiry begins when a disunified and con-

---

[30] For Dewey's commentary on the needed reform in logic see: *Logic: The Theory of Inquiry*, Chapter V.

fused state of affairs is encountered. This state of affairs blocks and impedes behavior because the habitual behavior of the person involved is inadequate to cope with the situation. The psychological or affective response of the person is one of doubt, as Peirce had observed, but the character of feeling on the part of the person is itself a product of the character of the situation in which he finds himself. Doubt is not something we have inside ourselves, and then project into the environment. We doubt because we live in an environment which in some of its aspects is contingent and therefore doubtful. Doubt is an uncomfortable, irritating, and anxiety-producing state and our effort is to pass from it to the comparatively settled, complacent, comfortable state that Peirce has called belief.

If this is to be achieved, however, something has to be done to the conditions that are responsible for the state of doubt. As we already know from Peirce's analysis, there are various kinds of ways that may be employed, but the most effective way is the general method of science or, as Dewey often called it, the method of intelligence.

A crucial step in the resolution of the indeterminate situation is to recognize it as a situation requiring inquiry, that is, to recognize it for its problematic character. The presence of an indeterminate situation is a prerequisite for inquiry, but as a situation it is whatever it existentially is, and it does not owe its character to thought or cognition. The first necessary achievement of an inquiry is to transform an indeterminate situation into *a problem*. When a problem is well formulated it is on its way to solution.

The third stage of inquiry is one of finding possible solutions to the problem and this comes about as we are able to grasp the structure of the situation and to see what the relevant facts in it are. The facts represent what must be taken into account in our efforts to deal with the problem. If we are able to determine the salient factual aspects of the problem we can anticipate certain possibilities and these possibilities are *ideas*. As we have already seen, both Peirce and Dewey conceived ideas as proposed plans of action—possible operations and in this sense the term is synonymous with hypothesis. Ideas are always hypothetical because they are anticipations of possible consequences; their function is one of pointing ahead and of directing action. This stage of inquiry, then, is one of developing possible plans for operations to be performed.

The fourth stage of inquiry is devoted to a logical evaluation of the relative merits of the proposed ideas and this involves determining the meaning of various proposals and their attendant factual connections.

The pragmatic rule indicates the hypothetical method of determining the meaning of an idea. If I act on the basis of H, where H stands for a possible operation, what consequences can be anticipated? All ideas we have developed are subjected to this logical treatment, and the selection of one course of action, together with the rejection of others, is made in terms of the foreseeable consequences.

The fifth and terminating step is to act on the situation in terms of the idea (hypothesis) chosen to guide the operations. To this point, inquiry has proceeded by means of a series of partial and tentative judgments. In the last stage a terminal judgment is made, and the object of this judgment is whether or not the situation, which originally was one of indeterminacy and disunity, has been transformed into a unified and determinate set of conditions. If it has been so transformed, our psychological experience is to move from doubt to belief, *but this psychological transformation is itself a product of the transformed situation.* The terminal judgment is, therefore, not subjective and personal, but objective and public. Both Peirce and Dewey agreed in this and, as we will see a little later, it was on this point that an important controversy developed between them and James.

Now what about truth? Is the terminal judgment in an inquiry concerned with establishing truth or falsity? Do these terms really make any sense in this context? If they do make sense, it is in ways that differ significantly from traditional philosophical conceptions of truth.[31] In one way it is more useful to use the term "true" and "false" as modifiers, for it is sensible to think of ideas leading us truly toward our goal or, conversely, leading us falsely so that we miss our objective. Or, at least at one time, it seemed meaningful to say that ideas are true in the sense that they work, but this phrase has been so misinterpreted and misused that pragmatists have given it up and it is now mostly used as a straw man by unfriendly critics who like to knock it over. From the standpoint of a logical definition, Dewey advocated and used the term "warranted assertibility" to denote the terminal judgment of inquiry and expressed agreement with Peirce's statement that truth is: "The opinion which is fated to be ultimately agreed to by all who investigate . . ."[32]

The ideas that emerge from the analysis by Peirce and Dewey of scientific inquiry that are most important to our purposes are such as these:
1) Ideas that enable us to transform the character of indeterminate and

---

[31] A valuable summary of the chief differences between pragmatic and traditional views of truth will be found in Dewey's *Philosophy and Civilization*, p. 23 ff.
[32] See: *Logic, The Theory of Inquiry*, p. 345.

disunified situations are adequate or warranted and, as emergents of the processes of inquiry, they become the means to help us in subsequent inquiries. The general process of inquiry is continuous and serial in character and this in the same sense that experience in general is continuous and serial. 2) Inquiry is always operational and experimental in character and is, consequently, objective and public in the same way that all scientific work is objective and public, both in its methods and in its results. Favorable affective responses follow the successful termination of inquiry, but these favorable feelings are not themselves the test of the hypothesis, for the test of it is whether or not the indeterminate situation was transformed. This is an objective public matter. 3) Meaning is always relative to the specific operations and consequences that establish it. There is no possibility of attributing universal truth to statements because there is no method by which this can be done. The limits of human knowledge are the limits of human experience and, as Peirce observed, "experience can never result in absolute certainty, exactitude, necessity, or universality."

We come now to the differences that developed in pragmatic philosophy, particularly the different interpretation of the pragmatic rule by William James. As we said earlier, James was greatly impressed by Peirce's approach to the problem of meaning and he added the pragmatic method to his own radical empiricism. James saw pragmatic method as a means of finding middle ground between the extremes of tough-mindedness and tender-mindedness, neither of which extreme he thought tenable. He made several formulations of the pragmatic rule[33] and agreed with Peirce that the meaning of a concept lies in its practical consequences. But James also believed that pragmatism could be interpreted as a theory of truth and that such an interpretation would make it possible to test some ideas from theology and philosophy that Peirce himself thought were rendered meaningless by the pragmatic rule. James' interpretation involved extending the meaning of the term "consequences" to include those that are ethical and psychological and therefore in a measure subjective, whereas Peirce had restricted them to those that are logical and scientific and hence public and objective. Out of James' extension of pragmatic method came the proposal that if a person believes a certain idea to be true, and if his belief in this idea has certain beneficial results in his experience, then on pragmatic grounds this belief may be judged as true.

[33] See for example: James, "What Pragmatism Means," in *Essays in Pragmatism*, New York: Hafner Publishing Company, 1948, p. 142. This famous paper was first published in 1907 and has been reprinted many times.

The most celebrated application of this principle occurs in James' essay, "What Pragmatism Means." In this paper he argues that if theological ideas, belief in the existence of God, for example, have favorable consequences in the lives of people, then to that extent the hypothesis that God exists must be true on pragmatic grounds. James qualified the statement somewhat by adding that the truth of the idea also would depend on its relations to other truths, but this qualification was not sufficient to stem the protests that were made against what Peirce and others considered an unwarranted extension of the rule.[34] Peirce, who had originally coined the term "pragmatism," eventually gave it up and substituted in its place the word "pragmaticism," which he said "is ugly enough to be safe from kidnappers."[35]

In the development of his own philosophical position, Dewey remained much closer to Peirce, particularly with respect to the public and objective character of consequences. He emphasized that James had recognized the instrumental function that ideas have in experience, but he also pointed out that James had not tried to develop any theory of logical forms based on the instrumental view. Much of Dewey's own work in logic was devoted to the effort to demonstrate that the rules of logic are themselves emergents of the processes of inquiry. He did not regard the name "pragmatism" as very useful in characterizing his own philosophical position. In the earlier part of his career he used the term "instrumentalism" to characterize his own work; in the later part of his life he called it "experimentalism." One of Dewey's most noteworthy contributions to the general pragmatic tradition was his relating of experimental method to the major aspects of value theory. Ethics was always a major philosophical interest with Dewey and he saw close relationships between value theory and broader social and educational questions. In the next section of this chapter we will turn our attention to the problem of value as pragmatists see it, and we will be particularly concerned in this connection with Dewey's experimentalism.

VALUE AND VALUATION

One of the areas both in philosophy and in general experience in which a philosophical tradition reveals its power—or lack of it—is the area of value and, specifically, ethics. It is in this aspect of experience

[34] See: *Ibid.*, p. 154.
[35] Buchler, ed., *op. cit.*, p. 255.

that the theories of reality, of knowledge, and of truth of a given philosophical approach converge to throw light on the most important class of problems human beings encounter. We have already seen that one of the great attractions Peirce's pragmatism had for James was the promise it seemed to offer for a middle ground between the extreme *a priorism* of various absolutist conceptions of value and the extreme relativism of many positivistic and materialistic approaches to philosophy. James' reinterpretation of the pragmatic rule, that extended the idea of consequences to include more than Peirce had intended, was his effort to make pragmatic method available for the analysis of ethical questions. We have noted that both Peirce and Dewey objected to James' broadening of the rule. Dewey himself agreed with Peirce that truth is public, and when he set out himself to study the relation of experimental logic to the problem of value he stuck with the principle that genuine validation is always objective and public.

Dewey's work in experimental logic had led him to the conclusion that the method of intelligence, which he equated with the general method of science, is applicable to any meaningful subject matter. This indicated, at least in the estimation of Dewey and his followers, that the processes of inquiry need not be limited to the kind of subject matters with which the natural sciences customarily deal. It is true that by far the most impressive accomplishments of controlled inquiry are to be seen in the natural sciences, the reason being that it is in those fields that the method has had its most rigorous and systematic application. But it should also be recalled that at one time—and that time was not so long ago—men fixated many of their beliefs about the nature of the physical world by other methods than the experimental approach.

The phenomenal advances of the natural sciences in the past four or five centuries is related directly to the development of methods of inquiry that are built around observation, hypothesis, and experiment. A major part of Dewey's philosophy is the call to submit other areas of human concern to the logic of controlled inquiry. Men encounter critical problems in other fields besides physics and biology, and the question is whether such areas as politics, education, and religion can also be unified and ordered in the same way that the natural sciences are unified and made rational. Leaving aside for the moment the question of whether scientific inquiry itself involves any value dimensions, when we come to consider problems of human association and endeavor in social life it is clear to us that these matters seem always to involve dimensions of value. In the face of a problematic situation, as for example in education, we are confronted by the question "What can we do?" and also by the question "What ought we do?" As is well known, the position of a very great deal of western philosophy is that we will never find the answer to the second kind of question by employing scientific method. For as it is often said, science deals with means and cannot deal with ends.

The application of experimental method to ethical questions is one of the most important contributions of American pragmatism to philosophy. It is also one of the most complex areas of pragmatic thought. In this section we cannot hope to give a full exposition of pragmatic ethical theory. We will outline the general nature of Dewey's argument and show something of how it relates to other parts of his philosophical position. In doing this we will concern ourselves with two general questions: 1) the nature and origin of ethical norms; 2) the process of valuation.

One of the facts of experience is that we not only interact with the environment in which we live, we also constantly place value on certain aspects of it and disvalue on others. We are seldom "neutral" for we actively desire and seek to possess some objects and ends and also to avoid others. Some objects and events show themselves to be of such importance and desirability that we idealize them; that is, we endow them with the character of ideals. These ideals, then, become leading ideas that guide our conduct in various ways amidst the contingencies of experience. These ideals function as norms or standards. They provide "bench marks" that enable us to make judgments about the desirability or undesirability of specific objects and events. One does not have to be a pragmatic philosopher—in fact, he does not have to be any kind of philosopher—to know that human experience is, among other things, an affair of judging and choosing in which certain general ideas or concepts exert a normative influence.

The philosophical question arises when we attempt to determine where those normative ideas come from and what their character is, particularly whether they are completely dependable or whether they work out only in certain kinds of circumstances and not in others. Perhaps it will help to understand the position taken by Dewey and other experimentalists if we give some notice to two extreme points of view on the subject of ethical norms. If we think of this question in terms of a continuum we can identify two polar extremes. One of these is occupied by various absolutistic theories about ethical norms and the other by various forms of ethical relativism.

There are different ways of conceiving norms in terms of absolutes, but they all involve certain common characteristics, namely, 1) that norms are universal in their reference and 2) they do not change with time and circumstance. Whatever character they are alleged to possess and whatever origins they may be thought to have, the important matter is that as values they have this character of universality and timelessness. We can anticipate with considerable confidence that the source of these absolute norms must be something other than nature itself because nature, at least as human beings experience it, does not exhibit any character of complete permanence, and everything that exists is subject to the temporal processes of the natural order. Those who think of ethical norms as universal and timeless, therefore, must conceive of the origins of these standards in some kind of transcendental fashion. This must also mean that ethical standards cannot be derived through empirical method because the limits of that method are the limits of experience.

In western culture two main accounts for the origin of absolute ethical norms have developed; many variations of these major themes have appeared in western philosophy, but in essence norms are alleged to possess their absolute character either because they are truths revealed directly from some transcendental authority, or because they derive from characteristics built into the very nature of reality and are knowable through rational (not empirical) processes. The first of these is exemplified in the Hebraic-Christian tradition, the second in the Greek tradition of ethical rationalism. The point is that whether values are thought to be the direct pronouncements of an almighty God or rational derivations from the very structure of Being, they are absolute and universal in their character and function.

At the other extreme are the relativists. Their central position is that values do not possess a character of universality and permanence because they are always functions of some kind of context. This context may be objective, in the sense of being cultural and historical, or it may be subjective in the sense of being personal and psychological. Cultural anthropology has been instrumental in demonstrating how wide and varied the structure of systems of practical ethics actually is. What is viewed as valuable—or at least tolerable—in one society or at one time in history may be viewed as evil and depraved in another society or at another point in time.

There now exists a tendency to scale down the extreme relativism portrayed by some of the earlier anthropologists and to identify a considerably wider community of ethical beliefs, but even when this is done there is still left over a broad spectrum of differences in ethical standards. This appears to be true even of the so-called sub-cultures within a society. Thus, there are often marked differences in certain value conceptions among social classes in a society granted, of course, that there is also a community of agreement within the society. Cultural relativists, therefore, are of the opinion that there is an overwhelming amount of empirical evidence against the belief that ethical norms actually are independent of particular cultural and historical contexts.

The other form of ethical relativism involves an underlying subjective element. In this case things take on value because they are objects of some person's interest and desire. We have already seen something of this in the ethical theory of the new realist Ralph Barton Perry. If "A value is any object of interest," then the fact of value derives from such psychological factors as wanting and desiring. Things take on the property of value when somebody actively needs and wants them. Unless something else is incorporated in the situation, this form of relativism would appear ultimately to reduce all values to the status of personal taste, which is about as relative as anything can get.

Dewey finds a certain amount of validity in both of these positions on the source and character of ethical standards, but he also finds grave defects in them. The absolutists are right, he thinks, in holding that we actually do possess general ideas or conceptions about good and that these general ideas are of importance in guiding our behavior and helping us make decisions. In this sense, we do empirically have ideals and these exert on us a sense of obligation; they are imperative. But the great fallacy in all absolutism lies in the effort to give these leading ethical ideas a transcendental and timeless character. The only way they can be said to have such a character is to hold that they originate outside experience, which in turn raises the question of how it is that they then can be said to function within experience as ethical imperatives. We do not have to endow our scientific ideas with a supernatural character in order to enhance their status; we know that it is the power of these products of experience to guide inquiry that compels us to admire them and cherish them. The absolutist, of course, replies that the case with ethical values is different because ethical values—if they really are ethical and values—exert a moral obligation or claim on the individual.

The experimentalist has an answer to this. It is true, he says, that ethical values do exert a moral claim on us, and in the same fashion scientific ideas also exert a claim on our behavior. We know that if we want our scientific inquiries to proceed fruitfully, we have to respect and act in accord with certain ideas and rules. If we do not behave in accordance with these rules our inquiries will be inept and without significant consequences and we stand little chance of reaching any desired objective. In this sense, the general ideas of scientific procedure do exert a claim on us. They demand, as it were, that we behave in such and such ways in the presence of certain kinds of situations. Yet, in the view of pragmatism, nobody can claim seriously that these rules for inquiry are anything other than the conceptualized products of antecedent inquiries. These rules are imperative because they have emerged from and been tested over and over in scientific work and in the process have been refined and increasingly perfected. The value they possess and the imperative character they have is owing to the consequences they produce, not to their origin.

Dewey's point is that ethical generalizations also are the products of human social experience. Why do we have to embalm them in some metaphysical fluid in order to appreciate the enormous impact they have in human life? Certainly these ideas have an ethical claim—they *are* imperatives—but this is because prior experience has tested and refined them and in so doing has demonstrated their value for application in future experience. The reason man is a "social animal" is because he has language and can share consciously in social life, and the reason he can become an "ethical animal" is that he can regulate his behavior consciously in terms of the shared moral experience of mankind. Ethical ideas exert a moral claim because they assist us in behaving wisely in the presence of problematic situations in which some value conflict is involved.[36] They are not separate from and set over against other kinds of ideas as absolutely different in kind. They are, in fact, as natural as anything else that functions in social life.

Thus, the function ethical ideas (standards, norms, ideals, etc.) have in experience is one of acting as *leading ideas*; in this role they help us make the decisions we are called upon to make in the presence of confused and problematic situations. In Dewey's experimentalism the process of valuation is essentially the process of intelligent inquiry and, as we have already noted, intelligent inquiry presupposes our possession of ideas that derive from antecedent experience and are relevant in some fashion to the matter in hand.[37] Before we turn to a consideration

[36] See Dewey's discussion of moral claims in: John Dewey and James H. Tufts, *Ethics*, New York: Henry Holt and Company, 1932, p. 236 ff.
[37] *Ibid.*, pp. 304–313.

of the process of ethical inquiry we will give attention to some ideas stemming from the relativistic end of the continuum.

It will be recalled that at the other extreme are found those conceptions of ethical standards that involve the relation of ethical norms to some kind of specific context. As we have seen, a context may be cultural-historical or psychological. In Dewey's estimation there is something important to be learned about value theory from these positions. For one thing, whenever we encounter some allegedly universal ethical standard, we know that this standard has a history. It has arisen in some kind of social context and it has had certain kinds of consequences. These matters are of great importance to us as we consider the relevance any particular idea may have for our own ethical deliberations.[38]

In the second place, whenever we encounter a problematic situation we do have a stake in the issue. The situation is problematic because the elements in the situation are blocking our efforts to realize some objective that we have an interest in. Thus, interest and desire do play a part in the ethical situation, for clearly if there is nothing desired and no need to be fulfilled, there is no problem, ethical or otherwise. Need and desire are elements in the situation that generate the ethical problem, but it is one thing to say that and another thing to say that desire and desirability are the same thing. The function of reflection is to guide impulse into reasoned response, and as we saw earlier, reasoned response is that behavior in which account is taken of future consequences. That an object or event is desired is simply an occurrence— a fact, but whether the object is *desirable* is a matter of reflective thought which attempts to estimate what effects will follow if this impulse is acted on.

We come now to the question of how the general method of inquiry can be employed in dealing with situations that have value dimensions. Situations of this character have their origins in experience and arise when habit becomes insufficient to guide our behavior. We are confronted by a state of affairs in which we do not know what to do. The question that is often asked is how a value situation differs from one that is ethically neutral. What is the difference between a moral act and one in which moral dimensions are lacking? By and large in Dewey's estimation, the difference is one of degree rather than kind, for every act, potentially, has moral dimensions.[39]

[38] See *Ibid.*, pp. 161–163.
[39] *Ibid.*, p. 178 ff.

Whenever the road of experience forks, whenever we are faced with the necessity to choose one way instead of another, the likelihood is present that the consequences of our chosen act will affect the lives and interests of other people and, certainly, the course of our own conduct and character will be affected. That the effect of some actions is minimal, nobody will deny, but Dewey believed that Aristotle was right when he observed that in a moral act not only must a man be aware of what he is doing and be able to choose, *the act itself must be a true expression of a formed and stable character.*[40] So, the moral quality of any act is, in part at least, owing to the fact that this particular act is continuous with the previous experience of the person, that it represents a deliberate and considered decision to act in a given way, and therefore is neither purely impulsive nor merely the product of routine habit.

Problematic situations that have ethical properties arise in the same way any problematic situation arises. There is an existential state of affairs in which we find ourselves. The situation itself is disunified and indeterminate. The road forks and there is nothing forthcoming from our previous experience that tells us what we should do—and yet, we must do something. At this point it should be emphasized that all ethical situations are specific and unique. What we are required to do is to find a way to act *under those circumstances at this point in time.* We are not called on to solve all problems or to make universal judgments or find some *summum bonum.* We are called on to find a way to act *now* that promises best to transform the indeterminate character of the events in which we find ourselves to one that is unified and determinate.

The situation that confronts us always is unique. It is unlike any that has ever existed before as well as any that will ever exist again. It is problematic because the residue of prior experience is insufficient to guide us under these circumstances, though such previous learning must provide a means for instituting inquiry if we are to deal with the situation intelligently. As a situation, it is not simply a matter of choosing between right and wrong, for if there are these two courses of action and these are plainly labeled in some way, *there is no problem.* It is true that much traditional moral theory proceeds on the assumption that ethical acts are essentially choices between alternatives that represent good and evil. If this is really the case then ethical actions represent merely the *will* to choose the *right* path and reflection plays a subservient role, if indeed it plays any at all. Dewey uses an example of a

40 *Ibid.*, p. 176.

bank clerk who is considering embezzling money. This clerk knows perfectly well that to embezzle the bank's money is wrong and in this sense there is no ethical problem at all. He may be trying to find some reason why it would not be wrong for him to take the money but, says Dewey, "He is not really thinking, he is merely permitting his desire to govern his beliefs."[41] It may seem a simple and trustworthy matter to say that to live an ethical life means to "follow the rules," the rules being the Ten Commandments or some other code, but what do we do when we are not clear what a given rule means under a particular set of circumstances? Things do not always come plainly labeled "good" and "evil"; if they did, there would be no need for reflection nor would there be any need for ethical theories.

The reason a genuinely moral act involves reflection is that the choice of action we must make is really a choice among competing goods. It is this fact that sets the problem for inquiry and also it is the condition that gives our ethical decisions the poignant quality they have. In demonstrating that moral problems originate when goods come into conflict with each other, Dewey uses the example of a man whose country has just declared war.[42] This person is a good and loyal citizen who loves his country and is devoted to its welfare. But he also harbors fundamental convictions that are anchored in his religious beliefs that war is evil and is really nothing but mass murder. But, he is told on good authority, the only way the nation can survive is to wage war resolutely and by any means possible to destroy the enemy. Unless total victory is achieved, the nation will be lost.

A man faced with these circumstances is not presented with the simple choice of good or evil. On the one hand, he is powerfully affected by his concern for the country he loves and wishes to preserve, but he is also torn in another direction by his deep-seated religious and ethical beliefs against killing human beings. Up to this time these values have not been in conflict and in reality have often seemed to reinforce each other. But they are in conflict now, and what is the universal ethical rule that can be invoked to settle this matter?

In ethical inquiry, as in any genuine act of inquiry, we search for a way to act that promises best to change the indeterminate character of the situation. The resources we have to assist us are the fruits of previous experience in the form of ideas. We attempt to foresee the consequences of possible action as best we can and to evaluate and

41 *Ibid.,* p. 174.
42 *Loc. cit.*

choose on the basis of our foresight. The idea we choose to act on is tested by the way it affects the situation that generated the problem. Can we be sure that in this kind of reflection we will always foresee all possible consequences? No, there can be no such assurance. If we act on the basis of the most careful reflection we are capable of, can we be sure we will do the "right" thing? No, not if by the "right thing" is meant that all situations are capable of being resolved satisfactorily for all concerned or that we are always able to perceive what means will best secure the ends we desire. Given the kind of world we live in, the quest for certainty is futile, for certainty is no more attainable in the making of judgments about value than it is in making scientific judgments.

The objections to Dewey's approach to ethical theory are numerous and of varied character, stemming as they do both from absolutist and naturalistic-relativistic sources. The absolutist's fundamental criticism is, of course, that Dewey refuses to grant a character of universality and permanence to ethical standards and that he insists that values originate in experience and must be tested in experience. There are many variations on this theme, but the common element in all of them is that ideas cannot have a normative function unless they are in some secure sense absolute and unless there is some ultimate Good to which all other goods are subordinate in the sense of being merely instrumental to the Ultimate. This Good may be the *eudaemonia* of Aristotle or the spiritual salvation of the New Testament, but however it may be conceived, all other goods are subaltern to it.

Although Dewey's own ethical theory is in the naturalistic tradition, he also receives severe criticism from others of that tradition, in large measure because he has refused to accept the belief that unexamined desire or preference is sufficient to determine value—in short, that to be desired means to be desirable. If ethical statements are simply expressions of our own desires and feelings, as much contemporary analytic philosophy holds, then a cognitive ethics is simply impossible, for statements of this kind are neither true nor false. It is permissible to say that they are meaningful, in the sense that they do communicate our own feelings and desires, but we can no more attribute truth or falsity to the imperative, "Love thy neighbor!" than we can to the imperative, "Shut the door!" Under this view, ethical norms function as axioms do in logical systems. They can be related logically to certain rules of conduct, but they cannot themselves be proven true.[43]

[43] See for example: Hans Reichenbach, *The Rise of Scientific Philosophy*, Berkeley, California: University of California Press, 1951, Chapter 17.

Dewey's answer—at least one of his answers—is that there is no substitute for knowledge in conducting any inquiry, whether the inquiry is concerned with science, with common sense, or with ethics. The conditions that control inquiry are those inherent in the situation. It is they that determine what is relevant and what is not. To the extent that we understand the factual structure of the situation are we able to make wise decisions to act. Even if we do not wish to agree that knowledge is virtue, this hardly means that ignorance is the best state of mind for making ethical decisions.[44]

Dewey has maintained that one of the underlying causes for this disjunction between knowledge and values, between fact and worth, is the ancient dualism that sets mind and consciousness over against a material environment of brute fact. Under this view, knowledge, science, inquiry can only deal with primary qualities inherent in the world of things while those qualities men prize for what they are in themselves are secondary and subjective. But a thorough-going naturalism recognizes that within nature things and events possess not only instrumental potentialities but also final qualities that are as much a part of their natures as any other qualities they may possess.[45] Once we set man and his experience apart from nature, we inherit all the dualisms that philosophy has to cope with, and so every generation struggles with the problem of being, the problem of knowledge, and the problem of value. But what is held to be a problem here, in the judgment of the naturalist, is a pseudo-problem, for it is an effort to find a way to account for our possession of what we do empirically possess, which is to say it is the effort to rejoin by elaborate means what should never have been put asunder.

MAN AND NATURE:
THE ONTOLOGY OF PRAGMATISM

It is often said that pragmatism as a philosophical tradition offers nothing but a method. Some have held that it cannot rightfully be called a philosophy at all because it has refused to be concerned with metaphysical questions except in a destructively critical way. It is true that pragmatists (James is perhaps in some measure an exception here)

---

[44] An interesting development of this point is found in: Charles S. Stevenson, "The Scientist's Role and the Aims of Education," *Harvard Educational Review*, 24:231–238.
[45] *Experience and Nature*, p. 96.

have declined to deal with the traditional "why" questions: "Why are we here? Why do we suffer? Why is there evil in the world?" We know that the pragmatic rule eliminates as meaningless those questions that do not lend themselves to the operations of inquiry, and "why" questions are generally of this kind. However, though such questions may be meaningless in the linguistic and scientific sense, they are genuinely expressive of the realities of experience that go on in a world which itself possesses basic attributes of contingency and unpredictability.[46]

In the early part of his career Dewey foresaw that one of the effects of the theory of organic evolution that would be most difficult for modern man to accept was a new concept of nature that departed radically from the idealized cosmology of the classic tradition, the anthropocentricism of the Hebraic-Christian tradition, and perhaps even the mechanistic determinism of Newtonian physics. Those worlds, each in its own way, displayed a character of completion and fixity. They seemed to provide a secure place for the human drama to be played out because they exhibited a basic character of rationality, lawfulness, and order into which it was possible to read the answers to the "why" questions. But the physics of relativity and the revolution in biology and all that has followed from these have changed our conceptions of the conditions under which we must live and work. There are various possible ways to react to the kind of world portrayed by modern science and in a certain degree contemporary philosophy has attempted some interpretation of the new cosmology and the place of man in the scheme of things. Pragmatism is one of the traditions in modern philosophy in which the consequences of a scientific, naturalistic outlook have been developed philosophically.

In the view of this tradition, traditional philosophies have been preoccupied with putting a sure, finished, complete character on the "world of real existence" and they often have shown themselves capable of going to any extreme to do it. But, says the pragmatist, regardless of what previous philosophizing says about the identity of the Real with what is sure and complete and perfect, empirically we do live in a world in which all is not finished and sure. The world we know in our experience is a mixture of the ordered and the indeterminate.

Even when classic metaphysics identifies the good with the Real, the fact still remains that something is left over that is uncertain, fluid, and changing. This was relegated in the classic tradition to the realm

---

[46] One of Dewey's most important contributions to naturalistic ontology is found in *Ibid.*, Chapters II and III.

of "becoming" or "appearance" or the "merely empirical," and yet, the pragmatist reminds us, the world remains what it is and always was—a suffusion of the indeterminate and the relatively stable. It was in this arbitrary separation of the seemingly permanent and the obviously transient that philosophy forsook the very conditions that brought it into being, for it is at the point where the unstable and the regular impinge, where the goods men desire are the most elusive, where choice demands struggle and action, that philosophy was born. If philosophy was indeed born of wonder, as Aristotle said, classic metaphysics converted it from wonder to contemplation.

The very fact that men do experience satisfaction indicates that nature is characterized by both the assured and the perilous. Satisfactions come as the result of difficulties being cleared up and of the consequent relief from tensions. If there were no hindrances, no blockings in the environment, if the path were always smooth and assured, there would be no tension and no satisfaction. When a desirable fulfillment does come it is taken as good because its possession was and continues to be uncertain and because it had to be striven after. Once a desired outcome is achieved and experienced, it becomes ideal. We make it ideal because prior experience has shown it to be worthy of desire and effort. In retrospect we commemorate its issue from struggle to assurance. Thus, the precarious nature of existence is, in a sense, the source of all trouble, but it also is the condition of all satisfaction and hence of all ideality.

If the world were not in its basic character partly a matter of contingency and indeterminacy, what role would intelligence have to play? We have already seen that to Dewey and other pragmatists the office of thinking is one of clearing up the dubious and making the situation assured; of passing from doubt to belief, in Peirce's terms. Thinking is like any tool or natural energy that may be employed to clear up the indeterminate by applying to it the regular and assured. Thinking is not an abrupt transition from a "natural" to a "rational" level; it is a process of reorganizing and reconstructing experience within a world of space and time. The problematic always lies where the unpredictable and the stable intersect and in this sense every act, idea, and existence is an experiment. Those whose wish it is to act wisely, to have their actions guided by intelligence, must be cognizant of the nature of the world, for those who do not understand how to use the processes of nature to advantage will be continually at their mercy. We may as well face the reality that nothing lasts forever. Any existent thing has its existence in some environmental context and all the forces operating in that context are never entirely compatible with its existence. Change is intelligible only as a relation of events and permanency is comparative, not absolute. An existence may endure for eons, but it cannot be forever.

There are always those who lament this and refuse to face it and, in the estimation of pragmatists, there are distinguished representatives of this group to be found in the history of philosophy. But, as Dewey has said, there is no occasion to gloat over or to mourn what is so clearly a fact of nature. If the goods we prize are not eternal, neither are the evils that plague us. If the game is not rigged in our favor, neither is it rigged against us. The call is to face up to the world we know and in which we must live. The way to make secure in the future those things that deliberation shows to be most worthy of preserving is by studying and inquiring into the course of events, assaying their interconnections and noting the final qualities for which we prize them.

Inquiry is the method of intelligence and, in the estimation of Peirce and Dewey, the method of intelligence is the general method of science. In having said this, we are brought full circle in our study of the liberal protest. In the preface to the first edition of *How to Think*, Dewey wrote:

> This scientific attitude of mind might conceivably be quite irrelevant to teaching children and youth. But this book also represents the conviction that such is not the case; that the native and unspoiled attitude of childhood, marked by ardent curiosity, fertile imagination, and love of experimental inquiry, is near, very near, to the attitude of the scientific mind.

SUMMARY: THE IMPACT OF THE LIBERAL PROTEST

We have now concluded our study of the liberal protest, and there remains only space enough to give some attention to the influence this movement has had on the character of American educational philosophy. Our consideration of the progressive protest against essentialism has been concerned mainly with the educational theory developed within this tradition and for which John Dewey took the main responsibility. Some attention has been given to the historic context out of which this philosophy developed but we have made no effort to portray the wide scope and the varied character the progressive movement assumed in the years between the turn of the century and the ending of the Second World War. For this reason the assessment made here will be confined largely to the impact of the liberal protest as this was evidenced in a systematic philosophical position in which educational theory had an organic relation with American pragmatism. In the last chapter of his *The Transformation of the School*, Mr. Lawrence Cremin advances a number of reasons for the abrupt decline of the progressive education movement. Though such considerations are outside the scope of our purpose in the present context, those who wish a broader understanding of the decline of progressivism and the resurgence of a militant conservatism should study the concluding chapter of Mr. Cremin's book.

It is interesting that both the friends and foes of Dewey's progressivism and his experimental naturalism have often found it useful to overstate the impact of this tradition. Conservatives have proclaimed it the cause of all our social ills, and it is not unusual to find adherents of progressive educational philosophy attributing every significant advance in the status of public education directly to it. For example, it seems reasonable to think that on historical grounds the following achievements may properly be claimed for the American educational system of this century.

1. Conceptions of the purposes of free public education have been extended and enhanced. The idea that every person should have educational opportunities appropriate to his own needs and abilities is probably more nearly realized in this country than anywhere else on earth. (It is granted that this achievement is incomplete and that the statement means somewhat different things in conservatism and in progressivism.)

2. The school curriculum has been liberalized and extended. A broader range of educational experiences is now available than ever before in history.

3. Conceptions of individual and group discipline have become more humane and in some ways more effective.

4. The importance, as well as the possibility, of enlisting child interest and purpose in the educative process have been demonstrated. (Here again the differing perceptions of conservatives and progressives of the meaning of this statement should be noted.)

5. The materials of instruction have been improved and many new devices and materials have been developed.

6. The value of orienting method and curriculum around scientifically established concepts of human development and the psychology of learning has been established.

That the liberal protest movement favored such developments and supported them at virtually every turn appears so well established as to be outside the possibility of serious argument. It is, however, quite another thing to attribute them solely or even mainly to the direct influence of educational progressivism. The extension of the scope of the curriculum, for example, has included many areas that progressives never particularly sanctioned, and certainly in the case of many narrow vocational courses it is fruitless to search for support of these in the educational writings of John Dewey. In the same way, progressives view the products of the "new technology" with mixed feelings, even though they have consistently favored and worked for the improvement of the materials of instruction. It does not appear necessary to go beyond the facts in order to say that many of these changes probably would have come about whether a rigorous protest movement in liberal educational philosophy had ever developed in this century.

The purpose of these remarks is not to belittle or denigrate the achievements of educational progressivism. But the fact is that the causes of cultural change are always complex and there have been many forces at work in this century besides the experimentalism of John Dewey and the varying interpretations placed on it by his host of followers. The fact remains, however, that the really foundational elements in Dewey's educational philosophy never received widespread testing in the progressive movement. Why this was so is a matter best left to the historians, and Mr. Cremin, for one, has already found some cogent things to say about it.

For Dewey, education is a process in which the latent, plastic powers and tendencies of the child are developed through a carefully planned sequence of experience in which experimental method is the basis of educational method. In this view the purpose of educational effort is the continuous growth of the person in the fullest possible sense. There is nothing that growth can be subordinate to for growth itself is that which is "given." Neither can education, which itself is a process of growth, be said to be subordinate to something else—particularly to some distant *summum bonum* that more often than not is endowed with a mystical character. Dewey believed that education is something more—considerably more—than the communication of established knowledge and that the method of education ought to reflect the principle that in the long view what the Greeks used to call "the art of knowledge" is more important than the products of that art, as valuable as they may be. Dewey's contention that the curriculum of the school should be a process of active work was closely related to his studies in psychology and philosophy. It has been suggested in this book that the

PHILOSOPHY OF AMERICAN EDUCATION

major difference between the pedagogy of progressivism and that of essentialism is that progressivism viewed the curriculum as an ordered series of active enterprises, whereas essentialism has always seen it as some ordered series of subject matters. It has also been suggested that most of the differences in practical methodology of the two traditions stem from this source.

The idea that knowing and doing are inextricably linked in the cognitive process was never grasped very firmly in progressive practice, and the "activity movement" that reached its highwater mark in the '30s proceeded at the practical level largely without any real psychological or logical foundations. That this lack of understanding on the part of teachers led to a great deal of questionable improvisation and playing by ear is well established, and if there was any connection to be found between what Dewey had called the method of intelligence and the cutting, coloring, and pasting that went on in many schools in the 1930s, it was not easy to locate.

What had begun as the "project method" developed by Mr. William H. Kilpatrick, one of the most celebrated of the interpreters of Dewey's educational philosophy,[47] grew into the "activity movement" of the 1930s and by the close of that decade had become formalized in a kind of "unit teaching" that often bore about as much resemblance to the active enterprises of the Laboratory School as the formalized Pestalozzian object lesson had to the Old Master's own work at Yverdon.

Probably no reform movement ever really succeeds, if by success is meant that the foundations of its ideology receive faithful translation into action. Certainly if this is the criterion of success, Dewey's long adventure into educational theory was a failure and, by the same token, so was that of Plato and Rousseau and Pestalozzi and all the others who came before him. Whatever else it may or may not have done, progressivism raised the question of what the purposes and means of education must be in an industrial, urban society, whose basic pattern is as different from the early industrialism of the nineteenth century as a Jupiter rocket is from a box kite. We have not mastered this question yet.[48]

Viewed in retrospect, Dewey's effort was to find the way to a new humanism, a humanism that would be built on the achievements and

[47] See his "The Project Method," *Teachers College Record*, 19:319–335 (1918).
[48] For a provocative view of the current status of progressivism see: William Van Til, "Is Progressive Education Obsolete?" *Saturday Review*, 45:56 ff (February 17, 1962).

potentialities of scientific method and the ethical postulates of democracy. In the evolution of this new humanism, education, he thought, must play a strategic role, but in many respects it must be a new education in which the insights of science will assist us in the fuller realization of our common humanity. Given the conditions that existed in American schools of the 1890s, some kind of reform movement probably was inevitable. It may well be that for the progressive movement the historical irony is that Dewey's influence could not have been greater. Perhaps one way to sum it all up is to say that this, the greatest of the protest movements against American essentialism, ultimately was sold out—unconsciously, to be sure—by those who in Sidney Hook's words "thought they could remain progressive while ceasing to be liberal."

PART FOUR

OTHER PROTESTS

... *We act as if the task of education were to infuse into the child or the adolescent, only abridging and concentrating it, the very science or knowledge of the adult—that is to say, of the philologist, the historian, the grammarian, the scientist, etc., the most specialized experts. So we try to cram young people with a chaos of summarized adult notions which have been either condensed, dogmatized, and text-bookishly cut up or else made so easy that they are reduced to the vanishing point. As a result, we run the risk of producing either an instructed, bewildered intellectual dwarf, or an ignorant intellectual dwarf playing at dolls with our science.*

—JACQUES MARITAIN

Education at the Crossroads, New Haven: Yale University Press, Inc., 1943, p. 59.

CHAPTER TEN

The Protest of the

Perennial Philosophy

In Part IV of this book we will concern ourselves with three traditions in philosophy and education that constitute significant protests against modern American essentialism in educational theory and practice. The first of these three traditions we will undertake to analyze has been given the name *perennialism* or the *perennial philosophy*. We took some brief note of the origins of this great tradition in Chapter II of this book when we were reviewing the contributions of antiquity to the western tradition in culture and philosophy. We observed in that connection that the perennial philosophy was formed from a great synthesis of the Hebraic-Christian tradition in theology and the Hellenic tradition in philosophy. Perennialism, therefore, presents for our consideration a view of the world and of man that in many important respects is very different from ideas about these matters that we have analyzed in the earlier parts of this book.

For example, the established or conservative tradition in American education is a product primarily of the modern world. We have seen that there are important elements of both the classic and medieval traditions still to be found in contemporary conservatism, yet this tradition in its basic structure exhibits the post-medieval and middle-class nature of its origins. In America the conservative tradition, differing as it does in certain important respects from European conservatism, has incorporated much of that strain of eighteenth century liberalism from which emerged the economic "rugged individualism" and "free enterprise" which are so clearly associated with the American character. Conservatism is also the tradition that has attempted to accommodate the tenets of supernatural religion to the spirit, methodology, and achievements of experimental science and thus to fashion a kind of "public philosophy" by which men may live in a culture characterized by science and corporate industrialism but by which they may also regulate their lives according to a tradition, many of whose roots lie in the supernatural. We have already seen how clearly the eclectic character of the conservative tradition is mirrored in the educational theory advanced and supported by that tradition and in the schools of our time.

It is important to understand that perennialism is not simply a kind of conservative philosophy of society and education, although it has on occasion been treated in the literature as if it were, just as some of the leading American spokesmen for the perennialist protest against American essentialism sometimes have been classified as educational conservatives. The protest of the perennial philosophy is not against simply the educational theories of the modern world—whether these be conservative or liberal. Its objections are not merely to miscellaneous ideas in science or philosophy, which for one reason or another it finds untenable. Perennialism is a strong and continuing protest against the pattern of contemporary western culture with its science and technology, its corporate industrialism, and its political and educational institutions, which in America, at least, have become almost completely secularized. It is, in effect, an invitation—or perhaps better, an insistence—that we turn our backs on the folly we have wrought and return to a pattern of culture that western man abandoned nearly half a dozen centuries ago. In this sense, perennialism is openly and frankly a proposal for cultural regression, for at the heart of its proposals is the demand that we return to those conceptions of nature, of man, of society, and of the nature of good from which we were tempted by the hollow and arrogant promises of natural science and middle-class economics.

Clearly, a proposal of this kind puts perennialism in opposition to modern conservatism and modern liberalism, for both of these recognize the inevitability of cultural change and social evolution, though as we have seen, the conservative and the liberal differ sharply on the question of the desirable rate of cultural alteration. Even so, both conservatism and liberalism represent efforts to combine the basic elements of modern culture into a workable synthesis. Both these traditions support democracy, capitalism, nationalism, and experimental science, although both of them continue to experience difficulty in accommodating these traditions to each other. Both the conservative and liberal traditions have accepted natural science and the profound alterations it has brought about in the pattern of western life, and both of them have found an important place for scientific studies in the curriculum of the schools. The invasion of the traditional humanistic curriculum by the natural sciences has created strains within American essentialism that at times seem almost intolerable, yet there is seldom found in the contemporary literature of the conservative tradition any serious proposal to eliminate natural science from the curriculum or to give it a truly subordinate role.

So far as education is concerned, perennialism has always found progressivism a natural and, usually, a mortal enemy. This is because it is in progressivism that the influence of modern naturalism and empiricism are most clearly seen and the perennialist believes that the major ills of modern society may be traced ultimately to these two elements. It is true that on occasion essentialists and perennialists have joined forces against the common enemy, progressivism, particularly in earlier decades of the present century when the progressive protest was far stronger than it is today. It is likely that this temporary truce was part of the cause for some commentators' listing of prominent American essentialists as educational conservatives. Any truce between essentialism and conservatism, however, is mostly a matter of convenience and is always uneasy. Though it is certain that perennialism has no love for progressivism, the important point is that the main thrust of the perennialist protest is against the established American tradition in education and, as has already been shown, the prevailing tradition in American education is essentialism. Mr. Robert M. Hutchins, certainly one of the foremost spokesmen for the perennial tradition in America, has for many years engaged progressives in lively combat over educational theory, but he has always been at his best when lambasting existing educational institutions, particularly the American university—that citadel of American essentialism.

If we are to understand the part that perennialism plays in the contemporary educational scene, we must see it as a vigorous and serious protest against the character of American society, and we must also understand that the proposals of perennialism for the righting of the wrongs that infest our system of education necessarily involve profound changes in the pattern of contemporary culture. In order to understand the proposals for educational reform that perennialists advocate so vigorously, we must engage in an analysis of a view of the world and man's place in it that had its origin in classic Greek thought, that reached its full flower in the works of Plato and Aristotle, and that ultimately was amalgamated with the Hebraic-Christian tradition in the great medieval synthesis. Our first step in this inquiry will be to survey the character of contemporary perennialism.

THE CHARACTER OF CONTEMPORARY PERENNIALISM

In some respects perennialists are more pessimistic about the future of western man than any other important intellectual group in America. The depth and intensity of this attitude, of course, vary from one spokesman for the tradition to another but the roots of their pessimism lie in the interpretation of history that often appears in perennialist literature. Under this view the decline of western society began in the fourteenth century and the event that precipitated this decadence was the abandonment of the classic belief in the independent existence of universals. This event came about as a consequence of the great medieval debate over the character of universals in which the Platonic, the Aristotelian, and various intermediate positions were argued by some of the greatest philosophic minds in Europe.[1] Briefly, the debate over universals was concerned with the question of whether universal ideas have a real existence and if they do, how the universal is related to the particular. For example, it may be asked whether there is a universal idea of man that has an existence that is independent of individual men and yet is in some way related to the individual natures of different men? We saw in an earlier chapter that Plato took the position that ultimate reality is composed of forms (universals) that exist prior to and independent of any particular things or events. Plato was convinced that particular things owe their natures to participation in these universals, but he never was able to develop a complete demonstration of the character of this relationship. The Platonic position

[1] This thesis that the alleged decadence of modern culture began with the defeat of logical realism and the ultimate triumph of nominalism has been developed in a brilliant and remarkable book by Richard M. Weaver, *Ideas Have Consequences*, Chicago: University of Chicago Press, 1948. Mr. Weaver is often spoken of as a conservative and has contributed to conservative publications. However he may be classified otherwise, the essentially Platonic argument he advances in this book indicates strong leanings toward the perennialist explanation for the sickness of contemporary society.

played an important role in the debate that developed in the medieval world in which it was argued as "Extreme Realism" by such able protagonists as Anselm of Canterbury (1033–1109). Anselm's position was that universals exist independently of thought or things; thus there is a universal form of man that exists prior to and independent of any particular person. As a Christian, he went beyond Plato in arguing that universals exist in the mind of God and, therefore, when we recognize truth our minds are in accord with the mind of God.

We also noted in passing that a serious difference over the status of universals developed between Plato and Aristotle.[2] Where Plato had insisted that the universal exists prior to and independent of particulars, Aristotle maintained that the universal (form) always is found united with matter in substantial entities. In Chapter II in which we took some note of the Aristotelian position, we referred to this principle of the union of form and matter as *hylomorphism*. Aristotle's position on the status of universals is known as *moderate realism*. In the medieval debate the most distinguished advocate of moderate realism was Thomas Aquinas (1225–1274) and this essentially Aristotelian doctrine was ultimately accepted as the philosophical position of the Church.

Certain intermediate positions on the question of universals developed, but the real challenge to logical realism was offered by a philosophical position usually known as *nominalism*. Nominalism is, in essence, the denial that general terms (i.e., universals) actually refer to anything that really exists and holds instead that universals are simply terms that have been found convenient for denoting objects that are similar. According to this idea, therefore, anything that is real is an individual thing. Any universal ideas we may have about individual things consequently are products of our own observation and classification and they have no reality beyond that; they are simply words. An early advocate of this position was Roscellinus (c. 1050–1122) who was forced by the Church to recant. The most celebrated advocate of nominalism, however, was William of Occam, a fourteenth century philosopher. Occam's nominalism was regarded as dangerous to various aspects of the doctrinal position of the Church, for if nominalism is accepted as a correct explanation of the character of universals, it becomes impossible to demonstrate philosophically certain important tenets of the Christian faith, for example, such important tenets as the

[2] Aristotle's criticism of Plato's doctrine of the forms is found in *Metaphysics*, Book I.

existence of God and the immortality of the soul. Therefore, since it is impossible to demonstrate these doctrines rationally, all that remains is the possibility of accepting them purely on the basis of faith. Such a position was rejected by the Church.

Many moderns may well wonder, of course, what the debate over these ideas has to do with events in the contemporary world, particularly since this great intellectual controversy occurred over five centuries ago. Perennialists, however, are of the opinion that the consequences of this debate have a great deal to do with the character of contemporary society and some of those in this tradition, whose pessimism about modern society runs deep, believe that the eventual triumph of nominalism paved the way for modern decadence. Mr. Richard Weaver, whom we have identified as a representative of this view, has said that the net effect of nominalism has been to deny the reality known by the mind and to put in its place that which we know through the senses. And, he argues, once this profound philosophical reorientation was achieved the west started down the road to modern empiricism.[3] It is the fact that we have continued to follow this road that explains the predicament in which modern man finds himself. This road has led us to rationalism; thence inevitably to materialism; to the arrogance of experimental science; to technology, which is the fruit of scientific materialism; and to industrial society in which man is no longer *homo sapiens,* but *homo faber.* Weaver is not very sanguine about the chances of our survival; ours, he points out, would not be the first civilization in history to disappear into oblivion.

If we do have a chance to survive, it will be realized to the extent that we can correct the momentous error that was committed. The road back to the point at which we were betrayed by our ancestors may be a long one, and our hopes of reaching it are by no means assured, but it is the only effort that can be worthwhile. We must recapture for ourselves the vision of the objectivity of truth which is possible only if universals have an independent reality of their own. If we can do this, we will again accept the view of man and nature encompassed in classical and medieval philosophy, and once this view is reinstated as dominant, the school, the church, and other of the great institutions of society will be purged of their ills and will once again become effective in the lives of men.

Not all contemporary proponents of the perennial philosophy profess as profound a pessimism as Mr. Weaver's, nor do they always argue

[3] *Ibid.,* p. 3.

that the whole course of western history has been determined simply by the triumph of nominalistic philosophy. On the other hand, there are few, if any, of this philosophical persuasion who do not believe that profound changes must occur in contemporary society if we are to escape a final disaster, and the model they most often present to us to guide our efforts is one in which the classic and medieval traditions in society and education predominate.

Contemporary perennialism in America is, in fact, represented by two major groups. The community of interest between these two groups is extensive but there is also a fundamental difference between them. Both these groups have had a very great deal to say about educational theory and practice, and there is wide agreement between them concerning the ills that are typical of American education. They often find themselves in close accord on proposals for remedying these ills. One of these groups is made up of men who identify themselves primarily, though not necessarily exclusively, with the original classic Greek philosophical tradition, particularly with Aristotelianism. Their approach to education, for example, is most often characterized by Aristotelian conceptions of human nature, the nature of society, science, and ethics. We will refer to this wing of modern American perennialism as *rational humanism*. The other main group is composed of those who represent the modern version of scholasticism, which is to say, of course, that they are the modern intellectual heirs of St. Thomas Aquinas and medieval scholasticism. This group will be referred to as neo-scholastics or neo-Thomists. The fundamental difference between the rational humanists and the neo-scholastics is that those in the former group are not identified with the Roman Catholic Church and do not subscribe necessarily to its theological doctrines; a survey of the literature, however, will reveal a sympathetic attitude on the part of many non-Catholic perennialists toward Roman Catholic theology. On the other hand, the neo-scholastics are composed partly of lay philosophers, some of whom are scholars of high distinction and who have made distinguished contributions to perennialist educational philosophy. Others of this neo-scholastic group are members of the Roman Catholic clergy, but they often approach the problems of education from philosophical as well as theological grounds.

The spokesmen for the perennial tradition who are best known to Americans probably are those we have classified as rational humanists, and it is all but certain that Mr. Robert Maynard Hutchins (1899–   ) is the best known of these. Mr. Hutchins began his career in educational administration when he was made dean of the Yale Law School at the age of 29. Subsequently, he was president and then chancellor of the University of Chicago and in 1951 joined the Ford Foundation. He has written and lectured for many years on the need for the reform of our educational institutions—particularly our institutions of higher learning.

A close associate of Mr. Hutchins at Chicago and a major contributor to perennialist educational thought is Mr. Mortimer J. Adler. Adler's approach to educational philosophy has been more explicitly and technically philosophical than has Hutchins'. The contributions of the two men have complemented each other admirably. Mr. Adler has been prominent in the "Great Books" movement and has served as one of the editors of *The Great Books of the Western World*. To the names of these men should be added those of Mr. Mark Van Doren, distinguished scholar, teacher, and man of letters; Mr. Stringfellow Barr, who along with Mr. Hutchins and with Mr. Scott Buchanan helped to reorganize St. Johns College, a liberal arts college in Annapolis, Maryland that more than any other contemporary institution embodies the perennial philosophy in education as this is interpreted by rational humanists.

The most gifted philosophers among the neo-scholastics are generally conceded to be Jacques Maritain who, although he was educated and reared as a Protestant, was converted to the Catholic faith and has become one of the most important philosophical voices of the Roman Catholic Church, and Etienne Gilson, a distinguished French medievalist, member of the Pontifical Academy of St. Thomas Aquinas in Rome, and Director of Studies in the Pontifical Institute of Medieval Studies in Toronto. Members of the clergy who among others have made significant contributions to educational theory are Father William F. Cunningham, Father William J. McGuchen, Mr. J. D. Redden and Mr. F. A. Ryan.

We may summarize the character of contemporary perennialism by saying that: a) it is a strong and continuing protest against much of the character of modern industrial society; b) it insists that the salvation of western society depends on our achieving a reorientation of our views of the universe and of man, which will involve a recovery of the classic and scholastic theses; c) the tradition today in America is represented by two groups, one secular and proceeding mainly from Aristotelian premises, the other religious and oriented about the Thomistic tradition. Although as we have noted, there are differences between these two groups, these differences being occasioned perhaps more by theology than by philosophy, there is also a great deal of common ground. One of the areas in which there is considerable commonality is that of educational theory. Both wings of this tradition have often launched bitter criticism against the character of American education. Our next step in the analysis of the perennial philosophy will be to examine the protest this tradition makes against the state of things in American schools.

THE PERENNIALIST PROTEST IN EDUCATION

In the first chapter of one of his earlier books Mr. Robert Hutchins has said that the confusion in American higher education is caused by three primary conditions in society: the love of money, a misconception of democracy, and a mistaken idea of progress.[4] The university is not free, and hence cannot be a true intellectual center, because it is always pursuing money, either from legislative bodies or private donors, usually from both, and always, of course, from students. The practical effect of the love of money is the emergence of the "service station" concept of education which means, says Mr. Hutchins, that a university must make itself "felt in the community." The expectation is that whatever immediate problems face society must be taken up and made the primary business of the university. Since the character of these problems varies from one period of time to another, the university expends its energy and resources variously on everything from agriculture to military weaponry, and the purposes for which the higher learning should exist are honored only in the breach. The American university persists in keeping underclassmen on its rolls because typically they pay more in fees than it costs to teach them (at least in proportion to the cost for upperclassmen and graduate students), since they can be entrusted to graduate students who can be made into teaching fellows and who will work for low wages.[5] Thus, the love of money helps perpetuate the confusion

---

[4] *The Higher Learning in America,* New Haven: Yale University Press, 1936; reissued in 1962 as a Yale Paperbound with a new preface by Mr. Hutchins. References here are to the latter edition. Many changes have occurred in American education since the publication of *The Higher Learning,* but Mr. Hutchins' criticisms appear to have about as much relevance as they ever had. In fact, it is possible to interpret many events of the last decade as fulfillments of his predictions.
[5] *Ibid.,* p. 8.

of collegiate education with university education and few Americans can tell the difference.

The scramble for money has increased manyfold in the years since the end of the last World War, primarily, of course, because of the vast sums of it that have been poured into universities by the federal government and by private business for various kinds of research. A whole new class of administrators has developed; the purpose these officials serve is to get as many research projects as possible for their institutions. The status of faculty members necessarily is determined more and more by the amount of federal or industrial money they have been able to garner. Says Mr. Hutchins, "The universities have demonstrated their willingness to do almost anything for money."[6]

The second source of confusion in American education lies in a misapprehension of what democracy means, particularly when the term is applied to educational theory. The major effects of the confusion over democracy are several. First, this confusion is responsible for the typical American belief that a young person should be allowed to stay in school as long as he likes, study whatever appeals to him, and be a candidate for any degree he finds attractive.[7] Thus, the typical American belief has developed that everybody has a right to the same amount and the same kind of education as everybody else. Another effect, and one closely allied to the two just noted, is that everybody in the country thinks he is an expert on education and rarely foregoes the opportunity to intrude himself into the making of educational policy. And when the citizens set out to tell the authorities how the public schools and colleges or the universities should be run, the confusion is many times compounded.

The other source of the confusion that affects education in our country is our misconceived notion of what constitutes progress. The fact is that we tend to identify progress with the accumulation of information and the development of science and technology. In their search for more and more information, the sciences have become increasingly specialized and, one by one, they have split off from their original source which, like most perennialists, Mr. Hutchins believes to be philosophy. The final triumph of empiricism came, he says, ". . . when the social sciences, law, and even philosophy and theology themselves became experimental and progressive."[8] Here we see again the major theme that runs through perennialist thought: the ultimate source of our troubles lies in our abandonment of logical realism—and therefore in our denial

[6] *Ibid.*, p. xi.   [7] *Ibid.*, p.13.   [8] *Ibid.*, p. 26.

of the power and importance of human reason—and our acceptance of nominalism and hence of empiricism. "And so," Mr. Hutchins says, "empiricism having taken the place of thought as the basis of research, took its place, too, as the basis of education. It led by easy stages to vocationalism; because the facts you learn about your environment (particularly if you love money) ought to be as immediate and useful as possible."[9]

Now it is perhaps only to be expected that a society as confused over educational policy as is our own would conceive education as serving fundamentally a vocational purpose, and, therefore, would not only ignore the importance of liberal education, but indeed would not even be able to define what the term "liberal" means when it is associated with the term "education." It might also be expected that such a society in its reverence for "facts" would see the process of teaching as essentially one of transmitting as much factual material to students as possibly can be done. Perennialists point out that there are grave difficulties with this idea. One is that facts do not stay current and therefore may not prove to be very useful, even if they are remembered. Another difficulty is that there is already such a bulk of factual detail, and it appears to be increasing in quantity at a geometric rate of progression, that nobody could possibly learn it all, even if he stayed in school until middle age. The third kind of criticism advanced by perennialists concerning education conceived as the transmission of factual material is that students simply do not have the maturity and experience needed to assimilate in any meaningful way either the kind or the vast amount of material schools try to transmit.[10]

It should be recognized that criticism of this kind necessarily is directed against the essentialist tradition in education, for it is that tradition, as we have seen in considerable detail, in which education is considered to be the transmission and absorption of organized factual material. It will also be recalled that spokesmen for educational progressivism have also criticized the prevailing tradition on the same grounds; much of the liberal protest is against the effort to prepare students for some distant future by transmitting to them various bodies of "essential

---

[9] Loc. cit.

[10] Objections of this kind have already been developed at some length in the chapter on essentialism and will not be repeated here in detail. Mr. Hutchins' writings contain many variations of these criticisms, one of his most forthright statements being found in: The Conflict in Education, New York: Harper and Brothers, 1953. A similar criticism will be found in Jacques Maritain, Education at the Crossroads, New Haven: Yale University Press, Inc., 1943, Chapter III. My references are to the paperbound edition of Maritain's book issued in 1960.

subject matters," and progressivists also have paid careful attention to the problem of meaning. As we will see later, and as might be expected anyway, progressivism and perennialism find very different kinds of philosophical reasons for their protests against essentialism, yet it is important to note that the protests of the two traditions *at the practical level* are very similar, if not identical. This in itself should be enough to correct the common belief that perennialism is simply a kind of conservative approach to education.

Perennialists find many things to criticize in the prevailing mode of education in America, but some of their strongest protests are against the vocationalism that they believe infests our schools, particularly our secondary schools and our institutions of higher learning. It is the considered opinion of most perennialists that the height of our educational folly is to be found in what we have done to the university, which once was the greatest educational institution ever developed in the west. The higher learning, in the judgment of perennialists, has become little else than a glorified training for various occupations. The colleges have long since lost any sight of what is meant by liberal education—even when they try to define it, they attempt to do so by listing an array of subject matters dignified by the word "discipline." The university has become a collection of professional schools in which a student can learn how to do almost anything except what is important. In the university research is now the great prestige-building activity; in many, if not most, institutions one of the cherished perquisites of the full professor is that he can reduce his teaching, particularly of underclassmen, or perhaps escape it entirely and concentrate on research. Therefore, Mr. Hutchins has said, it is small wonder that in America the chief opponent of liberal education is the professor who works in a university that has a reputation for research and professional training.[11] Nor is it surprising that the real commitment of a professor is to his own subject, rather than to his university or to the education of students. It used to be said that the university is a community of scholars but, says Mr. Hutchins, "This community, if it ever existed has now collapsed."[12]

There is a conflict in American education but fundamentally this conflict is not between teaching and research, for this struggle is simply symptomatic of a greater confusion. The real conflict exists because of differing conceptions of the aim of education. If we take the university,

[11] "An Appraisal of American Higher Education," *School and Society*, 90:214–218 (May 5, 1962).
[12] *Ibid.*, p. 216.

for example, we find that historically the purpose of this institution has been the pursuit of truth for its own sake, but gradually the idea has developed among us that the purpose of a university is to prepare people for their life's work. To the perennialist these two aims of a university education are irreconcilable. Since Americans are practically unanimous on the issue that higher education should prepare students for their chosen vocations, not only have universities become aggregations of professional schools, the older departments, that formerly considered themselves the curators of the liberal arts and sciences, are as vocationally oriented as the schools of library science, engineering, veterinary medicine, or any of the others that have grown up in this century.[13]

The dead hand of vocationalism is also everywhere to be found in our secondary schools. As a people, we have always thought that universal education could accomplish almost anything, but we really do not know what it can do because we have never tried it out. A very large majority of students in the American high school have simply pursued various kinds of vocational training courses that will provide them with "marketable skills" but which contribute nothing to their education. Essentialists, to be sure, are in strong accord on the policy that the intellectually gifted student should study only the academic subjects, particularly those that prepare for entrance to college. However, the conservative tradition is badly split on what to do with those students who have no intention of going to college and who cannot cope with the essentials of the academic high school curriculum. As noted previously, Arthur Bestor and others of the Council for Basic Education are generally in opposition to including vocational courses in the curriculum for non-college-bound students, though in the long run a substantial part of their argument for the essentials turns out to be instrumental in character. However, James B. Conant is the conservative voice to which contemporary Americans attend most closely, and Conant has consistently advocated the inclusion of vocational courses in the high school program for students who are not going to college. In fact, in his book

[13] See for example: *The Higher Learning in America*, Chapter II. A study conducted by the University of Michigan Survey Research Center, *Public Concepts of the Costs and Utility of Higher Education* by Angus Campbell and William C. Eckerman, Ann Arbor, Michigan: University of Michigan Institute for Social Research, 1964, indicates that a preponderant number of the American public think that training for a good job is the most important objective of a college education. To perennialists this is simply one more link in a long chain of evidence that shows the complete inability of Americans to conceive of what liberal education is or what its values are. It is also an example of the typical American inability to distinguish between collegiate and university grade education.

Slums and Suburbs[14] Conant proposes that the plight of slum children can be alleviated by giving them vocational training courses that are tied directly to the current labor market in the local community.

Such a proposal as this is profoundly distasteful to perennialists for at least two major reasons. The more immediate reason they point out is that narrow, excessively practical skills quickly lose their relevance in a technology as dynamic as that of contemporary America. Much of the unemployment today is suffered by people who have only a few vocational skills that have been outmoded by automation or other technical advances in industry. In one of his newspaper columns, Hutchins, addressing himself to the current employment situation, observed that those who have Ph.D.s in physics can sell them without difficulty, but those who have only marketable mechanical and manual skills find few takers in the labor market. Since the latter group is composed in large measure by adolescents who got little or nothing in high school but vocational training, the unemployment rate among youth up to age nineteen is twice that of adults and growing constantly larger. Viewing these events in another context, Mr. Hutchins has said that Conant's proposals to tie vocational education directly to local labor markets will do nothing but make the situation worse.[15]

Perennialists, however, advance a far more serious criticism of vocational education than that we have just considered. To train a young person in school simply to do some such servile task as cosmetology, automobile mechanics, or television repair, and this at the expense of his *education*, amounts purely and simply to the debasement of human nature. Hutchins, describing the curriculum in cosmetology pursued by a young girl in a public technical high school, noted after listing the courses she is required to take in driver training, homemaking, physical education, etc., that "This is the education of a slave . . . not the education of a free citizen of a society that hopes to remain free. It is barbarous."[16] If we are serious about democracy, Hutchins insists, we are either going to have to learn how to *educate* all citizens or we will be forced to change our form of government. If all men are to be rulers, which is what democracy means, then all men must be educated as rulers; nine-tenths of them cannot continue to be trained as slaves. The alternative to educating all men as rulers is to return to a form of govern-

---

14 New York: McGraw-Hill Book Company, Inc., 1961.
15 Robert M. Hutchins, "That Candles May be Brought," *Graduate Comment*, Wayne State University, 3:1–4 (April, 1960), p. 4.
16 *Loc. cit.*

ment in which a small elite will rule the great uneducated, slavish masses. This will represent a tacit, if not an explicit, agreement with the ancient Greek conviction that some men are by nature fit only to be slaves. In the judgment of perennialists, we are operating our schools as if most men were fit only for servile occupations, not for the obligations of free citizenship.[17]

There is much more in a similar vein that could be said about the character of the perennialist protest against the existing state of things in American education. However, since we have examined the major kinds of criticisms advanced by perennialists, and since there are other important directions our inquiry into the perennial tradition must take, we will next turn our attention to the position on educational theory and practice that American perennialists assume. Before we turn to this matter directly, it seems desirable to give a little thought to how the perennialist thinks the confusion that besets contemporary society and education can be cleared up—providing, of course, that it can be cleared up. The fact of the matter is that it is difficult to determine from reading the literature of modern perennialists precisely what their position is on this matter. What is involved is the question of the role the school can (and should) play in society; specifically, can the school right itself, change its program, and purge itself of its ills, even when the society in which the school exists does not change, or if it does change, when the direction taken is worse instead of better? There is much in the perennial tradition to indicate the belief that corruption in the school is the result of corruption in the society in which the school exists. Under this view, therefore, it may be concluded that the reform of education can come only after the reform of society has been achieved. Parenthetically, we might remind ourselves again that perennialism represents a protest against the whole character of modern western society, not simply against certain ideas about education that are current in this society. Therefore, we would seem justified in concluding that the needed reform in education cannot occur until a complete reform in society has been achieved. The character the school possesses at any particular time is a function of the social context in which the school exists. Evidence in favor of this view is not difficult to find in perennialist literature.

For example, Hutchins in his book, *Education for Freedom*,[18] raises the question, "What is wrong with our educational system?" The an-

---

[17] Hutchins, *The Conflict in Education*, p. 66.
[18] Baton Rouge: Louisiana State University Press, 1943, p. 48.

swer, he says, is *nothing.* "There is never anything wrong with the educational system of a country. What is wrong is the country. The educational system that any country has will be the system that country wants." One does seem justified in concluding from these remarks that the only salvation for education lies in a reform of society and that education can be altered significantly only when such a reformation has been achieved.[19]

On the other hand, there is much to be seen in the behavior of perennialists to indicate that they really believe organized education has the power to effect desirable changes in society. For a great many years, spokesmen for this tradition have expended their energies and intelligence in promoting reform movements in education, particularly in higher education. The ordinary observer has usually been led to believe that the leaders of this protest movement promise improvements in society as a result of improvements in education. If Hutchins really believes, for example, that sick societies can only have sick schools, why has he devoted his considerable talents to promoting so many reform movements in education, particularly when there seems to be so little evidence that the condition of American society is improving, at least by any criteria he or his associates have offered? According to the initial thesis, these efforts would necessarily have to be viewed as futile. Perhaps the reorganization of St. Johns College, the Great Books movement, the Hutchins reform efforts at the University of Chicago properly can be viewed as last acts of desperation performed in the face of an impending catastrophe, but for some reason this explanation does not ring true. These do not look like the acts of desperate men; they look much more like the concrete plans of men who believe that the ills of society can be made to yield to the power of education. We cannot resolve this apparent contradiction here, but we recommend it for the reader's consideration for it is an example of the confusion that so often obtains over the question of the relation of the school to society.

Thus far in our inquiry, we have given systematic attention only to the criticisms the perennial philosophy makes of contemporary society and education. We are now ready to turn our attention to ideas about education that are advocated by this tradition. We will consider how such matters as the objectives of education, the curriculum, and the role of the teacher are conceived by perennialists.

---

[19] Jacques Maritain has also indicated that it is too much to expect teachers to make up for the evils and insufficiencies in a culture. See: *The Education of Man: The Educational Philosophy of Jacques Maritain,* eds., Donald and Idella Gallagher, Garden City, New York: Doubleday & Company, Inc., 1962, p. 82.

THE PERENNIALIST APPROACH
TO EDUCATIONAL PRACTICE

In earlier chapters of this book, the author raised serious doubt that philosophy of education can properly be considered as a series of deductions from some set of *a priori* principles. The reasons for this doubt have already been indicated and will not be repeated here. The reason for mentioning this matter again is that the perennial philosophy is an outstanding example of the approach to educational theory that seeks to derive directives for educational practice from certain philosophical statements that serve as initial premises. We should remember this as we consider the exposition of the perennialist educational theory that follows.

The Aims and Means of Education

In his most celebrated treatise on education, *Education at the Crossroads*, Jacques Maritain has said, ". . . the chief task of education is above all to shape man, or to guide the evolving dynamism through which man forms himself as a man."[20] He observes also that, "nothing is more important for each of us, or more difficult, than *to become a man*." The art of education, therefore, is essentially that of helping individuals to realize the nature that is inherent in them and what education must be will depend necessarily on what this human nature is. Therefore, in order to know what human education *must* be, we are required to direct our attention to the nature of man, for it is here that the answers to our most urgent educational questions will be found. Once we know the ultimate ends toward which education should proceed we will be then, and only then, in a position to know what means we must employ to realize these ends.

These things being so, it follows that the ultimate ends of education are universal. They do not change with time or culture or any circumstance. The reason for this is that the purpose of education is to actualize a potential nature, and since all men have the same potential nature the ends pursued in the art of education must always be the same. It is in this sense that perennialists hold the ultimate ends of education to be absolute and universal.[21] What constitutes these ultimate aims, says the

[20] Page 1.
[21] One of the clearest statements of this position ever made is to be found in: Mortimer J. Adler, "In Defense of the Philosophy of Education," *Philosophies of Education*, Forty-first Yearbook of the National Society for the Study of Education, Part I, ed., John S. Brubacher, Bloomington, Illinois: Public School Publishing Company, 1942, pp. 227–249. See particularly p. 221 ff.

perennialist, is not simply a matter of opinion or prejudice. What they are can be known in absolute fashion; in other words, they can be demonstrated rationally. This means that any person sufficiently intelligent enough to understand the argument must necessarily concur in the judgment of what the ultimate and absolute aims of education are. And, further, this means that there can really be only one philosophy of education. There are, of course, many kinds of opinions about education circulating in contemporary society and often various combinations of these are advertised as philosophies of education. That these collections of opinion and prejudices are spoken of as philosophies of education, is clear evidence of the debasement to which philosophy has been subjected in an age dominated by nominalism and empiricism. To put the matter simply, philosophy of education, as the perennialist sees it, deals with two things—and only two, viz.: the ultimate aims of education which are its first principles, and the general means, which are its secondary principles. These first and secondary principles can be known in an absolute manner, and this is what is properly known as philosophy of education. Anybody who denies the absolute and universal character of these principles or the possibility of their being known in an absolute and universal fashion is simply denying that there can be anything properly called philosophy of education.[22]

If we pause for a moment to take stock of the progress of our inquiry, we find we have two major ideas. We have learned that, according to the perennialist view, the ultimate aims of education are the same for all men in all times and under all circumstances, and the general means for realizing these aims are also universal. In addition, we have established that perennialists believe the ultimate aim of education is "to make a man." Now, the next step in understanding this position is to understand that the aims of education, being derived from the nature of man, must necessarily always be the same *because human nature is always and everywhere the same.*[23] It is obviously of great importance in this tradition to be able to demonstrate in complete fashion that human nature itself is universal and unchanging, for it is on this proposition that much of the educational argument necessarily depends. We will come to a consideration of this demonstration a little later. For the moment, having determined what the ultimate aim of education

22 *Ibid.*, p. 222.
23 This is also the general position of John Wild whose connection with educational conservatism was noted in Chapter V. In the chapter on philosophical realism, it was proposed that Wild's position be included in the perennialist philosophy since his realism is largely in the orthodox Aristotelian tradition.

is, we will give some brief attention to what the means in general are.

When we come to consider the question of educational means it is necessary for us to make certain distinctions. For one thing, the ends of education, while universal, are also plural and education, therefore, necessarily deals both with moral development and with intellectual development. Intellectual development in turn must be subdivided into the speculative and the artistic. Thus, we see that the means employed must be adapted to the nature of the educational end being sought, and these are somewhat different in moral education from what they are in intellectual education. We will give closer scrutiny to the question of educational method in another section; what is important to note here is that education always involves the exercise of a person's own powers, whether he teaches himself or is taught by another. The means of education in general, therefore, are the exercise of the natural powers men have and since all men have the same natural powers, the means in general are the same for all men. We have already seen that the means will vary depending on the type of education being considered since the powers involved in moral education are different from the powers involved in intellectual education. Now that we have established the perennialist's belief in the universality of the objectives and general means of education, we are ready to explain in more detail his conception of the educative process.

The Art of Teaching

The purpose of education is "to make a man" and the means by which this is done is the exercise of the individual's own powers. The art of teaching, therefore, is the art of stimulating and directing the activity of these powers so that they are developed and perfected. One of the most important sources from which perennialists draw their ideas about the art of the teacher is a treatise by St. Thomas Aquinas, *De Magistro* (*Concerning the Teacher*).[24] We have already noted that St. Thomas was one of the most important scholars involved in the great medieval synthesis of classic philosophy and Hebraic-Christian theology and his interpretation of Aristotle's realism remains the accepted position of the Catholic Church on the question of the status of universals. Aquinas himself was one of the greatest teachers at the University of Paris and it

[24] *De Magistro* is part of a larger work, *De Veritate*. My citations here are to an edition titled *The Teacher—The Mind*, trans., J. V. McGlynn, S.J., Chicago: Henry Regnery Company, 1959. A much more complete explication of St. Thomas' theory than can be given here will be found in: Herbert Johnston, *A Philosophy of Education*, New York: McGraw-Hill Book Company, 1963, Chapter 7.

is likely that he drew on his own considered experience as a teacher as well as on philosophy and theology in the formulating of his views of the educative process.

In the first sentence of his *Metaphysics*, Aristotle said that, "All men by nature desire to know." This means that the final end toward which certain natural powers of the intellect tend is that of grasping truth for its own sake. However, like all natural powers of the organism, the rational powers exist originally only as potencies. Some cause must function to move them from potentiality to increasing degrees of actuality. This process is what we usually refer to as education—particularly when we wish to make a distinction between education and training. The art of teaching, therefore, is the process of converting the natural powers of reason from potential to actuality, and the real question is what the source of causation is that makes this possible. Since St. Thomas' analysis is Christian as well as Aristotelian, he first demonstrates that the primary cause of human knowledge must be God. God is the primary cause since he created man's nature, which is in part intellectual, and if man's nature were not intellectual—that is, in Aristotle's terms, if men did not by their nature desire to know—there would be no human knowledge. God, then, is the primary cause of knowledge, but he has created man in such a way that man is capable of being the secondary principal cause of his learning, since it is through the use of his own natural powers that man learns.

The Thomistic position on this point involves a distinction between two forms of potency. One of these is the potency that is active and complete in the sense that it has the power to result in a complete act. A well known example of this is the power of the body to heal itself. The other kind of potency is passive in nature and is exemplified by a pile of sticks that has the potency to become a fire but does not have within itself the power to ignite itself. Thus, if it is to become a fire, an agent external to the wood must ignite it (i.e., cause it to burn) because the pile of sticks does not have within itself the power to effect this change. Now, according to St. Thomas, the potency of the human intellect is of the same kind as the power of the body to heal itself; that is, knowledge exists in the learner in the sense of active potentiality. If this were not true, man would not be able to gain knowledge for himself without the help of another person. It is a fact, however, that men can gain knowledge for themselves without the help of another through the process of natural reason we speak of as *discovery*. The other way of learning is through the process of *instruction* which is the way most formal instruction proceeds and which, of course, involves the activities of a *teacher*. The major question we are concerned with here is what the function of the teacher is.

The Thomistic answer is that the function of the teacher when he teaches a student is analogous to the function of the physician when he heals a patient. The physician heals the patient by cooperating with and assisting nature, furnishing medicines and other means that nature can use to effect a cure. The physician, therefore, is the *secondary cause* of the patient's recovery; the principal cause is the natural powers of the body to heal itself. This is not to say that the ministrations of the physician are unimportant; it is to say, however, that the physician's efforts are a cause only in the secondary sense. If this were not true, no one would be able to recover his health without the aid of a physician, and everyone knows that sick people sometimes do recover without medical assistance. There is wide agreement, however, that the services of a physician promote and expedite the recovery of health.

In the process of learning the teacher plays the same kind of secondary causal role that the physician plays in the healing process. The active cause of the pupil's learning is the operations of his own natural powers of intellect. "Consequently," says St. Thomas, "one person is said to teach another inasmuch as, by signs, he manifests to that other the reasoning process which he himself goes through by his own natural reason. And thus, through the instrumentality, as it were, of what is told him, the natural reason of the pupil arrives at a knowledge of the things which he did not know."[25] Thus, the intellect is not to be viewed as analogous to a pile of sticks that can be changed into a fire only as an external cause is brought to bear on it, and the teacher's role is not that of a torch bearer who thrusts fire into the dry wood to kindle it and thus is the active cause of the conflagration. St. Thomas also maintains that teaching is not the communication to the student of knowledge possessed by the teacher. Rather, the knowledge that is in the student's intellect is caused by the student's own intellectual activity. What the teacher does is to present certain signs (words, symbols, etc.) that stand for things that then may be not present to sense and from these signs the intellect of the student derives the things not present to sense and causes them to exist in his own mind. It is in this way that the teacher's activity plays a mediating role in the learning process.[26]

These ideas about the self-activity of the learner and the role of the teacher as secondary and ministerial, constitute a major source of the perennialist protest against the pedagogy of essentialism. We have al-

[25] *The Teacher*, trans., J. V. McGlynn, S.J., p. 17.
[26] *Ibid.*, p. 23.

ready seen in detail that essentialism as a theory of education is built around the assumption of an irreducible core of subject matters to be transmitted to all and the conception of the teacher as the agent who transfers these subject matters into the mind of the student. The structure and functioning of our entire educational installation in this country derive from this conception of education. In considering this aspect of the American approach to education, Maritain has said bluntly, ". . . any education which considers the teacher as the principal agent perverts the very nature of the educational task."[27] And he has reserved some of his bitterest criticism for a system of schooling that is devoted to cramming students with predigested, overorganized, synthesized subject matters—usually through the medium of textbooks. This condemnation of the conception of the teacher as a kind of intellectual pumping station is a major theme in the educational philosophy of the perennial philosophy, and this is as true in the case of such contemporary rational humanists as Messrs. Hutchins, Adler, and Van Doren as it is of neoscholastics.

It may also be recalled that this same element is part of the major protest of progressivism. We have already seen in an earlier chapter that John Dewey denied that education could be (much less should be) considered primarily as the transmission of organized information. He also insisted that the self-activity of the student is the means by which the educative process goes on, and he conceived the role of the teacher as one of mediator, guide, and perhaps, one might even say, ministerial agent. We already know that in the case of progressivism this conception of the art of teaching makes a great deal of difference with respect to the way the curriculum and organization of instruction is conceived. In the next section of the present chapter, we will see that the way the perennialist views the art of teaching also makes for profound differences between his conception of the curriculum and that of the prevailing essentialism. In this connection we should not attempt to make more out of this striking similarity between the progressive and perennialist protests than the facts warrant. There are, to be sure, vast differences in the way in which human nature is viewed in these two traditions. The fact remains, however, that both of them view education as a *process* in which the self-activity of the learner is the principal cause of his learning, and they both agree with Aristotle that it is important to know the difference between the art of knowledge and its products. It is possible that Maritain has been more aware of this similarity between the two

27 *Education at the Crossroads*, p. 32.

protest movements than have the leading figures among the rational humanists. Maritain has had kind things to say on occasion about the achievements of progressivism, though he has necessarily deplored the naturalism and pragmatism out of which it developed, and in saying these things he has insisted that a major contribution of the progressive movement has been to reassert that the dynamic factor in education is the self-activity of the student. Even when allowance is made for the differences in underlying philosophical conceptions, one can hardly help being struck by the similarity of this statement to many made by John Dewey and others of the progressive tradition.

The Curriculum

The purpose of education, as we have seen, is "to make a man" and the art of teaching, as the perennialist sees it, deals with the processes by which the individual realizes in actuality the intellectual powers he possesses in potential. We should perhaps remind ourselves again that "making a man" does not mean that human nature can be shaped and molded like a ball of wax, nor does it mean that the role of the teacher is one of pumping pre-processed material into the mind of the student. With these things in mind, we are now ready to consider the program of studies that perennialists believe to be necessary in achieving the objectives of the educational process.

The key to understanding the perennialist curriculum and, in fact, the whole perennialist protest against essentialist pedagogy, is the idea of *liberal education*. In the chapter on essentialism we saw that although this term is prominent in essentialist writing, it is often difficult—if not impossible—to know with any precision what is meant by conservatives when they talk about liberal learning. The most usual approach is to attempt to define it in terms of organized subject matters in which some subjects are liberal and some are illiberal. But we also saw that Aristotle warned against trying to define liberal education in this way for, as he pointed out, some arts may be liberal or illiberal depending on the purpose for which they are learned. We should also recall that the concept of liberal learning, as opposed to illiberal, had its origin not only in Greek philosophy, but also in the realities of Greek social organization. Given the Greeks' attitude towards productive work and their idea of the deleterious effect of labor on the human personality, it is not difficult to understand the difference between liberal and servile learning as it was viewed in the Hellenic world. Nor is it difficult to understand Mr. Hutchins' protest that a girl trained in her high school to do little else than drive automobiles, perform household chores, and arrange coiffures is being trained as a slave—a slave in the modern manner, to be sure, but still a slave.

The process that makes a man, and not simply a slave, is liberal education. The end towards which the intellectual activity of the student tends is that of the development and perfection of the natural powers of intellect that all men possess. The model that modern perennialists take is the Greek ideal of liberal learning, particularly as this was conditioned by medieval thought, and the model of collegiate and university education they follow is one that emerged in the flowering of medieval culture in the thirteenth and fourteenth centuries. When classic learning passed over into the medieval world, it took the form of the "Seven Liberal Arts." Commentaries on the liberal arts were prepared by various late classical and early Christian scholars including the Romans, Varro and Quintillian, and St. Augustine, who was one of the most influential as well as one of the most learned of the early church fathers. However, the most famous treatise on the liberal arts undoubtedly was an allegory, *The Marriage of Philology and Mercury*, written by Martianus Capella in the fifth century, and containing virtually all the learning of the classic era that survived in the early middle ages. There is some reason to think that this may be the dullest book ever written, though any generalization about this dubious honor is admittedly dangerous. However, dull or not, it is said to have been used more widely in the early middle ages than any other textbook on the ancient learning.

Capella followed Plato's original example in dividing the liberal arts into two categories: The Trivium and the Quadrivium. The Trivium is made up of grammar, rhetoric, and dialectic.[28] The Quadrivium is composed of arithmetic, geometry, astronomy, and music (really harmony, since it was concerned with the mathematical relationships involved in musical harmony). Thus, the arts in the Trivium are the literary arts and those of the Quadrivium are the mathematical arts. In their recommendations about the content of the curriculum American rational humanists usually have stayed close to the original medieval model. Mr. Hutchins, for example, has maintained that in the contemporary world the liberal arts should be viewed as four in number: rhet-

[28] In this sense, dialectic is a form of logical discourse called "disputation" in which the effort is made to examine all sides of an issue and discriminate truth from error. The "disputation" was a standard teaching procedure in the medieval university.

oric, grammar, dialectic, and mathematics. Mastery of the liberal arts, he has said, means mastery of the arts of reading, writing, and reckoning.[29] The liberal arts constitute general education and should be pursued by every student, whether he plans to terminate his education at the secondary level or whether he plans to enter the higher learning and ultimately one of the learned professions. It is the liberal arts that bring out the common human nature in all of us and, since this nature is the same for all men, the liberal arts are for all men. There is no place in the curriculum for "electives;" all students must pursue the same curriculum.

The liberal arts are, in the strict sense of the word, ways of doing things; that is what the word "art" means. Thus, there are the arts of rhetorical analysis, grammatical analysis, and logical analysis. Taken together they constitute the art of reading. The art of mathematics is, of course, the process of quantitative and geometric analysis. Thus, the liberal arts are disciplinary in character; that is, they develop the natural powers of intellect and lead towards the perfection of these powers. In this sense they are instrumental. In Mr. Hutchins' own words, "The liberal arts are, after all, the arts of reducing the intellect from mere potentiality to act."[30] However, an art, being a mode of action, requires something to be acted upon. Education, it will be recalled, proceeds through the activity of the student's intellectual powers, but there must be some material on which these powers may be brought to bear. What, according to perennialists, should this be? A major answer to this question has been supplied by rational humanists and given such emphasis that almost all Americans have heard of the "Great Books" even if they are innocent of any other knowledge of the perennialist tradition in education.

The content that is appropriate for liberal education, say the perennialists, are the *permanent studies* and these are found in their most universal and, therefore, in their most valuable form in the great literary products of the west. They are in short the *great books*; the classics. A classic, as perennialists are fond of saying, is a book that is contemporary in every age. It is held further that these books must be a part of liberal education because a person cannot understand developments in the modern world and in his own times unless he has studied these

---

[29] *The Higher Learning in America*, p. 82 ff. See also his remarks to the first class entering the college at the University of Chicago, reprinted in *The Social Frontier*, 5:98 (January, 1939).
[30] *The Higher Learning in America*, p. 115.

classics.[31] Moreover, in liberal education the major portion of the time of the student is to be spent in reading, discussing, and analyzing the great books. "The reading of these books is not for antiquarian purposes," Adler has cautioned; ". . . the intent is not archaeological or philological . . . Rather the books are to be read because they are as contemporary today as when they were written, and that because *the problems they deal with and the ideas they present are not subject to the law of perpetual and interminable progress.*"[32] The program of St. Johns College in Annapolis, Maryland, which we have already identified as being the purest American example of the rational humanist's ideal of collegiate education, is essentially one of reading and analyzing the great books. Therefore, it is very likely the only college in the country that really provides the opportunity for a liberal education as that term is understood in the perennial philosophy. Meantime, American colleges, dominated as they are by educational essentialism, see their mission as transmitting portions of organized subject matters—largely through the medium of textbooks. And, ". . . textbooks," Hutchins has said, "have probably done as much to degrade the American intelligence as any single force."[33]

Liberal education, which is designed to discipline the intellectual faculties of the student, is preparatory to university education and is essential to it. Mastery of the liberal arts, therefore, is prerequisite to admission to the university. We have already seen something of the bitterness with which perennialism attacks the professionalism and empiricism that pervade the American university and we will forego any repetition of it here. Although no perennialist has ever succeeded in purging an American university of these ills—and Mr. Hutchins must receive credit for having tried the hardest—the ideas of perennialists on this subject are perfectly lucid. The clearest model for the university emanating from contemporary rational humanism is that furnished by Hutchins. We will consider its general outlines briefly.

First of all, the university is to be considered an *educational institu-*

---

[31] *Ibid.*, pp. 78–79.
[32] Mortimer J. Adler, "The Crisis in Contemporary Education," *The Social Frontier*, 5:140–145 (February, 1939), p. 144. Italics are in the original. For another discussion of the actual workings of the curriculum, together with a description of the St. Johns program, see: Mark Van Doren, *Liberal Education*, New York: Henry Holt and Company, 1943. My citations are to the edition by the Beacon Press issued in 1959, pp. 144–165. The present character of the curriculum at St. Johns is described briefly in *The College Handbook*, ed., S. D. Karl, New York: College Entrance Examination Board, 1961.
[33] *The Higher Learning in America*, p. 78.

tion, not, we might note, a heterogeneous collection of research institutes in which a little teaching is done on the side. Hutchins, for one, has said that he recognizes the importance of the fact finding and accumulation of data to which the empirical sciences are devoted. But he also has said many times and in many ways that a university is not the place to do these things, the reason being that these activities inevitably obscure the true purpose of a university. The major reason for the confusion and atomism that are characteristic of our university is that there is no unity in it. Every subject matter, every department is fractionated and specialized beyond belief. It is no longer a matter of members of different departments being unable to communicate meaningfully with each other. The malaise of specialization has spread until even faculty members within a department have no common intellectual ground. On the other hand, the medieval university was unified intellectually and that which proved the unifying principle was theology. Knowledge, both speculative and practical, was unified and ordered; all scholars had mastered this order and those who aspired to be scholars knew what there was to be mastered.

However, Hutchins, along with others of the rational humanists, has acknowledged that given the conditions of the modern world, there is no possibility of making theology the great synthesizing and unifying discipline it once was in the university.[34] Hutchins has pointed out that if we eliminate from theology the ideas of faith and revelation we will find ourselves in about the same philosophical position as the Greeks, which is to say that we will regard metaphysics as the highest form of knowledge and employ it, as the Greeks did, as the great unifying discipline in the higher learning. Here, of course, is one of the major points of difference within modern perennialism. Although neo Thomists agree with Hutchins and his associates that metaphysics is the highest form of rational knowledge, they insist that unless education is anchored in the revealed truths of theology it remains rootless.[35]

Whereas liberal education is the proper enterprise of elementary and secondary education, the higher learning deals with organized knowledge or the sciences.[36] In the university, as it is envisioned by Hutchins, there

[34] See: *The Higher Learning in America,* p. 97 and Van Doren's *Liberal Education,* pp. 142–144. This and what follows from it bears out our earlier observation that contemporary rational humanists are in many respects closer to Aristotle than to St. Thomas.

[35] For example see: William McGucken, S.J., "The Philosophy of Catholic Education," *Philosophies of Education,* ed., Brubacher, Chapter VI, p. 256.

[36] Perennialists use the term "science" in the same sense as the Greeks used it, namely to denote any organized body of knowledge in which principles and conclusions are

would be three divisions or faculties: metaphysics, natural science, and social science. Students in the university would study in all three and emphasis would be placed on the interrelations among them. Since metaphysics is the highest form of knowledge, being speculative in character and dealing with first principles, social and natural science are necessarily inferior to it and, in fact, dependent on it for their own first principles. Hutchins would allow a student some degree of specialization in one of the subordinate fields, but this would not be at the expense of study in depth in the other two divisions.

Empirical research and practical training would be banished from the university and organized in a series of technical institutes. Those preparing for the learned professions would be *educated* in the university and given their *practical training* in a technical institute. Thus, a student who aspired to be a physician would not only study natural science, which is the science directly related to the art of medicine, he would also study metaphysics, which is superior to all empirical science, and social science which is also related to the knowledge required for an educated man and for a physician. The actual practice of the art of medicine would be acquired in a technical institute attached to a hospital. The technical institute would also be the place in which empirical research would be conducted and the results fed back into the university where the new material would be integrated into the existing bodies of knowledge. The major tasks of the faculties of the university, therefore, are those of organizing, unifying, and teaching.

The general view of an educational organization that emerges from contemporary rational humanism is ordered around three levels: elementary education, secondary (collegiate) education, higher (university) education. We have seen in some detail that collegiate education is concerned with liberal education and the mastery of the liberal arts and that the university is concerned with the sciences and the perfection of the intellectual virtues. There is not much to be said about the rational humanist's ideas concerning elementary education for these have received little attention in the literature of this tradition. Messrs. Hutchins and Adler have rarely said anything about the education of young children except in brief passing remarks, and Van Doren's observations in his *Liberal Education* (p. 88 ff.) are so random and fragmentary as

related. A simple body of factual material is not science even if there are no errors in it and it is eminently useful in the practical sense. Hence, in this view, the data in a telephone directory are not scientific knowledge but mathematics, metaphysics and theology are.

to furnish little insight or guidance. Apparently, there would first be a level of elementary education extending from entrance to school to about the end of what we now call the sophomore year of high school.[37] The main purpose of elementary schooling would be to introduce the child to the rudiments of the liberal arts, which are reading, writing, and reckoning, and to prepare him for the intellectual work of the college. The years of collegiate education would span the period from the junior year of high school to the end of what we now call the sophomore year of college. When a student could give a demonstration of his mastery of the liberal arts, he would be given the bachelor's degree. By definition and by historical precedent, the A.B. degree means mastery of the trivium and the quadrivium. Only those who had mastered collegiate education would be admitted to the university.

There are, of course, many questions that occur immediately about what is to happen to those who are unable to make their way very far up this educational ladder. Clearly, this proposal is for a highly selective system of education, and it seems certain that relatively few will survive very far beyond the end of elementary schooling. The perennialist will remind us, of course, that this organization will enable all individuals to do what most of them are debarred from doing under our existing system—namely, getting as much liberal education as they can profit from. Presumably, once the school has done as much for a student as it can, in view of his own potentialities, its obligation ceases. Unemployment, for example, may be a social problem of great importance and vast dimensions, but in this view it is hardly an educational problem.

With respect to matters we have just been considering, there is a wide area of agreement between the rational humanist and the neo-Thomist. We have seen that both agree on the general aims of the educative process, the nature of the teaching process, and the function of the liberal arts. There are, however, differences of opinion on certain practical aspects of curricular organization that are worth giving some attention to. In this connection we will consider certain proposals advanced by Maritain for the organization of the curriculum.

According to Maritain, there are three principal stages in the educative process. These correspond with the three major stages of human growth, as well as with three distinct stages of human knowledge. Thus, child-

---

[37] It seems clear that if the proposals of the rational humanists were to be put into effect the high school, as we have known it, would disappear. Part of its work would be allocated to the elementary school and part to the college. See: Van Doren, *Liberal Education,* p. 98.

hood corresponds with the years of elementary schooling, adolescence with the years of liberal education, and young adulthood with the years of the higher learning. Specifically, Maritain has advocated a Stage I, involving seven years of elementary education (ages six to twelve); a Stage II covering seven years and involving the humanities (ages thirteen to nineteen); and a Stage III which is the period of the advanced studies taken in the university. The elementary stage is divided into an initial period of four years, corresponding to primary education, and a three-year period corresponding to the intermediate grades in our conventional elementary schools. Stage II would be divided into a three-year period of secondary education and a four-year period of college. The A.B. degree would be awarded at age nineteen, the average age at which students would complete pre-university education. In university education the normal time required for the master's degree would be three years, with two to four years for the Ph.D. In the purely organizational sense, this does not represent any very great departure, either from the program advocated by Hutchins and the rational humanists, or from the traditional organization of American schools.[38] Within this general outline, however, are certain important differences.

At the elementary level Maritain stresses the difference in the mental life of childhood as compared with that of adolescence and adulthood. He makes much of the fact that childhood is the time of intense imagination in which knowledge must be given the child somewhat in the manner of a story. Childhood is the time in life when reason slowly gains ascendance over imagination, but this process cannot be hurried nor can it be imposed on the child. Maritain lays stress on what he calls the "vitality and intuitiveness" of the child. Granted that the excess of animal spirits and lack of internal rational controls in the child can lead to mischief, nevertheless the "vitality of spirit" is the great resource to be used in the education of the young child. In various places in his writing, and always in the strongest terms, Maritain has inveighed against the idea that a child is simply a small adult who must be stuffed with simplified, diluted adult knowledge. Here we may note again that even though there are many and profound differences between the educational philosophies of Maritain and Dewey, here, at least, they meet on common ground in forming a protest against the prevailing American essentialism.[39] The same kind of protest can be found by careful search in the

[38] Maritain's description is in a long footnote on pp. 66–67 of *Education at the Crossroads*.
[39] See: *Ibid.*, pp. 60–61 and compare with Dewey's *Democracy and Education*, p. 257 and pp. 242–244 of the present volume.

literature of rational humanism, but it is usually there by implication or in the form of side remarks.[40]

Maritain's interpretation of the liberal arts differs in certain important respects from that of the rational humanists who, as we have seen, tend to interpret these arts in the sense they had in the medieval period. The fact, says Maritain, that the liberal arts took the familiar form of the Trivium and Quadrivium was more an accident of history than anything else, and he suggests that whatever is considered to be the liberal studies in any historical period ought to depend on the kind and amount of humanistic knowledge extant in that period. Since the corpus of knowledge in our own time is far greater and very different from that of the medieval era, our conceptions of liberal learning ought also to be different.[41] In his opinion, one of the most notable additions to the liberal studies that must be made is the natural sciences.

Maritain would place first in the curriculum what he has called "the pre-liberal arts." These would include grammar and linguistics, logic, modern languages, history, and in connection with it, geography. In the liberal arts proper, the Trivium would consist of eloquence (presumably rhetoric in a wide sense of that term); literature and poetry; and art, which would include not only the fine arts, but also the applied arts and technology, these being employed, of course, in a humanistic mode and not with any reference to vocationalism. The Quadrivium would be made up of mathematics, including its history; physics and natural science and the history of science; social sciences and the history of civilization; philosophy, to include philosophy of nature, philosophical psychology, metaphysics, epistemology, and social philosophy (ethics, politics, etc.). Thus, Maritain has been more forthright in making the Quadrivium that part of the liberal arts that is substantive in nature and not exclusively formal, as the rational humanists tend to interpret it. In a footnote to page 70 of *Education at the Crossroads*, Maritain speaks directly to a point on which rational humanists have not always been clear; namely, that the great books have other purposes than furnishing the apparatus for mental gymnastics.

There are also differences between Maritain's idea of a university and that advanced by the rational humanists. Briefly, Maritain holds that the purpose of the university is one of teaching universal knowledge. Hence, there would be four "orders of subjects" each of these to be taught in an "Institute" which would be organically linked with the

[40] The most extensive remarks in this vein with which I am familiar are to be found in Van Doren's *Liberal Education*, pp. 88–93.
[41] See: *The Education of Man*, ed., Gallagher, pp. 90–93.

other "Institutes." The first order of subjects would be the useful and applied sciences, e.g., technology, applied arts, agriculture, business administration, etc. The second order would include medicine and psychiatry, law, politics, education, economics, etc.; these are practical studies that relate to man and human society and hence either belong to the domain of art or to ethics. The third order would embrace the speculative sciences and fine arts, viz., mathematics, natural sciences, social sciences, history, literatures, music, fine arts, etc. The highest institute in the university would teach the fourth order of subjects which would include philosophy in all its branches together with theology and the history of religions.[42] Beyond the teaching institutes, Maritain envisions a series of Institutes of Advanced Research devoted to the extension of knowledge in all branches of human endeavor. He advocates that these research institutions ought to complement each other in their work but that they ought to be separate and distinct. Maritain agrees with the rational humanists that when research and teaching compete with each other in the university it is usually teaching that suffers from neglect.

If we were to look for the greatest difference between the educational philosophy of the rational humanists and that of the neo-Thomists, we would find it to lie in the conception of the role religion and theology should play in the education of man. We have already observed that the neo-Thomist believes that as enlightened as the rational humanists have shown themselves to be in their understanding of the real meaning of liberal education and the purpose of the higher learning, their philosophy of education is incomplete because they fail to include theology and religion in their educational formulations. Maritain, writing as a Catholic as well as a philosopher, agrees that in a society based, as ours is, on religious pluralism religious instruction cannot be made compulsory in the schools, but he has suggested that ways can be found in communities to provide students with instruction in religion. And he has maintained further that if the university is really to be a center for the teaching of universal knowledge, theology must be included, for it is as much a part of knowledge as physics or mathematics.[43]

In concluding our consideration of the curriculum as it is viewed in the perennial tradition we may make the following summary observa-

[42] *Education at the Crossroads*, pp. 75–83.
[43] For examples of Maritain's position on this point see: *Education at the Crossroads*, pp. 71–75; 82–83; *The Education of Man*, pp. 75–81; *Modern Philosophies and Education*, ed., Brubacher, pp. 83–88.

tions: First, although there are some differences over details to be found, there exists a very wide area of agreement among adherents of this tradition over basic educational questions. Secondly, although perennialists are critical of progressivism on a number of major points and reject the naturalism inherent in it, their major educational criticisms are directed squarely (and necessarily) at essentialism, the prevailing tradition in America. Third, the major difference in the educational philosophy of rational humanism and that of the neo-Thomists stems from somewhat different perceptions of the significance theology has for our understanding of the educative process.

We turn now to a consideration of the philosophical foundations that underlie the educational philosophy of the perennial tradition. Some of these have already been mentioned incidentally in Chapter II and in the present chapter. However, our present purpose is to give a systematic, though necessarily abridged, account of some of the philosophical bases of perennialism.

EDUCATION AND THE NATURE OF HUMAN NATURE

In beginning our inquiry into selected elements of the perennial philosophy, we will do well to recall Maritain's injunction: "The chief task of education is to shape man." This means that the immediate directives for what the education of man should be emerge from a consideration of what man is in his fundamental nature. Education, therefore, is properly considered to be a branch of ethics and, specifically, a part of social ethics. However, there are also other kinds of knowledge that must be taken into account when we consider human nature; for example, biology, psychology, and epistemology are also sources of knowledge about the nature of man. And, since ultimately man is part of a great world system, we must turn to metaphysics for certain important understandings. We cannot pretend to give any complete exposition of the world system as it was conceived either in Aristotelian or in Thomistic philosophy. All we can do here is to indicate in general outline the nature of man as it is conceived in those philosophies and to show the import this conception has for the philosophy of education. The exposition here will be arranged around certain propositions which are as follows:

1. All men share in the same human nature and this nature is constant; it does not change. (This has been mentioned but not clarified.)
2. Since all men have the same nature, all men have the same natural powers. (This has been mentioned as being an important point, but we have not inquired very far into its meaning.)
3. By virtue is meant the perfection of a natural power and since all men have the same natural powers, the virtues are the same for all men. (We have yet to determine what this means.)
4. Education is concerned with the development of man's rational powers, that is, with the formation of the intellectual virtues. (We have already discussed this idea, but we will investigate it further.)
5. Since the aim of education is the formation of the intellectual virtues, and since these virtues are the same for all men, the aim of education is the same for all men. (This is the conclusion we will reach.)

Thus, our major interest is in the nature of man and what can be derived from it to guide educational policy, but before we can turn directly to specific consideration of man, we must give some heed to the nature of the world system in which this human nature exists and of which it is a part.

Man and Nature

We have already had occasion to note that a major point of disagreement between Plato and Aristotle lay in their conception of the relation of the universal to the particular. Plato had conceived reality in terms of universal ideas or forms to which particular things are related in some way. Aristotle was never satisfied with the Platonic metaphysics because it separated the universal (form) from the particular and since there seemed to be no way to get them united, it became necessary to assign an inferior status of being to the things that make up the world of sense experience. Aristotle's solution to the problem lay in his conception of substance as the union of form *in* matter. Thus, in this hylomorphic relationship all substantial existences are composed of matter that is indissolubly linked with form. The universal, therefore, is always *in* the thing. Intellectually, we can conceive of "prime" matter, that is, matter that is completely unformed, but we never encounter it in nature. Similarly, we can think abstractly of pure form—the universal existing independently of matter—but this does not occur in the natural world. We have already seen that this "moderate realism" that was originally developed by Aristotle played an important part in the great medieval controversy over the character of universals and became the view accepted by St. Thomas Aquinas and ultimately the accepted view of the church. We should remember that both the contemporary rational humanist and the neo-Thomist argue their case from the position of moderate realism.

Thus both Aristotle and St. Thomas were realists and accepted the principle of independence quite as much as any contemporary realist. The independently existing world is made up of substantial entities and the relations that obtain among these entities. A substantial thing, a table, for instance, is composed of matter which is given the character peculiar to a table by the union of matter with the form "tableness." In this way the form of a thing makes it what it is. Both chairs and tables are material objects and, therefore, there is a material cause involved in their existence, but tables are different from chairs and, therefore, there is also a formal cause involved. It is the difference in the forms involved that makes the difference between chairs and tables.

The universe is made up of innumerable corporeal bodies related to each other in various ways. In considering the question of how the world comes to have the character it exhibits, Aristotle maintained that a complete analysis must take into account four kinds of causation: the material cause, the formal cause, the efficient cause, and the final cause. To illustrate how these various kinds of causation are involved, let us consider that a miscellaneous pile of timbers, lumber, bricks, metals and so on do not constitute a house. However, in order that a house may come into existence, there must be material available. Hence, the piles of material are the *material cause* of the house. Since it is a house that is to come into being and not a barn or garage, there must be a plan for the house involved in its construction. This plan, which is usually the ideas of the architect preserved in the form of blueprints, corresponds to the *formal cause*, that which makes the structure the kind of thing it is. However, material and formal causes, though necessary, are insufficient to bring a house into existence, for the building materials must be acted on in terms of the plan. Thus, the activities of carpenters, masons, plumbers, painters, etc. are the *efficient cause* of the house. Aristotle indicates that there is still one other element of causation involved, namely, the use to which a house is to be put or, as he called it, the *final cause*. And, as we know, the purpose or final end of a house is to be lived in. Thus, the matter that once had the forms of trees, clay, metallic ores, has assumed new forms and has become a house. These four aspects of cause operate in every act of becoming, which is the development from potential to actual. Aristotle's point is that in every case, there must be something to be moved, something to move it, a course of development and a goal towards which the whole process moves. However, if we take another look at the four forms of causation, we can see that actually there are only two causes: *the formal* (which includes the efficient, formal and final) and *the material*. When we speak of a thing coming into being, we really mean that there is a movement from matter to form. The stack of building material becomes (takes the form of) the house; the acorn takes on the form of an oak tree. Thus, for any object, matter is the "stuff" that has the capacity to become that object: bronze or stone is matter for a statue, stone and wood are matter for a house. In other words, matter is *potentiality* and is capable of taking on form and thereby realizing the actuality inherent in it. It should be noted that Aristotle gave a wider meaning to "matter" than we ordinarily do in modern speech ("timber" is the original meaning of the Greek word translated in English as "matter."). Thus, such qualities as courage and bravery are matter that can become a soldier and, even in our common speech we may speak of a certain statesman as "good presidential timber."

Furthermore, change is always a movement from potentiality to actuality and therefore what a thing will become is already inherent in its nature. This is another way of saying that the *actual is prior to the potential*.[44] Experience indicates this to be true. If an acorn develops into anything, it becomes an oak tree for this final end is inherent in its nature. Not all acorns realize their potential for some are eaten by animals and others fall on stone or barren ground. However, we know there is nothing that can be done to cause the acorn to become a petunia or a fir tree. Similarly, the final end of an egg is to become a chicken, though it may wind up as part of a potato salad and therefore never realize its potential. Thus, in nature all things change and develop according to the pattern of movement from potentiality to actuality, and all development is toward the final ends inherent in the natures of things. And this represents, of course, a teleological conception of nature because the cause of movement is an ultimate end that lies ahead, not the efficient cause that as we may say figuratively, "pushes from behind." The view of modern science, and therefore the view most

[44] Aristotle's development of this idea will be found in Chapter 8, Book IX of *The Metaphysics*.

familiar to us, involves a concept of causation in which there is only efficient cause, and this means that any cause must be antecedent to its effect.[45]

Thus, the Aristotelian universe is one of constant process in which things come into being and pass away and in which the movement is from potential to actual and the whole thrust of nature, so to speak, is upward toward the realization of complete actuality. Since all becoming must have a cause, that is, must have motion imparted to it, there must be something that ultimately is the cause of all motion in nature but itself is unmoved. Otherwise, in our analysis of cause we will fall into an infinite regress in which cause-effect relations appear to go back and back forever with no starting point. That which is the origin of all motion and therefore the cause of all things in Aristotle's philosophy is the Unmoved Mover, which is the source of all motion, but is not itself moved. He indicated that this prime mover is uncreated, dependent on nothing else for its existence, and thus is pure actuality. In Thomistic thought the Unmoved Mover becomes God.[46]

The Dimensions of Human Nature

If we look at nature through the eyes of a scientist—or even with the vision of common sense—we see that there are two great strata of existence in nature. We usually speak of these as the "animate" and the "inanimate" levels of nature, and more often than not, common sense seems to indicate that the distinction is an absolute one. Even if it should be discovered that a block of stone contained the same chemical elements as a squirrel, and in exactly the same proportion, common sense still indicates that a block of stone is not a squirrel and there is nothing that can be done to make it so. Common sense would say, of course, that the squirrel is "alive" and the stone is not. Things that are animate have something that inert things do not have, and this something is life (*psyche*).[47] In operational terms, to be a living thing, that

---

[45] Aquinas accepted Aristotle's conception of causation. In this respect there is a certain difficulty in scholastic philosophy over the significance of "efficient cause." See for example: Etienne Gilson, *The Elements of Christian Philosophy*, New York: New American Library of World Literature, Inc., 1963, Chapter 8.

[46] For Aristotle's discussion of the Unmoved Mover see: *Metaphysics*, Book XII, Chapter 6, 1072b, Ross translation.

[47] The Greek word *psyche*, generally translated in Latin as *anima* and in English as *soul*, is never conceived by Aristotle in the sense it has come to be understood in the Christian tradition. Aristotle rejected the idea that *soul* could be conceived as existing apart from a body.

is, to have psychē, is to have certain natural powers related to living and, at some levels of organic life, to knowing, and these powers are not possessed by inanimate things. This is Aristotle's position.[48]

There are, however, differences among animate things with respect to the natural powers they possess. Some kinds of organisms are capable of doing things that other animate bodies cannot do. Once again, this fact can be observed and living things can be classified according to the powers they exhibit. According to Aristotle, there are three levels at which organisms function. These levels are: the vegetative, the sensate and the rational. At the vegetative level of organic life living things exhibit the powers of reproduction, nutrition, and growth. A plant, for example a radish, possesses all these powers. It can take the elements in the environment (chemical elements in the soil, air, water, light, etc.) and convert them to its own form. The radish not only has the power to grow, but also the power to reproduce its kind.

As everyone knows, the natural powers of nutrition, growth and reproduction do not exhaust the natural powers possessed by living organisms, although such organisms as radishes do not possess powers beyond these. There is a level of life at which we find living things exhibiting not only vegetative powers, but also those of sense perception and locomotion. And we, like Aristotle, call these organisms *animals* and we distinguish them from plants (vegetables in the wide sense of the word). Animals have, in addition to vegetative powers, the power to receive stimuli from distant objects, as for example through organs of sight and hearing, and they have certain internal powers of memory and imagination. Animals also have powers of locomotion and their actual environments are more extensive than that of a sessile plant.

For all the species of organisms, save one, the vegetative and sensate powers mark the limits of their natures. There is, however, another level of organic life at which there are other powers. These are the natural powers of responding to abstractions, of deliberation, of anticipating outcomes—in short, of behaving rationally. Only the human species is possessed of these natural powers of reason which Aristotle refers to as *nous*. It must be understood that when Aristotle is discussing this third

[48] Here is a fundamental difference between the Aristotelian and Darwinian conceptions of nature. Aristotle's conception involves no idea of organic evolution in which new species evolve from less complex levels of organization. As was said in another connection, Aristotle's conviction was that the species are immutable and the world has always existed in its present form. Darwinism postulates a continuity in nature in which it is impossible to make an absolute distinction between the inanimate and the animate levels of nature.

level he is not talking about anything mystical or supernatural. The rational powers of the human species are as much a part of nature as the reproductive or sensate powers, and we know of their existence in the same way we know about the other natural powers—through observation and analysis.

We can now conclude that in Aristotelian terms there are three major dimensions of human nature. First, as men, part of our nature is shared with plants and animals. The human species exhibits the same powers of nutrition and reproduction as do radishes and dogs. Moreover, men have the same powers of sensation and locomotion as do cats and turtles. But man also has rational powers, and no other kind of creature has these. The thing that makes man different from all other living creatures, therefore, is *nous*, the rational powers. And, hence, we have the famous Aristotelian definition: "Man is a *rational* animal." Man is a member of the genus animal, but he is differentiated from other animals by his rational powers and is thus a separate species.

We need now to remember the hylomorphism on which Aristotle's analysis rests. In all things (animate or inanimate) there are two principles involved: the material and the formal and, as we have already considered, it is the formal that gives a thing its nature and makes it different from other things. For example, a chair may be made from any number of kinds of material: steel, wood, aluminum, plastic, bamboo, or stone. A chair may be made of any of these and still be a chair. We see, therefore, that the material factor does not determine the nature of a thing. It is the form (universal) locked up, so to speak, with the matter (wood, metal, etc.) that makes an object a chair and not a table or an automobile. Thus, we can say that though there are differences among chairs, for example, between camp chairs and lounge chairs, these differences are *accidental* and not *essential* for they are all chairs. Thus, by essence we mean the nature necessarily possessed by a thing, as contrasted with its "non-necessary," or accidental qualities.

We now begin to see what is meant when perennialists speak of human nature being everywhere the same and never changing. Obviously, what is meant is that the *essential* nature of man does not vary, but this does not mean that there are no differences *among* men. Aristotle or Aquinas or any other perennialist knew quite as well as do contemporary psychologists that the differences within the human species are innumerable, but Aquinas and Aristotle would remind us that these differences are accidental and not essential. And certainly, one of the major criticisms of contemporary perennialists is that a great part of the confusion over educational policy in the modern world traces back to the failure to distinguish between essential and accidental qualities. Whether a person is male or female has nothing to do with the fact that he is a member of the species *man* and, hence, sex is an accidental quality. The difference between a man and a goat, however, is an essential difference, because man is a rational animal and a goat is not, and there is nothing anybody can do to turn a goat into a man. Since the dimensions of human nature coincide at the vegetative and sensate levels with those of goats, man has the capacity to behave like a goat when he allows the appetites of sense to over-ride his rational powers. This has been known to happen.

The neo-Thomist agrees with the essentially Aristotelian conception of the rational humanists that man is a rational animal and that it is the natural powers of reason that differentiate man from all other species of animals. Thomists are also in agreement that metaphysics, the science of first principles, is the highest form of rational knowledge. We can anticipate, however, that the original dimensions of human nature as seen by Aristotle must be viewed by Thomists as incomplete. Aristotle saw man as an organism, existing within nature, subject to its processes, and possessing the nature he has by virtue of the formal principle or universal, "manness" or "humanness." To Aristotle the soul (in the sense of psychē) is the form of the body, linked with matter to form an individual. The soul, therefore, must lose its existence when the body perishes, for form is never found except in union with matter. This conception of soul is plainly in opposition to the truth revealed in the scriptures that the soul is immortal and survives the disintegration of the body. Since the immortality of the soul is one of the most fundamental of the basic doctrines of Christian theology, a correction— or at least a reinterpretation—of Aristotle had to be made.

The general direction in which St. Thomas argues for the immortality of the soul is that the soul of man is different from other kinds of forms in nature. This difference lies in the power of the human soul to gain abstract knowledge *in addition to* its power to inform and give motion to the body, which, we have seen, the souls of other animals also possess. Man is capable of abstract knowledge in which the object of knowing is *form*, not matter. In this sense, man can know in an immaterial way. Moreover, it is argued, only an immaterial substance can perform acts that produce *concepts*, which clearly are immaterial. The soul of man, then, must be an intellectual substance that has an existence of its own and does not have to be involved in matter in order to be, yet as the form of the body it shares its own being with the body and gives unity to human nature. Aquinas then argues that intellectual substances are incorruptible and since the human soul can be shown to be an intellectual substance, it must necessarily be considered to be incorruptible. And this is to say that the human soul is immortal.[49]

Thomism maintains, therefore, that the immortality of the soul can be demonstrated philosophically, that is, through reason. The salvation of the soul, however, is a matter belonging to theology and is known through revealed truth. The import these matters have for us here is that the dimensions of human nature, as it is viewed by neo-Thomists, are considerably wider than that of the contemporary rational humanists, who see man largely in Aristotelian terms. Certainly one of the clearest statements of the Thomist view of man, and one that demonstrates the various elements that have gone into the making of the Thomist view, is to be found in a passage from Maritain's *Education at the Crossroads* (p. 7):

> In answer to our question, then, "What is man?" we may give the Greek, Jewish, and Christian idea of man: man as an animal endowed with reason, whose supreme dignity is in the intellect; and man as a free individual in personal relation with God, whose supreme righteousness consists in voluntarily obeying the law of God; and man as a sinful and wounded creature called to divine life and to the freedom of Grace, whose supreme perfection consists of love.

We should remember that we started our inquiry by considering the perennialist's statement that the purpose of education is "to form man." The meaning of this statement is that education is the process of developing the natural powers that are potential in human nature. In this section we have determined what these powers are, according to perennialists, and we have also seen that while American rational humanists are content to view man largely in philosophical terms, neo-Thomism insists that the ultimate nature of man transcends the natural powers that make him a rational animal. The ultimate educational question that must be answered is, "What is the end of man?"

All things in nature develop from potency to act; there is a final end inherent in the nature of all existences. If the purpose of education is "to form man," we must know what the final end of man is. This is the supreme ethical question, but it must also be the supreme educa-

[49] For an explication of St. Thomas' argument see: Etienne Gilson, *op. cit.*, Chapter 9.

tional question, for the means that are employed in the process of education are intended to assist in realizing this ultimate end. In the next part of our inquiry, therefore, we will concern ourselves with the ethical question.

The Virtues and the End of Man

The main idea around which we will develop our inquiry is that some natural powers, but not all, are capable of being developed and perfected through *habit*. It is necessary to make a distinction here because some powers are not capable of being developed through habituation. Examples of these are the sensory powers. Experience in seeing or smelling does not make our visual or olefactory powers stronger, nor can school experience improve the innate intelligence of an individual. Education can only develop the potential that is present. There are, however, certain powers that are capable of development through habituation and these fall into two main categories: the intellectual and the volitional.

The perfection of these natural powers, that is, the development of them from potentiality to actuality, is what is meant by *virtue*. From the standpoint of the essential nature of man, therefore, there are two kinds of virtues: the intellectual virtues and the moral virtues. The intellectual virtues are the perfection of man's natural powers of reason. The moral virtues are the perfection of the powers of volition. In both cases this perfection is achieved through forming right (i.e., good) habits. Thus education is the process through which the intellectual virtues are formed through good habits, and moral training is the process of habituation that leads to the realization of the moral virtues. A habit is a right habit when it perfects a power in terms of the final end of that power. Since the dimensions of human nature extend below the strictly human level of intellect and will, there are also vegetative and sensate powers that are capable of development through habit, though in the case of these powers, this is necessarily in a sense different from the development of the intellectual and moral virtues.

The perfection of the intellectual and moral virtues, however, cannot be held to be the ultimate end of man. This was agreed both by Aristotle and St. Thomas. The final end of man must be something that exists in and of itself alone and is not desired for the sake of anything else. The perfection of natural powers is the means to the final end, but this is not the end itself. With Aristotle this final end is expressed in the untranslatable Greek word, *eudaemonia*, usually ren-

dered in English as *happiness* or *well-being*, by which he meant the ←
activity of the soul's powers in accordance with reason. All men desire
happiness, Aristotle maintained, but a man can achieve this state only
as he is able to exercise his powers to the proper degree and in balance
and harmony. Over-indulgence works to prevent the attainment of
happiness, but so does ascetic repression of natural powers. To attain
happiness a man must have enough means to sustain himself—a hungry man can not act nobly or attain happiness, and neither can a man
who must spend his days in servile work. Happiness is not a passive
state; it involves the active exercise of various powers in proper proportion to each other. The highest kind of activity of which man is capable is *contemplation*, that is, thought that is concerned with the first
principles of things. This is the nearest man can come to pure thought,
and when he is engaged in this activity, he is nearest to the Unmoved
Mover.

Since revealed truth, as well as philosophic truth, is involved in the
Thomistic view of man we can anticipate that Aristotle's view of the
ultimate end of man as being attained through the perfection of the
moral and intellectual virtues must necessarily be considered incomplete
by Thomists. In terms of Christian theology, therefore, the ultimate
end of man must be supernatural, not natural, and it must be that of
attaining a supernatural and eternal union with God. The ultimate ←
knowledge is knowledge of God. The formation of the intellectual and
moral virtues is an important part of the process of realization of
man's ultimate end, but it is only part. Here we come again to the root
of the difference between the educational views of the two major groups
in modern perennialism. The major differences between them with
respect to educational philosophy are owed primarily to their different
conceptions of human nature.

We may return now to the five propositions that were stated at the
beginning of this part of the discussion. The purpose of our inquiry
has been to clarify the meaning of these statements. We cannot claim
that we have demonstrated their truth because such a demonstration
would require far more space than is available and would make it necessary for us to consider many things that have not even been mentioned.
Our analysis has served, however, to throw light on what perennialists
mean by the statements.

With respect to the first proposition, we find that all members of a
species have the same specific nature and this nature does not change.
For example, the species *man* is differentiated from the genus *animal*

by that which is essential in human nature, namely the natural powers of reason. Thus, all men have the same specific nature. Further, any differences that are found among men are accidental and not essential. With respect to the second proposition, we have seen that since all men have the same nature, they all have the same powers. We have found the dimensions of human nature to extend from the lowest level of soul, the vegetative, through the sensate, and culminating in the rational. Some of these powers, particularly at the rational level, are susceptible to development through habit and these are the virtues. The most important of these, as we have found, are the moral and intellectual virtues, which are the perfection of natural powers at the level of rational soul. And so, as was stated in our third proposition, the virtues since they are perfections of powers we all possess, must be the same for all of us.

The fourth and fifth propositions are those with which we dealt originally in our survey of the pedagogical position of perennialism. We now can see how these propositions are related to the perennialist's view of man. The intellectual virtues are the perfection of the rational powers and the right habits through which they are perfected are formed through *education*, which is the activity carried on in the school. The chief aim of the school, therefore, is to contribute to realization of the ultimate end of man by helping him perfect his natural powers of reason. The school also has some responsibility for the formation of the moral virtues, but this is not its main area of concern. The family, the community, and the church also have major obligations for development of the moral virtues.[51]

The purpose of education is the formation of the intellectual virtues, and since these virtues are the same for all men, the purpose of education must be the same for all men. Hence, the fundamental strategy of education should never be laid around accidental differences. There should not be one kind of aim for some students and another kind for others. All men are rational beings and they have the right to the kind of education that will develop their supremely human qualities—that is, they have the right to *become men*. The school abrogates this right when it substitutes narrow vocationalism, which is really the training of the sensate powers of the animal, for liberal education which develops the natural powers of intellect and leads to the ultimate perfection of these powers in the intellectual virtues. Human nature is complex and multidimensional. There are various levels of powers to be perfected

[51] See for example: *The Education of Man*, ed., Gallagher, Chapter 5. Compare with Van Doren's *Liberal Education*, pp. 58–65.

but, in the words of one of the most distinguished perennialists of the last century: "Everything has its own perfection, be it higher or lower in the scale of things; and the perfection of one is not the perfection of another."[52]

Knowledge and Truth

We have now concluded the major part of our inquiry into the connection between the perennialist view of man and the leading ideas about education in that tradition. Before we conclude our study, however, we should give some attention to the way in which this tradition views the knowledge process and the conception of truth associated with it. We have already discussed some matters relevant to this aspect of the perennial philosophy, most notably those concerning the human intellect as a complex of natural powers. Our purpose now is to learn something about how the perennialist thinks these powers function in perception and cognition.

In one of his most important essays on education Maritain[53] has said that the fundamental element underlying an educational tradition is the philosophy of knowledge inherent in that tradition. By way of example, he contrasts the position of Thomism with that of empiricism on the question of the relation of sensory knowledge and rational knowledge. Empiricism, he points out, denies the distinction made by perennialists between sense knowledge, which apprehends things only as singulars and "only as enigmatically manifested by the diversified physical energies they display," and the intellect, which is spiritual in its nature and knows things as they are in their essential nature through its power to abstract the universal from that which is presented to sense. Empiricism, therefore, according to Maritain, since it equates all knowledge with sense impression, also maintains that all human knowledge is simply animal knowledge, more complex than that of other animals, of course, but still based on the animal level of the sensate soul. This means that as it is viewed in empiricism, human thought is simply a response to environmental stimuli and reflective thought occurs only in the presence of problematic situations, as Dewey, for example, has maintained. As the perennialist sees it, the results of this conception of knowledge are disastrous in the educational process. Maritain believes, with Dewey, in the power of thought to control and improve

[52] John H. Cardinal Newman, *The Scope and Nature of University Education*, New York: E. P. Dutton, 1958, p. 100.
[53] "Thomist Views on Education," *Modern Philosophies and Education*, ed., Brubacher, Chapter III.

the environment, but he is sure that Dewey, and all empiricists with him, has a completely erroneous view of the nature of human thought:

> On the contrary, it is because every human idea, to have a meaning, must attain in some measure (be it even in the symbols of a mathematical interpretation of phenomena) what things are or consist of unto themselves; it is because human thought is an instrument or rather a vital energy of knowledge or spiritual intuition (I don't mean "knowledge about," I mean "knowledge into"); it is because thinking begins, not only with difficulties but with *insights*, and ends up in insights which are made true by rational proving or experimental verifying, not by pragmatic sanction, that human thought is able to illuminate experience, to realize desires which are human because they are rooted in the prime desire for unlimited good, and to dominate, control, and refashion the world. At the beginning of human action, insofar as it is human, there is truth, grasped or believed to be grasped for the sake of truth. Without trust in truth, there is no human effectiveness.[54]

Aristotle said in the first sentence of the *Metaphysics*, "All men by nature desire to know." Thus, there is no problem relating to the "why" of human knowledge. Men tend to know in the same sense that smoke tends to rise and unsupported bodies tend to fall. This tendency of man toward knowing is simply one of the facts of nature. The general outline of the cognitive processes is common both to Aristotle and to St. Thomas. Any cognitive situation involves the three elements we have noted in earlier chapters: a subject (knower), an object (that which is known) and the relation that is established between the subject and object. Since both Aristotle and Aquinas agreed to the principle of independence, they agreed that the object exists independently of the mind. The external senses (smell, sight, sound, touch, taste) are the avenues through which the external reality impinges on the organism. All knowledge originates in sensory experience; there can be nothing in the intellect that was not first in the senses. The impression that comes from without activates the sense organ and it produces sensation. It should be noted that this is a very different account from that rendered by behavioristic psychology. In behaviorism, a sensory stimulus is held to be the efficient cause of a response, but in the Aristotelian and Thomistic account an external reality is a necessary condition for an act of knowing, but it is not the efficient cause of it.

The act of perception is the creation of an image in the mind of the subject which is identical with the external reality except that this image is spiritual (non-material) while the external reality is material. In this

[54] *Education at the Crossroads*, p. 13.

process the sensation affects the internal senses (imagination, memory, etc.) and they create an *intentional image,* which is comparable to some extent to what in modern psychology would be called a percept. Next the active intellect, which exercises its power to eliminate accidental qualities and thus reveal the essence of a thing, presents to the cognitive intellect the form (essence) of the object. The cognitive intellect, thereupon, expresses the essence of the object in terms of a concept or universal. The acts of the intellect are: apprehension (conception), that is, making the thing present in and to the intellect but without affirming or denying it; judgment, which is the process of affirming or denying; reasoning, which is the process of going from known truth to unknown truth. The criterion for the truth of our judgments is the one we have already considered in connection with modern realism—the principle of correspondence. Truth means the conformity of the mind with reality.

It is in this way that the perennial philosophy explains how it is that we can know things as they really are, that is, in their essential natures, and thus is able to demonstrate the possibility of objective truth which is known for itself and not merely for some instrumental purpose. The object of knowledge for the human intellect is essence, the universal, which is abstracted from the numerous data of sense impression and which, through the operations of reason, leads us to consequences. Thus, for the perennialist, the Truth exists and can be known, but this knowing is not easy and is possible only when the faculties of reason have been developed by education, which is the major role of the school. For those perennialists who recognize not only rational truth, but also revealed truth, there is another dimension. The revealed truths of the supernatural order must be transmitted and interpreted for children and youth, for otherwise these truths would never be gained by the young.

SUMMARY

We have now completed our inquiry into the educational theory developed and supported by the perennial tradition in philosophy. We have also seen something of the kind of philosophical support perennialists offer for their practical ideas about educational policy. Perennialism holds that the ultimate ends of education are capable of being demonstrated and can be known in an absolute fashion. In this sense, there is only one *philosophy* of education, for philosophical knowledge is that knowledge that is capable of rational demonstration from first principles. In this chapter we have not attempted any such complete demonstration. We have only sought to show that the major beliefs in the perennialist's educational philosophy derive immediately from the philosophy of human nature of that tradition.

Since in this book we are concerned with the philosophy of American education, the perennial philosophy has been presented as a protest against the prevailing essentialism. In other historical periods, perennialism has been the prevailing tradition and has been influential in determining the character of whatever educational arrangement prevailed. Perhaps in some countries of the contemporary world this tradition is still the dominant one. It is submitted, however, that this is not the case in the United States. Perennialism has furnished the basis for a penetrating and, on occasion, a devastating criticism of educational essentialism, but it has not succeeded in making fundamental changes in the nature of American education. Whether it ever will succeed is, of course, a speculative matter that cannot be settled here.

It has been noted that in some respects the protests of perennialism at the practical level of educational policy are similar to those made by Dewey and the progressives. Both these traditions are critical of the essentialist's emphasis on the transmission of organized subject matter as the primary aim of formal education and, since other practical considerations about the operations of the school follow directly from this conception, perennialists and progressives have sometimes found other common ground for practical criticism.

Beyond the practical level, however, the differences in outlook between progressivists and perennialists are enormous. In a sense, both of these philosophical traditions that underlie the two bodies of educational theory are humanistic. Both of them agree that the purpose of education is "to make a man." The issue over which they differ is the question, "What is man?" We have seen how strategic the answer to this question can be for educational theory.

CHAPTER ELEVEN

The Marxist Protest

In our days everything seems pregnant with its contrary . . . At the same pace that mankind masters nature, man seems to become enslaved to other men or to his own infamy. Even the pure light of science seems unable to shine but on the dark background of ignorance. All our invention and progress seem to result in endowing material forces with intellectual life, and in stultifying human life into a material force.

—KARL MARX

The established tradition in American education has been described in this book as an expression of a cultural pattern that is essentially middle class in origin and character. Important elements in this pattern have been identified as capitalism, nationalism, democracy, and experimental science, together with the supernaturalism of the Hebraic-Christian tradition. We have noted the continuing efforts of conservatism to unite in some kind of acceptable synthesis the spirit and achievements of modern science with the older supernaturalism. We have also seen that the educational policies developed and supported by the conservative tradition reflect the essentially middle-class character of conservatism and its eclectic approach to the problems of society.

The conservative tradition in America has been severely challenged once in the present century by liberal elements who instigated a reform

From an address delivered by Marx at the anniversary of the *People's Paper*, 1856. Reprinted in Karl Marx and Friedrich Engels, *Selected Works*, Moscow: Foreign Language Publishing House, 1962; Vol. I, pp. 359–360.

movement of considerable proportions which had as one of its facets the progressive movement in education. However, the liberal reform movement itself arose from within the middle class and its leaders, by and large, were fundamentally middle class in origin and outlook. Though liberals have long advocated far-reaching reforms for social institutions, including schools, these reforms were not to be abrupt and revolutionary, but rather were to take the form of a steady and persistent advance toward improving conditions in the modern industrial world. Certainly, the liberal has sought the transformation of society and the elimination of many elements in the conservative pattern, but he has proposed that it be done through non-violent means and within the existing procedural framework. Furthermore, it is a well-established point of liberalism that the school as an institution has a part to play in social reform and the improvement of the lot of man.

However, in this century the established tradition has had to withstand another protest movement that has not been gradualistic in its strategy, a protest that has condemned the middle-class gradualism of the liberals as completely as it has the traditionalism of the conservatives. The political reality of revolutionary socialism is a product of our own century, but its origins lie in the nineteenth century. The end of February, 1848, was a fateful time in the history of the west, for it was then, on the eve of the Revolution of 1848 in France, that a small pamphlet, written in German, was published in London. It bore the title, *The Manifesto of the Communist Party*. Its authors were Germans, Karl Marx (1818–1883) and Friedrich Engels (1820–1895) and its opening lines were meant to be the death-knell of the old order: "A spectre is haunting Europe—the spectre of Communism. All the Powers of old Europe have entered into a holy alliance to exorcise this spectre . . ." The closing passage of the *Manifesto* has served for more than a hundred years to send chills down the spines of western conservatives and liberals alike: "The Communists disdain to conceal their views and aims. They openly declare that their ends can be attained only by the forcible overthrow of all existing social conditions. Let the ruling classes tremble at a Communistic revolution. The proletarians have nothing to lose but their chains. They have a world to win. Working men of all countries, unite!"[1]

[1] The *Manifesto* has been reprinted many times. My references are to: Karl Marx and Friedrich Engels, *Selected Works*, 2 Vols., Moscow: Foreign Languages Publishing House, 1962; Vol. I, pp. 33–69.

PHILOSOPHY OF AMERICAN EDUCATION

It has often been said, even by those who hate the very sound of his name, that Marx is one of the genuinely important figures in human history. There are, in fact, as Mr. C. Wright Mills has pointed out, several Marxes.[2] There is Marx, the political agitator and polemicist; he has had few peers in this role. There is Marx the economist; after him, economic theory could never be the same. There is, of course, Marx, the philosopher of history and, we may ask, is there also a Marx, the educational philosopher? The answer to this question must be in the negative. Marx had relatively little to say about education and whatever comments he made are scattered through his voluminous writings.

It may seem reasonable to ask, therefore, why attention should be given in a book on American education to a body of doctrine that originated outside the stream of American tradition, that has been disavowed by American liberals and conservatives alike, and which has little to say directly about educational policy. There are, in fact, several reasons for giving attention, although it must necessarily be brief, to certain aspects of Marxian thought. In the first place, there are few who will deny that the protest movement that began in the nineteenth century with such figures as Marx and Engels, and found political reality in the Russian Revolution, constitutes the most powerful and the most dangerous threat to established traditions and institutions in the world today. The dimensions of this threat are so well known that there seems little point in discussing them here.

In the second place, one of the major threats deriving from Marxian thought has been that of the educational system of the Soviet Union. As is well known, an important part of the strategy of a resurgent American conservatism has been to make invidious comparisons of the American system of education with that of the Soviet Union, which has been held by some conservatives to be superior in every important respect to our own.[3] Whether this alleged superiority of Soviet education is owed to the influence of Marxian ideas or to some other influences is a difficult and complex question that cannot be settled in these few pages. But, since the U.S.S.R. is supposed to be the great example in this century of what Marxism means when it is translated into concrete political and social reality and since Soviet schools have been rated so

[2] *The Marxists*, New York: Dell Publishing Co., Inc., 1962, p. 41. See also Chapter 2.
[3] For example see: *Report on Russia by Vice Admiral Hyman G. Rickover, USN*, Hearings before the Committee on Appropriations, House of Representatives, Eighty-sixth Congress, Washington, D.C.: United States Government Printing Office, 1959.

high by some Americans, it seems worth giving attention to whatever ideas of Marx can be related to educational theory. In the third place, certain ideas of Marx provide insight into the human situation, particularly under conditions of industrial society, and into the prospect for improving man's lot in the modern world. We have considered this matter in connection with other traditions and found it important in its effect on educational theory and we propose to do the same thing with Marxism. We do not intend to make the educational system of the Soviet Union a major subject of this chapter. References to Soviet school policies will be useful at certain points in our inquiry, but our major enterprise is to study the character of the protest Marx and his followers launched against bourgeois society and whatever ideas about education we may find to be involved in this protest.

MATERIALISM AND DIALECTICAL DEVELOPMENT

Marxism is undoubtedly best known—and most feared—for its economic theory, but Marx developed his theory of history long before he turned his attention to demonstrating that capitalism had within itself the seeds of its own destruction. In the field of philosophy by far the greatest influence on Marx's thought was the idealism of Hegel. In the chapter on idealism in this volume we saw something of the character of Hegelian thought: the Absolute Mind that is within itself the whole of reality; history as the concrete manifestation of the developing processes of this Supreme Consciousness; the inherently logical character of the development of this Consciousness in terms of a dialectic pattern, which is the synthesis of opposing forces. Marx rejected Hegel's idealism, but he saw in Hegel's dialectical and historical method a means to the development of a scientific interpretation of history. "What distinguished Hegel's mode of thought from that of all other philosophers," Engels said in commenting on Marx's *Critique of Political Economy*, "was the tremendous sense of the historical on which it was based."[4] It is true, Engels agreed, that Hegel was thoroughly idealistic, but he always related the development of his argument to history and believed that the events of history constitute a test of the validity of the argument. What Marx and Engels proposed to do was to unite Hegel's dialectical method with materialism. In this view, the world is to be

[4] *Selected Works*, Vol. I, p. 372.

taken as it is for what it is. Its existence is not to be attributed to the creative act of some supernatural force nor dependent for its reality on any form of consciousness. The priority of matter is asserted in place of the priority of consciousness, as in idealism. Consciousness derives from matter.[5]

Marx's materialism, however, is not to be viewed as a kind of mechanism in which inert matter is pushed and pulled about by separate forces. Matter is essentially dynamic in nature, always in process of change and transformation. Development and change follow the dialectical laws inherent in the nature of things. Therefore, if we are to inquire into the nature of anything in order to understand it, we must inquire into its history. What a thing is seen to be at any particular point in time does not reveal the real nature of that thing. It is the direction and rate of development that are important. Presumably, this is true of all phenomena of nature, but Marx's great achievement was the application of this dialectical materialism to the phenomena of human society. In the preface to his "A Contribution to the Critique of Political Economy" Marx relates how he came first to a study of Hegel because of a controversy in which he was involved when he worked on a radical newspaper in the Rhineland. This experience convinced Marx of the inadequacy of his own philosophical knowledge and in consequence of this he embarked on a critical study of Hegelian philosophy. "My investigation led to the result," he said, "that legal relations as well as forms of state are to be grasped neither from themselves nor from the so-called general development of the human mind, *but rather have their roots in the material conditions of life* . . ."[6] Thus, if we are to understand institutions or laws of any particular time these must be studied in terms of their history—the conditions from which they have emerged and the direction in which they are tending. This is the essence of dialectical method.

From this beginning Marx worked out the basic theses of his theory of society and history. In social life men necessarily enter into certain kinds of relations over which they have no control. These are relations

---

[5] In the preface to the second edition of *Capital* Marx makes this observation about Hegel: "My dialectic method is not only different from the Hegelian, but is its direct opposite. To Hegel, the life-process of the human brain, i.e., the process of thinking, which, under the name of 'the Idea,' he even transforms into an independent subject, is the demiurgos of the real world, and the real world is only the external, phenomenal form of 'the Idea.' With me, on the contrary, the ideal is nothing else than the material world reflected by the human mind, and translated into forms of thought." *Capital*, Vol. I, New York: The Modern Library, no date, p. 25. All my references in *Capital* are to the Modern Library edition.
[6] *Selected Works*, Vol. I, p. 362. Italics mine.

involved in economic production, and the sum total of these relations constitute the economic structure of society, the base on which everything else in that society rests. Therefore, in any given period the character of all institutions—legal, political, educational, religious or whatever—is a function of the existing modes and forces of production current in that society. Perhaps the most momentous effect of the economic base is that it determines the class structure of a society. It is a matter of historical fact that class structure in different periods has varied, and it is Marx's point that these variations have been the result of different economic bases, that is to say, variations in the class structure of societies are the result of objective, historical conditions.

All development is dialectical in nature and, at the level of human society, the dynamic takes the form of the struggle of social classes. The conditions leading to this clash and struggle of interests are described by Marx as follows:

> At a certain stage of their development, the material forces of society come in conflict with the existing relations of production, or—what is but a legal expression for the same thing—with the property relations within which they have been at work hitherto. From forms of development of the productive forces these relations turn into their fetters. Then begins an epoch of social revolution.[7]

For example, given the economic base of capitalism in which the institution of private property is the basic element, society consequently is divided into two classes. Those who own the means of production, i.e., the capitalists, and those who have nothing to sell but their own labor, i.e., the workers. One of the elements in the economic base is what Marx called, as in the quotation above, "the existing *relations* of production," by this he meant the system of ownership, which under capitalism is that of private ownership of the means of production, and prevailing ways of distributing and exchanging commodities. The other element which Marx refers to as "the *forces* of production" consists of the raw materials, tools, technical skills, etc. involved in the processes of production. As the historical period of capitalism begins, the relations of production are harmonious with the forces of production and there is a period of dynamic and creative growth. But eventually the point is reached at which a contradiction develops between the forces and relations of production. The expanding productivity, which creates surpluses of goods, is inimical to the interests of the owning class. This class reacts by suppressing technological advance in various ways and in the end, it is capital itself that is the real barrier to production. The

7 *Ibid.*, p. 363.

practical effect of this contradiction is that the mass of the people are without work and on the verge of starvation. The "epoch of social revolution" Marx speaks of in the quotation begins when this exploited proletarian mass becomes politically conscious and adopts revolutionary methods to change the economic base. The conflict that develops between the forces of production and property relations cannot be resolved within the institutions of capitalism. According to Marx, no amount of social reform effort, legal or otherwise, can possibly suffice to ease the mounting tension to prevent the ultimate disintegration of the old order. In Marx's view, the transition from one historic period to another is never easy, gradual, or peaceful. Said Engels in his preface to the *Manifesto*, ". . . the whole history of mankind (since the dissolution of primitive tribal society, holding land in common ownership) has been a history of class struggles, contests between exploiting and exploited, ruling and oppressed classes . . ."[8]

The economic base of a society, which, as we have seen, includes the relations and the forces of production, determines the superstructure of social institutions and relationships of that society, and hence determines the way in which society is divided into classes and the kind of relationships that obtain among these classes. The class structure in feudal society, for example, is different from that under capitalism, and the relations of a feudal lord to his serfs is different from the relations of the owning class to the workers under capitalism. The reason for these differences is objective and historical; it derives from the character of the economic base of society.

The institutions that rise above the economic foundations as a superstructure are not only functions of basic economic conditions in a historical period, they are always employed by the dominant exploiting class to further its own purposes. The legal structure of a society exists to protect the interests of the class in control, although its true origin and character may be hidden behind a gloss of abstractions about "natural rights" and "eternal ideals of justice." In the *Manifesto* Marx and Engels ridiculed the pretensions of the bourgeoise about the objectivity of law and justice. ". . . Your jurisprudence is but the will of your class made into a law for all, a will whose essential character and direction are determined by the economical conditions of existence of your class."[9] Engels, writing at a later time and discussing the ways in which abstract legal concepts and systems of law develop, observed: "The justice of the Greeks and Romans held slavery to be just; the justice of

[8] *Ibid.*, p. 28. This refers to the English edition of 1888.
[9] *Ibid.*, p. 49.

the bourgeois of 1789 demanded the abolition of feudalism on the ground that it was unjust."[10]

In the same way, and for the same reason, the nature of the family and the character of relations between the sexes, together with the relations of parents and children, vary from one historic period to another. Bourgeois society makes its ideas about the family into holy myths and supports them with theological pronouncements about marriages being made in heaven and wedlock a holy state ordained by God. "On what foundation is the present family, the bourgeois family, based?" the authors of the *Manifesto* demand. And they answer their own question: "On capital, on private gain. In its completely developed form this family exists only among the bourgeoisie. But this state of things finds its complement in the practical absence of the family among the proletarians, and in public prostitution. The bourgeois family will vanish as a matter of course when its complement vanishes, and both will vanish with the vanishing of capital."[11] And with the question of education, the same thing holds. Bourgeois education in its aims and operations is determined by the economic structure of which it is both a product and a tool. In highly developed bourgeois societies the educational system conceals its origin and nature behind a screen of genteel abstractions about "the pursuit of truth for its own sake" and the "general enlightenment of mankind." Lenin lashed out at this pretension:

> The more cultured was the Bourgeois state, the more subtly it deceived, asserting that the school can remain outside of politics and thus serve society as a whole. In reality the school was wholly an instrument of class domination in the hands of the bourgeoisie; it was permeated throughout with the spirit of caste; and its aim was to give to the capitalists obliging serfs and competent workers.[12]

In the *Manifesto* the promise was made that under communism the influence of the bourgeoisie over education would cease, and this, of course, as a matter of historical necessity. The tenth measure for action proposed by Marx and Engels in the *Manifesto* is for free education for all children in public schools, the abolition of child labor in factories, *and the combination of education with industrial production,* this last being Marx's most important proposal for educational practice.

We have now seen something of how the superstructure of society develops in terms of the economic base. The class structure, the legal

[10] From "Supplement on Proudhon and the Housing Question" (1873), *Ibid.*, p. 624.
[11] *Ibid.*, p. 50.
[12] Quoted in George S. Counts, *The Soviet Challenge to America,* New York: The John Day Company, 1931, p. 318.

system, the nature of such institutions as the family and the school, political processes and institutions, are what they are, and what they necessarily must be, because of the objective conditions that have produced them. At the top of the superstructure of society is what Marx called *the state*. In this sense, the state is not simply the government, that is, the institutions that carry on the routine and administrative affairs of society. The state is the coercive power in society, described by Marx as "the standing army, police, bureacracy, clergy, and judicature."[13] This coercive power is always available and when the interests of the dominant class are threatened seriously and these threats cannot be contained by political or other means, the full force of the state will be invoked. Marx dismissed the idea of the state's being neutral and above class considerations as pure nonsense. "The state," said Engels, "is nothing but the organized collective power of the possessing classes, the landowners and the capitalists, as against the exploited classes, the peasants and the workers."[14] Nor will this condition change until the conditions that produce it change. Until capitalism falls, the state will be in the service of the exploiting class.

In this section, we have noted some of the main ideas involved in Marxian theory. These may be summarized as follows: (a) a conception of nature as material in character, all else being derived from matter; (b) nature developing in terms of a dialectical pattern in which the struggle and eventual synthesis of opposing forces is the dynamic factor; (c) the applications of dialectical, and, hence, historical method to understanding the nature of human social organization, and an interpretation of the struggle of social classes as the dynamic element in social change; (d) the theory that the relations and forces involved in economic production are the determining factors in society and shape the character of that society. These ideas are all fundamental in Marx's conception of the historical process and the rise and fall of social systems, a matter to which we will now give some attention.

THE COURSE OF HISTORY

According to Marxian thought, there are five major stages in human history. These are: primitive communism, slavery, feudalism, capitalism, and socialism (i.e., communism). Each successive stage has developed out of the preceding one (primitive communism being, of course, the

---

[13] *Ibid.*, p. 516. [14] *Ibid.*, p. 604.

initial state of human society) according to the historical process we have already considered in the preceding section. The character of each of these social systems is determined by the relations and forces of economic production in that system. The transition from capitalism to socialism is the most important question in Marxism, and it is the matter to which Marx himself gave the most attention. However, the development of socialism out of capitalism is only one (and the last) historical development of society. It is necessary that Marx's theory of history account not only for the fall of capitalism but also for previous transformations and developments of society if it is to be truly comprehensive in its conception of the historical process. There are certain difficulties involved in Marx's conceptions of the development of slavery and subsequently the transition from slavery to feudalism,[15] but these are too involved to be treated in this short account. Briefly, the course of historical development is as follows:

As human history begins, men live under conditions of a primitive communism in which the means of production are the natural environment. They are food gatherers and hunters and in order to survive the rigors of nature are forced to work together. The means of production and the proceeds of production are held in common. There is as yet no conception of private ownership of the means of production. There is no owning class, and hence there is no exploitation.

The historic period that succeeds the era of primitive communism is that of slavery. Now both the forces and relations of production have changed. Tools and techniques are much improved in comparison with their primitive counterparts. Agriculture, handicraft manufacturing, and animal husbandry are well advanced. Surplus wealth appears (i.e., economic goods in excess of those needed to sustain the population), the way is now clear for exchange of goods and the accumulation of wealth, and the division of society into an exploiting class—the owners —and the exploited class—the slaves. Thus, a class structured society emerges, and the relations of production are those of master to slave. The slave is his master's chattel. A master can do anything with a slave he chooses to do: buy him, sell him, punish him, kill him, if he wants to. Slaves receive enough for their subsistence, but that is all they get. Whatever a slave produces beyond that needed to keep himself alive and in working condition is surplus value and, of course, accrues to the owner.

[15] For a more detailed discussion see: George Lichtheim, *Marxism: An Historical and Critical Study*, New York: Frederick A. Praegger, Inc., 1961.

Eventually, the relations and forces of production change and humanity enters the new era of feudalism. Technological improvements have changed productive forces somewhat. The various forms of agriculture have become more efficient, the beginnings of factory manufacture can be seen. It becomes to the advantage of the owning class for the workers to have some psychological involvement in the productive process and therefore to exercise some of their own ingenuity and initiative —this, of course, in contrast to the slave who felt no involvement and whose attitude was passive. And so the slave becomes the serf who owns some of the tools of production and who pays the feudal lord with part of the fruits of his labor, keeping whatever is left for himself. Thus, the exploitation of the serf is nearly as bad as that of the slave under conditions of the previous historical period and, as was true under slavery, there is an intense class struggle developed between the exploited class and to the owning class.

We come now to the advent of the fourth stage of historical development which is that of capitalism. The relations of production under capitalism are those of an owning class (the capitalists) to a working class (the proletariat). Members of the proletariat are free; that is, they are not owned by the capitalists and they cannot legally be bought or sold or killed. The forces of production have also changed. The simple handicraft system and the guilds of medieval craftsmen have given way to large and increasingly complex manufacturing establishments. The major source of energy is no longer human and animal muscle power, but steam and, later, electricity. Capitalism requires much more from workers than either slavery or feudalism demands. Industrial production involves complicated machinery and processes and workers must be capable of being instructed in the use of machines. It is to the advantage of the owning class, therefore, that the workers have personal freedom and at least the illusion of a certain amount of political freedom. Under the conditions of advanced capitalism it is also advantageous for the working class to have a certain amount of schooling— at least the elements of literacy.

In Marx's day the desirability of popular education, however, ran counter to another important aspect of the early capitalism, the employment of children in factories. In England, which was the most advanced industrial nation in the early and middle nineteenth century, there were included in a series of "Factory Acts" provisions that children employed in factories were to receive a certain amount of schooling—actually a few hours per week. Marx's comments on the quality of this "schooling" are withering. He quotes from reports of factory inspectors concerning the total lack of fitness of the teachers in the factory schools, many of whom were not sufficiently literate to keep the class register or even to spell their own names in the same way on different occasions.[16] To Marx, of course, the sham of factory education of children was but an example of the merciless exploitation of the working classes by capitalists. However, as scornful as he was of capitalism's real contribution to the education of the common people, he did discover in the combined work-study program provided under the factory acts an idea for the universal education that would develop when capitalism and all its attendant evils have succumbed to the historical process. We will return to this matter in a later portion of this chapter.

The transition from capitalism to socialism is the last and most crucial episode in the historical process, according to Marxists. It is also the point of greatest interest for us in this chapter. The Marxist protest is against bourgeois, capitalist society and the institutions and philosophies of that society. Hence, Marxism is in various ways a protest against all the educational traditions we have considered thus far. Therefore, we will give a somewhat more extended consideration of this period than has been given to those that came before. In thinking about Marx's ideas about the transition from capitalism to socialism we must be sure to keep certain things in mind. For one thing, we should remember the principle that the mode of production in a society determines the nature of the institutions, processes, and ways of life of that society. We have already discussed the importance of the relations and forces of production which are the economic base on which the superstructure of society is erected. In addition to this idea, which is the basis of Marxian social philosophy, there are two other ideas closely associated with it.

First, since it is the mode of production of material life that determines the character of social processes, according to Marx, "It is not the consciousness of men that determines their being, but on the contrary, their social being that determines their consciousness."[17] This is a conception of great importance and we will need to refer to it again in various contexts. For the moment, we may note Marx is saying that the very way in which we perceive the world is a function of the mode of production that obtains in the historic period in which we live. What we consider right and what we consider wrong, what is just and what is unjust, what is to be desired and what is to be avoided are all judgments

16 See: *Capital*, Vol. I, p. 437. See pp. 436–440 for Marx's complete description of the education of working class children.
17 "Preface to the Critique of Political Economy," in *Marx and Engels, Selected Works*, Vol. I, p. 363.

made with reference to certain objective conditions that exist and serve to determine our perceptions. Hence, Marx is denying that there is some ultimate source, usually alleged to be universal and unchanging, from which our ethical principles derive. Ethical principles are emergents of history; they are naturalistic in their origin. In Marx's thought, therefore, not only are ethical conceptions relative to historical periods, they are also relative to the demands and needs of social classes. This must be true because all social orders existing in the historical period between primitive communism and the advent of socialism are divided into opposing classes whose needs and interests are diametrically opposite. Each class seeks to make its own claims prevail, but neither class can seriously maintain that its claim can be justified in terms of some higher law or absolute. The last resort, said Marx, is force:

> The capitalist maintains his rights as a purchaser when he tries to make the working day as long as possible, and to make, whenever possible, two working days out of one. On the other hand, the peculiar nature of the commodity sold implies a limit to its consumption by the purchaser, and the labourer maintains his right as seller when he wishes to reduce the working day to one of normal duration. *There is here, therefore, an antimony, right against right, both equally bearing the seal of the law of exchanges. Between equal rights force decides.*[18]

It is often maintained, of course, that there is a more or less objective community of values to which all men customarily subscribe, regardless of history or class status. After all, it is said, truth, goodness, security, love, beauty, and so on, are goods that are universally desired. In essence, Marx's answer is that perhaps they are, but the very way in which these abstractions are conceived is a function of historical circumstances. What is justice to the capitalist is injustice to the worker. The security of the owning class is bought at the expense of the insecurity of the workers. There is no community of value in the practical sense because the needs and demands of social classes cannot be reconciled so long as there is an exploiting class and an exploited class. This is the case under capitalism and, given the base on which the superstructure of capitalism rests, it cannot be otherwise so long as that system endures. The proletariat, therefore, can never be free of exploitation until class distinctions and class struggles cease, and this condition will come only with the advent of socialism.

The other matter we need to bear in mind as we consider Marx's conception of the transition to socialism is the principle enunciated by him in his "Preface to the Critique of Political Economy."[19]

[18] *Capital*, Vol. I, p. 259. Italics mine.   [19] *Selected Works*, Vol. I, p. 363.

No social order ever perishes before all the productive forces for which there is room in it have developed; and new, higher relations of production never appear before the material conditions of their existence have matured in the womb of the old society itself. Therefore mankind always sets itself only such tasks as it can solve; since, looking at the matter more closely, it will always be found that the task itself arises only when the material conditions for its solution already exist or are at least in the process of formation.

Each of the succeeding stages of history, therefore, beginning with primitive communism, develops only as the preceding stage has exhausted itself. The transition from capitalism to socialism must occur in a country in which capitalism has run its course. Just prior to the breakdown of the old capitalistic order certain symptoms will appear. The polarization of society will be virtually complete. The two great classes, the capitalists and the proletariat, whose interests are diametrically opposed, will be in a state of continuous struggle. The owning class will have grown smaller in number and the proletariat will have grown larger, to a considerable extent because of the impoverishment of small shopkeepers, farmers, etc., and their consequent descent into the propertyless proletariat. Economic crises grow in frequency and in severity. Riots and strikes are common. The aging capitalism no longer has the flexibility and viability to recover from periodic crisis. The owning class, feeling its domination threatened, uses the coercive power of the state without mercy to keep down the increasingly revolutionary actions of the masses, which by now have become politically conscious.

The final act in the drama is a revolution in which the capitalistic class is overthrown, the proletariat institutes a dictatorship in which the coercive power of the state is converted to the uses of the now dominant working class as it seeks the transition to socialism. The conversion from one social system to another cannot be abrupt and immediate. In one instance Marx described the nature of the transition in this way:

> Between capitalist and communist society lies the period of the revolutionary transformation of the one into the other. There corresponds to this also a political transition period in which the state can be nothing but the revolutionary dictatorship of the proletariat.[20]

The first stage initiated by the new dominant class is state ownership of the means of production. Out of this emerges the first stage of socialism in which workers are rewarded according to what they produce. This period has not divorced itself completely from certain aspects of capital-

[20] "Critique of the Gotha Programme," *Ibid.*, Vol. II, p. 32.

ism, yet it is a classless society. The change that has occurred in the economic base, that is, the abolition of private ownership of the means of production, has destroyed the class basis of the old society. Hence, there is no exploitation and no class struggle. The final and highest form of society is reached in pure communism. Under these conditions the last manifestations of the old order have disappeared and all men will "contribute according to their capacities and be rewarded according to their needs." In this final stage, the state will disappear because it will have no reason for being. The only function of the state is the protection of the interests of the dominant class and under communism there are no social classes and no selfish interests to protect. This does not mean there will be no institutions to regulate and administer the routine affairs of society. It means that the need to coerce has vanished. Exploitation of human labor is gone. There is no need for extrinsic motivation for man to labor. He is now free to express freely his own uniquely human nature—to live like a man. And so, in the next stage of our inquiry, we will concern ourselves with the question of what it means to live like a man. To answer this question we must turn our attention to Marx's conception of human nature.

THE NATURE OF MAN

We can anticipate at the beginning that whatever conception of human nature Marxists may hold, it must be one that is consistent with the materialist philosophical position of this tradition and also one that is defensible in empirical and historical terms. Philosophies of human nature, whatever their character may be, are always concerned with describing the major characteristics of the human species, discovering the essential differences that set man apart from other species of animals, and, as a consequence of these ideas, with stating some final end for man. For example, in the chapter immediately preceding this one we saw that Aristotle (and subsequently the Scholastics) saw man as an animal, part of whose nature is identical with that of animals but who in addition possesses the unique powers of reason. The essence of man, therefore, in the perennial philosophy is reason and man is a rational animal.

The approach of Marx and Engels to the question of the nature of man is historical and scientific. Human nature, and that which is unique to it, is a product of historical development. Man is what he is because of the conditions involved in his development from less complex organisms, and the fundamental factor is that of *labor*. This thesis is stated by Engels:

> Labour is the source of all wealth, the political economists assert. It is this next to nature, which supplies it with the material that converts it into wealth. *But it is infinitely more than this.* It is the prime basic tradition for all human existence, and this to such an extent that, in a sense, we have to say that *labour created* man himself.[21]

Having stated his thesis, Engels then proceeds with his argument that the human species developed from apes and that the major factor in this evolutionary development was labor. The decisive event in the development of the human species was the accomplishment of walking upright and thereby freeing the hand for work. "Thus," said Engels, "the hand is not only the organ of labour, *it is also the product of labour.*"[22] The hand, of course, is only one of the members of the organism, yet the development of this one member affected the development of others, and man not only learned to labor with his hands but also to speak. And so the simple, primitive gregariousness of the ape becomes the society of human beings and work becomes cooperative, that is, social. This, in the judgment of Engels, is the crucial element in human nature and in human society. He asks, "And what do we find . . . as the characteristic difference between the troupe of monkeys and human society?" The answer, he says, is "labour."[23] An animal only uses whatever may be present in the environment but man adapts nature to his own ends—he masters it—and the fundamental element in this mastery is human labor.

We are not concerned here with the technical adequacy of Engel's evolutionary theory. The important matter is his idea of the historic role labor has played in the development of human nature and the strategic part this idea plays in Marxian conceptions of the nature of man. Marx and Engels regarded the control man had achieved over nature with the greatest respect and enthusiasm. The conquest of nature not only shows the power of human labor, they thought, but also shows the intimate relation of man with the rest of the processes of nature, and exhibits the falsity of all those philosophies that rest on the familiar dualisms of mind *and* matter, man *and* nature, soul *and* body. Man is a part of nature, an animal evolved from more primitive species. But, "Man is the sole animal capable of working his way out of the merely animal

[21] Engels, "The Part Played by Labour in the Transition from Ape to Man," *Ibid.*, Vol. II, p. 80. Italics mine.
[22] *Ibid.*, p. 83.   [23] *Ibid.*, p. 84.

state—his normal state is one appropriate to his consciousness, one to be created by himself."[24] The essence of man, therefore, is his urge to create and to recreate his own environment, not simply to adjust to it as other animals do. The urge to labor is not simply a reaction to external stimuli; it is of the very nature of man himself. If for Aristotle man is a rational animal, for Marx and Engels he is a *working* animal. It is through labor that his fundamental nature is realized.

The role of human labor is to give man mastery over the physical world and to make possible the realization of man's own nature, but since the time of the emergence of the human species from the original condition of primitive communism, events have conspired against it. Man has conquered nature, but in having lost control of the productive forces that have given that control, he has lost himself. Said Engels in the introduction to *Dialectics of Nature:*

> In the most advanced industrial countries we have subdued the forces of nature and pressed them into the service of mankind; we have thereby infinitely multiplied production, so that a child now produces more than a hundred adults previously. And what is the consequence? Increasing overwork and increasing misery of the masses and every ten years a great crash.[25]

Such is the course of human alienation.

Ever since human society emerged from primitive communism to slavery the mass of men have been alienated from themselves; they have always worked under compulsion—first under slavery, then feudalism, and finally under capitalism in which the process of alienation has reached its highest point. Under capitalism human labor is simply a commodity that is bought and sold on the market, and man becomes merely a means and not an end. Hence, the worker is most with himself when he is not working and most alienated from himself when he is at work. The work he does is not in response to the deepest urgings of his own nature, but rather is extraneous to it. Marx said the worker feels most free when he is performing purely animal functions and least free when he is performing the distinctively human activity of labor. This is the irony of history, and it can never be eliminated, man can never be united with himself, until the capitalist period of history ends and mankind gains control of productive relations and processes. The historical effect of labor has been to create private property, the property of someone other than those who labored

[24] Engels, *Dialectics of Nature*, New York: International Publishers Co., 1940, p. 187.
[25] *Selected Works*, Vol. II, p. 75.

to produce it. "Capital is dead labor," Marx said, "that vampire-like, only lives by sucking living labor, and lives the more, the more labor it sucks."[26]

For most of human history man has been exploited and hence alienated, but it is under the conditions of capitalism that this alienation has reached its highest point. The relations of production under the factory system are such that work has become completely dehumanized. The interest of the worker is set off against the interest of the factory owner, but more than that, in their work men are set over against each other. Factory management assigns to each worker a simple, routine, repetitive task that is done over and over again (in Marx's day for as long as 14 or even 18 hours a day). It was this simplification and routinization that made it possible to employ very young children in the early factory system of production, the horrors of which Marx described and documented in great detail. The work that is natural to man—the labor that in the view of Engels has served to make the species what it is—is free spontaneous activity in which through communal effort men seek to transform the environment in accordance with their desires. Under conditions of factory production, however, labor is neither spontaneous nor free. It is forced labor performed for another; it is wage slavery. And it is under these conditions, Marx points out, that "the relations connecting the labor of one individual with that of the rest appear, not as direct social relations between individuals at work, but as what they really are, material relations between persons and social relations between things."[27] And it is in this sense that a contradiction develops within human nature itself, for under these conditions labor is not the essence of man. In fact, it contradicts the very character of humanness, and that which is at the very heart of this contradiction is acquisitiveness—greed. Man is thus engaged in a struggle with himself to free himself from the despotic rule of this inhuman and dehumanizing force, which is objectified socially in the person of the capitalist.[28]

We should remember that "it is not the consciousness of men that determines their existence, but on the contrary, their social existence determines their consciousness." Alienated man, who is not the real

[26] *Capital*, Vol. I, p. 257.
[27] *Ibid.*, p. 84.
[28] There are marked differences of opinion about how certain ideas of Marx concerning human alienation should be interpreted. An important point of controversy is whether the primary alienation is within the individual and subsequently projected into social relations or whether alienation in social relations is the prior con-

man, is what he is because of objective historical conditions. Before man can lose his alienated state he must become conscious of himself. Self-consciousness is the key to freedom, and the burden of the fulfillment of this, in Marx's philosophy, is laid by history on the proletariat. The first step in this process is that the proletariat must become class conscious. When this class consciousness has become sufficient, the proletariat will revolt and in its act of revolution change the conditions that created alienated man. Thus, when the social relations in society are brought into harmony with the forces of production, all mankind will be freed from its condition of alienation and men can live like men. As one writer has said, "The promise of the Marxist vision is of man united with himself, his comrades, and his world."[29]

In his long history alienated man has turned to religion. In Marx's view, religion has always been an emotional outcry of great intensity, expressing the essential misery of the human species. It has also constituted a protest against the conditions that produce this misery. But religion has also served to prevent men from recognizing and rising against the conditions that perpetuate their misery. Institutionalized religion has been a means employed by the exploiters to keep the masses in subjection.[30] Engels, for example, discussing the situation in Britain remarked: "Now, if ever, the people must be kept in order by moral means, and the first and foremost of all moral means of action upon the masses is and remains—religion."[31]

In his own conception of the nature and function of religion, Marx was influenced by the German philosopher, Ludwig Feuerbach (1804–1872). Feuerbach had interpreted religion to be a projection of human needs and aspirations, although, he pointed out, this projection is necessarily illusory and distorted.[32] Religion is a form of self-alienation because it involves a duality: an imaginary and ideal world portrayed by religion and the real world in which men live and suffer. Marx was attracted by Feuerbach's naturalistic explanation of the religious phenomenon, that is, that the world portrayed by religion has its origin and finds its basis in the "real" world of secular life. But Marx also

---

dition. See for example: Robert C. Tucker, *Philosophy and Myth in Karl Marx*, London and New York: Cambridge University Press, 1961, Chapter IX, and Sidney Hook, *From Hegel to Marx*, Ann Arbor: University of Michigan Press, 1962, pp. 3–8.

[29] Robert S. Cohen, "On the Marxist Philosophy of Education," in *Modern Philosophies and Education*, ed. Brubacher, p. 192.

[30] *Ibid.*, p. 188.

[31] "Socialism: Utopian and Scientific," in *Selected Works*, Vol. II, p. 113.

[32] Ludwig Feuerbach, *The Essence of Christianity*, London: John Chapman, 1854.

believed that Feuerbach had left the real task undone. "Feuerbach," he wrote, "resolves the religious essence into *human* essence. But the human essence is no abstraction inherent in each single individual. In its reality it is the ensemble of the social relations."[33]

Feuerbach's failure to perceive that religious feeling is itself a product of historical and social conditions allowed him to reach a conclusion that was common in those days, as well as in these, that religious feelings are a part of man's essential nature; that is, that man, we might say, is by nature "a religious animal." Since he is religious by nature, man always tends to project his needs and desires into a perfect world of illusion, and this vision—distorted though it may be—is a true expression of his longings and a protest against their lack of fulfillment. It was with this in mind that Marx in his earlier career wrote the famous line, "Religion is the people's opium." If man has an essential nature, it is not one that is carried in the genes. Rather, Marx maintained, it derives from social life, and this means, of course, that the character of economic forces and relations is the determining factor. The religious phenomenon, therefore, is a social phenomenon and can be studied and understood in empirical and historical terms. The conditions that give rise to religion are the conflicts that develop in society and are caused by economic conflict. When these conditions disappear, that is, when men gain control over economic and natural forces, they will no longer be at the mercy of these forces and they will gain control over their own history. The alienated condition of man will pass away, and the myths and illusions of religion will no longer have a part to play. This cannot be, however, until the historic age of capitalism has spent itself and the proletariat can institute the classless society under socialism. Marx, himself, did not believe that the working-class movement, as he knew it, should make anti-religion a part of its strategy. The energy of the working class, he maintained, should be directed against the conditions that generate religion. When those conditions have been changed, the rest will follow as a necessary course.[34]

It is also in his critique of Feuerbach that we find the key to Marx's conception of the nature of human knowledge and the character of truth. As a materialist, Marx necessarily rejected the idealistic account

[33] *Theses on Feuerbach, Ibid.*, p. 404.
[34] See on this point: Sidney Hook, *From Hegel to Marx*, p. 293. Also see in this same volume Hook's complete discussion of Marx's *Theses on Feuerbach*, pp. 272–307.

of the knowledge process, but he also found in idealism, particularly in Hegel, the element that was missing in previous materialism, whether that of the ancients or that of the eighteenth century. This element was the essentially active aspect of the knowledge process, which in idealism is the activity of mind. Typically in materialism the act of cognition had been conceived as essentially passive in character. The mind passively receives the impact of stimuli coming from the external object and, thus, mind is simply a spectator of an independent reality. Such a view, Marx thought, was incapable of accounting for the role that human action has in the process of knowledge and consequently in social life. The fact of the situation, as he saw it, is that knowing always involves acting on and, therefore, transforming the object. In the second of his *Theses on Feuerbach*, Marx observes: "The question whether objective . . . truth can be attributed to human thinking is not a question of theory but is a *practical* question. In practice man must prove the truth, that is, the reality and power, the this-sidedness of his thinking."[35] Now, the question is, how do we prove the truth?

Marx had thought the idealists right in their emphasis on the dynamic, active character of cognition, but since idealism is built on the priority of consciousness and the immateriality of the object, the only possible criterion for truth is that of coherence, a matter we discussed in some detail in an earlier chapter. On the other hand, the only conceivable criterion of truth available to materialism is correspondence, which we have also seen, involves certain difficulties, and these are sufficient in Marx's judgment to render correspondence inadequate as a theory of truth. In the last sentence of his second thesis on Feuerbach, Marx says: "The dispute over the reality or non-reality of thinking which is isolated from practice is a purely *scholastic* question." What Marx is saying here is very similar to what C. S. Peirce and subsequently, John Dewey said; namely that a statement that cannot be put to the test of action is a meaningless statement. As in the pragmatism of Peirce and the instrumentalism of Dewey, ideas are always hypothetical in character. They are not simply copies of an external object. *They are plans for guiding action.* To prove their truth, therefore, our ideas must be brought to action and the condition that must be satisfied is that the consequences anticipated in the idea must be realized in the experimental application of the idea. Our desires and aspirations do not constitute the truth of our ideas. As Sidney Hook has said, "There

[35] *Selected Works*, Vol. II, p. 403.

is no will to believe in Marx but a will to action, in order to test belief and set additional grounds for further action if necessary."[36] As with the pragmatists, truth is something that happens to an idea. Truth is not universal and unchanging. It must change as the conditions that generate it change. In this sense, it is historical and dialectical.

Marx's theory of knowledge and truth is consistent with his historical and social theories. If the basic motive in human nature is action, freely directed at changing the environment in accord with men's own needs and desires, then ideas are not divorced from action but are one aspect of human activity. Any effort is specious that seeks to cut theory off from practice and make it something higher and more important than mere action. This was one of Marx's fundamental objections to Feuerbach, who he said, "regards the theoretical attitude as the only genuinely human attitude, while practice is conceived and fixed only in its dirty-judaical form of appearance."[37] Thus, Feuerbach, for all his materialism, winds up in essentially the same position as classic western philosophy, which consistently gives theory a separate and higher status than mere practice. Parenthetically, we may anticipate that Marx's theory of the relation of idea and action has important implications for his conception of education and for the kind of protest against educational conservatism that is inherent in the Marxist philosophy of human nature. In fact, philosophy itself is seen by Marx not as simply an explanation of the character of the world, nor, as it sometimes seems to be, an apology for it, rather it should represent a wholehearted effort to convert the world to the needs and uses of humanity. This conviction finds expression in one of the best known and most frequently quoted statements from Marx's writings: "The philosophers have only *interpreted* the world, in various ways; the point, however, is to *change* it."[38]

THE EDUCATION OF MAN

We have completed our survey of certain of the important elements in Marxian thought. We now turn our attention to the connection these ideas have with certain conceptions about education that are

[36] Hook, *op. cit.*, p. 285. See also on Marx's theory of knowledge: C. E. M. Joad, *Guide to Philosophy*, New York: Dover Publications, 1936, pp. 474–476.
[37] *Selected Works*, Vol. II, p. 403.
[38] This is the last of the eleven *Theses on Feuerbach, Ibid.*, p. 405.

either explicit in the thought of Marx or are implicit in it. As was noted initially, neither Marx nor Engels had much to say about education directly. Whatever statements were made were scattered through their writings in various kinds of contexts. Furthermore, there is comparatively little extant in the way of commentary on Marxian ideas of education, except that emanating from the Soviet Union and in which the ideas of Marx have been warped in whatever way seemed necessary to accommodate them to the prevailing line of the Communist Party of the U.S.S.R. Since the purpose of the present inquiry is not to survey the character of Soviet education, but to consider the protest inherent in Marxian thought against the character of conservative middle-class educational practice, we will confine our attention to what Marx himself had to say that may be relevant to this protest.

We may begin by saying that Marx took universal education seriously. This observation may be thought to be innocuous enough, since every tradition we have considered thus far also has taken it seriously. We should perhaps remind ourselves, however, that when Marx lived and wrote the idea of free, universal education was very far from being established and it was also in conflict with the prevailing practice of employing young children in factory production. It is virtually axiomatic that universal education cannot exist until it is made legally compulsory and until it is completely tax supported. Some idea of how radical an idea the notion of free, universal education was in the middle of the nineteenth century can be gained if we consider that it was one of the measures called for in the *Manifesto* along with a heavy graduated income tax and socialization of industry, communication, and transportation. Marx and Engels knew well enough that the principle of free education in public schools for all children would remain a mockery unless the labor of children in factories was abolished or, at least, greatly curtailed, or unless education could be combined in a humane and fruitful way with productive work.

It is a fact of history, now so well established as to be outside serious argument, that free, public education is itself a product of industrial society. In previous periods of history it was virtually unknown even as a serious idea, and certainly unknown as a concrete reality. This means that universal education is not only a product of industrialism but of capitalism, and, if Marx's thesis that the superstructure of society, which certainly would include the schools, is a product of the economic base, then the character and function of education is determined by the productive forces and relations inherent in capitalism.

The term "school" is simply an abstraction whose meaning is determined by the social context in which it exists and which determines its function. Thus, Marx in his critique of the program of the German Workers Party, written in 1875 pointed out the equivocative character of the party's proposition on education. The program of the party had called for: "Universal and *equal elementary education* by the state. Universal compulsory school attendance. Free instruction."[39] Marx inquired:

> What idea lies behind these words? Is it believed that in present-day society (and it is only with this that one has to deal) education can be *equal* for all classes? Or is it demanded that the upper classes also shall be compulsorily reduced to the modicum of education—the elementary school—that alone is compatible with the economic conditions not only of the wage-workers but of the peasants as well?[40]

Marx evidently believed these questions to be rhetorical. A society that is divided into an owning class and a working class will never have free and equal educational opportunity for all children. Such a society will not provide opportunity for education of the masses above a minimum level (in Marx's day this meant elementary schooling) and it most surely will not reduce the education of the dominant class to the common level. Furthermore, Marx raises the question of what happens when in some of the United States higher education is also made free, referring, presumably, to the land-grant colleges established under the Morrill Act of 1862. What happens, he said, is that the upper classes have the costs of their higher education free, these costs being defrayed by the general tax revenues. The poor, of course, get nothing, and he adds, "The paragraph on the schools should at least have demanded technical schools (theoretical and practical) in combination with the elementary school."

The statement in the program of the German Workers Party that Marx found most repugnant was that education should be conducted by the state. He believed that financial support, minimum qualifications of teachers, subjects to be taught, and perhaps the supervision of instruction should be prescribed in law. But he maintained the government and the church should be excluded from any influence on the school. In this position he approached the ideals of Jefferson and other liberals of the eighteenth century, which were that education should be carried on for the general enlightenment of mankind and the school should not be in the services of any element of society

39 *Ibid.*, p. 34.   40 *Loc. cit.*

whether it be class, state, or church. However, given the vast differences between the Marxian view of history and that of the eighteenth century liberals, it must be that education can never function as a true source of enlightenment for mankind so long as it goes on in a class structured society. We noted in an earlier part of this chapter how Marx excoriated the "factory schools" that British capitalists had been forced by the Factory Acts to establish. In his view, the school, prior to the advent of socialism, is inevitably the tool of the dominant class—it is used by the capitalists to further their own ends. Is this not immoral? This question can be answered only in the context of Marx's ethical relativism. From the standpoint of a thoroughly class-conscious proletariat, it is a monstrous immorality, but the consciousness of men is determined by their social existence and the capitalist is only doing with the school what must be done within the context of capitalist society. This is one of those historical conditions that can be settled *only by force*. In the period prior to the revolution the proletariat, now become socially conscious, will attempt to use the schools to further the class-consciousness of the masses and pave the way for the final struggle that will transform society.

Once the complete transformation of society has been achieved, the old forms of education will disappear and man will develop his full nature by participation in social life.[41] Men will no longer be chained to machines doing endlessly repetitive tasks that dehumanize them. They will rather be capable of doing all kinds of labor and these labors will be true expressions of the whole man. In this sense, Marx's view of the future is idyllic. In that future he saw a man, "hunting in the morning, fishing in the afternoon, raising cattle in the evening, and even judging food, without ever being either hunter, fisher, herdsman, or food taster . . ."[42] Between the last days of the old order, however, and the ultimate realization of the new historic period, there lies a time of transition—the "realm of necessity." For this transition period Marx proposed that the old forms of education be retained but modified to meet the needs of the working class.

The modification he proposed was one of combining education with productive work. He gives credit to a British factory owner, Robert Owen, for initiating this idea in his mill at New Lanark, Scotland in 1799. Owen opened a school for the children apprenticed to him by the

[41] In this conception Marx reactivates the Greek idea that "the city educates the man."
[42] On this point see: Horst Wittig, "Philosophical Origins of Communist Pedagogy," *Soviet Survey*, No. 30 (October–December, 1959), pp. 77–81.

poor-law authorities and sought to give them moral, physical, and intellectual training. Said Marx:

> From the factory system budded, as Robert Owen has shown us in detail, the germ of the education of the future, an education that will, in the case of every child over a given age, combine productive labour with instruction and gymnastics, not only as one of the methods of adding to the efficiency of production, *but as the only method of producing fully developed human beings.*[43]

Marx's objection to the plight of children in the factories was not only that they were overworked but that the work they did was completely uneducative. ". . . The children employed in modern factories and manufactures," he said, "are from their earliest years riveted to the most simple manipulations, and exploited for years, without being taught a single sort of work that would afterwards make them of use, even in the same manufactory or factory."[44] In its essence, Marx's proposal was to implement the original idea of Owen more fully and make it the standard practice in elementary education. In 1866 he prepared a memorandum on education for the German delegation to a meeting of the International Workingmen's Association. In this memorandum he followed the general idea first advanced by Owen. Education was to have three closely related aspects: intellectual education; physical training or gymnastics; and polytechnical training, by which he meant instruction in the scientific principles underlying all production processes, together with instruction in the use of the tools of production. He proposed three levels of schooling and at each level productive work was to be related to the intellectual learning of the children. The first level was for children of the ages from nine to twelve years who would do two hours of productive work in a shop or at home. At the second level there would be four hours of work for children of the ages thirteen and fourteen. The third level would include those up to seventeen years who would do six hours of work each day.[45] Those who have any familiarity with the educational system of the Soviet Union will recognize this as the "polytechnical education" that has played an important part, off and on, in Soviet pedagogical theory and practice and has seen a revival under the educational reforms initiated by Premier Khrushchev beginning in 1958.

[43] *Capital*, pp. 529–530. Italics mine. For Engels' description of the work of Owen at New Lanark see: "Socialism: Utopian and Scientific" in *Selected Works*, Vol. II, pp. 125–126.
[44] *Capital*, p. 530.
[45] I am indebted for the details of this program to Horst Wittig, *op. cit.*, p. 79.

There is reason to believe, however, that in the Soviet Union there is less interest in developing the human personality through a union of intellectual and productive work than there is in producing technicians who will carry farther the industrialization of the country and ensure, if possible, the military superiority of the U.S.S.R.

However that may be, the idea of the fusion of knowing and doing in the form of polytechnical education is surely the most important of Marx's ideas on education. We have already seen enough of his thought on this subject to know that it is at the heart of Marxism's protest against bourgeoise educational practice. As Marx saw it education is not only the tool of the dominant class, it is also the product of the classic philosophical dualism of mind *and* body, idea *and* action. This dualism, as we have already seen in other contexts, seems always to find expression in an educational theory that sets up theoretical, rational learning as the highest and most desirable (and, therefore, that which is appropriate for free men) and then in opposition to it puts active, physical, productive work as low, base, and servile (and, therefore, that which is appropriate for slaves). Marx condemned this educational dualism not only because it was the dominant conception of bourgeoise society, but also because he thought there was evidence of its ineffectiveness. Marx had a very low opinion of the education demanded by the Factory Acts for children working in industries, but even so, he noted with approval a discovery of the factory inspectors that, "the factory children, although receiving only one half the education of the regular day scholars, yet learnt quite as much and often more." He also agreed with the observation of a Mr. Senior, made at a Social Science Conference in 1863, that upper class children waste their time and energies in the long hours of the school that is divorced from any practical activity or productive enterprise.[46]

Marx's idea of combining theoretical and practical activities clearly is consistent with his conception of the knowledge process. We have already seen that he rejected any conception that makes mind merely a spectator of an external reality and insisted that in any act of cognition the object itself is changed. Thus, Marx's operationalism would appear almost by necessity to demand a theory of education that stresses the essentially dynamic interrelatedness of knowing and doing. Since he was confronted with the fact of child labor in factories, and since his major concern was with the economic system, it is perhaps only to be expected that he would work out whatever ideas about

[46] *Capital*, Vol. I, p. 529.

education he might have within the context of the factory system. This, of course, is in contrast to Dewey who, a half century later and in the context of another philosophy of society, worked out the connections of his instrumentalist theory of knowledge with the theory of education. Nevertheless this aspect of the Marxian protest against essentialism is similar to that of Dewey, or, for that matter, to the protest of any theory of education that involves an operational theory of knowledge. Marx did not believe that the purpose of education is one of transmitting information for absorption by learners, apart from any real social contexts, any more than he believed that human labor, when freely performed, is slavish and degrading to the personality. Marx believed that the purpose of education should be to develop the powers inherent in the human organism so that man could become human and live like a man. He did not believe, however, that this could be accomplished so long as capitalism endured because in that historic period the exploration of one man by another is inherent in the nature of things.

This observation brings us to a consideration of the part existing modes of education play in human alienation. As we have already noted, the idea of human alienation in Marx's thought is a tricky one. This is owed partly to the fact that Marx's position with respect to it changed with the maturing of his own thought and partly to a recent preoccupation of various commentators with equating Marx's ideas to certain contemporary views on psychotherapy.[47] We have already seen how Marx criticized Feuerbach's acceptance of a human essence, conceived apart from the complex of social relations that obtain in any historical period. This enabled Feuerbach to explain religion in terms of the essential nature of man and to explain human alienation in terms of man's being torn between an illusory world of perfection, which by his very nature he projects, and the real world of imperfection and suffering in which he finds himself.

Now a little thought will indicate that a somewhat similar case can be made for the alienation of man by traditional modes of education, for these too invariably involve a dualism consisting of a world of pure ideas, universals, forms, etc., that are alleged to be the proper subject matter of education, and a world of process and becoming in which there is no possibility of *truth* or of grasping truth for its own sake, but only of opinion and practical action, which is animal-like and servile.

[47] For example, Erich Fromm, *Marx's Concept of Man*, New York: F. Ungar Publishing Company, 1961.

As is well known, the view of human nature that accompanies the former view is that man in his essence is rational; he is a "rational animal," and any mode of education that centers on practical activity and the union of idea with action, alienates man from himself—since the essence of his selfhood is reason. It is easy to see that this kind of conclusion must be excluded completely in Marxian thought. But it is possible to argue the other way and maintain that classic forms of education alienate man from himself because they create an illusory world of pure thought (universals, essences, "first principles," etc.) and ignore the world of labor and practical activity, which is the real world. Thus, under this view man is alienated because in his education he is torn from the real world to one of illusion. Classical philosophy, and hence classical education, is a distorted projection of man's longing for a world of stability, dependability, and universal truth in the face of his real existence in a world that is precarious, changing, and in many respects unpredictable.

To argue in this vein is to repeat the error Marx found in Feuerbach; it is to escape from the clutches of one absolute only to fall into those of another. The nature, or essence, of man, according to Marx, is a product of historical conditions that can be determined and studied scientifically. In the same sense, the conclusion of classic philosophy that the essence of man is reason is a conclusion that was produced by a determinate set of economic and social relations existing at a particular time in history—namely, in the historic period of slavery in the Hellenic world. It is the product of a class-stratified society in which the mass of men (in the Greek world the slaves and, since the idea was carried over into the middle ages, in the medieval world the serfs) are systematically exploited by the dominant class. The view that the essence of man is reason is the product of the same set of social relations that produced the distinction between liberal and practical education and led Aristotle to the conclusion that some men by their nature are fit only to be slaves. Thus, the dominance of the classical dualism, and its expression in educational policy, together with the splitting of thought from action in labor, are *results* of objective conditions. One is not the cause of the other, for they are all consequences of the economic base that determines the character of a society and its institutions. As with the case of religion, these dualisms will pass away when the conditions that produce them cease to exist. This is to say that they cannot be eliminated until capitalism is eliminated. When true communism is achieved, the dualism of thinking and acting will be gone entirely, but for the "realm of necessity" it will be possible to mitigate its effects by combining intellectual education, physical training, and useful labor in the schools.

In his own protest against educational essentialism, John Dewey and many of his associates had called for a fusion of thinking and acting in the education of children. Dewey advocated the use of active occupations in the school and developed the program of his own laboratory school in terms of a sequence of active enterprises. Dewey, however, gave little weight to the actual production of commodities in the school, whereas Marx did. They both believed that education of the intellect could never be separated from other aspects of development with fruitful results. Marx never worked out in detail either his theory of knowledge or his theory of education as Dewey did, but it is possible for us to see that in certain respects their protests against the reigning tradition are similar. On the other hand, the differences between the two in this respect are as great as the differences between revolutionary socialism and American liberalism. Dewey believed that the school could be a means for social progress and the gradual improvement of society and the common lot of man. But Marx's historical determinism indicates that in any period before the coming of socialism, the school can only be the tool of the dominant class and hence, can have little or no influence in the direction of social reform. The school in the transition from capitalism to socialism, under the dictatorship of the proletariat, can be employed by the proletariat to further the aims of the revolution and eventually to usher in the new era in human society. It is the treasured belief of American liberalism that by bold and thoughtful political action the evils and insufficiencies that characterize the older order can be mitigated and our institutions—including our educational institutions—can be transformed so that they will serve human needs and aspirations. And it is the belief of the liberal that this can be accomplished without social upheaval, violence, and bloodshed. The simple fact is that Marx considered such a belief naive.

SUMMARY: THE MARXIST PROTEST

We have now concluded our brief inquiry into the character of the Marxist protest against the conservative tradition in education and the kind of society of which that tradition is a part. In conducting this inquiry we have traced out in their general formulation certain of the major themes that predominate in Marxist thought. Marx's protest is not aimed exclusively at western conservatism, although it is the outstanding example of what he considered the fundamental rottenness of the bourgeoise society that is destined by history to disappear. His protest is also against what he considered the opportunism and political naivete of liberalism. Needless to say, he thought the perennialist philosophy, whose own protest we have already considered, to be reactionary, inimical to the welfare of the masses, and a dangerous hangover from feudalism. ("The mortgage that the peasant has on heavenly possessions guarantees the mortgage that the bourgeoise has on peasant possessions.")[48] Marxism is thus a conscious protest against the major historic traditions of the west. Purely as an intellectual protest it is provocative enough, but the political reality that it has assumed in the U.S.S.R. is the determining factor in the political character of our world. In this book we have not undertaken any investigation of the social system of the Soviet Union or its educational policies. These are subjects for long and complicated inquiries into matters that go far beyond the possible scope of our efforts here. Sidney Hook has characterized Marxism as "an ambiguous legacy" and truly this ambiguity seems reason enough to make us doubt that Marx could either have predicted the course of events that took place in Russia in this century or that he would approve of what developed there.

The fact that there are numerous insufficiencies, obscurities, and outright errors in Marx's writings has been documented in numerous sources and it is not within our purpose to repeat them at length in this brief chapter. It must suffice here to indicate a few of the major difficulties inherent in the Marxian tradition. First, Marx's theory of history, which was one of his most important contributions, has shown itself inadequate as a means of interpreting the events of this century. The power of any scientific theory, and it should be remembered that Marx considered his interpretation of history to be scientific, lies in its predictive powers and only secondarily in its power to account for events that have already occurred. As has been pointed out many times, Marx's theory has been inadequate to predict that a communist revolution would occur in Russia when it did and subsequently that one would occur in China. In fact, revolutions of this kind should never have occurred in either place, since at the time of both revolutions those countries were not well advanced into the industrial age nor into capitalistic economy. According to a fundamental principle of Marxism,

48 Marx, "The Class Struggles in France, 1848–1850," *Selected Works*, Vol. I, p. 187.

no social order ever perishes until all the productive forces inherent in it have developed, but not by the widest stretch of the imagination could this be thought to be true of either China or Russia at the time revolutions occurred in those countries. This failure of prediction in itself is sufficient to require us to doubt the correctness and the usefulness of Marx's historical determinism.

In the second place, Marx's conception of the class-stratification of society as being a function purely of the economic base is now seen as an over-simplification. This is not said as a denigration of Marx's contributions to scientific sociology, to which full credit is regularly given by social scientists who are not Marxists and who therefore do not think Marx said the last word about the origin and nature of social classes. Contemporary sociology recognizes the existence of class stratification but finds it far more complex than the simple polarity of an all-powerful owning class of capitalists and an increasingly impoverished proletariat. Granted that economics is closely related to class structure, it still does not follow that all class structure and all class relations are determined simply by the forces of economic production. The nature of social stratification is an empirical question and, while Marx believed that his analysis of it was indeed scientific, with the perspective now available to us it is apparent that there was a kind of economic mystique inherent in his thought that in many respects effectively obscured the complexity of human relations as they existed in his time and as he predicted they would be in the future.

Third, it now seems clear that Marx completely underestimated the potency of politics and particularly the power of political democracy. It will be recalled that, according to his view, politics is a part of the superstructure that develops on the economic base of a historical period and, thus, the character of political life is determined by that base and cannot function in independence of it. In other words, political power can never be disassociated from economic power. Perhaps it is true that politics are never separate from economics, but the history of the present century shows, among other things, that, at least in America, trade unionism did succeed in improving the working conditions and remuneration of factory workers, that the horrors of child labor in industry were eliminated, that the mass of working people—the proletariat—have improved their lot significantly instead of becoming increasingly impoverished and wretched. And, it is submitted, these have been achieved almost entirely by political means and without bloodshed. Certainly they have been achieved by means that are far short of revolutionary. This is not to say that all problems are solved. Unemployment still seems to be a built-in feature of modern capitalism, although the amount of it today is far short of what it should be under Marx's predictions. Poverty and economic misery are still present in our own country which is the richest nation ever to exist. Support for public education varies greatly from state to state and is cruelly meager in some parts of the nation. The successes we have had, however, give us reason to believe that these difficulties also can be made to yield to resolute and dedicated effort that is essentially political in character. In view of all this, what can we say about the Marxist protest—is it completely false?

In thinking about this, let us consider that nobody ever asks whether Plato is true or false. In fact, we would regard the question of whether Platonic philosophy is true or false as completely fatuous. There is not much question but that we could say the same thing about Plato that was said about Marx a few paragraphs above, namely, that Plato's writings also contain many insufficiencies, obscurities, and outright errors. The value of a philosophy lies in the power it has to help us think for ourselves about the great problems and issues of our own age. It is this enormous potency in Platonic thought that has kept it alive and vital for nearly three thousand years, and it is this same quality in Marx that keeps his thought alive, in spite of all the outrages that have been committed in the name of it. The real question is whether in the great protest that Marx raised against the character of western society and its institutions anything remains that is pertinent to our own times—specifically to our educational problems. The answer to be given here is in the affirmative.

In the first place, although we have a long history of dedication to the idea of free, universal education, we apparently still have to learn that in America educational opportunity is linked closely to class status. It is true that our conceptions of social class stratification are different from those of Marx and undoubtedly more accurate, but the fact remains that for the mass of children the amount and kind of education they will receive and the life work they will pursue is determined in considerable measure by the social class into which they are born. To admit this goes directly against the basic instincts of a majority of Americans, but the fact is so well documented as to be beyond argument. It has long been a commonplace of educational sociology that the American public school is thoroughly middle-class in its orientation and that it discriminates systematically against lower-class children, usually unconsciously and, therefore, unusually effectively. The plight of the Negro child in the slum school is the most dramatic example of this in our time, but it is only one example. This is not the place to record statistics about high school drop-outs, the few Negroes and other members of submerged minority groups enrolled in institutions of higher learning, and the lack of opportunity for these people to enter the learned professions. But until we have put our own house in order, we will do well to ponder Marx's biting question addressed to the German Workers Party in 1875:

> Is it believed that in present-day society . . . education can be *equal* for all classes? Or is it demanded that the upper classes also shall be compulsorily reduced to the modicum of education . . . that alone is compatible with the economic conditions not only of the wage-workers but of the peasants as well?[49]

In the second place, whether Marx was right about the source of human alienation or not, the fact remains that this is one of the realities of our own day and Marx's description of it comes close to matching the clinical accounts of psychotherapists. The loss of a feeling of self-identity on the part of modern man is a theme that is treated in somewhat different ways by those of varying philosophical viewpoints. We have already seen that Dewey considered it mainly in terms of the need to develop a new individualism that would be in the modern age what the old individualism was historically. In the next chapter we will see that the existentialists handle it entirely differently. It may well be that the loss of identity in the modern world is not a function of capitalism, which is what Marx thought it was, but a product of *industrial society*, which does not necessarily have to be equated with capitalism—as in the Soviet Union, for example. Marx's observations on the effects of machines on factory production, the routinization of human effort in productive work, and the dehumanizing effects of it, were acute. Yet he did not know the production-line techniques that have transformed the industrial processes of our own day nor did he anticipate the emergence of the "automatic factory" in which active human labor is reduced to the vanishing point. It has long been fashionable for critics to point out that Marx failed to anticipate or to predict this or that occurrence. And certainly in many ways this is correct. He foresaw the proletariat as becoming increasingly impoverished and reduced to the verge of penury and starvation. What he did not foresee is the modern industrial worker who performs the motions of an automaton

[49] *Selected Works*, Vol. II, p. 34.

for forty hours a week on an assembly line and spends his "free" time with a can of beer while squatting in front of a television set. It seems a fair question to ask, who is the more alienated? We will no doubt do well to remember Marx's bitter observation, "The animal becomes the human and the human the animal."

We can already foresee a time when a large percentage of the population will not engage in productive work, because this work will be done by machines. In fact, we have already been told that an electronic computer can do the work of a high school graduate. Yet, there is little evidence that we have any conception of what this means for our educational efforts or what will be required of the school in the times ahead. There seems little doubt that with respect to this question educational essentialism is completely without resources and, in their present state, the other traditions we have considered thus far lend little, if any more, assistance. It may be, of course, that the following lines from *Capital* are simply oracular and, therefore, may mean whatever they are interpreted to mean, but in the brave, new world that lies ahead, we are certain to have our own encounter with the fact that, "the relations connecting the labor of one individual with that of the rest appear, not as direct social relations between individuals at work, but as what they really are, material relations between persons and social relations between things."

There remains only to be mentioned Marx's protest against the arbitrary division of theory and practice which, in educational terms, is seen so clearly in the bifurcation of learning into liberal and practical. We have already discussed this kind of protest in other contexts and there is little that can be added at this point. Marx took a unitary view of human nature, believing that ideas are inseparably united with action. He sketched in outline—but only in outline—a system of education that would unite thinking and doing in the form of productive work. If his ideas on this subject are outmoded, it is because the industrialism he knew is outmoded. He did not advocate "polytechnical" education in order simply to produce mechanics and technicians, rather, he said, it is the only way to produce complete human beings. In this he is reminiscent of Rousseau, who at an earlier time had said in a famous book on educational theory:

> Instead of making a child stick to his books, if I employ him in a workshop, his hands labor to the profit of his mind; he becomes a philosopher, but fancies he is only a workman.[50]

[50] Jean J. Rousseau, *Emile*, trans., William H. Payne, New York: D. Appleton and Company, 1898, p. 153.

CHAPTER TWELVE

The Existentialist Protest

*And, to say all in a word, everything which belongs
to the soul is a dream and vapor, and life is a warfare
and a stranger's sojourn, and after-fame is oblivion.
What then is that which is able to conduct a man?*

—MARCUS AURELIUS

About the time of the ending of World War II, Americans began to
be aware that new developments in philosophical thought were taking
place in Europe. The early harbingers of these events reached our
shores largely in the form of literary works—stories, novels, and plays—
by certain French writers. These writings usually had an alien, somewhat gamey flavor that made them provocative and intriguing, as well
as difficult to understand. This new movement went under the name
of "existentialism" and in the early days this term mostly raised the
vision in Americans of Left-Bank bohemianism and drinkers of absinthe.
The major themes of the existentialist writers were dim and murky
with anxiety, despair, death and alienation predominating. It was
thought in the beginning that these woeful expressions were simply
the result of the horrors of a great war and the disillusionment and disenchantment that inevitably are the aftermath of such upheavals. In
time, however, it began to be known that existentialism was more than
a literary cult, in fact, much more. The realization developed that,
fundamentally, existentialism represents an approach to philosophy that
dates back well into the nineteenth century and one that is different
both from the classic, system-building approach and from the contemporary analytic schools. The effects of existentialist thought began to

Marcus Aurelius, *Meditations*, quoted in B. A. G. Fuller, *A History of Philosophy*,
New York: Henry Holt and Company, 1938, p. 234.

390

be felt in the field of theology, and perhaps with good reason, since some of its main historic roots lie in that area. It also made its presence felt in psychology, particularly in the field of psychotherapy.

In the American world of academic philosophy, however, existentialism has not fared as well. The interests of American philosophers have for more than a generation revolved mainly around technical, analytical work, particularly with analysis of language and with logic and scientific method. This preoccupation of academic philosophers with such technical and abstruse matters in many ways has been fruitful for the philosophical enterprise, but it has also caused the philosopher to lose touch with the rest of mankind—even with those men who are intelligent and educated, but who have not been trained in the rigors of philosophical analysis and who, therefore, usually do not know what contemporary philosophers are talking about. In too many cases they have come to the conclusion that they could not care less. Given some encouragement, however, a considerable portion and perhaps all of mankind is incurably philosophical. Mr. Crane Brinton, for example, has observed that it is as hopeless to ask people to do without metaphysics as it is to ask them to do without sex relations.[1] People are not simply "interested in" the character of the universe in which they live and the relation they have to the scheme of things; they are *concerned* with these matters. They are not only concerned in their own amateur ways with the historic categories of philosophy—with ontology and epistemology and ethics—they are also concerned, as the existentialists have demonstrated, with themselves. And this concern with the character of one's own existence is different in certain important respects from the concerns of either the classic or the modern traditions in philosophy. The question of the nature of *existence* or *being* has been a matter of debate ever since the birth of western philosophy, and the development of this question has usually taken the form of great speculative systems of metaphysics in which the nature of man himself has been reduced to some essence that in itself not only *describes* the nature of man but also *prescribes* it. Man, thus, is reduced by the philosophers to an abstraction. But something apparently keeps telling common men, and perhaps also philosophers in their unguarded moments, that the real problem of existence is not one of abstraction and essences, but the problem of *my* existence, *here* in this world. The existentialist approach to philosophy is in agreement with this common feeling, or intuition, or

[1] *The Shaping of the Modern Mind,* New York: The New American Library of World Literature, Inc., 1953, p. 13.

whatever it is. Thus, in a sense, existentialism proposes to do what Socrates did for the philosophy of his own time, namely to abandon physical nature as the center of interest and the attempt to develop some all-encompassing scheme to explain everything and, instead, to make *man* the central concern of philosophy. "Know thyself" was Socrates' admonition. "The unexamined life is not worth living." And in a much later day we find one of the leading figures in modern philosophical thought, Karl Jaspers, saying, "Man is everything." If existentialism is capable of being defined, and there is some question whether it can be, it is possible only to say that as philosophy it is concerned with the actual character of human existence and the calling of men to a realization of their essential freedom.

As we come to our inquiry into the general character of the existentialist protest, we are confronted immediately with two major difficulties. In the case of the traditions with which we have dealt up to now—and this holds true whether these are educational or philosophical traditions—we have been able to work, at least for the most part, with well developed, systematic bodies of thought. We have been able, therefore, to develop reasonably systematic surveys of the ideas involved, to indicate certain lines of argument, and to come to reasoned philosophical and educational conclusions on the basis of the argument. It is important for us to realize in the beginning that with existentialism this is exceedingly difficult. Existentialism is not *a philosophy* in the sense that idealism or pragmatism may be said to be. It is not systematic in the usual sense of that word and it has no ambitions to become so. In fact, one of the major protests of existentialist thought against traditional philosophy is that conventional philosophers have sold out everything—particularly man—to the interests of some system. It is sometimes said that existentialism is an approach to philosophy rather than a system of philosophical thought. This view is somewhat clearer, but there is a question as to whether even this observation is really adequate. Existentialist philosophers, as might be expected, are, above all, individualists. There is some commonality of thematic material among them, but each approaches a theme in his own way, and its development in the hands of one man is usually very different from that of another. Thus, our first major difficulty is that our inquiry into existential philosophy simply cannot have the relatively neat intellectual character of our previous efforts.

The second difficulty has to do with the fact that almost nothing has been said in the primary literature of existentialism about education. It is a broad generalization to say that no major figure in existential philosophy has had anything significant to say about education, yet it is true. There simply is no indication that educational policy is regarded by existentialists as important. Existential thought has much in it that is directly relevant to religion and to what in the broad sense, at least, we would call psychology, but of education there is little said directly. Why this should be so is a provocative question to which the present author has no good answer. As a general rule, the great names in western philosophy have found something, and some of them have found considerable, to say about educational matters. In our previous inquiries we have been able to locate specific connections of one kind or another between philosophical ideas and educational ideas. In the present context, however, this is not going to be easy. We will either have to draw inferences of our own with respect to the relation of existential thought to educational policy, or to consider the inferences drawn by others. This is probably not very satisfactory, but it is the best we can manage.

In this chapter we will do the following things. First, we will give brief attention to the historical development of the existentialist tradition in philosophy so we may have some grasp of its general character. Secondly, we will consider some of the major themes of contemporary existentialism and the ways in which they have been developed. And last, we will consider what these matters may indicate for educational thought. In adopting this procedure, of course, we are again giving up the pattern of analysis we have used for all the traditions except Marxism. In our procedure we have begun with the specific educational ideas involved in a tradition and then gone on from them to more abstract matters. In most cases we have had before us a real school or a body of practice that served as a model; for example, the existing elementary and secondary schools of the conservative tradition or the historic Laboratory School of the Deweyan tradition. With the existentialists this is impossible. Where is there to be found an "existentialist school"? For that matter, does the term "existentialist school" make any sense? Perhaps it does, but if it does, we are left with the task of making our own model. Whatever this may turn out to be, it is certain that its nature must reflect in some way the historic character of existentialist thought, a matter that will engage our attention in the next section of this chapter.

THE DEVELOPMENT OF EXISTENTIALISM

In our brief sally into the history of existentialist thought, we will consider the contributions of four men who are generally conceded to be major figures in existentialism. They are: Soren Kierkegaard (1813–1855), Friedrich Nietzsche (1844–1900), Martin Heidegger (1899–   ), and Jean-Paul Sartre (1905–   ). We will have occasion to consider other names also but, in general, our attention will be addressed to these four. Modern existentialism is generally thought of as beginning with Kierkegaard, but it is possible to find the development of existential themes in much earlier sources. Certain portions of the Bible, the Book of Ecclesiastes, for example, express ideas that have recognizable existentialist content. The same may be said for certain parts of the works of St. Augustine and of Blaise Pascal, the French mathematician and philosopher. The Russian writer Fyodor Dostoevsky also is often considered to be a forerunner of existentialism and his "Notes from Underground" are thought by many to be a rich mine of existentialist thought. It was the thought of Kierkegaard, however, that more than anything else started the modern trend, and we will begin our account with him.

By conventional standards, Kierkegaard's life was a tragic failure. Physically, he was deformed by a hunchback. His constitution was frail and he suffered from chronic illness. Psychologically, he was introverted and solitary. He did not achieve the ordinary felicities of family life, though he seemed to long for them throughout his life. In a single act of self-denial he broke his engagement with a young woman whom he loved deeply and the consequences of this act never left him. It is a fairly common interpretation to hold that the character of Kierkegaard's thought is a direct product of his physical abnormalities and perhaps of his psychological crippling.[2] However this may be, in the present context we are interested in the *grounds* on which Kierkegaard's thought rests and not on the causes of it.[3]

Kierkegaard's thought was a protest and one of the greatest, matched perhaps in the modern age only by that of Marx. It was a protest not only against the age in which he himself lived, but also against the historical continuum that led up to it. In a sense, his protest was two-pronged—against philosophy (he did not consider himself a philoso-

---

[2] For example, Theodor Haecker, *Kierkegaard, The Cripple*, trans. C. V. O. Bruyn, London: The Harvill Press, 1948.
[3] This distinction is important and was first pointed out in Chapter V of the present volume.

pher) and against conventional religion. Insofar as philosophy is concerned, Hegel was for him the arch enemy. Yet Hegel was only the leading representative in the nineteenth century of the whole fallacious tendency of classic philosophy to submerge the individual and make of him only an abstraction, whose identity rests in the fact that he is a part of something more all-embracing. This idea may have had its highest development in the hands of Hegel, but his conclusions were implicit in the whole course of western philosophy.

In an instructive piece of analysis of Kierkegaard's protest, Mr. William Barrett[4] has observed that there are two ways to react to Kant's analysis of the term *being*. Kant had maintained that there seems to be no real way to conceive of *being*. It is possible to think of a thing, a table or a lamp, for example, and then think of the table or the lamp existing, but nothing seems to be added to the first concept by the addition of the concept of being. Therefore, Kant concluded, to predicate existence of a thing adds nothing and, in fact, it appears there is no way of conceiving of being as simply being. Barrett's point is that one way of reacting to this conclusion is that of the positivists and other scientific philosophers. In the view of these people, knowledge is operational—it is *about* something that is capable of being observed and manipulated. Existence is obviously something that it is not possible to observe or experiment with and, therefore, the positivists gave it up, calling it and all such matters metaphysical and hence superfluous.

Kierkegaard's reaction was diametrically opposite. It may be that existence cannot be conceived rationally, but if this is so it is not because it is amorphous and vague. It is because it is so immediate and enveloping that mind cannot cope with it. Therefore, I do not know *existence*. I *experience* it. It is the reality of the self. Existence is had, and the supreme manifestation of this having is when man is confronted with the necessity of choice. This is a major theme in Kierkegaard's thought and in modern existentialism. Thus, the main elements in Hegel's idealism that Kierkegaard attacked are objectivity and determinism. We have already considered in the chapter on idealism some of the main elements in the Hegelian system. In this system the dialectical workings of the Absolute are objectified in the phenomenal world. The world process is all-inclusive and completely logical in its character. Whatever happens in history *must* happen. Whatever is, is right. If the

---

[4] *Irrational Man: A Study in Existentialist Philosophy*, Garden City, New York: Doubleday and Company, 1958. My references are to the paperback edition published in 1962. On the point referred to above, see page 158 ff.

world is itself the necessary unfolding of the Idea, then what happens to individual freedom? It would appear that the only answer is that what we call individual freedom is simply our awareness and acceptance of necessity. To Kierkegaard this is the most repugnant conclusion it is possible to reach. Such a conclusion closes the door forever on the possibility of freedom of the self to choose in an uncertain world in which genuine possibilities exist. And so, in opposition to Hegel's objectivity of history, Kierkegaard emphasizes the essentially subjective existence of the individual and his passionate involvement in his existence. To the determinism of Hegel he opposes the freedom of the individual to choose and the necessity of this choosing, together with the individual's awareness of the crucial character of his choice.

Aside from Hegel and classic philosophy, Kierkegaard's major target for criticism was organized Christianity, and his protest was against the Danish State Church of his time. He thought, as we have seen, that the net effect of western philosophy had been to submerge the individual in the Absolute, to deny the validity of subjective truth, and to obscure the reality of individual experiences. In its own way, organized religion had done the same thing. When Greek rationalism, which insisted that the only truth is objective truth, was synthesized with Christianity, religion itself fell victim to a rationalistic reductionism. Theology became a matter of proving propositions through rational argument, and faith, which emphasizes the commitment of the individual, had to assume a secondary role. Further, the church as an institution was ignoring the individual subjective element that is always paramount in religious experience. It was engulfing the individual and the realities of his own experience. "Man," Kierkegaard said, "has forgotten what it is to be a Christian."

Religious truth can never be grasped merely through reason. There is, in fact, in Christianity a paradox that reason can never comprehend, much less resolve. Basic to the Christian creed is the idea that God, *the eternal*, revealed Himself *in time* in the person of his Son, Jesus. In the light of reason this is a contradiction. It is absurd. Yet this is the basic tenet of the Christian faith for without it there is no Christianity. For Kierkegaard, therefore, there can be no rational resolution of the paradox inherent in Christian doctrine and what is left is faith. But faith, itself, is a response to uncertainty; to have faith means to choose and, hence, to take a risk. By faith is meant that there is an inherent contradiction between the inward passion of the self and the uncertainty of objective truth. However, when man places himself in this relationship to God he is *in* truth—which also may appear to us of a later day to be absurd, since it places a different meaning on truth from that to which we are accustomed.

Kierkegaard, however, would remind us that we are victims of the belief that truth is a matter of group opinion—of the crowd. In this view, one only has the truth, so to speak, when he has the crowd on his side. This is Kierkegaard's blow against mass society and the creeping "groupiness" we have come to know so well in our own day, but it is also more than that. By "crowd" he means not only the mass of society in the 1850s or, for that matter, in the 1960s, to which men give their allegiance and which, in turn, determines their ideas and their concepts of the truth. The "crowd" is also the whole body of doctrine which holds that to be a man means to belong to a species of rational animals. Given this view, says Kierkegaard, there are no individuals, only specimens. To be with the crowd is to be in *untruth*. Truth, for him, lies in the individual's own unique experience. In this sense it is subjective, for man always stands alone. His existence precedes his essence.[5]

The fundamental condition of man Kierkegaard finds to be one of despair. This is a universal condition. He says that just as in the medical sense no man is ever completely healthy, so there is no man who is outside despair. The only possible exception is the true Christian (i.e., the man who stands completely in the relation to God that Kierkegaard defined as true Christianity). But even the devout Christian, who is not completely the true Christian, is also in despair. Kierkegaard describes despair in such terms as: "disquietude, a perturbation, a discord, an anxious dread of an unknown something, or of a something he does not even dare to make acquaintance with . . ."[6]

Despair is the sickness unto death, but this is not to be taken in the usual literal sense we mean when we speak of a mortal sickness in which death is the last phase of illness. To the Christian, death is not the last thing, for it is the beginning of life in eternity. The agony of despair consists in not being able to die. The self cannot die of despair in the sense that the body can die as a result of illness. According to Kierkegaard, despair takes three forms: despair at not being conscious of selfhood; despair at not being willing to be oneself; despair at willing to be oneself. The investigation of these modes of despair con-

---

[5] On this point see Kierkegaard's "That Individual," reprinted in Walter Kaufmann, ed., *Existentialism from Dostoevsky to Sartre*, New York: Meridian Books, 1956, pp. 92–99.
[6] *The Sickness Unto Death*, trans. Walter Lowie, Garden City, New York: Doubleday and Company, Inc., 1954, p. 155.

stitutes Kierkegaard's most remarkable treatise on human psychology.[7] The terrible feeling of despair is the price we pay for our existence as conscious selves in a world in which all things are possible. But the experience of anguish and dread is not morbid, for it is our experience of freedom.

We may summarize Kierkegaard's original and extremely important contributions to existentialist philosophy under three major categories. First, there is Kierkegaard's interpretation of the essentially subjective nature of human existence; his insistence on the complete freedom of the individual to choose and to become what he wills himself to become; his consequent denial of determinism and of the priority of essence over existence. Secondly, there is his protest against institutionalized Christianity that seeks to understand and make clear that which is paradoxical and absurd and therefore outside the possibility of human reason. The church is an institution that engulfs men as individuals, encouraging them to act like sheep, effectively preventing them from the personal encounter with God that is the only true religious experience. Third, there is Kierkegaard's analysis of the human condition as being one of despair and anxiety, at the root of which lies the necessity for choice in a world that is completely undetermined. These three themes have been taken up and developed in various ways in contemporary existentialism and, therefore, we will return to them again. Before we come to consider the character of the existentialist philosophy of our own day, however, we must give some attention to the contributions of another historical figure, the German philosopher Friedrich Nietzsche.

Nietzsche was without doubt one of the authentic geniuses of the nineteenth century, but his genius often was as erratic as it was brilliant. His intellectual development was precocious. He assumed the university chair in classical philology at Basel when he was only twenty-four years of age. This in itself was a remarkable achievement. Like Kierkegaard, Nietzsche suffered ill health throughout his life and in the end he was engulfed in a hopeless insanity. As in the case of Kierkegaard, we can hardly escape attributing the restless, passionate, often tragic character of his philosophy to the structure of his own personality and the tragic events of his own life. Neitzsche's philosophy, however, is far more than simply the expression of a tormented soul, although it certainly is that. Neitzsche foresaw with great clarity the problems that were to haunt man in the twentieth century, problems that many of us have not even faced up to, much less solved. His statement of and

[7] *Loc. cit.*

reactions to these problems is one of the great contributions to modern philosophy and their influence on the development of contemporary, existentialism is decisive. In our brief overview here we will consider three major thematic elements: his atheism, his ethical relativism, and "the will to power."

In Nietzsche, as in Kierkegaard, there is a basic religious theme, but this theme received a very different treatment by Nietzsche. Kierkegaard was a profoundly religious man who attacked conventional organized religion because, in his judgment, it prevented the individual's confrontation of God and thus made real religious experience impossible. Nietzsche's reaction to the character of religion in the nineteenth century was different. The awful fact, he said, is that God is dead and we have killed him. There was nothing novel about atheism in Nietzsche's time, but his development of the consequences of "the death of God" in the modern world is overwhelming. In the second chapter of this book it was pointed out that a fundamental conflict exists in modern culture because in the post-medieval world the older supernatural view of man and the world is in direct conflict with other traditions that deny such a view. The further point was made that in the medieval world institutionalized religion—the church—was the great universal institution that formed the community of western man. In our analysis we attributed the breakup of this community to the development of new, conflicting traditions, and one of the most potent of these was natural science. And so we may say that with our science we have killed God. We must, however, enlarge the meaning of "science" so that it extends beyond the currently restricted sense of that term. We have killed God with reason, with rationalistic philosophies, as well as with rationalistic science. We have killed Him with our pretensions to objective truth. Kierkegaard believed the church had killed religion, but he believed that God exists and can be known, although not in the formalistic sense that the church prescribed. Nietzsche went beyond and insisted that religion is dead because God is dead. From now on, each of us is on his own. We are no longer cuddled up with each other in an all-embracing community in which our fears and anxieties are sublimated and made to go away. We are on our own—whether we know it or not.

A major reaction of modern civilization to all this is that if we will only stop thinking about it, it will go away. The conservative tradition, for example, proceeds in the belief that there is no real contradiction between the older supernaturalism and the new universe of science.

Conservatism seeks to make science (in the broad sense) a kind of sub-department of God. What the conservative tradition does not know—or, at least, is unable to admit—is that the sub-department has destroyed the whole establishment, and all that is left is the *individual*. In his most powerful exposition of these events, Nietzsche portrays a madman who runs about in the market place crying, "I seek God! I seek God!" Various people, who do not believe in God, make fun of him and ask whether God has got lost or gone on a voyage or is hiding somewhere. But the madman with his frenetic stare ignores their jibes and cries, "Whither is God? I shall tell you. *We have killed him*—you and I."[8] And then come the prophetic words: "Is not the greatness of this deed too great for us? Must not we ourselves become gods simply to seem worthy of it? There has never been a greater deed; and whoever will be born after us—for the sake of this deed he will be part of a higher history than all history hitherto." But the madman saw that the people did not understand him and he ran around to several churches singing requiems for God and when he was asked why he did it, he said, "What are those churches now if they are not the tombs and sepulchers of God?" The men in the market did not believe God exists but they had no apprehension of the awful consequences of the fact that they had killed him. They had yet to learn that when He died all the alleged absolutes of conventional morality died with Him—leaving the individual.

The root of Nietzsche's ethical relativism lies in his prediction that a new episode in history is to begin, an era that will be nihilistic in so far as the old, conventional values are concerned. He thought he saw the beginning of a "more manly, a warlike age," and this age was to be preparatory to a time in which men would "carry heroism into the pursuit of knowledge . . ." For this first new stage of history new men would be required, men of valor and strength of character—in short, men whose character is marked with "style." What will not be needed are the meek conformers, the subscribers to Kant's categorical imperative, which Nietzsche described as "the highest formula of a government official." For men of the new age the imperative is: "Live dangerously." Nietzsche was influenced by the Darwinian conception of nature as evolutionary. In this view, life is in a continuous process of evolutionary development in which new types appear. Nietzsche believed that "the death of God" marked the beginning of a new historical period and the emergence of a "new" man. The fundamental motive of all life is not

[8] "The Gay Science," reprinted in Kaufmann, ed., *op. cit.*, pp. 104–106.

to adjust supinely to the pressures and necessities of the environment. The motive of all life, wherever it is found in nature, is the *will to power*.

In this conception, Nietzsche, who presumably had renounced all metaphysical absolutes of conventional philosophy, appears to invent one of his own. The will to power is not simply the will to self-preservation. It is not the effort to experience pleasure and to avoid pain. Hedonism, Nietzsche maintained, is no answer to the nature of value. It may be true that increase of power and mastery brings feelings of pleasure with it, but pleasure exists and is experienced in the increase of power. Value and power are identical and the ethical principle for man is self-aggrandizement. An approach to ethics that equates value with power recognizes that pain and suffering cannot be avoided for they are necessary elements in the experience of those who live dangerously. What Nietzsche warns us against is the easy pessimism into which hedonists are prone to slip, since they make their value judgments on the basis of pleasure and are therefore appalled by the ubiquity of pain. He warns us also against the trap of conscience, that tool of conventional Christian morality with its mawkish, sentimental approach to morality and its exploitation of feelings of guilt that constitute a sickness in the human mind. The antidote for sickness of the spirit is the will to power. But there is a difficulty here, and apparently Nietzsche never found his way out of it. If the will to power exists only for itself; if power leads only to the striving for more power; do we not come ultimately to the brink of nihilism? If there is a final answer to the problem of nihilism, and perhaps we should admit the possibility that there is none, it is not to be found in the thought of this great precursor of contemporary existentialism.

We have now come to the point at which we will consider the contributions of two contemporary figures to the development of existentialist philosophy. In the case of Heidegger and Sartre we will simply identify the major ideas in their thought and reserve more extended comment on these ideas until we come to the point of examining the leading themes of current existentialism. It will be apparent that the ideas developed by contemporaries bear strong resemblance to those we identified in Kierkegaard and Nietzsche, although their detailed development is often somewhat different. A paramount interest in the philosophy of Heidegger is the philosophical problem of being. In his work with this concept, Heidegger was partly influenced by the German philosopher Edmund Husserl. In this brief account we cannot attempt any consideration of Husserl's influence; however, Heidegger was also influenced by certain ideas we have already encountered in Kierkegaard.

The nature of *being* is the primary concern of that branch of philosophical thought called ontology and Heidegger has maintained that the real purpose of his philosophical studies is to develop a philosophy of *being* rather than a philosophy of existence. There are no trickier words in the philosophical vocabulary than the simple verbs *to be* and *to exist*. The interpretation of the meaning of these terms is one of the perennial problems of western thought. Heidegger's major conclusion with respect to the different ways in which the word "exist" can be used is that it is man alone who can be said *to exist*. Other kinds of things *are* but they do not exist. Trees, rocks, and animals are, says Heidegger, and angels and God also are, but they do not exist. This does not mean necessarily that these things are unreal or illusory; it means that man exists in a way that is different. A fundamental difference is, of course, that man has consciousness.[9] Man can exist authentically, however, only as he dissociates himself from the world in which things merely are, that which in common speech we would call "the everyday world." So long as we remain in this world we are not conscious of our own existence. According to Heidegger the only form of being with which we truly are in contact is the being of man. Man can exist authentically, however, only by undergoing certain kinds of experiences in which he is aware of himself as one who exists. Fundamentally, these experiences are of the kind Kierkegaard had called anguish or anxiety—"the sickness unto death."

In the experience of anguish man sees himself for what he is. He is in the world, but he does not know why he is there. God does not exist and, consequently, the existence of man is forlorn. He has no home nor refuge. And, as was foreshadowed in Kierkegaard, he is existence without essence. In this conclusion, Heidegger, as did Kierkegaard, departs from the well-travelled path of classic philosophy. Both Kierkegaard and Nietzsche had found that human experience was characterized by infinite possibility, although they came to this conclusion by somewhat different routes. But Heidegger emphasizes that the existence of man is limited, that for a time all things may be possible, but this time ends because the existence of man is finite. Death puts an end to all possibility, and all men must die. The authentic person is one who is able to face up resolutely to the fact that his existence is a "being for death."

---

[9] This point is made in Heidegger's "The Way Back into the Ground of Metaphysics," in Kaufmann, ed., *op. cit.*, p. 214.

Hence, for the authentic man the thought of death, though it pervades the whole of human existence, is not morbid, but it does account for the tragic character of the human condition.[10] In Heidegger's view, however, man should pass beyond the condition of anxiety and anguish. The world is unfriendly and it is cruel, but the point is not to attempt to reconcile man, through philosophy or science, with the fact that this is the way things are. The authentic person is one who will face up to the fact of his existence and, through what Heidegger called "the resolute decision," take his destiny into his own hands. This, too, was foreshadowed in Kierkegaard and Nietzsche.

We turn our attention now to the major ideas in the existentialism of Jean-Paul Sartre, the French philosopher. Sartre's thought is better known in the United States than is that of Heidegger. This is partly because Sartre's works have been more generally available in English translations and partly because his literary works, which are built around existentialist themes, have been read widely in this country. One of the fundamental concerns in Sartre's philosophy is the ontological question of being, which we have already seen to be the major concern of Heidegger. Perhaps the most important aspect of Sartre's treatment is his distinction between two forms of being: being-in-itself and being-for-itself. By being-in-itself Sartre means the self-contained being of things. What we in common speech call "objects," that is, trees, stones, chairs, tables, etc. are being-in-itself. They are what they are in themselves. On the other hand being-for-itself is the realm of human consciousness and the essential fact of consciousness is that it is always outside of and ahead of itself. We project ourselves into the future, or perhaps behind into the past, but we are always outside ourselves. In this sense, we transcend ourselves and the being of man is always for itself. If this were not true, we would simply be being-in-itself. It will be noted that this dualism of being in Sartre is in some ways comparable to the dualism developed by Descartes, which we considered earlier in this book. There is also a resemblance between Sartre's being-for-itself as the realm of consciousness and Heidegger's principle of transcendence or "passing beyond" ourselves.

Sartre restates and makes an important part of his philosophy the theme we have already discovered in Kierkegaard: existence precedes essence. Sartre completely disavows the idea that there is some universal

---

[10] For a discussion of Heidegger's position on this point see: Robert G. Olson, *An Introduction to Existentialism*, New York: Dover Publications, Inc., 1962, pp. 197–201.

concept "Man" that exists prior to the existence of particular men and determines their nature. What this means, Sartre says, is that "man exists, turns up, appears on the scene, and only afterwards, defines himself."[11] There is no universal idea of human nature because there is nothing to conceive it. God does not exist and, therefore, the idea of man does not exist in the mind of God. Man is whatever he conceives himself to be, and whatever he may become is whatever he wills himself to become. Said Sartre, "Man is nothing else but what he makes of himself. *Such is the first principle of existentialism.*"[12] It is important to understand that not only is man free to choose what he will become, but he is also *responsible* for what he chooses to become. At the beginning of this chapter we adopted a definition of existential philosophy that indicated two objectives for existentialism: an examination and analysis of the nature of human existence *and* the calling of men's attention to the fact of their freedom *and its consequences.* This second part of the definition receives powerful development in the hands of Sartre.

The conditions of existence are not only that man is whatever he has chosen to be, but that whenever we choose we are not choosing only for ourselves, *but for all mankind* and, therefore, the responsibility we inescapably bear is far greater than merely choosing for ourselves. "In fact," Sartre says, "in creating the man that we want to be, there is not a single one of our acts which does not at the same time create an image of man as we think he ought to be."[13] Whenever we choose, the choice made is one we affirm to be good. Choosing is never the simple matter of distinguishing good from evil and choosing one or the other. We are incapable of choosing evil, anyway, and so our choices are made among competing goods. According to Sartre, "We always choose the good, and nothing can be good for us without being good for all." This being the case, the responsibility that weighs on all men is simply incalculable, and it is this fact that is the source of anguish, anxiety and despair. Like Kierkegaard, Sartre believes that there is no man outside the condition of anguish and despair. There are, of course, people who do not exhibit the obvious clinical symptoms of anxiety, but they are hiding their anxiety and running away from it. Even when we attempt to discuss the crucial character of our decisions and maintain we are choosing only for ourselves, we are lying and in so doing we choose the lie for all mankind.

11 *Existentialism,* trans. Bernard Frechtman, New York; Philosophical Library, 1947, p. 13.
12 *Loc. cit.* Italics mine.   13 *Op. cit.,* p. 20.

PHILOSOPHY OF AMERICAN EDUCATION

Like Nietzsche, and subsequently Heidegger, Sartre is an atheist. For him, the root of human anxiety is in the fact that man exists, must choose, and does not find God present to put the responsibility on. But Sartre insists that the non-existence of God is not a matter for rejoicing among existentialists, and they do not stoop to cheap tricks to get rid of Him. Sartre comments wryly, "The existentialist is strongly opposed to a certain kind of secular ethics which would like to abolish God with the least possible expense."[14] In some ways, perhaps, it would be better if God did exist. His existence would make possible a universe of permanent and dependable values. The real point of the non-existence of God, Sartre says, is exactly the way Dostoevsky put it, "If God didn't exist, everything would be possible." As the existentialist sees it, this is the situation precisely: God does not exist; everything is possible; consequently, man is in despair, for there is nothing to which he can cling. Therefore, *man is condemned to be free. Condemned* is a strong word, but it is the right one to use because man did not create himself and did not ask to be thrown into the world, but when he is in the world he is faced with the necessity of choice and the necessity for shouldering the responsibility for what he chooses. Thus, Sartre continues the theme that is a major one in existentialist philosophy—indeterminism. Man's nature is not predetermined by any universal; existence comes first, and the behavior of man is not determined. He is what he chooses to be.

THE PROTEST OF EXISTENTIALISM

We have now concluded our historical survey of the development of existential philosophy. In our survey we have confined our efforts to the thought of two important figures in the nineteenth century, Kierkegaard and Nietzsche, and to two contemporary philosophers, Heidegger and Sartre. There are, of course, other men who have played important roles in developing the existentialism of our own time, but there is wide agreement among students of this philosophical tradition that the contributions of the men to which we have given our attention form the basis of existential philosophy. It is our purpose in this chapter to consider the nature of the protest that existentialism makes against the character of modern society and its institutions, particularly, of course, the protest of existentialism against western conservatism. Our ultimate objective is to assess what the protest of existentialism means for educa-

[14] *Ibid.*, p. 25.

tional ideas. In this next part of our inquiry, therefore, we are going to consider three themes that are major elements in contemporary existentialism, and the point of our analysis is one of seeing how these themes constitute protests against the established tradition.

The Human Situation

As anyone knows who reads the papers and the popular magazines, ever since the close of World War II there has been a steady outpouring of sentiment about the fact that this is "the age of anxiety." It is customary for various kinds of evidence to be brought out to prove why this should be so. Certain horrible events of the war—the death camps, the gas chambers, the reeking piles of burning human bodies—show that what we are pleased to call civilization is simply a very thin and fragile veneer that, being stripped away, reveals underneath the savagery and brutality that is human nature. It was during this same war that what may well be the "ultimate weapon" emerged—or at least its ancestor did. Crude and inefficient as this ancestor may have been by contemporary standards of technology, it was sufficient to destroy two great cities in a matter of seconds and hence to change forever the character of warfare. Only shortly after the end of this war, technologists succeeded in partially freeing an object from the earth's gravitational field and sent it spinning in an orbit around the earth. The fact that this feat was first achieved by Russians instead of by Americans was an occasion for the development of a profound mass anxiety in the United States. On the basis of these facts, and many others we will not pause to mention, the conclusion is reached that our age of anxiety is unique. Man is afraid of other men, but more and more *he is afraid of himself.* He now has the means to destroy himself completely—and perhaps he will. Thus, it is said, living under such awful and unprecedented conditions as these, we are prone to anxiety and all the classic symptoms of this malady are everywhere to be seen. Our fears are not merely rational and therefore concrete. The fears of our age are in many respects insubstantial, irrational, and without any discernable reference. They are of the free-floating kind, accounts of which fill the notebooks of every psychiatrist. What all this argument boils down to—if it boils down to anything—is that the anxiety of our time is a response, although a neurotic response, to certain objective conditions which lie for the most part outside the self and are explainable, therefore, in terms of the cause-effect relations of behavioristic psychology or the psychodynamics of the Freudian schools of psychology. The existentialist, however, has a different account.

Existentialism, by and large, is willing to agree that the condition of contemporary man is forlorn, that he is in despair and anguish. But what makes contemporary man think he has any private option on this condition? Kierkegaard described the human condition of anguish and despair with a passion and power that probably never will be equaled, yet he knew nothing of megaton bombs and "overkill." William James, who, it is often said, comes the nearest of any American philosopher to existentialism, spoke of "metaphysical wonder" and "cosmic sickness." Yet in his day men were still politely shooting at each other with cannon. Ours certainly is not the first age of history in which the threat of mass-annihilation was a reality. The Black Death killed more men than atomic or nuclear weapons have, and its workings were as mysterious to medieval man as those of a hydrogen bomb are to most people today. It may be, of course, that crises in society in various historical periods serve to bring to the fore philosophical thought that emphasizes the plight of the individual caught in the net of circumstance. This was true, for example, of the Stoic philosophy that developed in the declining years of the Roman Empire. It is one thing to say, however, that social crisis emphasizes and calls our attention to the unique condition of man and quite another to say that it is the cause of it. In the view of existentialism, one of our major difficulties is that we are prey to the hedonistic ethic Nietzsche warned against. In this view of ethics, happiness is the ultimate end and is equatable with pleasure, which itself has materialistic origins. Poor men think they would be happy if they were only rich, but when they become rich they find they are not. Hungry men think they would be happy if only they had food in abundance, but the satiation of hunger does not bring happiness. Insecure men think they would be happy if they only had financial security, but when they attain that security they are restless and bored to the point of nausea. Mr. Ralph Harper in considering these same matters concludes that ". . . the materialistic ideas of the nineteenth century are as good as achieved. And this, of all times, is the time for the greatest anxiety, mass anxiety."[15]

The structural elements of the existentialist's position on the question of the human situation are at hand. We have already identified them in our previous inquiry into the origins of the existentialist tradition. There is agreement within this tradition that to be a man means to be in despair—to experience anguish. Presumably, this has always been

[15] Ralph Harper, "Significance of Existence and Recognition for Education" in *Modern Philosophies and Education,* Fifty-fourth Yearbook of the National Society for the Study of Education, Part I, Chicago: University of Chicago Press, 1955, pp. 215–258; p. 217.

the human condition but certain events in the modern world have conspired to increase the intensity of human experience. There are two major things that can be said about the human situation in our day: first, our awareness of the contingent nature of existence; and, secondly, our realization of the inherent particularity of human existence. We will now elaborate these two ideas briefly.

First, with respect to contingency, when we say that a thing or event is contingent we mean that it may either be or not be. There is nothing that makes its existence necessary. In this sense, "nothingness" or non-being is as much a possibility as being. It is possible to garner a great deal of evidence from our experience in the everyday world to show that contingency does seem to be a built-in character of the conditions under which we live. Pragmatists, particularly, have emphasized the inherently contingent and unpredictable character of the world with which we interact. The very way in which John Dewey defined intelligence and its methods reveals his conception of nature as always in process, unfinished, undetermined in many of its basic features. A major effort of western traditions in philosophy, however, has been to banish contingency as a basic trait of reality and to insist on the necessity of Being. Plato denied the reality of the world of sense, in which the contingent character of existence seems so obvious, and posited as real a perfect world of unchanging forms whose existence is timeless and absolute. Aristotle could not conceive of a specific act of creation in which the world was created out of nothing. Therefore he subscribed to the idea that the world had always existed in the same form and the species are immutable.

On the other hand, a fundamental tenet of the Hebraic-Christian tradition is that the earth was created by God and therefore, its existence is contingent. There was a time when the world did not exist, and contingency must be an aspect of its being. Strictly speaking, there is no way of knowing why God created the world. This is something that is a mystery, forever outside the possibility of human understanding, and simply must be accepted. There are other doctrines of the church, however, that mitigate the effects of the Christian doctrine of contingency and make the prospect more tolerable. Not so for the existentialists, however.

For the existentialist, even such Christian existentialists as Kierkegaard, it is a mistake to try to water down our awareness that contingency is of the very nature of things. Kierkegaard was a devout Christian who believed in the existence of God as ardently as any man ever did, and he believed that man had fallen from God through original sin. He did not believe, however, that man could ease his alienation from God by any act of reason or simply through good works. The nature of God's existence and His creation of the world are a mystery in which there are elements of paradox. Therefore, whether Christianity is based on an unfathomable mystery, as in Kierkegaard, or whether God is dead in Nietzsche's sense, the fact is that the being of the world —and, therefore, the being of man—is without meaning. It is absurd. It is absurd because there is nothing to give it any meaning. That is, there is nothing outside man himself. The condition of man is that he is in the world. He does not know why, and there is no way for him to find out why. It is in anguish that man realizes that the source of value and of meaning lies within himself. He is called upon to shoulder the responsibilities that once were believed to belong to God.

To this fundamental awareness of the contingency of existence, the existentialist adds the fact of the particularity of human existence. We have already seen that a major protest of existentialist philosophy is against the effort of western philosophy to reduce the human being to an abstraction—an essence or universal. The net effect of this, as Kierkegaard said, is to make man a specimen instead of an individual. The fact of human life is that man exists as an individual. There is no structure of Being, call it God or whatever, that determines any essential nature of man as an individual. The existence of man is finite and he lives in the knowledge that he must one day die. His existence, as Heidegger said, is a "being for death." Therefore, even in our moments of greatest joy and happiness, our experience is pervaded by a sense of nostalgia and despair, for we know that this joy cannot endure. The individual is unique and therefore irreplaceable. Whatever he is he has chosen to be and when he dies, there is no one to fill the vacant place. The way we have most often taken in our attempts to escape from the awful fact of the indeterminacy of existence and our finite nature is to run to the crowd in the hope that by submerging ourselves in the group, in the institution, we will find some surcease. But the crowd, whatever form it may take, is always untruth.

The Fact of Freedom

We have already seen that one of the most important ideas in the existentialist tradition is that man is free to choose and that his choices are undetermined by external conditions. In this sense, existential philosophers emphasize the principle of indeterminism as opposed to various deterministic theories of nature and human behavior. Although the idea of freedom of human choice plays an important part in the thought of most existentialist philosophers, it has remained for Sartre to pay the closest attention to this point. In this section we will consider briefly some of the aspects of Sartre's analysis.

William James once made a distinction between two forms of determinism: "hard determinism" and "soft determinism." To illustrate what he meant by hard determinism he used a verse from Omar Khayyam which expresses the thought that at the beginning of time every event was determined and there is nothing in the nature of things that can change it. Under this view, James says, "The future has no ambiguous possibilities hidden in its womb: the part we call the present is compatible with only one totality. Any other future complement than the one fixed from eternity is impossible."[16] James himself did not subscribe to the doctrine of hard determinism, but he paid it a grudging kind of admiration because he thought it was forthright and did not try to dodge the issue. His contempt was reserved for soft determinism, a position he considered "a quagmire of evasion" in which the term "freedom" might be interpreted in any number of conflicting ways. Soft determinism, said James, because it mingles ideas about good and bad with ideas about cause and effect, always winds up in a dilemma, one of whose horns is pessimism and the other subjectivism. Neither of these alternatives is very attractive and James himself believed that the way between the horns of the dilemma is to see the world as characterized throughout by pluralism and indeterminism.

From what we have already considered in existentialism, it seems clear that existentialists must reject hard determinism and therefore there is no point in pressing this matter any further. The concern of Sartre in discussing the problem of freedom was to eliminate soft determinism also as a possibility. His major thesis is expressed as follows: "Man cannot be sometimes slave and sometimes free; he is wholly and forever free, or he is not free at all."[17] It will be recalled that in our discussion of freedom and determinism in other contexts we found that the traditional view is that two elements are always present in any act of choice: an external, objective state of affairs and an internal or subjective motive. Man has powers of reason, but these powers are not

[16] "The Dilemma of Determinism," reprinted in *Essays in Pragmatism*, New York: Hofner Publishing Company, Inc., 1948, pp. 37–64; p. 41.
[17] *Being and Nothingness*, trans. Hazel E. Barnes, New York: Philosophical Library, 1956, p. 441.

capable of producing action and, therefore, it is necessary to conceive of another kind of power—volition or will. In the classic view, the intellect informs the will and the will initiates an act. A virtuous act is one produced by a good will that has been informed by reason. This is to say, the action has been willed freely and, therefore, the individual can be held responsible for it. Moreover, the classic view included, in addition to the faculties of intellect and will, the passions. The good life—the ethical life—is one in which the passions are regulated and kept in bounds by reason and will.

Objections to the classic view that have developed in modern philosophy differ mainly with respect to the emphasis placed on the elements involved in an act of choice. Mostly, these objections involve a denial of the "freedom of the will," or, perhaps the denial that there really is anything that can be called *the will*. Extreme behavioristic theories emphasize the external, objective situation and insist that all behavior is the reaction to stimuli and that man's actions are determined by external causes over which he has no control. In this view, of course, "free will" means nothing. Logically, the ultimate position of this view is hard determinism, but most people have fought shy of the ultimate conclusion and have attempted to substitute some variant of soft determinism. Sartre's reply to this kind of determinism, whether hard or soft, is that the objective situation is never sufficient to initiate action. Our actions are always in terms of our own perceptions and apprehensions of the external situation and these are always freely chosen by us.

Another form of modern determinism places emphasis on the internal motives—the passions. In this view of behavior, whatever action we take is the result of the superior strength of one passion over others. Our behavior, therefore, is determined by the relative strength of our motives. The most powerful passion wins, so to speak, and we do what we have to do. To this kind of argument Sartre replies that the existentialist takes no stock in the power of passion. "He will never agree," Sartre says, "that a sweeping passion is a ravaging torrent which fatally leads a man to certain acts and is therefore an excuse. *He thinks that man is responsible for his passions.*"[18] In Sartre's opinion, it makes no sense to talk about the strength or weight of passions as if they were physical things capable of being submitted to operations of measuring and weighing. If it makes any sense at all to talk about "the weight of passions" the conclusion is that a passion has just as much weight as we give it. Thus, Sartre is not denying that external circumstances are

[18] *Existentialism*, pp. 27–28. Italics mine.

411

involved in our actions or that we do have motives. What he emphasizes is that our apprehension of external conditions and the character of our own motives are themselves products of our own choices.

Sartre also raises objections to the kind of psychological determinism inherent in Freud's work. A key idea in Freud is that behavior is determined by the unconscious part of psychic life, the id, which is primitive and irrational. Since Sartre's criticism of Freud is complex and would take more space than is available in this chapter, we will not pursue it farther, except to say that Sartre asks if Freud's theory is correct, how are we to explain certain things that happen in psychoanalytic therapy —patient resistance, for example?

Now, having seen something of how Sartre dismisses major theories of determinism, we return to a restatement and summary of his own views. The fundamental premise is that man is free and makes his own choices. His behavior is self-determined and the responsibility for it cannot be placed anywhere except on himself. The only limit placed on his freedom is that he cannot choose not to be free. The choices we make are made in terms of a goal that we have set for ourselves; Sartre calls this "a project of the for-itself." In order to understand his point here, we must consider that his views are different from those found in conventional psychology. Sartre maintains that there are two aspects of consciousness: the non-reflective and the reflective. Our original choices—our project of being—is made by the non-reflective consciousness. The part played by the reflective consciousness is not to select the project of being, but to make us aware of the motives we have. Even before we begin to deliberate, we have already made up our minds.

Sartre illustrates this with an anecdote that has been retold many times. A young man comes to Sartre and asks his advice. This young man is faced with the necessity of making a decision. He can stay with his mother in occupied France and take care of her, or he can rejoin his comrades in the Resistance and try to escape the country and join the Free French who are fighting the Nazis. Sartre's point is two-fold: first there is no point in giving this young man any advice because he had already made up his mind before he sought advice; secondly, the young man made his decision at the level of non-reflective consciousness—where all such choices are made—and he, himself, cannot change his own choice through any process of reflection.[19] In this sense, voluntary deliberation is always a deception of oneself.

[19] *Existentialism*, pp. 29–33.

The fact that we determine our project-of-being by our own choice is the source of anguish. Given Sartre's conception of the matter, it must be conceded that we make this choice alone without the possibility of any help from God or from any human being. The responsibility is ours and cannot be transferred elsewhere.

Alienation and Authenticity

We will conclude our survey of the major themes of contemporary existentialism by considering two questions. These are questions that are treated in various ways by people of differing philosophical and psychological outlooks. There is no denying, however, that they are matters of very wide interest today. These questions are as follows: First, what is the meaning and the source of human alienation as it is viewed in existentialist philosophy? Secondly, what does it mean to live *authentically?* What is the *authentic* person?

In our consideration of other philosophical traditions we have seen that human alienation is an important question. Marx, for example, treated the question at length and, it will be recalled, in the latter part of his career affirmed that the alienation of man is a consequence of certain objective historical and social conditions. The promise of Marxism is that in the course of historical events, when conditions change, man will overcome his alienated state and will be with himself. In this sense, at least, Marxist philosophy is optimistic about the human condition. A similar kind of optimism can be found in the ranks of the pragmatists. Dewey was concerned with the loss of individuality in the world of modern industrial society and he agreed that the older individualism, that had its origin in the pre-industrial world, was no longer tenable. His middle-class liberalism indicated, however, that a new individualism is possible and organized education can play a part in helping us find our way to it. Even William James, who differed significantly from Dewey temperamentally and, to some extent, philosophically, attempted valiantly to maintain an attitude of optimism in the face of the contingency and unpredictability of existence. This kind of optimism is lacking in the existentialist view. In any common meaning of the term, existential philosophy is pessimistic in its view of the human condition.

A major root of this pessimism is the existentialist's conviction not only that man is alienated, but that alienation is an irreducible condition of human existence and hence can never be overcome. Sartre's conclusion that "man is condemned to be free" is an eloquent statement of the case. As we have seen in previous contexts, there are at least three dimensions of this freedom and the consequent alienation of man. In the first place, man is forever alienated from the source of his being. This is explained somewhat differently by Christian existentialists and by atheistic existentialists, but their explanations, in the end, turn out to be similar. Christian existentialists, of whom Kierkegaard is a major example, hold to the existence of God and the belief that for Him being does have meaning. The gulf, however, between man and God is so vast that there is no way by which man can apprehend this meaning. The significance of the Christian doctrine of the fall of man is that man has become an alien in the world, that, as Heidegger has said, man is forlorn. The atheistic existentialists, on the other hand, maintain that only the existence of God could give meaning to existence, and since He does not exist, there is no possible meaning at all. In either case, man is alienated from the source of his being and this alienation cannot be overcome.

Man is not only alienated from the source of his existence, he is also an alien in the world in which he must live. Heidegger, it will be recalled, insists that man is simply thrown into the world, for no reason apparent to him. Sartre has said that the central principle of existentialism is that man simply appears on the scene, again for no known reason. Both Sartre and Heidegger emphasize the inherently contingent character of the world and maintain that this contingency indicates a complete lack of intrinsic meaning. There is no ultimate ground of being, philosophical or theological, that furnishes a source of value. The world is being-in-itself and man in his existence is hampered by the in-itself. It is his adversary. Thus, man is set over against the world and there is no possibility that he can ever achieve an harmonious adjustment to it. Man is not only alienated from the world, he is irrevocably alienated from it.

Even this is not all the story, for man is not only alienated from the source of his being and from the world, he is also alienated from other selves—from society. In accepting this principle, contemporary existentialists follow the course set by Freud rather than that taken by pragmatism, for Freud had maintained that man cannot ever hope to establish the kind of social harmony with others that is implicit in pragmatic and other modern philosophies. Existentialism emphasizes individuality and the fact that every man stands alone in the world. This does not mean, however, that existentialists think interpersonal relations are unimportant, nor does it mean that this philosophical tradition advocates a withdrawal by the individual to the existence of a hermit. The point is that existentialists consider the problem of human relations to be a crucial problem in philosophy, but their interpretation of it is different from that encountered in most contemporary philosophies and psychologies. The basic condition of interpersonal relationships is one of tension and conflict. "The other" is set over against me as my adversary. As a subject (being-for-itself) all other selves become objects (being-in-itself) just as for another self I become an object for him. Thus, my relations with other persons are marked with tension and conflict that can never be resolved. As we have already seen, the existentialist has profound contempt for two major efforts of contemporary man to escape the conditions of freedom that are forced upon him by the nature of existence: one of these is the escape to the crowd. The crowd, Kierkegaard said, is always untruth, but those who seek this way out try to conform to the ways of the crowd, to become "socially adjusted," which means that they never do anything without thinking first about the reactions of other people. In fact, their main goal in life seems to be not to offend anybody. The other effort is exemplified in the behavioristic psychologists and the "group-dynamics" advocates who regard themselves as "social engineers" who can manipulate human behavior at will and, through the application of scientific method, can create whatever human nature and whatever human society they desire. Their "social technology," of course, is based on an assumption of determinism.[20] What these "engineers" do, in the judgment of the existentialist, is to make human beings into laboratory subjects and do all they can to eliminate subjectivity and choice. The point of existentialism is that these efforts, abhorrent as they are in themselves, always fail because the human spirit is capable of rising above them. It may be that most men today are "other directed," to use a popular phrase, but the facts of existence are such that they need not be, and it is part of the mission of existentialist philosophy to call attention to the essential freedom of man. This brings us then to the other idea with which this section is concerned; namely, "authenticity."

What does it mean to be an "authentic person" or to live "authentically?" Naturally, there are differences among existentialist philosophers on this point stemming mostly from differences among them concerning the nature of human existence. However, there are also common elements. In the broadest sense, to live authentically means to live in full awareness of freedom. To achieve this, we must be aware that

[20] The scientific realism and behaviorism involved in this approach was discussed in Chapter V.

human existence is absolutely unlike the existence of things. We must not only understand, but take to heart, Sartre's distinction between the in-itself and the for-itself and Heidegger's insistence that the locus of human inauthenticity is the condition of being-in-the-midst-of-the-world — that is, the everyday world of things. Sartre and Heidegger have somewhat different conceptions of the nature of the everyday world of things, but they are in agreement that the authentic person is one who transcends it, and this can only be achieved through the experience of anguish. The authentic person is one who faces up to the real character of existence, who recognizes both the freedom and necessity of choice, and who chooses freely with complete realization that he is responsible for what he has chosen.

There is an element of irony here, for it seems clear that the more authentic we become, the more we are with ourselves instead of with the crowd, the greater our isolation from other individuals becomes. If the existentialists are right, if the only significant choices are those we make ourselves for ourselves, then it must be that nobody can really help us—we stand alone. The price of authenticity is anguish.

We will conclude our survey of contemporary existentialism by summarizing the various kinds of protests that existentialists make against modern society and the character of modern life. First of all, we have found existentialism to be a protest against conformity in all its possible aspects. It is as much a protest against institutionalized religion as it is against the institutional character of the classic tradition in philosophy. We may add to this also the protest existentialism makes against the institutionalized science of our day and against the willingness of many people in these times to reduce man simply to a scientific object. There are many people who have switched their conformity to metaphysics for a conformity to scientism, and they have succeeded in transforming man from a metaphysical essence into a scientific specimen. The kind of protest against conformity for which existentialism is best known today is against conformity to mass society. The problem undoubtedly is more acute now than it was in the nineteenth century, although both Kierkegaard and Nietzsche saw the situation with great clarity. The "other-directed" person was as well known to them as he is to us. The difference between the pressure to conform in their day as compared to our own may be a difference of degree rather than of kind, but even as a difference of degree it is overwhelming. There is a whole popular literature, as well as a technical one, on this point and we will not press the matter further in this limited context.

A second major protest is against determinism in any form, whether this be the mechanistic determinism of the behaviorists or the psychological determinism of the Freudian schools of psychology. Existential philosophy insists that man is free and that, whether he likes it or not, he is faced with the necessity of choice. There is a radical difference between man and the rest of existence. Man, in Sartre's term, is being-for-itself, he is constantly transcending himself and hence is not subject to the law of identity. Things are whatever they are in themselves; they are being-in-itself. But man is what he becomes and what he becomes is a matter of his own choosing. He may choose authentically as a man or inauthentically to be a member of the crowd, but he must choose because there is nothing anywhere on which he can place the responsibility. It is a common thing, of course, for us to look for something to blame for the predicament in which we find ourselves: if I had not been born in a slum; if my parents had not treated me so badly when I was a child; if my genetic inheritance had not been so unfavorable; if I had been able to go to a better college; if I were not a Jew or a Negro or something; and so on and on through all the familiar litany of excuses. But the admonition existentialism addresses to us is that we are what we have chosen to be. It is easy to misunderstand this, of course. Existentialists are not talking about magic. They are not saying that a person born into slavery could have chosen to be born into royalty or that a person born a Negro could have chosen to be born a white. Their point is that man can rise above history and assert his own freedom. The point is not what the content of our choices is, so much as the fact that we make choices and shoulder the responsibility for them. How we act in the face of circumstance is our own doing.

Existentialism may also be interpreted as a protest against all efforts to reconcile man with the world. It has sometimes been said, by Dewey, for example, that the mission of western philosophy has been a concealed effort to banish all that is harsh, banal, and annoying in existence to some limbo of non-being or the "merely empirical" and to enshrine the true, the good, and the beautiful as the real attributes of Being. Theology, like philosophy, has been concerned to assure us that existence has a built-in meaning to it; that if we could only get the "big picture" we would see that what in the partial and finite view appears meaningless and even evil is but an aspect of that which is complete and good. In common language, the effort of a very great deal of philosophy and theology has been to assure us that, in the long run, everything is going to be all right. If man is alienated in this world, he will lose his alienated condition in the next. If man is alienated under the conditions of capitalism he will be with himself when socialism is established.

The existentialist protests against the effort to explain away that which so evidently is the condition of human existence. Men can know, even without the assistance of philosophers, that there is much in human life that is without any apparent meaning, that death is the reality that confronts all men, that each man must live and choose for himself, that the world in many respects is alien and unfriendly. The charge existentialism lays on us is to face up to the realities of human existence and the fact of human freedom and not to sell our birthright as men for a mess of philosophical and theological pottage. Existential philosophy is a condemnation of all the abstractions and rationalistic reductionisms that serve to blind us to the fact that existence inherently is absurd and the only meaning life has is that with which we ourselves invest it. There is more to be learned about human existence in poetry, art, and myth than in all the intellectual posturings of the metaphysicians and the scientists.

Existentialism is also a protest against absolute norms for value, however their allegedly absolute character may be conceived. It represents a position of ethical relativism in which the individual chooses his own norms. This view does not necessarily dismiss tradition as unimportant, but it does label blind acceptance of tradition as an inauthentic choice. What is also notable is that blind rejection of tradition also constitutes an inauthentic choice. The inability of behavioristic psychology, which concerns itself with outward behavior and ignores the essentially subjective condition of human existence, to distinguish between an authentic and inauthentic acceptance of tradition (or of anything else) is evidence, to the existentialist, of the poverty of scientific psychology.

EXISTENTIALISM AND EDUCATION

We have come now to the last part of our inquiry into the nature of existential philosophy and the protest it makes against existing modes of life and education in contemporary American society. As was noted in the beginning, in seeking to locate connections of some kind between existential philosophy and ideas on education, we are at a disadvantage.

This disadvantage lies in the fact that the major figures of this tradition have had little to say about education. And, it must be confessed, when some important spokesman for existentialism has said anything about education, his pronouncements have seemed to originate more in his own educational experience than in his existentialism. Further, the amount of commentary on the implications of existential thought for educational theory is not very extensive, at least in comparison with other traditions we have considered. This means that we are left, in considerable degree, to our own devices.

In the beginning of this chapter we described the existentialist tradition as one which views the mission of philosophy as analyzing the basic character of human existence and calling the attention of men to their freedom. It seems reasonable to expect that existentialists would think that the educative process should take its major direction from this principle. If this inference is correct, we should expect also that such practical aspects of education as the nature of the curriculum, the role of the teacher, and the character of educational method will be consciously designed to achieve the mission of existentialism. Generally speaking, the efforts of various commentators on existentialist ideas concerning education has been to demonstrate that this is the case.

With respect to the character of the curriculum, for example, there seems to be considerable agreement that to achieve the aims of education, as these are stated or implied in existential philosophy, education must be conceived as liberal education.[21] The difficulty here lies in determining what is meant by the term "liberal education." The fact of the matter is that we get little help in clarifying the idea because what is offered by way of explanation are, on the one hand, platitudes made popular by educational essentialism ("freeing the mind from ignorance and confusion") and on the other hand the attempt to define liberal learning in terms of certain subject matters. In the first chapter of this book the reader was invited to try his hand at analyzing how it is that a realist, an idealist, and an existentialist can come to such close agreement on the nature of the curriculum if it is the philosophical ideas of these writers that dictate their conceptions of the curriculum. Those who did not accept the invitation originally may find it instructive to do so now.[22]

[21] As examples, see: Harper, op. cit., p. 227 and George F. Kneller, Existentialism and Education, New York: Philosophical Library, Inc., 1958, p. 122 ff.
[22] See ante, p. 13.

In his widely-read essay on existentialism and education, for example, Mr. Ralph Harper considers the question of the curriculum. In so doing, he advocates the following ideas: 1) everybody must be taught certain things—reading, arithmetic, writing, history, etc.; 2) The pupil is not the one to decide what he should learn. This is the teacher's prerogative. It is not injurious to be made to learn arithmetic or read the Bible or the *Odyssey*; 3) The human mind always works in certain ways and, therefore, it is essential for man to learn logic, for it leads to truth.[23] Even though the author salts his discussions of these matters with existentialistic-sounding phrases and observations, this seasoning is insufficient to mask the fundamentally conservative flavor of the discussion. It may well be that these are good and worthy ideas about the curriculum—at least conservatives have maintained for a long time that they are. The question would seem to be: what do they have to do with existentialism? Are they even consistent with existentialist ideas? One thing, at least, seems certain: *one does not have to be an existentialist to accept them.*

If an existentialist does not believe that the pupil decides what he should learn, then who does he think can decide? If Sartre is right that man appears on the scene and chooses; if the authentic choice is that which one makes for himself—and which he alone can make, then what happens to authenticity in this educational scheme of things? On one occasion, at least, Sartre tried his own hand with this question and was finally forced to find refuge in the last haven available to an existentialist—the paradoxical nature of existence. He defends a requirement that everyone should master the essentials, but when he is brought up against the fact that the essentials are universals, he simply says that we should do what everybody else does but be like nobody else. How this can be consistent with other aspects of his thought is something on which considerably more light is needed.[24] Simply to label the matter a paradox does not seem particularly helpful.

There is evidence in the writings of both Sartre and Heidegger of their belief that the humanistic studies are the most valuable. It is in various forms of art that the existence of man in all its poignant character is most clearly portrayed. Since truth for the existentialist derives from human subjectivity, since truth is a relationship in which man places himself, literature, the graphic arts, music and myth are far more the source of truth than the sciences. There is, in fact, in the

[23] Harper, *op. cit.*, pp. 234–236.
[24] On this point see Kneller, *op. cit.*, pp. 122–123.

literature of existentialism a strong anti-scientific strain. There is evidence that Nietzsche foresaw accurately the problem of extreme specialization that is characteristic of both the pure science and the technology of our own time. He advocated the now familiar antidote of liberal education to counteract it. The major existentialist objection to science is, of course, that it is cold, aloof, and objective in its approach to nature and to man, and that as an intellectual enterprise it is concerned only with abstractions. Its effects have been unfortunate enough in warping our conception of physical nature, but when the methods of science have been applied to human nature, the results have been simply disastrous.

Those who seek to draw inferences about the role of the teacher from various principles of existential philosophy seem most often to advocate the Socratic method as a model.[25] In some ways, at least, this seems to be a reasonable choice. By almost any existentialist criterion, Socrates appears to have been an outstanding example of the authentic individual. His humanistic approach to philosophy and his insistence on man as the focus around which inquiry should be developed are themes that find an important place in contemporary existentialism. The way in which Socrates conducted his teaching, at least as it is portrayed by Plato, and the kind of relationship he established with his students are also in apparent agreement with various ideas we have discovered in existential philosophy. It is true that Socrates did not give lectures, or prepare course outlines, or administer comprehensive examinations. There were no entrance requirements to his school, because he had no school. There were no administrators and no tuition and no overhead. His method of teaching was one of asking questions, refining answers, asking more questions, and pushing the issue until some acceptable conclusion was reached. He himself did not give answers and always maintained that he was ignorant and was only asking for enlightenment from those with whom he was conversing. All of these things appear to indicate that Socrates and his famous method is an appropriate model for existentialist education. There is something more, however, that needs saying about the Socratic method.

There is, for one thing, the question of what the method of Socrates is supposed to yield. It is true that in initiating an inquiry, Socrates invariably began with some situation that was common in Athenian life. The movement of his thought was inductive, *proceeding from the immediate and particular to the abstract and universal.* Aristotle de-

[25] For example, Kneller, *op. cit.*, pp. 133–135.

scribed Socrates' work as, ". . . busying himself about ethical matters and neglecting the world of nature as a whole *but seeking the universal in these ethical matters, and fixed thought for the first time on definitions . . .*"[26] As we have noted, Socrates' example of neglecting nature and centering attention on man is something the existentialist can admire. But, we should ask, what about the rest of Aristotle's observation? The method of Socrates was aimed at reaching abstractions—universals, or essences. The method itself is built on the supposition that there are universal and absolute principles of ethics, and these in the hands of Plato became the Forms. Moreover, the method also rests on the principle that ideas are innate in the individual. The ideas exist in the soul, but in order to be known they have to be brought to consciousness, and this is the purpose of Socrates' method. Knowing is a process of *recollection* in which, of course, the direct transmission of information can play no part at all. But knowing is the apprehension of that which is already present in the soul, and that which is in the soul is *abstractions*. It would appear that at this point the existentialist finds his Socratic model turning against him. Unless any methodology that involves the teacher asking questions is to be classified as "Socratic," and this would appear to do violence to the Socratic-Platonic tradition, then there is a real question that certain principles in existentialism actually imply the method of Socrates. After all, the claim has also been made that a teaching machine can be programmed to teach like the gadfly of Athens![27]

There is also found in the commentary on existentialism and education a strong emphasis on the character of the personal relationships between teacher and pupil. The usual thesis is that, under the influence of existential ideas, the teacher-student relation will be more personal and, to use the fashionable term, more "interactive."[28] According to this view, the only really important thing about education is the relationship established between the student and the teacher. What this relation should be—or perhaps better—*can be*, depends on whose existentialism is taken as authoritative. If, for example, Sartre's analysis of personal relationships is accepted as authoritative, it appears that the pupil-teacher relation can never be other than one of tension and conflict. Each of the persons involved is the adversary of the other.

[26] *Metaphysics*, Bk. I, Chapter 6. Italics mine.
[27] Lawrence M. Stolurow, *Teaching by Machine*, Cooperative Research Monograph No. 6, Washington, D.C.: Department of Health, Education and Welfare, 1961, p. 60.
[28] See Harper, *op. cit.*, pp. 229–233.

The teacher seeks to make the student an object that he can manipulate in accord with his own ideas and for his own purposes. For the student, of course, the role is reversed; the teacher is his adversary, who stands in opposition to his own freedom. Sartre's philosophy even raises the question of whether language can serve a true mediating function among individuals, and surely there is in his approach the belief that no one can really do anything important for anyone else. The same kind of question can be raised about the efficacy of student counseling and guidance, an activity that has become of great importance in contemporary secondary schools. If a person's project-for-being can be made only by the individual at the level of non-reflective consciousness and if reflective consciousness serves usually as a means of self-deception, then the question is whether the counselor-client relationship can really be productive of anything. The anecdote of the young man's soliciting Sartre's advice about whether he should stay with his mother or return to his comrades in the underground is an example.

Sartre's ideas, at least when they are taken for their face value, do not seem to lend much comfort to the educational enterprise, even when this enterprise is interpreted in somewhat unconventional terms. For this reason, among others, persons interested in the implications of existential philosophy for the practical affairs of education or for counseling and psycho-therapy often have tended to shy away from Sartre and to pay more heed to the work of such philosophers as Karl Jaspers and Gabriel Marcel. We have not included either Jaspers or Marcel in our survey of existentialism and there is no space available now to make any analysis of their ideas. Those readers who elect to pursue a study of the influence of these men may possibly find a closer relation between their brands of existentialism and ideas about education.[29] The question, at least, ought to be left open.

The foregoing remarks, although they are somewhat critical of contemporary efforts to relate existential thought in some logical sense to educational policy, are not meant to indicate that the existentialist protest has no significance for those interested in the philosophy of education. In the opinion of the present author, a primary difficulty lies in attempting to resurrect the familiar approach to educational philosophy, that is, in taking some principles of existentialism *a priori*

[29] See: Gabriel Marcel, *The Philosophy of Existentialism*, trans. Manya Horari, New York: The Citadel Press, 1961; Karl Jaspers, *Man in the Modern Age*, New York: Henry Holt and Company, 1933.

and then trying to show something that is entailed logically. It is suggested here as a possibility—if nothing else—that a more revealing approach to the problem of existential thought and education may be found if we consider the protest of existentialism as essentially nihilistic in character. Nihilism is not a nice word to most people, particularly to Americans, who have a way of thinking that technology can solve all problems, including those of interpersonal relations. What is meant here is that existential philosophy offers no schemes for social reform and progress. It does not promise us that everything is going to be all right in some kind of future. Kierkegaard did not initiate a program to reform the Danish Church; he told us how to be a Christian in spite of the church, and how to escape from the crowd. Nietzsche did not advocate the establishment of social democracy and communal harmony; he said that some men could rise above the herd and become super-men. The herd would remain. Sartre and Heidegger do not tell us that man can be reconciled to the world, rather they insist that he can learn to live in a world that is forever alien, and to live authentically.

Existential philosophy is a protest against an age in which the individual is reduced to his social security number and a computer card with holes punched in it. It is a protest against mass society, mass religion, mass education, mass communication. It does not tell us how to change the character of this society. In fact, there is reason to believe that existentialists may not think this is very important. The important thing is not what happens to a man, but how he chooses to meet it. And this, they tell us, is solely up to us. It is suggested, therefore, that instead of attempting to tame this rebellious offspring of philosophy, instead of trying to gentle it and dull its bite, we take it for the passionate and in many ways, the irrational protest it makes against the established order of things. There is no point in looking in the literature of existential philosophy for the blueprints of a new order in which all problems will be solved. There is the chance, however, that when we begin to think obstinately about the education of *the individual* in mass society, the protest of existentialism will be heard and appreciated for what it is.

SUMMARY

The purposes of this chapter have been to survey the historical development of existentialist philosophy and to make some estimate of its possible relation with contemporary questions of educational policy. With respect to the existentialist tradition itself, it has been portrayed as a protest movement against the character of modern society and, specifically, against contemporary developments in science and philosophy, especially as these relate to interpretations of the nature of man. The view presented here is that the protest of existentialism is nihilistic in the sense that it presents no formula for a reconstruction of society in which the individual automatically will realize his identity and self-integrity. Rather, we have seen that a common theme developed by various existentialist philosophers is that adversity, the necessity of choice, and, hence, disquietude and anxiety are inherent in human experience and can never be eliminated by any means. Existentialism emphasizes the importance of our understanding that how we face up to the events that confront us is a matter of our own choice and the responsibility for this choice can never be transferred. Hence, the emphasis is on the individual and not on the environment in which he finds himself.

With respect to the other purpose in the chapter, that of making some estimate of the import of existentialist philosophy for ideas about education, we found the task exceedingly difficult. In various ways organized education itself displays many of the qualities of mass organization, aloofness, and contempt for individuality that existentialism condemns in society at large. The conclusion offered here is that there is little or nothing in contemporary existentialism that indicates how the school as an institution might be reformed—or even any indication that such a reform might be thought by existentialists to be important. There does appear to be a possible inference that a man's education can only be a product of his own choosing, and his alone. Perhaps, there is also the promise that a man can become educated— even in spite of the school.

Epilogue

In the body of this book I have endeavored to present as completely as the limits of space permit a panorama of contemporary American educational theory and its various connections with social and philosophical traditions. In bringing the work to a close, I propose to make some brief observations about the functions of philosophy of education and the prospects for the educational enterprise in the years ahead.

At the beginning of his famous treatise on government, James Mill observed:

> Notwithstanding the portion of discourse which has been bestowed upon this subject, it is surprising to find, on close inspection, how few of its principles are settled. The reason is that the ends and means have not been analyzed, and it is only a general and indistinguishing conception of them which is found in the minds of the greatest number of men. Things in this situation give rise to interminable disputes; more especially when the deliberation is subject, as here, to the strongest action of personal interest.

Those who have made their way through the twelve chapters of this book are now aware that in educational policy, as in political policy, there are interminable disputes and many of these disputes can be traced to conflicts among traditions and hence, to conflicts of social and personal interests.

A major difficulty in the study of the philosophy of education is that systematic theories of education seem always to be hortatory in character. People rarely take their educational theory dispassionately, and a major reason for this is the common perception—however dim it may be for some—that educational policy inevitably is linked with fundamental values and aspirations.

For example, it is now a common criticism of educational progressivism that under its influence the schools have been run on the basis of slogans, to the exclusion of either common sense or systematic knowledge. Consequently, a resurgent conservatism presently holds up to public ridicule such slogans as "we learn by doing," "the whole child," "rich experience," "functional learning," "the needs of children," "social adjustment," and numerous others. These slogans are represented as the shibboleths of a decadent radicalism that has sapped the vigor of American education and, hence, of American society.

The irony is, however, that the resurgence of orthodoxy is itself proceeding largely by means of slogans. As we have noted before, a very large part of the contemporary literature of educational essentialism is polemical and hortatory. The new conservatism presents us with its own slogans: "intellectual discipline," "the wisdom of the race," "the pursuit of excellence," "educational standards," "liberal education," "elimination of frills and fads," and "minimum essentials." More often than not, such rhetorical devices as ridicule, satire, and name-calling have taken the place of reasoned discourse and logical argument. Since so much of what has gone under the name of educational philosophy can be said to be little more than evangelizing for one or another point of view, it is small wonder that contemporary citizens, subject as they are to one propaganda barrage after another, are either submerged in a welter of conflicting slogans, or have resolutely identified themselves with a body of doctrine from which nothing seems likely to dislodge them.

One of the most interesting aspects of the commotion over educational policy that began with the end of World War II, and still continues, is the almost complete lack of concern with empirical evidence. This "great debate," as it is sometimes called, has been almost entirely ideological in character. When people argue from ideological grounds, rather than from the grounds of evidence, their statements are likely to become increasingly extravagant and their voices shrill. We have had a great deal of this in the last twenty years.

The most important question in educational philosophy, I am inclined to think, is the same as that which Mill identified as the main question of political theory, namely, *the adaptation of a means to an end*. It appears to me that the question of appropriate means is an empirical matter and must be settled—if it is to be settled at all— on the grounds of careful observation and experimental evidence. The question of ends is predominantly an ethical matter and one that is inextricably bound up with the question of means. I am advocating, therefore, that the main function of the philosophy of education should be normative; that is, it should concern itself with ends for education that are desirable and relevant in a given social context, together with the means that appear likely to be of service in attaining those ends.

In carrying on its normative function, the philosophy of education must concern itself with a variety of kinds of evidence. There are numerous subject matters that bear on the questions of the ends and means of education. Some of these subject matters lie within the field of philosophy itself, particularly those that are concerned with ethics. Other pertinent sources are to be found in the natural and social sciences. Philosophy, it seems to me, has always been at its best when it has sought to take the evidence available in any historic period about the nature of the world and of man and to synthesize it into as inclusive a conception of the nature of things as the existing state of knowledge has made possible. There is, of course, a danger in this synthetic function of philosophy because views of man and the universe that at one time seemed reasonable, and in fact had useful functions in society, have a way of becoming resistant to the effects of new evidence and, hence, of losing their relevance and viability.

At the beginning of my discussion in this book, I suggested that a major source of the confusion and acrimony that beset educational theory in our time lies in the conflict of major ideas about the nature of man, the character of the universe in which man lives, the nature of the good, and the nature and limits of human knowledge. These are matters that are major concerns of philosophy, but I do not believe the conflicts can be settled solely by philosophers; at least, I can find very little evidence in the history of philosophy for any such likelihood.

For one thing, it appears to me that ethics is altogether too important a matter to be left to the philosophers alone. There is no question but that the philosopher is uniquely qualified by his training and experience to investigate questions of a technical character concerning the nature of ethical discourse and the linguistic and other special problems involved in such discourse. This technical work can be of great assistance to the rest of us who are faced with the necessity of making decisions about ends that are worth achieving and means that are most appropriate for realizing them. We should remember, however, that philosophers do not have any exclusive option on moral wisdom and sensitivity. Very few of them claim to have any such option.

Hence, I should say that questions about the ends of education lie partly in the province of philosophy and partly in such fields as history, the social and behavioral sciences, the natural sciences, and educational practice. Since somebody has to take the lead in formulating the manifold questions of educational policy and in organizing inquiries into them, I am assuming that this is primarily the province of the educational philosopher. However, it is also necessary to insert a word of caution here. Those who regard themselves as educational philosophers have no exclusive option on educational wisdom anymore than general philosophers have an exclusive option on ethical wisdom. The day of the universal genius is past. There is too much knowledge that bears on the important questions of educational policy for any one person to master. The only conclusion I can see emerging is that we will either learn how to think cooperatively *and* obstinately about the problems of education in our time, or we will continue simply to formulate bodies of doctrine, broadcast slogans, and scapegoat each other. So far as I can see, there is nothing that guarantees we will approach the problems of educational policy on the basis of reason and experiment; there is the real chance that at the present time there are too many irreconcilable differences to make intelligent inquiry possible. In any event, a major effort will be required if any kind of workable synthesis is to be achieved.

I would suggest that if we really intend to engage in a rational conversation about the ends and means of education appropriate to the last part of the twentieth century, we will need to park our metaphysics at the door. There are two reasons for saying this, one of them philosophical, the other practical. The philosophical reason has to do with the question of whether metaphysical statements really mean anything, and the practical question has to do with whether anything could be inferred from such statements that would have any significance for educational policy, even if they could be shown to be meaningful. So long as the belief persists that the business of educational philosophy is to deduce statements about the practice of education from statements about the nature of being, or some other kind of *a priorism*, we will get nowhere. In fact, the only possibility I can see is the continued advocacy of conflicting prejudices, largely through the medium of slogans.

One of the most important contributions of analytic philosophy has been to call into question the widely-held belief that values are genuine only if they are grounded in some transcendental principle, which, of course, may be conceived in either metaphysical or theological terms. There is no space here to examine the various arguments that have led analytic philosophers to this conclusion, and I will only add the practical observation that if it were true that values are values only if they derive from transcendental absolutes, then we are in a sorry plight indeed. I can see no evidence that we are any nearer to agreement on metaphysical principles now than we were a thousand years ago, and if the absolutists are right, there is little hope of agreement on educational values or any kind of ethical matters.

A major point of importance, it appears to me, lies in giving serious attention to something that seems obvious, yet often is overlooked by many of us in discussions of practical ethics. I refer to the fact that there is a community of value among us, and the dimensions of this community are extensive. One thing our study of contemporary philosophies of education has revealed is at least an abstract agreement on such ideas as the importance of the development of intelligence and the value of personal commitment to human dignity and social justice. The important differences with respect to these matters among educational traditions are not occasioned by the metaphysical or epistemological bases on which they (some of them, at least) are alleged to rest. The differences stem rather from the meanings attributed to the terms and the relative importance placed on them. I am suggesting that what we need is not agreement on a common metaphysics, but agreement on a common method that will enable us to evaluate proposed courses of action in terms of their foreseeable effects, not only their effects on the immediate situation, but on the whole course of events, in so far as they can be anticipated.

Such a method will necessarily require two kinds of activity that rightly can be called philosophical. First, it will require a much closer attention to the importance of language than has usually been employed in educational discourse. The existing literature of educational theory is not only saturated with the slogans of contending factions, it is also replete with words having the most diverse referents, with concepts that are loose and slippery, and with hortatory sentences disguised as statements of fact. There are also long lines of argument whose real premises are so concealed that the unwary is trapped into agreements he would never make if he knew what he was doing. It is here that a judicious application of the techniques of linguistic analysis can make an invaluable contribution to the philosophy of education. I emphasize the importance of judicious application because there are signs that certain enthusiasts have already concluded that the philosophy of education need involve nothing but the analysis of language. We need occasionally to remind ourselves that while empirical questions can be clarified by linguistic analysis, they cannot be solved merely by analytic methods.

The other kind of activity I regard as a legitimate and important part of the philosophy of education is methodological. Here I refer to the activity of formulating and selecting means to be employed in the effort to realize educational ends. It is a widely held belief that questions of educational method, in the last analysis, are the province of certain specialists; psychologists and other behavioral scientists, curriculum experts, and those who conduct empirical research in various aspects of the technology of educational method. When I say that educational method is too important a matter to be left to the educational scientists, I intend in no sense to belittle the roles the scientists and the practitioner must play in the educational enterprise. I only am pointing out that somebody has to keep before us the fact that means and ends are so interrelated that one without the other is simply an abstraction. This should be a major part of the educational philosopher's responsibility.

I have already indicated my opinion that there is a considerable community of agreement in this country in so far as high-level abstractions are concerned. For example, conservatives and liberals agree that *democracy* is a conception of the utmost significance in modern social life. We have also seen that American essentialists insist that the primary purpose of formal schooling is intellectual training, and that John Dewey always maintained the development of critical intelligence is one of the important ends of the educative process. Conservatism, liberalism, scholasticism, Marxism, and existentialism all maintain that the inherent dignity of the human being must be a supreme consideration. It is when adherents of these traditions begin defining such terms as democracy, intellectual training, and human dignity, and, particularly, when they indicate what steps should be taken to realize them in society and in the process of education, that the real differences become apparent. It should be remembered that when a person, or an institution, adopts a method of procedure, a commitment to certain ends is involved, for different methods—if they are genuinely different—lead to different effects. The art of education is to adapt a means to an end so that the ends that are truly prized and desired may be achieved as fully as conditions permit. This must be a major concern of the philosophy of education.

Thus, it seems to me, the heart of an approach to educational philosophy must be methodological and it must be critical and experimental. It must employ as fully as possible both the techniques of analysis that contemporary philosophy has shown fruitful and the general canons of scientific method that have demonstrated their power in the natural sciences.

There are some conditions today that augur well for the forward progress of American education. Certainly, one of these is a widespread consciousness of the supreme importance of education in the modern world and the increasing willingness of citizens to support it. I am aware that this frame of mind is corrupted somewhat by narrow and excessively utilitarian motives on the part of many among us. Nevertheless, it seems encouraging that the mass of people apparently at last realize the strategic role universal education must play in an industrial society that is to prosper—or even survive.

On the other hand, I must confess that there are some signs that do not seem so promising. American essentialism apparently has emerged substantially intact from its encounter with the progressive protest, although in the process of this encounter the conservative tradition had to make some compromises and yield some concessions. In doing this, the character of the tradition has changed in certain respects. In the first stage of its resurgence, educational conservatism was aggressive and shrewd in ridiculing the weaknesses of the progressive movement, in ignoring its achievements, and in exploiting the widespread anxiety of the post-war years. But when one comes down to it, what to this time has a resurgent conservatism offered us besides a return to educational tradition, flossed up cautiously here and there with such methodological devices as ability grouping, phonetic reading methods, team teaching, and technological gadgetry of various kinds?

There is evidence available that protagonists of the conservative tradition, encouraged by their initial successes, are already beginning to feel self-satisfied. This tradition rarely has recognized that there is any particular problem about the aims of education, except, of course, the maintenance of tradition. Mr. Conant has reported that talk about educational aims engenders a vast sense of weariness in him. Mr. Martin Mayer in his widely-read book, *The Schools*, has dismissed the subject of the aims of education as "the dullest and most fruitless of human pursuits." Views of this kind are tenable only if those who hold them are certain that the ends of education are so well known and so firmly established that any discussion of them is superfluous and any deviation from them is simply a form of heresy. Those who hold to this notion of the fixed character of educational aims are thereby enabled, as for example, Mr. Conant, to define education as "that which goes on in schools." There is reason to suspect that a great many in the teaching profession are in agreement with these sentiments.

In the times immediately ahead it will be necessary for American society to reappraise and, in many ways, to redefine both the aims and the means of education. This is not something we are free to choose or not to choose; it is being forced upon us. I am convinced that much of what has been done by educational conservatives in the past two decades will be seen in historical perspective as not much more than a delaying action, designed to postpone as long as possible the inevitable confrontation with the changed conditions of a new age.

Certainly, it will be unfortunate, and possibly disastrous, if we continue to think of the major problems of educational policy as being whether team teaching is superior to the self-contained classroom or whether teaching machines are superior to flesh-and-blood teachers. Such questions are of the same order as those about whether screwdrivers are superior to hammers or whether chain saws are superior to both. We already have some reasonably good techniques for assessing the effectiveness of different educational techniques. As yet, we have not shown ourselves very able at discerning what ends are relevant to the conditions of life in a society that is being transformed.

In this book I have tried to show something of the social and philosophical context out of which the new answers to the old questions of the ends and means of education must emerge. It has been said that those who ignore the past are condemned to repeat it. My point in writing this book has been to help those who will shape the educational policy of the future to understand perhaps more fully the context in which their work must begin and the myriad forces with which they must contend.

Index of Names

Adams, G. P., 215n, 266n
Adams, John, 55, 58, 72n, 73, 74n
Addams, Jane, 214n
Adler, Mortimer J., 314, 323n, 328, 332, 334
Alcott, Amos Bronson, 162
Allen, Dwight W., 97n
Anselm of Canterbury, Saint, 311
Aquinas, Saint Thomas, 30, 311, 313, 325–327, 333n, 341, 345–348, 352
Aristotle, xii, 8, 12, 22, 24, 26–28, 30, 114, 142n, 175, 183, 186, 228n, 237, 294, 296, 299, 310, 311, 325, 326, 328, 329, 333n, 340–346, 348, 349, 352, 369, 371, 383, 408, 421, 422
Augustine, Saint, 30, 330, 394
Aurelius, Marcus, 390
Babbidge, Homer D., Jr., 95n
Babbitt, Irving, 73n
Bacon, Francis, 208
Bagley, William C., 57n, 91n
Baker, Melvin C., 216n
Barnes, Hazel E., 410n
Barr, Stringfellow, 314
Barrett, William R., 395
Bell, Bernard Iddings, 61n, 85n, 89n, 100
Berkeley, George, 131–136, 166
Bestor, Arthur E., Jr., 83n, 85n, 86n, 90, 91n, 94, 99n, 106, 107, 110n, 114n, 117n, 319
Billington, Ray Allen, 96n
Black, Max, 20
Bode, Boyd H., 259, 260
Bolster, Arthur S., 96, 99n
Bonaparte, Napoleon, 35
Brinton, Crane, 391
Broudy, Harry S., 11n
Brown, W. Burlie, 99n
Brubacher, John S., 13n, 87n, 127n, 159n, 185n, 323n, 333n, 338n, 351n, 373n
Bruyn, C. V. O., 394
Buchanan, Scott, 314
Buchler, Justus, 263n, 266n, 273n–275n, 278n, 279n, 287n
Buckley, William, 66, 68n, 73n, 100
Burke, Edmond, 57, 58, 65, 70, 73, 74n, 100, 179
Burnett, Joe R., 13n
Burns, Hobart W., 12n
Burtt, Edwin A., 47n

Bush, J. N. Douglas, 110n
Butler, Nicholas Murray, 171n
Calkins, Mary W., 134n
Campbell, Angus, 319n
Capella, Martianus, 330
Carlyle, Thomas, 68
Chalmers, Gordon Keith, 102n
Chesler, Mark, 71n
Chodarov, Frank, 100n
Clapp, Harold L., 110n
Clark, Fred G., 36n
Cohen, Robert S., 373n
Coleridge, Samuel Taylor, 68
Conant, James B., 85, 101, 107, 108, 319, 320, 432, 433
Condorcet, Marie Jean, 201
Counts, George S., 258, 259, 362n
Cremin, Lawrence A., 210, 212n, 258n, 301, 302
Cunningham, William F., 314
Curti, Merle E., 68n
Darwin, Charles, 36n, 75, 264, 265, 268, 273, 344n
Demiashkevich, Michael, 57
Descartes, René, 12, 125, 128, 131, 165, 403
Dewey, Jane M., 215n
Dewey, John, 12, 21, 114, 145n, 195, 203n, 206n, 207n, 209, 215–226, 228n, 229–239, 241–261, 263–271, 272n, 273, 276–278, 283–285, 287–289, 291–304, 328, 329, 336, 351, 352, 354, 375, 382, 384, 388, 408, 413, 417, 431
Dickinson, G. Lowes, 25n
Dostoevsky, Fyodor, 394, 397, 405
Drake, Durant, 169n
Eastman, Max, 215n
Eckerman, William C., 319n
Edwards, Anna C., 216n, 224
Emerson, Ralph Waldo, 162
Engels, Friedrich, 355n, 356–358, 361–363, 369–373, 377, 380n
Evans, M. Stanton, 60n
Fadiman, Clifton, 94
Feuerbach, Ludwig, 373–376, 382, 383
Fichte, Johann Gotleib, 136
Field, Marshall, 214n
Finn, James D., 88n
Frechtmann, Bernard, 404
Freud, Sigmund, 412, 414
Froebel, Friedrich, 179, 236

434

Parker, Francis H., 212, 214, 216, 217
Pascal, Blaise, 394
Payne, William H., 389n
Peirce, Charles Sanders, 46n, 215, 262–266, 273–288, 299, 300, 375
Perry, Ralph Barton, 145n, 163n, 167–169, 172, 174, 190–192, 291
Pestalozzi, Johann Heinrich, 303
Phenix, Philip H., 85n, 114n, 117n
Philonous, 135
Pickard, W. A., 27n
Pitkin, Walter B., 163n
Plato, 8, 10, 12, 24, 26–28, 111n, 124, 128, 142, 143, 164, 180, 181, 236, 266, 281, 303, 310, 311, 330, 340, 387, 408, 421, 422
Plotinus, 143n
Pratt, James B., 169n
Price, Kingsley, 11n
Quintilian, 330
Ratner, Joseph, 257n
Redden, J. D., 314
Reichenbach, Hans, 45n, 296n
Reisner, Edward H., 35n
Rice, Joseph Mayer, 211–214
Rickover, Hyman G., 62n, 110n, 111n, 357n
Rimanoczy, Richard S., 36n
Rippa, S. Alexander, 69n
Rogers, Arthur K., 169n
Roosevelt, F. D., 205n
Root, E. Merrill, 69n
Roscellinus, 311
Rosenzweig, Robert M., 95n
Ross, 343n
Rossiter, Clinton, 55n, 58n, 72n
Rousseau, Jean Jacques, 64, 179, 187, 199, 201, 303, 389
Royce, Josiah, 171n
Runes, Dagobert, 162n
Ruskin, John, 68
Russell, Bertrand, 144n, 145n, 186
Ryan, F. A., 314
Santayana, George, 169n
Sartre, Jean-Paul, 394, 397n, 401, 403–

405, 410–414, 416, 417, 420, 422–424
Savage, Willinda, 215n
Schelling, Friedrich Wilhelm von, 136
Schilpp, Paul A., 215n
Schmuck, Richard, 71n
Schultz, Theodore W., 40n
Scopes, John, 75
Sellars, Roy W., 169n
Skinner, B. F., 172n, 177, 180
Smith, Adam, 199
Smith, Wilson, 93n
Socrates, 392, 421, 422
Spaulding, E. G., 163n
Spencer, Herbert, 187
Stalin, Joseph V. (Dzugashvili) 257
Steele, Richard, 39
Stevenson, Charles S., 297n
Stolurow, Lawrence M., 422n
Strauss, Anselm L., 272n
Strong, Charles A., 169n
Tawney, R. H., 39n
Thorndike, Edward L., 171–173, 177, 179, 180
Tocqueville, Alexis de, 58, 72n
Tucker, Robert C., 373n
Tufts, James H., 292n
Van Doren, Mark, 314, 328, 332n, 333n, 334, 335n, 337n, 350n
Van Til, William, 303n
Varro, 330
Viereck, Peter, 64, 65n, 67, 68, 70, 72n, 74n, 103n, 201n
Watson, John B., 177n, 180, 267
Weaver, Richard M., 310n, 312
Wess, Harold B., 67n
White, Andrew Dickson, 264n
Wild, John, 13n, 87n, 107, 117, 170n, 185, 186, 324n
Wittig, Horst, 379n, 380n
Woodring, Paul, 107, 108, 111n
Woody, Thomas, 212n
Wormser, Rene A., 69n
Wright, Chauncy, 263

Index of Subjects

Ability grouping, 107
Alienation
  in existentialism, 413–415
  in Marxism, 371–374, 382, 383, 388, 389
Axiology, defined, 9 (see also Ethics)

Behaviorism, 167–169, 171–174, 176–178, 180, 181, 267, 352
Capitalism, 35–40, 66–69, 204, 205
  and concepts of human nature, 37–40
  Marxist critique of, 360–362, 364–368
  and natural law, 36, 37

Coherence theory of truth, 145–148, 157, 158
Conservative tradition, 57–80
  and capitalism, 66–69
  and criticism of contemporary education, 60–63
  and democracy, 71–74
  on human nature, 63–66
  and nationalism, 69–71
  origins of, 57, 58
  resurgence of, 58–62
  and science, 74–79
Correspondence theory of truth, 181–184, 353
Council for basic education, 84n, 86n, 94, 117
Culture and education, 1–3, 22–24
Curriculum, 84–87, 220–225, 239–246, 329–339, 379–381, 419–421
Democracy, 40–44, 71–74, 207, 208
  and education, 44
Determinism, 77–79, 155, 156, 372–374, 410–412, 415, 417
Empiricism, 45, 351, 352
  and science, 46, 47
Epistemology, defined, 9
  of idealism, 131–137
  of Marxism, 374–376, 383, 384, 389
  of new realism, 165–167
  of perennialism, 351–353
  of pragmatism, 270–287
Essentialism, 81–121
  philosophical requirements of, 115–119
  practical problems of, 92–115
    determining essential subjects, 93–102
    mass education, 103–111
    retention and transfer of learning, 111–115
  thesis of, 82–92
    on nature of curriculum, 84–87
    on purposes of education, 82–84
    on the school in society, 90–92
    on the teacher's role, 87–90
Ethics, 9, 41, 42, 50, 148, 149, 158–160, 184–192, 287–297, 366, 367, 379, 428–430
Evil, problem of (see Idealism)
Existentialism, 390–425
  on authenticity, 402, 403, 415, 416
  on education, 418–424
    curriculum, 419–421
    role of the teacher, 421–423
  on human freedom, 409–412
  on the human situation, 397, 398, 400, 401, 404, 405, 406–409, 413, 414

nature of its protest, 394, 395, 405, 406, 416–418
  on origins and character of, 394–405
    contributions of Kierkegaard, 394–398
    contributions of Nietzsche, 398–401
Experimentalism, as philosophy (see Pragmatism)
Greek tradition, 24–28
  body-soul dualism, 24, 25
  theory of education, 26, 27
  theory of knowledge, 27, 28
Hebraic-Christian tradition, 28–30
  conception of human nature, 28, 29
  synthesis with Greek, 30
Hylomorphism, 25, 311, 345
Idealism, 122–160
  absolute idealism, 136–145
    and the problem of evil, 141–145
    and religion, 140, 141
  and contributions of Berkeley, 131–136
  and contributions of Descartes, 125, 126
  and contributions of Locke, 128–131
  on individual and society, 149–154
  and origins of Marxian philosophy, 358, 359
  and the priority of consciousness, 125–127, 135, 136
  on relation of mind and matter, 127–136
  on truth, 145–148, 157, 158
  on value, 148, 149, 158–160
Independence, principle of, 165, 341
Knowledge, theory of (see Epistemology)
Liberal education, 26–28
  Greek conception of, 26, 27
  in perennial tradition, 329–332, 337, 338
Liberalism, 198–214
  and capitalism, 204, 205
  and concepts of human nature, 203, 204
  and democracy, 207, 208
  and nationalism, 205, 206
  origins of, 198–202
  and science, 208, 209
Man, nature of, 24–26, 28, 29, 50, 51, 63–66, 172–181, 268–272, 339–348, 369–376
Marxism, 355–389
  character of its protest, 384–389
  on dialectical development, 358–363
  on education, 376–384
  on nature of man, 369–376
  origins and character of, 356–358

on philosophy of history, 363–369
on theory of knowledge, 374–376
Materialism, 126, 358, 359
Mental discipline, 98, 113, 114, 237, 238
Metaphysics, 8, 49, 50, 136–139, 142, 164, 165, 297–300, 340–343, 402, 403
Mind, 125–141, 165–167, 173, 271, 272, 352, 353
Morals (see Ethics)
Nationalism, 32–35, 69–71, 205, 206
and education, 34, 35
Naturalism, 45, 272
and science, 45–47
Natural law, as laws of nature, 35–37, 46, 47, 75, 175, 176
Natural law, as moral law, 185, 186
Nominalism, 311, 312
Ontology (see Metaphysics)
Perennialism, perennial philosophy, 307–354
on conception of nature, 340–343
educational theory of, 323–339
on aims and means of education, 323–325
on curriculum, 329–339
on art of teaching, 325–328
on ethics, 348–350
on human nature, 339, 340, 343–348
on knowledge, 351–353
origins and character of, 308–315
protest in education, 315–322
Philosophy, 8–16
categories of, 8–9
relation to education, 10–16, 17–20, 428–432
Pragmatism, 262–304
interpretation of experience, 268–270
interpretation of meaning, 270, 271
the pragmatic maxim, 273–278
interpretation of mind, 271, 272
interpretation of selfhood, 272, 273
interpretation of truth, 278–283, 286, 287
on logic as inquiry, 282, 283
ontology of, 297-300
origins and development of, 262–267
influence of Darwin on, 264
influence of experimental psychology on, 267
influence of idealism on, 266, 267

on value, 287–297
Programmed learning, 88, 89, 422
Progressivism, 197–304
on educational method, 228, 246–254
as the liberal protest, 197, 198, 300–304
on nature of curriculum, 239–246
origins and development of, 209–229
on purposes of education, 231–239
on relation of school and society, 254–260
Puritanism, 39, 40
Rational humanism, as part of perennial tradition, 313–315
Realism, 161–193
basic theses of, 164, 165
extreme realism of Plato and Anselm, 310, 311
moderate realism of Aristotle and Aquinas, 311
new realists, 162–164
behavioristic interpretation of consciousness, 167–169, 171–174
epistemological thesis of, 165–167
resurgence of in twentieth century, 162–164
scientific realism, 169, 170
and interpretation of human nature, 178–181
theories of value, 184–192
truth as correspondence, 181–184
Reality (see Metaphysics)
Science, 44–48, 74–79, 208, 209
Scholasticism (see Thomism, also Perennialism)
Self and selfhood, 124–126, 138, 139, 151–154, 156, 272, 273, 395
Socratic method, 421, 422
Soviet Union, 33, 357, 377, 380, 381, 385, 386
Teleology, 186, 341–343
Theory and practice, relation of, 4–8, 323, 426–429
Thomism, 30 (see also Perennialism)
as part of perennial tradition, 313–315
on role of teacher, 326, 327
Truth, 27–29, 145–148, 157, 158, 181–184, 278–283, 286, 287, 353, 396, 397
Values (see Axiology, also Ethics)